Interpreters of Judaism
in the Late Twentieth Century

The B'nai B'rith History of the Jewish People
is a project of the
B'nai B'rith Commission on Continuing Jewish Education.
The first five volumes appeared during the years 1959–1964
as the B'nai B'rith Great Books Series.
Their republication occured in 1985,
and two new volumes were published in 1992 and 1993.
In its entirety, it has been selected to be part of
the B'nai B'rith Judaica Library whose purpose is
to promote a greater pupular understanding
of Judaism and the Jewish tradition.
The volumes in the series are

Creators of the Jewish Experience in Ancient and Medieval Times
Creators of the Jewish Experience in the Modern World
Concepts that Distinguish Judaism
Great Jewish Thinkers of the Twentieth Century
Contemporary Jewish Thought
Frontiers of Jewish Thought
Interpreters of Judaism in the Late Twentieth Century

The B'nai B'rith History of the Jewish People

INTERPRETERS OF JUDAISM IN THE LATE TWENTIETH CENTURY

Edited by Steven T. Katz

B'nai B'rith Books
Washington, D.C.

Jerusalem • London • Paris • Buenos Aires • East Sydney

Library of Congress Cataloging-in-Publication Data

Interpreters of Judaism in the late twentieth century / edited by Steven T. Katz.
p.   cm.—(The B'nai B'rith history of the Jewish people)
Includes bibliographical references and index.
ISBN 0-910250-22-7   ISBN 0-910250-23-5 (pbk.)
1. Judaism—20th century. 2. Judaism—Doctrines. 3. Holocaust (Jewish theology)
4. Jewish scholars.
I. Katz, Steven T., 1944–   . II. Series.
BM603.I58   1993
296'.092'2—dc20   92-47421

DEDICATION

This volume was made possible
through the generosity of
Alan D. and Lauren M. Weinberger.

Alan D. Weinberger offers the following tribute:

For my parents,
Theodore and Shirley Weinberger,
in honor of the 51st year of their marriage.

They taught me that:

There is nothing like a dream to create the future.

–Victor Hugo

*Honor thy father and thy mother; that thy days may be long
in the land which the Lord thy God gives thee.*

–Shemot/Exodus 20:12

Printed in the United States of America by
McNaughton & Gunn, Inc., Saline, Michigan
Typesetting: Computape (Pickering) Ltd., North Yorkshire, England
Index: Elliot Linzer
Production Coordinator: Felice Caspar

*This book is printed on acid free paper, and meets the guidelines for
permanence and durability of the Committee on Production Guidelines
for Book Longevity of the Council on Library Resources.*

Contents

Foreword

Interpreters of Judaism in the Late Twentieth Century together with its companion volume *Frontiers of Jewish Thought*, which was published in 1992, expand to seven volumes the multi-volume work which was originally called the *B'nai B'rith Great Books Series*, and which was retitled in 1985, *The B'nai B'rith History of the Jewish People*. Under the plan of the editor, Simon Noveck, the first five volumes presented the inner content of Jewish tradition, the achievements of the great leaders and thinkers, the ideas, beliefs and religious movements of Judaism. In fact, they comprise a history of the Jewish People until the 1950's.

These five volumes are found on the shelves of countless family libraries, and in the studies of thousands of teachers and rabbis throughout the world. Rarely do these volumes appear pristine. They were created to serve as texts for the classroom and for informal Jewish education, and that is how they have been used. There is nothing obscure in them. They were written with an enviable clarity, and they inspire a curiosity about the ideas and accomplishments they describe. Because of the freshness and vigor of each essay, for more than thirty years these five volumes have been central texts in Jewish education in the United States.

In 1985 I organized a new edition which supplemented each essay with annotated bibliographies that reviewed the literature relevant to the essay's subject and published subsequently. The new edition proved to be very popular, and it rapidly went into a second printing. Its success highlighted the obvious limitation that the series stops at mid-century, and that there were important new developments in Jewish thought, new views on old subjects, and important new subjects which the series did not cover. As sound as the series was, it would become a period piece if it was not taken forward, and what better way to honor the achievements of the original fifty contributors and their editors Simon Noveck and Abraham Millgram than to build upon their work and strive to equal the quality of their efforts.

It is now more than six years since I asked my good friend Steven Katz of Cornell University to consider the potential value of expanding the series with the purpose of carrying forward the intellectual history of the Jewish People from the 1950's to the end of the century. He believed the idea to be worthy, and he accepted my invitation to conceive and edit two new volumes, one devoted to critical issues and subjects in Jewish life, and the other focused on the principal interpreters of Jewish thought during the past forty years.

I shall forever be grateful to my friend Robert Damus who during my first weeks as a student at St. John's College, Cambridge, in October, 1968, suggested I join him for lunch in Steven Katz's rooms at Jesus College saying "You two Jewish guys from the States ought to know one another." The relationship that began then has flowered into a rich friendship of which this book is an offspring.

Steven Katz conceived the scope of this volume, and we both benefitted at an early stage of our work from the advice of our dear friend and teacher Pinchas H. Peli of blessed memory. Steven then enlisted the participation of a noteworthy group of essayists who when taken together with their editor may be justly described as among the principal figures in Jewish Studies in the 1990's. They are the intellectual heirs to the nearly fifty scholars, teachers and rabbis who contributed to the first five volumes. Because of the effective collaboration between the authors and the editor, I believe the readers will find this volume to be free of unnecessary density and exceptionally well-written. All of the essays were written specifically for this volume.

Now another volume is being planned, what will be the eighth in the series, and its purpose will be to examine the growth of the State of Israel since 1948 and its impact on the life on the Jewish People.

The B'nai B'rith Commission on Continuing Jewish Education comprises a dedicated body of lay leaders who devote themselves to the creation of programs which achieve a greater understanding of Judaism and of the Jewish contribution to civilization. Three successive chairmen of the Commission guided its return to book publishing – Abe Kaplan, Dr. A. J. Kravtin and Arthur Recht – each of them giving generously of their time and counsel to what is a complicated enterprise, and a true labor of love. During these years Milton Smith of Austin, Texas, a senior member and officer of the Commission, played a central role in these efforts to publish important books and to have them used in the widest range of educational settings. Milton's legion of friends know that he would give any one of them the shirt off his back, but they also know he would much rather give them a book to read. His enthusiasm, encouragement and high standards have lightened my burdens, and increased the success of our book publishing program. In February, 1993, he became the Chairman of the Commission, and this volume is the first to be published during his term of office.

This Commission continues to enjoy the support, advice and commitment of Philip M. Klutznick who as the President of B'nai B'rith oversaw its establishment and placed its work at the center of the B'nai B'rith agenda. The *B'nai B'rith Great Books Series* was begun under his watchful eye. Today, B'nai B'rith's current President, Kent E. Schiner, encourages the Commission's activities in every way he can.

Among my professional colleagues I owe the greatest debt to Dr. Sidney M. Clearfield, the Executive Vice President of B'nai B'rith, who is providing the leadership and environment necessary for a Jewish educational program of quality to flourish. Within the Department of Continuing Jewish Education the administrative support and deep devotion which Felice Caspar and Sandra Wiener provide have made this project proceed in a competent and orderly manner.

B'nai B'rith seeks to serve the Jewish People through a comprehensive set of programs which are devoted to the transmittal of one's Jewish identity from one generation to another, at the core of which are the ethics and values of Judaism. A tradition cannot endure or be passed on unless it is well understood, and the living faith which is Judaism is constantly in a state of creative tension and growth. *Interpreters of Judaism in the Late Twentieth Century* amply reflects the vigorous intellectual life of the Jewish

People today. With thanks to Steven Katz for an editorial job superbly accomplished, B'nai B'rith offers this book as both a chronicle and a contribution to the process of Jewish renewal.

MICHAEL NEIDITCH
Director
B'nai B'rith Commission
on Continuing Jewish Education

Washington, D.C.
11 March 1993
18 Adar 5753

Introduction

The past quarter century has been a period of great creativity in the area of Jewish thought. First-class minds have continued to wrestle with both old and new issues confronting the Jewish people. The Holocaust and the growth of the State of Israel have been the causes of ferment in Jewish thought. Much of this intellectual activity has centered around these two monumental and transformative events, particularly the Holocaust, for thought still has difficulty grasping the unprecedented attempt to physically exterminate an entire people. But these two *topoi*, important as they are, do not exhaust the subjects that have been philosophically and theologically consequential in our time. The more traditional legacy of German philosophy in its various guises, Kantianism, Hegelianism and Existentialism, has continued to be felt in important ways, as has the impact of American naturalism and pragmatism, especially among those influenced by Mordecai Kaplan. Then again, the diversity of philosophical and theological opinions expressed have ranged from right to left, from orthodox to self-proclaimed pagan, from Zionist to state-denying, from secular to messianic. Indeed it is difficult to think of a time that has evidenced more intellectual, religious, ethical and political diversity than our own. And this not only because of political and denominational divisions within the Jewish community but also because new and challenging issues, in particular matters relating to sex and gender, have arisen and need attending to. We do live in interesting times.

In the present collection of original essays, each examining the work of one of the foremost thinkers of our time, an attempt has been made to describe and analyze this diverse conceptual scene. Ranging over the wide geographical expanse of the Jewish People, from Israel, through Europe and on to America, the present volume offers the most current, comprehensive, and sophisticated introduction available to contemporary Jewish thought.

What is most impressive about the present effort is that each contribution not only provides competent exegesis of the thought of the individual thinker under review but also offers serious and meaningful criticism of what is living and what is dead in his work. The contributors to this volume are distinguished scholars, experts on their subjects. Accordingly, the studies that comprise this volume are themselves, insofar as philosophy and theology advance through criticism, significant contributions to the ongoing conversation which is contemporary Jewish thought.

This volume was initiated by Dr. Michael Neiditch, B'nai B'rith's Director of Continuing Jewish Education. With its recently published companion entitled *Frontiers of Jewish Thought*, which I had the pleasure of editing last year, it extends the five volume *B'nai B'rith History of the Jewish People*, edited by Simon Noveck and Abraham Millgram, and is a worthy addition to its illustrious predecessors. Like them, this collection embodies the best Jewish scholarship of its generation, and like them it makes this sophisticated scholarship available to an educated lay Jewish audience. Written in a style free of technical jargon, the essays in the present work seek to make it possible for the wider Jewish community to become a serious partner in the philosophical and theological dialogue that is so central to their future as Jews.

Here a note about three stylistic matters is in order. First, as Editor I have allowed each author to transliterate Hebrew words in the manner s/he prefers rather than imposing an artificial uniformity throughout the volume that would have made some of the contributors uncomfortable. Second, in the copy-editing of the manuscript, as in *Frontiers of Jewish Thought*, the copy editor has followed recent practice of not italicizing most Hebrew words that have become a quite regular part of the English language. Third, some small diversity in the form of the Bibliographies that accompany each essay has been allowed in order to accommodate individual authorial preferences.

II

In the creation, execution and production of this volume I have incurred a number of significant debts. First of all, I would publicly like to thank the contributors to this collection who have made my job as Editor a relatively easy one. Second, I must thank Dr. Michael Neiditch of B'nai B'rith, who invited the Editor to undertake the work, and offered wise counsel whenever he was called upon to do so. Third, the careful and diligent work of Ms. Felice Caspar of B'nai B'rith on all phases of the production of this book is much appreciated.

Closer to home, I have benefitted greatly from the help of Mrs. Raihana Zaman and Mrs. Phyllis Emdee, both of the Department of Near Eastern Studies at Cornell University. Their constant willingness to lend a hand, always with a smile, is greatly appreciated. And lastly, and as always, I am indebted in countless ways to my wife Rebecca, and to my patient and loving children, Shira, Tamar and Yehuda.

STEVEN T. KATZ

Eliezer Berkovits

CHARLES M. RAFFEL

Reading Eliezer Berkovits' varied writings, one is struck by the double image of a not-so-gentle warrior fighting to uncover the essence of Jewish religious faith on two widely different fronts. On the broad modern battlefield, he relentlessly challenges the skeptic, the scientist, and the searcher to consider the possibilities of a commitment to faith or at least to look on from the perspective of a committed and enlightened believer. A life devoid of faith, he seems to argue, is not worth living. On a narrower battlefield of traditional Judaism, as a committed insider of the Orthodox community, he argues passionately that tradition not only must learn from the best values of secular modernity but must adapt to them as well. He is interested not only in suffusing modernity with traditional faith and faith in tradition, but is equally committed to modernizing tradition.

Berkovits' biography provides a glimpse of a man passionately committed to a life of both theory and practice—a philosopher-theologian involved in both communal leadership and scholarly activity. He was born in Transylvania in 1908, when the area was under Hungarian domain (it currently is part of Romania), and received a traditional yeshiva education culminating in rabbinical ordination from the Hildesheimer Rabbinical Seminary. In 1933 he completed a doctorate in philosophy at the University of Berlin and, upon graduation, acquired a firsthand knowledge of world Jewry, serving Orthodox congregations in Berlin, Leeds, Sydney, and Boston. After twenty-two years in the rabbinate, at age fifty, Berkovits changed the focus of his career to become chairman of the Department of Jewish Philosophy at the Hebrew Theological College in Skokie, Illinois. There he was known as a dynamic and forceful teacher, public lecturer, and scholar. Berkovits' overarching philosophical vision and theological concerns reveal a deep imprint from his early rabbinic career. His approach in the classroom, lecture hall, or print, has been refreshingly direct, practical, and geared to the widest concerns of the Jewish community. Berkovits has used philosophic analysis and his knowledge of traditional Jewish sources in order to face real problems and to offer real solutions. He has had a lifelong commitment to addressing important problems and controversial issues. A case in point is Berkovits' crusade for understanding and expanding the role of women in Orthodox Judaism, a focus of some of his early essays, the subject of a detailed halakhic analysis in Hebrew in 1966, and the topic of a book scheduled for publication in 1990, Berkovits' eighty-second year. A recognized leader within religious Zionism throughout the first two phases of his career, Berkovits realized a personal dream and began a third phase in 1975 when he immigrated to Israel. The term *retirement* hardly applies for Berkovits' prodigious scholarly output has continued with a sharpened focus on revitalizing the status of halakha within the state of Israel.

In his writings, he successfully handles many roles: philosopher, theologian, social critic, polemicist, and controversialist. In 1956 he published a sustained critique of Arnold Toynbee's views on Jewish history and Judaism, *Judaism: Fossil or Ferment?* and in 1959, *God, Man and History*, which contains Berkovits' philosophy of religion in general and Judaism in particular. His independent and original analysis of biblical theology, *Man and God*, was followed by a prize-winning philosophic critique of Hermann Cohen, Franz Rosenzweig, Martin Buber, Mordecai Kaplan, and Abraham Joshua Heschel, *Major Themes in Modern Philosophies of Judaism*. Perhaps the easiest introduction to the full range of Berkovits' concerns and methods is a collection of twelve short essays, ranging from "The New Morality," through "The Status of Woman within Judaism," to "Exile and Redemption," in a volume entitled *Crisis and Faith*.

One may best be introduced to the depth, substance, and style of Berkovits' oeuvre through overviews of three representative works: his post-Holocaust theology, his philosophy of halakha, and a phenomenological examination of prayer.

Post-Holocaust Theology

Berkovits' most accessible theological statement for the general reader is his attempt to make the case for the possibility of belief in God in the modern era. In *Faith after the Holocaust*, he offers a concise yet relatively complete plan of attack. First, he identifies the moral dimensions of the problem, from the obscene wickedness of the Nazi death machine to the pointed apathy and even resistance to offering help on the part of governments that knew of the atrocities yet failed to respond. Second, he labels as pernicious and explodes the myth that the Jews who went to their deaths were somehow responsible for their own victimization. Third, he lays bare the doctrinal elements of anti-Judaism within Christianity which formed the background for persecution and destruction of Jews. Fourth, Berkovits offers a perceptive analysis of the death-of-God movement within Christianity, which, in his view, is an attempt to dismantle, if not transcend, some of the major weaknesses of the Christian view of man and the world: "What we see today in 'radical theology' is a rebellion among Christians against a concept of God and redemption that indeed treats man as a worthless creature, incapable of responsibility of his own, as well as a radical rejection of the notion of a world that is so fallen and so corrupt that its only hope is to be replaced by another-worldly Kingdom of God."[1]

All this work is necessary preparation for Berkovits' main thrust—to carve out an authentically Jewish view or response to the problem of evil. He labels as defeatist and as a misrepresentation of the totality of existence and experience the Jewish corollary to radical theology: "There is a simple way to resolve the crisis of faith presented by the Jewish death-camp experience. One may meet the problem with a resolutely negative approach and say that what happened was only possible because God has abandoned the Jew, because He is not concerned with what happens to man. One might cut the Gordian knot with the classical formula: 'There is no justice and there is no judge!'"[2]

His counterargument is based on an emotional appeal to recognize that good also exists and existed also in the concentration camps: "It is true that nowhere on earth and never before in history could one experience the absurdity of existence as in the German death camps; but it is also true that nowhere else in this world and never before could we experience the nobility of existence as there and then."[3]

Berkovits then begins to recount, while he confesses his own fears and trembling, the superhuman ability of some in the death camps to preserve their dignity, to persevere amid the horror, and in the ultimate sacrifice to die by sanctifying God's name. (Berkovits perhaps underestimates the response that good, at such a price, loses meaning outside of a faith experience.)

There is much left for Berkovits to teach the skeptical reader. He attempts to guide the reader along by revealing the roots of the problem within Jewish tradition. He signals the seriousness of his approach by moving beyond, at the very outset, the "evil as punishment for sin" view: "There is suffering because of sins; but that all suffering is due to it is simply not true. The idea that the Jewish martyrology through the ages can be explained as divine judgment is obscene. Nor do we for a single moment entertain the thought that what happened to European Jewry in our generation was divine punishment for sins committed by them. It was injustice absolute; injustice countenanced by God."[4]

The outlines of Berkovits' framing of the problem and its solution share a methodological similarity—neither the problem nor the solution is new. Through his close reading of selected, representative biblical and rabbinic texts, the key image which conveys the dialectic of faith and doubt is God's hiding his face (*Hester Panim*), the paradoxical experience of the believer, in time of despair, of the palpable absence of God's presence.

The problem of evil, which represents a challenge to faith, may be magnified by the terrors of the Holocaust, in Berkovits' view, but the theological problem is essentially the same. "The experience of God's 'absence' is not new: each generation had its Auschwitz problem. Neither is the negative response of resulting disbelief new in the history of Jewish spiritual struggle: each generation had its radical theology. Yet, the men of faith in Israel, each facing his own Auschwitz, in the midst of their radical abandonment by God, did not hesitate to reject the negative resolution of the problem."[5] This stance, as Berkovits notes, is epitomized by Job, who exclaims (13:15): "Though he slay me, yet will I trust in Him; But I will argue my ways before Him."

Though not fully trumpeted by him as such, the dialectical relationship of *Hester Panim*, of God's presence and absence, the believer's ability to persist in a faith relationship with God despite the heaviest of losses and in the presence of apparent divine indifference, is the cornerstone of Berkovits' answer to the problem of evil. Berkovits identifies as "the explanation" his own version of the familiar free-will defense, which attempts to explain why an omnipotent God tolerates evil. The answer involves God's initial and unbending commitment to the nature of man as a being who is capable of choosing good or evil: God is, if you will, so invested in preserving man's freedom that He restrains himself from intervening when man chooses evil.

For Berkovits, then, the question shifts from the specific problem of evil to the more general problem or mystery of creation: "The question therefore is not: Why is there undeserved suffering? But, why is there man? He who asks the question about injustice in history really asks: Why a world? Why creation?"6 Berkovits' own conclusion is that a mature understanding of the existence of moral evil and God's transcendence are connected: "He who demands justice of God must give up man; he who asks for God's love and mercy beyond justice must accept suffering."7

The final step in Berkovits' multidimensional approach to the problem is to underscore that the persistence of the Jewish people throughout history, and particularly the creation of the State of Israel against all odds and in defiance of all rational explanations, is a powerful indication of God's presence in history: "Eliminate Israel from history and there is no need for any reference to God. Without Israel everything is explainable and 'expected.' Economics, power politics, and psychology will explain all.... Because of Israel the Jew knows that history is messianism, that God's guidance—however impenetrably wrapt in mystery—is never absent from the life of the nations."8

Although every step of his efforts in *Faith after the Holocaust* would merit further analysis and refinement, Berkovits' achievement should not be underestimated—it is a concise, sophisticated, yet accessible defense of the possibility of maintaining faith in a divine being despite the terrors and challenges of rampant moral wickedness and depravity.

Philosophy of Halakha

Halakha, the Jewish ethical-legal system taken in its broadest sense, may cast a foreboding and inflexible image of doctrinaire, religious imperatives to a nonobservant bystander. Berkovits' goal in *Not in Heaven: The Nature and Function of Halakha* is to rehabilitate a truer image of the functioning of halakha, based on classical sources and interpretations, to shed light for both an involved participant and a more skeptical observer.

He begins by harnessing several well-known talmudic sources to demonstrate that biblical law, as interpreted, expanded, and contracted through the generations of rabbinic interpreters, has evolved, not in a vacuum, but in a close and decisive relationship with a number of primary ethical concerns. In discussing the roles of "common sense", "the wisdom of the feasible", and "the priority of the ethical" in halakhic decision making, Berkovits rehearses in a concise and convincing manner several cases to substantiate the following representative conclusions: "A number of other halakhic arrangements were, in fact, corrections upon biblical laws under the pressure of economic needs.... We have seen how interrelated pragmatic and moral considerations are in the Halakha."[9]

The hallmark of halakha, in Berkovits' portrait, is the opposite of its "popular" image; upon close examination, its inner workings reveal not rigidity but a purposeful and consistent flexibility based on a compassionate assessment of the human predicament: "As is the way of Halakha, great efforts are made to retain the meaning of the legal principle and yet to find solutions to the daily problems arising from the confrontation between the written word and the ethical needs of the concrete situation."[10]

This theme, a debunking of the image of the cold aloofness of the halakhic system, is reflected in the title of the work. Berkovits seconds Rabbi Joshua's claim in the Talmud (Baba Metzia 59b) of the significant human role in halakhic decision making by reaffirming that the Torah is "not in Heaven."

This false image of halakha arose in part because of the historical reality of the diaspora, which produced a "twofold *Galut* of Halakha—its exile from reality and its exile into literature and codification." Jews living under foreign rule, hostile or otherwise, could not construct and live the entirety of their social and political reality according to Jewish law. In part in reaction to diaspora conditions, halakha abandons its inherent oral (and inherently flexible) framework and is codified in written terms and as a result is "straitjacketed."[11]

Berkovits envisions the possibility of a major restoration of halakha to its original function: a bold, creative (and, in his view, classical) flowering of halakha in the state of Israel. Berkovits' dream calls for a new cadre of rabbinic leadership, in touch with the classical principles of Jewish law yet equally aware of all aspects of the modern reality, who boldly develop and carry out a plan of action. His summary overview includes creative and suggestive solutions to such controversial issues as qualifications of witnesses in a rabbinical court, restrictions on autopsies, balancing agricultural economic needs with Sh'mitta (Sabbatical year) observance, marital and divorce laws in light of the modern status of women, and conversion by non-Orthodox rabbis.

Each solution involves a return to the sources and the reassertion or application of a previously rejected minority view from the Talmud. Berkovits substantiates this method by explaining the function of the minority view in decision making. If, because of changing social, economic, or political circumstances, the minority view attains greater validity or cogency, it should be elevated to majority status and adopted as law.

Berkovits' first explanation is paradigmatic. According to the majority opinion, one who transgresses ritual commandments is disqualified to serve as a witness in a rabbinical court. The minority view, that "only a person who does not deal honestly with his fellow man is not to be treated as a witness," is recorded in the talmudic debate. According to Berkovits, the prevailing norms of ritual observance have changed, and the minority view should today be reasserted as law. He asks rhetorically: "Can we in all honesty say that a Jew who does not observe the dietary laws is not to be trusted as a witness? ... Dare we in good conscience disqualify as witnesses the majority of the Jews, who in their interpersonal relationships are no less honest and trustworthy than the Jew who does observe the dietary laws?"[12]

In this and the other cases, Berkovits argues that he is not reinventing the law but restoring it to its original intentions. Change in historical reality requires the substitution of the minority view to realign the law's balance and aim. Similarly, Berkovits would seem to call for liberalizing the rabbinic restrictions on autopsies to further medical research and to explore options for allowing the land of Israel to lie fallow every seventh year, which maintain the spirit of the prohibition and do not violate Israel's agricultural economy. He also calls for marital and divorce laws that take into account a more egalitarian view of the status of women. Finally, to preserve Jewish unity among the varied ideological denominations, he argues for a more lenient conversion process, in line with halakhic rulings, that would go to great lengths to satisfy all concerns.

Berkovits' suggestions, some of which he has substantiated more fully elsewhere, are not fully worked out in the book, nor are they meant to be. Rather, he has creatively sketched out a plan for the formation of halakha within Israeli society, a "restoration," as he calls it, for the future. Before evaluating these visions, one must at least applaud his daring, for demonstrating the courage to dream in what may be called, even in understatement, a politically charged minefield.

Overall, Berkovits' philosophy of halakha, as crystallized in *Not in Heaven*, confirms and expands upon clear trends and tendencies he expressed in earlier articles on selected issues of halakhic concern. He reveals a firm and explicit commitment to a process of halakha which is greatly informed by a respect for human freedom, by an awareness of the decisive influence of human reason, a heightened sensitivity to changing social, cultural, and economic realities, and the predominant role of ethical values. Not only must halakha change out of necessity with the times, but in Berkovits' view, the only authentic halakhic process, from its very inception, is the one that is ideologically committed to change. The decisive role which ethics, changing social circumstances, and human reason play in Berkovits' portrait has startled, if not shocked, many of his modern Orthodox colleagues. Several have questioned whether Berkovits has indeed thrown the baby out with the bathwater by pushing Orthodox ideology beyond its breaking point and thereby aligned his view of halakha with a classical Conservative view of the evolving nature of halakha. Nevertheless, Berkovits emerges as the forerunner of a new generation of modern Orthodox thinkers, represented by Irving Greenberg and David Hartman, for example, who, each in different ways, attempts to carve out a major role for creative human initiative in response to dramatic social change as part and parcel of the authentic halakhic enterprise. It is to Berkovits' credit that his theoretical forays are invariably linked (particularly in his Hebrew works) to practical, documented plans of his proposals for change.

Prayer

In his remarkable book on the nature of prayer, Berkovits addresses, in an understated tone, a number of philosophical and theological issues. The result is not only an inventive essay on prayer, which translates several significant midrashim into a modern idiom, but a revealing glimpse of Berkovits' view of the inner recesses of Jewish values and practice. The relationship between individual and communal prayer receives a sensitive examination. How may spontaneous, personal, deeply felt expressions of gratitude, despair, or supplication be harmonized into an obligatory format of thrice daily communal prayer? Berkovits emphasizes that individual prayer should be maintained as part of one's own personal quest, yet communal prayer is Jewish prayer par excellence. He summarizes the ultimate limitations of individual prayer:

> Individual prayer, elicited by specific occasions, may imply that man seeks, praises and thanks God only occasionally, whereas man's dependence and God's nearness are perennial. Every occasion is an occasion for prayer. Finally, we found that individual prayer may be selfish and unethical prayer, completely forgetful of the interests of one's fellow-men. We may, therefore, say that individual prayer is problematic because of the insufficiency of the subjective experience of the individual alone; because it takes insufficient cognizance of the objectively ever acute human dependence on God; and because it tends to overlook the intricate web of interdependence between all human destinies.[13]

The life challenge for a Jew is to invest his being into the life of the community through communal prayer in which he "transforms the obligatory prayer into the voice of his own heart." Rooting prayer both in the Jewish people's experiences in history and in light of eternity, Berkovits labels prayer not only a "national preoccupation" but a "national profession."[14] The realization that the form of prayer is communal and the text of prayer is anchored consistently in the first-person plural leads Berkovits to zero in on a concise and haunting formulation of Judaism itself:

> The concept derives directly from the specific nature of Judaism. Judaism is not a religion of individual souls but that of a people. This again is due to the fact that Judaism is not a creed in the sense that one should be saved by faith alone; in Judaism one must implement one's belief and one's deeds. The deed, however, is life in its entirety, and life in its entirety is never life in isolation, not even that of the individual. The whole of life, in all its manifestations, personal or political, ethical or economical, individual or social, must be lived with the awareness that it is being enacted by man in the presence of God.[15]

Berkovits' far-ranging discussion includes an insightful defense of a philosophical objection to prayer: how can man, through selfish requests and demands on God, hope to steer an omniscient being away from His original intent and plan? Berkovits sees the question arising not only from Kant's modern complaints about the illogic behind this kind of prayer but adumbrated in the writings of "Talmudic and Midrashic teachers of Judaism [who] saw clearly that prayer was—in a sense—tactless, that it was a form of molesting the Almighty."[16]

Berkovits' answer, that "prayer is possible only because God desires to be imposed upon by man,"[17] formulates a neatly nuanced portrait of God's omnipotence which welcomes and takes note of man's creaturely dependence as part and parcel of the overall divine scheme. This slim volume includes several other theological, philosophical, and practical questions, which Berkovits adroitly handles.

Assessing the Contribution

Writing in praise of his mentor, Rabbi Yechiel Yakob Weinberg, Berkovits admired, among his many virtues, his insistence in evaluating talmudic commentaries by which "he felt obligated to accept or to reject their ideas in accordance with what he himself found to be true or false." Berkovits' own writings are marked by this same independent insistence and impatience, but on a much larger canvas. He shows little patience for the moral bankruptcy of

Western civilization. Rather, he idealizes a religious piety that, for him, is the ultimate courageous response in the face of adversity. In this universe, it is crystal clear who and what are good and who and what are bad. Berkovits is not interested in being a stylist; his strong points of view are conveyed through a deliberate three-part plan, which he also learned from his mentor; "clarity, simplicity and depth."[18] This straightforward, aggressive approach can be refreshing, challenging, and, at times, heavy-handed and dismissive. But Berkovits is one of a handful of thinkers and critics of whom one may honestly say that he pulls no punches.

Another acknowledged master and mentor, the medieval thinker Judah Halevi, lurks in the background of much of Berkovits' overall plan. In an early work, he labels Halevi "the solitary figure among Jewish philosophers of religions who succeeded in recognizing the independence of the religious realm, combining with it a healthy respect for the faculty of reason in its own domain."[19] The dramatic tension of Halevi's magnum opus, *The Kuzari*, is worthwhile to recollect for the light it sheds on Berkovits' enterprise. Halevi's alter ego attempts to provide the impetus for the king's conversion to Judaism by arguing on two fronts: first, an internal critique of philosophy as incapable of providing the ultimate step to both a relationship to the divine and truth itself, and, second, an appreciation of Judaism as the unique vehicle to the ultimate experience of the divine.

Berkovits emerges as a modern-day Halevi, battling and demeaning the vanity of a secular and amoral existence by exploring the higher experiential truth offered by the religious realm. It is an approach that admires reason and exploits reason to lead to the beginnings of a path that transcends reason. If success is defined by the number of conversionary experiences engendered by Berkovits' provoking thoughts, one may only speculate. But if success is defined by his stimulating challenges to an atheological contemporary mind-set, Berkovits' writings, on a popular and accessible level, are more than welcome, forceful additions to the debate.

Of the works reviewed here in some detail, his *Faith after the Holocaust* provides a serious, sophisticated, traditional, and nuanced Jewish theodicy. Ultimately, for the contemporary reader, the answer it offers, the possibility of faith, either transcends logic or is devoid of it. But it attempts to balance the debate, both in combating radical atheologians and those who base their theological statements on the absolute uniqueness of the Holocaust. As such, it is an impressive, controversial, challenging, if not ultimately convincing work.

Berkovits is at his best when the combative fire is toned down or sublimated. His *Not in Heaven* works most effectively as a clear introduction to an innovative and creative approach yet traditional (read Orthodox) to the ethos and inner workings of halakha. At the close of the book, when outlining a plan for Orthodox leadership of the future, Berkovits partially reveals his goal. The pedagogical step prior to reinfusing halakha with its original breadth and dynamism is "to interpret the teaching and its meaning for the searching, questioning, doubting contemporary Jew."[20] Berkovits' portrayal is certainly a significant start in achieving this goal. In addition, *Not in Heaven* may surprise some contemporary readers with the unanticipated image of a daring, pragmatic, and compassionate Orthodox thinker. But its impact on Orthodoxy and the Orthodox com munity, both in North America and Israel today, considering their own current ideological bent, would seem to be marginal.

Berkovits' work is targeted on two different fronts: his attempt to explain the dimensions of Jewish thought to the general reader and his attempt to stimulate positive change within his own Orthodox community. Although the full nature of Berkovits' relationship to American and Israeli Orthodoxy is beyond the scope of this essay, a brief comment would seem necessary. As the Orthodox community moved, on the whole, in the direction of the right, toward a greater conservatism, Berkovits moved to the left, favoring more change and openness. As with other prophets in their hometown, Berkovits' suggestions, whether a proposed change in the wording of the marriage contract to avoid the problem of *agunot* or for a revised and modernized yeshiva curriculum of study, received more sustained praise outside of the Orthodox community than within it. At times, within the Orthodox community, he was damned with faint praise, misunderstood, challenged with pointed hostility, or ignored. Part of the problem is ideological, in that Berkovits' outlook did not capture the emerging consensus of Orthodox rabbis and laity. A contributing factor would also seem to be the geographical distance between Chicago, Berkovits' base, and the mythic seat of American Orthodoxy in New York.

Although *Not in Heaven* is designed for and works best for a non-Orthodox audience, Berkovits' theological positions, which reveal his role as defender of the faith, are of enduring value in enabling a committed traditional Jew to reassemble and realign his or her faith under the shadow of the Holocaust. Berkovits skillfully enables his reader to root the problem and the defense of faith in the texts and context of traditional Jewish thought. To put it simply, although his approach is not geared to motivate or substantiate a leap of faith, he may provide enough impetus to maintain or restore faith.

In his masterful work on prayer, Berkovits addresses his dual audience equally well. The book as a whole shows off Berkovits' great strengths and abilities. He tackles difficult philosophical or theological questions clearly and concisely, uses the wealth of talmudic resources which he controls to clarify and illuminate, and, most impressively, provides access to the inner dimensions of what Judaism is all about.

Berkovits' polymathic achievements deserve an appreciation and evaluation beyond the scope of this short essay. Such an evaluation, which has already begun, needs to be carried out by a committee of scholars. His post-Holocaust theodicy has received intensive and careful scrutiny, as have his readings of the major trends in modern Jewish thought.[21] His views on biblical theology and his apparent affinity, acknowledged or otherwise, for religious existentialism should merit separate attention. In addition, the impact of Berkovits' assessment of the future of Christianty in the modern era, particularly in the arena of Christian responses to the Holocaust, would be a welcome contribution to the contemporary religious dialogue. Berkovits' entire theological plan and his philosophy of halakha require serious examination in the context of Orthodoxy and Orthodox thought in the twentieth century.

A contemporary and perhaps nostalgic traveler, who feels uneasy amid the chaotic diversity of modern Jewish thought, might envision the following images of a rescuer or guide—a rabbi deeply rooted in classical Jewish learning, an authoritative traditionalist, who is passionately committed to communicate, without condescension, a love of learning, the knowledge of learning, and the complex feelings of a knowing believer's faith; a philosopher-theologian, equally familiar with ancient, medieval, and contemporary thought, whose built-in homing device is for the truth, free from artifice and pretense; a lover of Zion and of all of Israel, firmly rooted in history and deeply pained by history, who, from Jerusalem, sees hope and plans for redemption with great anticipation. Eliezer Berkovits' achievements, although they have as yet received far too little attention, well encompass all these images.

[Eliezer Berkovits passed away August 25, 1992 in Jerusalem.]

Notes

I wish to thank Dr. Berkovits for clarifying some details of his personal biography in a letter to me dated January 4, 1989.

1. Eliezer Berkovits, *Faith after the Holocaust* (New York, 1973), p. 75. Berkovits' other work on the Holocaust, *With God in Hell: Judaism in the Ghettos and Death Camps* (New York, 1979), examines the expressions of religious faith among Holocaust victims.
2. Ibid. p. 70.
3. Ibid., p. 76.
4. Ibid., p. 94.
5. Ibid., pp. 98–99.
6. Ibid., p. 105.
7. Ibid., p. 106.
8. Ibid., p. 158.
9. Eliezer Berkovits, *Not in Heaven: The Nature and Function of Halakha* (New York, 1983), pp. 15, 19.
10. Ibid., p. 32.
11. Ibid., p. 91.
12. Ibid., p. 94, 95.
13. Eliezer Berkovits, *Prayer* (New York, 1962), p. 59.
14. Ibid., pp. 61, 56.
15. Ibid., p. 55.
16. Ibid., pp. 74–75.
17. Ibid., p. 75.
18. Eliezer Berkovits, "Rabbi Yechiel Yakob Weinberg: My Teacher and Master," in *Tradition* Vol. 12 No. 2 (Summer 1966): 6–7.
19. Eliezer Berkovits, *God, Man, and History* (New York, 1959), p. 10.
20. Berkovits, *Not in Heaven*, p. 117.
21. See Steven T. Katz, *Post-Holocaust Dialogues: Critical Studies in Modern Jewish Thought* (New York, 1983), pp. 94–140, 268–86.

FOR FURTHER READING

Works by Eliezer Berkovits

Crisis and Faith, New York, 1975. This series of short essays is a good introduction to Berkovits' wide variety of concerns.

Faith after the Holocaust, New York, 1973. Berkovits' defense of the possibility of religious belief in the modern era, premised on the denial of the uniqueness of the Holocaust, is examined in this work.

With God in Hell: Judaism in the Ghettos and Death Camps, New York, 1979. This impassioned essay focuses on the courageous responses of traditional Jewry to the horrors of Nazi persecution.

The Jewish Woman in Time and Torah, New York, 1990. This monograph offers an analysis of the status of women in halakhic Judaism.

Major Themes in Modern Philosophies of Judaism, New York, 1974. This volume is Berkovits' critical work revealing his vigorous animadversions on the philosophies of Hermann Cohen, Franz Rosenzweig, Martin Buber, Mordecai Kaplan, and Abraham Joshua Heschel.

Not in Heaven, New York, 1983. In this monograph Berkovits explores, as its subtitle indicates, "the nature and function of Halakha" in contemporary times.

Prayer, New York, 1962. In this concise, nuanced essay, Berkovits neatly addresses a variety of knotty philosophical and theological problems. (Currently out of print, but should be available in libraries that maintain a substantial Judaica collection.)

Works about Eliezer Berkovits

Katz, Steven T., *Post-Holocaust Dialogues: Critical Studies in Modern Jewish Thought*, New York, 1983. The most sustained critical study of Berkovits' thought and methodology may be found in two separate chapters of this book.

Fox, Marvin, "Berkovits' Treatment of the Problem of Evil," *Tradition* (Spring 1974). An extensive review of *Faith after the Holocaust*.

Other reviews of individual works may be gleaned from the pages of *Tradition* and *Judaism*.

Eugene B. Borowitz

DAVID ELLENSON and LORI KRAFTE-JACOBS

A native of Columbus, Ohio, Eugene Borowitz (1924–) received his undergraduate training at the Ohio State University. Upon graduation, he enrolled in the Hebrew Union College in Cincinnati, where he received rabbinical ordination in 1948, as well as earning the degree of Doctor of Hebrew Letters in Rabbinic Thought. In the 1950s he served as founding rabbi of the Community Synagogue in Port Washington, Long Island, New York, and was enrolled in the Union-Columbia joint Ph.D. program in Religion, where he completed all work except for the dissertation. Upon assuming the position as director of the Religious Education Department of the Union of American Hebrew Congregations, Borowitz switched to Columbia's doctoral program in Education and received an Ed.D. In 1962 Borowitz became a full time member of academia, joining the faculty of the Hebrew Union College–Jewish Institute of Religion in New York. He has served there for over three decades as one of the leading theologians of the American Jewish community. He, perhaps more than any other Jewish religious thinker in the modern setting, has been responsible for a renewed interest in theology among contemporary American Jews. From his earliest volumes, *A Layman's Introduction to Religious Existentialism* (1965), *A New Jewish Theology in the Making* (1968), and *How Can a Jew Speak of Faith Today?* (1968), to his more recent *Choices in Modern Jewish Thought* (1983), Borowitz has insisted that Jews approach questions of faith and doubt, God and authority, autonomy and community, with the utmost seriousness. His popularization of religious thought to an

American Jewish community otherwise more sociologically inclined and his insistence that an attempt to address these issues is of considerable moment to the Jewish people are undoubtedly among his greatest contributions to the life of American Jewry.

As editor of *Sh'ma* magazine, a journal of lively Jewish debate and discussion to which persons from all sectors of the community contribute, Borowitz has facilitated dialogue on numerous issues of pressing concern to the American and Jewish communities. An active contributor to various debates within the pages of his journal, Borowitz has displayed an absolute commitment to democracy and pluralism in *Sh'ma*, always allowing the community to speak in all its many voices. Through these thoughtful journalistic and scholarly efforts, Borowitz has become a person of considerable renown on the American Jewish scene.

Borowitz has also served as a prominent Jewish representative to the Christian world. His authorship of *Contemporary Christologies: a Jewish Response* (1980) grew out of an address he was invited to deliver to the predominantly Christian American Theological Association. A significant theological achievement, the book also testifies to the recognition and respect his work has earned among the most prominent non-Jewish theologians in the United States today. Furthermore, his important place in the academic world is reflected in the positions he has held as a visiting professor at universities such as Columbia and Princeton and in his occupancy of the Albert A. List Chair of Jewish Studies at the Harvard Divinity School during the 1982–83 academic year.

Finally, on the denominational level, Borowitz has emerged as arguably the leading thinker of contemporary Reform Judaism and has devoted considerable efforts to articulating a Reform Jewish theology appropriate to the latter part of the twentieth century. While others within the Reform Movement have staked out theological and ideological positions, Borowitz's prominence within Reform is demonstrated by the central role he played in the drafting of the 1976 San Francisco Centenary Perspective. He served as chair of the Central Conference of American Rabbis' Committee that wrote this successor statement to the 1885 Pittsburgh Platform and 1937 Columbus Platform. It stands alone as the most articulate and representative declaration of the Reform movement's position on the doctrines of God, Torah, and Israel. His three-volume commentary on the Perspective, entitled *Reform*

Judaism Today (1979), clearly establishes him as the dominant
theological voice within the Reform Judaism of his generation. It
is in view of the significant positions he occupies in these distinct,
though interrelated, worlds that this essay will analyze and describe the contours and content of his thought as they have
emerged in his vital and productive career.

Eugene Borowitz, perhaps more directly than any other contemporary liberal Jewish thinker, addresses the challenges that the
modern world has presented to the creation of an authentic
present-day liberal Jewish theology. Throughout his career, he
has clearly identified the issue of religious authority—in technical
parlance, the nature of the epistemological warrants put forth for
the legitimization of Jewish life and thought—as the central one
confronting the modern Jew. Borowitz, as a "modern," rejects the
traditional rabbinic notion, articulated in the modern era by
Orthodox Jews such as Rabbi Samson Raphael Hirsch and Rabbi J.
David Bleich, that Jewish law is immutable, divinely legislated,
and absolutely obligatory. Instead, informed by modern notions of
history, Borowitz recognizes that Jewish law has developed over
time and place. Moreover, as in the case of women, that law is seen
as all too humanly constructed.[1] Furthermore, for all its many
difficulties, the central notion of modern moral thought—"that
only an autonomous ethics is worthy of a rational person"[2]—
derived as it is from the teachings of Immanuel Kant, is one that
Borowitz is not prepared to abandon completely as he confronts
contemporary matters of Jewish faith and practice. Given these
cultural conditions and the beliefs in individual autonomy, human
freedom, and historical development that arise from them, Borowitz asks how an authentic Jewish religious life and thought can
be reconstructed. The boldness with which he phrases the questions, as much as the answers he supplies, are key to understanding the importance his thought holds for the modern liberal Jew.

Borowitz has devoted considerable energy toward analyzing
the contributions of other Jewish thinkers. This sustained analysis
is not only insightful and the source of much of his fame. It is also
important to him as one who stands within the tradition of
modern Jewish thought. He notes that the Jewish responses to
emancipation have been more social than intellectual, focusing on
practical efforts to address the problems engendered by modern-

ity's challenge to Jewish faith.[3] Although he does not minimize the importance of these practical efforts, he is no less interested in questions of form and truth. This commitment to methodological and theological development characterizes his own writings and sheds light as well upon his critical investigation of other Jewish theologies. Two works in particular illustrate Borowitz's agenda in examining other Jewish thinkers: "The Problem of the Form of a Jewish Theology," which confronts the issue of method, and *Choices in Modern Jewish Thought*, in which he analyzes the major systematized models of modern Jewish thought.

In the first of these, Borowitz seeks to make explicit (in his own work and others') the form of the thought pattern that underlies all the theological particulars of a given system; that is, he does a "morphology of contemporary Jewish theologies" to discern the fundamental commitments characteristic of each.[4] His critiques of Abraham Joshua Heschel, Leo Baeck, Mordecai Kaplan, and Martin Buber clearly reflect his own commitment to covenant theology. He finds Heschel's, Baeck's and Buber's methods unacceptable because they slight the people Israel—Heschel by reducing Israel to its status as the recipient of revelation, Baeck by justifying Jewish particularity instrumentally, and Buber by fragmenting the community into a collection of individuals. By contrast, Borowitz is unpersuaded by Kaplan's method because he cannot accept the latter's elevation of Israel at the expense of God. None of the methods he examines strikes the balance he requires between God and Israel, between Judaism as a religion and Judaism as an ethnicity.[5]

Choices in Modern Jewish Thought echoes this agenda. Borowitz makes an effort to separate description from analysis and is largely successful in doing so, but he candidly acknowledges his own position, making "no claim to be writing ... as an objective historian of ideas."[6] And though here the analysis of various Jewish theologies is more detailed and more substantial, still the challenge each must face is whether it can do justice to this dual commitment to God and Israel. If either element of covenant is subordinated to the other, the covenant is unworkable.

Both of these works indicate the depth of Borowitz's concern with questions of form and truth. They demonstrate as well the ultimate reason he is interested in these questions—because he believes that Judaism must "be understood and explained in a convincing fashion, that is, in terms of ideas which carry weight with people today," if we are to find a satisfactory way of being modern and Jewish.[7]

Borowitz, like such among his liberal predecessors as Hermann Cohen and Leo Baeck, affirms the significance of autonomy and reason as categories of absolute value for the modern Jew. Yet living in a post-Holocaust situation, he recognizes the limits of classical liberalism. In the twentieth century, reason and reliance on the innate goodness of humanity have shown themselves to be "unreliable, if not destructive."[8] As he writes elsewhere, "I think it is only an understatement to say that, in our day, the self-confidence of humanism is ludicrous.... Secularity no longer is self-assured and triumphant. If anything, its moral collapse has been so thoroughgoing that it threatens to destroy whatever little faith in humankind we can still manage to muster."[9] Liberal Jews today simply cannot share the confidence their Reform ancestors possessed in autonomy, the icons of contemporary Western culture, and the notion of "progressive" revelation whereby the social and religious insights of each succeeding generation were regarded as representing an improvement over the preceding one's. In short, faith in secular culture and its accompanying beliefs, though not abandoned, has been muted.

Borowitz's reliance on, yet distance from, the categories of autonomy and reason he inherited from the legacy left him by the proponents of Enlightenment thought within the Reform Jewish camp is paralleled by the approach he takes to the thought of Martin Buber. It is impossible to understand Borowitz's writings without a genuine appreciation of the seminal role Buber's notion of relation plays in his thought. Buber has taught Borowitz that "all real living is meeting" and that the moments of I-Thou relation we experience in the world are the most significant glimpses of the divine we appropriate in our lifetimes. Yet Borowitz also recognizes, from both a Jewish and a modern perspective, the inherent limitations in Buber's thought for the modern liberal Jew. For all Buber's emphasis on relation, Borowitz still finds him too focused on the lone individual and not sufficiently appreciative of the role tradition ought to play in the life of the committed Jew. Buber's excessive emphasis on the autonomy of the individual and his refusal to allow the tradition and Jewish law to inform his consciousness and guide his conduct are contained in a letter Buber wrote to his close friend and colleague Franz

Rosenzweig. Anxious for encounter with God, Buber discredited
the role the law and community could play in facilitating such a
meeting. "I cannot," Buber wrote, "admit the law transformed by
man into the realm of my will, if I am to hold myself ready for
the unmediated word of God directed to a specific hour of my
life."[10] As a result, for Borowitz, Buber's notion of relation suffers
from the disintegrative tendencies of an excessive individualism
insufficient to provide for the social cohesion the contemporary
world, and particularly the Jewish community, so desperately
needs. For in the present situation, the task confronting the individual Jew is not primarily one of affirming autonomy and individual personhood. It is the challenge of creating institutions in
which Jews and all persons can have a sense of confidence and
hope. It is nothing less than the reconstitution of Jewish communal life that provides a sense of urgency to modern Jewish life
and thought.

Hence Borowitz turns to the classical Jewish notion of covenant to respond. This idea, though not understood in the Orthodox sense as "objective law," is a precise reflection of Borowitz's
methodological commitments, about which he is clear. In his
essay on method entitled "The Problem of the Form of a Jewish
Theology," Borowitz calls upon Jewish theologians to face "the
holistic question,"—that is, to look at the total context of which
each individual religious motif is but a part. This attention to the
conceptual structure of our theology forces us to acknowledge
our primary commitments and to recognize the way in which our
particular theological conclusions are derived from our fundamental patterns of thinking.

Borowitz fully accepts the modern principle of individual
autonomy, which is to him as important as Jewish tradition. Yet,
as we have seen, he is highly critical of those whose wholesale
affirmation of modern culture ignores the moral bankruptcy of
faith in science and the idea of inevitable progress. Unwilling to
choose between a method that subordinates our autonomy to the
divine will and one that subordinates the divine will to our own,
Borowitz embraces a method that seeks to give primacy to both
God and humanity by emphasizing their relationship. "Humanity remains central to our belief, but it is no longer pre-eminent.
Thus faith, that humankind is created so as to be God's partner in
completing creation, has an old and, indeed, unique Jewish foun-

dation. The Bible calls such a two-sided, God-humankind relationship, covenant."[11]

For Borowitz, covenant does not restrict our freedom but presupposes it. He writes, "Though God's sovereign rule of the universe is utterly unimpeachable, people under the covenent need not surrender their selfhood to God. If anything, to participate properly in the alliance they must affirm their freedom for they are called to acceptance and resolve, not servility. They are given commandments, not mere instinct."[12] In this way he seeks to preserve the insights of the Enlightenment without eclipsing the role of God. He calls for a balance between belief in and reliance on God, on one hand, and the affirmation of our own autonomy, on the other. Preserving this dialectic constitutes the fundamental methodological concern that underlies all of Borowitz's work.

To begin, he speaks of God, for it is the reality of God that leads to the "covenanted ethnicity" that Borowitz sees as essential for authentic Jewish existence in our time. "It is clear," Borowitz writes, "that Judaism requires a belief in God."[13] Borowitz acknowledges that human beings cannot know God's essence, yet it is clear that his own conception of God is a personal one, far removed from the ideal of a Hermann Cohen, who asserted that God was an ideal necessary to integrate a philosophical system. Rather, Borowitz, like the ancient rabbis and the prophets, wants to reassert "the reality and nearness of God."[14] God, for him, is the ground for human dignity and worth. "The self gains its worth," he contends over against the claims of an Enlightenment rationalism, "not from itself but from its relationship with God."[15]

Like Judah Halevi and other great thinkers in the Jewish past, Borowitz contends that history is "the laboratory of Jewish theology."[16] History, he feels, testifies to the existence of a "commanding-forgiving" God.[17] Borowitz acknowledges that this God sometimes appears to withdraw from the historical arena, and this he finds intellectually problematic.[18] Still, he affirms the reality of God's presence in history and asserts that God is no mere social projection. God is real, and Borowitz believes that a personal/relational model is the most appropriate one for "thinking about the God with whom I stand in relation."[19] Borowitz's emphasis is thus not on what we can say about God but on how God can be known. God can be known as we know other persons, in I-Thou encounter, "characterized by immediacy, intimacy, and privacy. It is the kind of knowing ... which ... cannot be observed or accurately reported, but only experienced. We know God in this way."[20]

God does not stand as the only pole upon which an authentic Judaism must be built. Indeed, "the axis, the pivot, of the Jewish religion ... [is] not an ideal of God, but the life of Torah. The root religious experience of Judaism ... is the positive one of hearing God's commandment.... It is the sense that God wants us to act in Godlike ways. It is the feeling of mitzvah. It is Torah."[21] This emphasis on "the life of Torah"—a life of commandments and deeds—should not be viewed in Orthodox terms. Here again we see Borowitz's commitment to the dialectic of covenant, which centers around the dual affirmation of God and the people of Israel. Both share in the development of Torah. As he does elsewhere, Borowitz here employs the model of human encounter to understand the roles of God and Israel: "If God gives, and that is all, change is limited.... If only man creates—then ... the laws are too easily changed and the values tend to disappear. Neither the older orthodoxy nor the older liberalism will do. My understanding of revelation involves both man and God actively. Its best analogy is human relationship." It is from this analogy that Borowitz draws his belief in contentless revelation. Just as personal relationship requires fulfillment in action without thereby dictating which acts are appropriate, so with revelation the individual "fills in the content of the law—that is his honorable role—but he does so in response to the living presence of God who is the source and the criterion of the appropriateness of his action."[22] God does not supply the content of revelation, but neither are we to fill in this content in isolation from God's presence.

The content of Torah, though fundamentally ethical, cannot be restricted to ethics, warns Borowitz. Here he distinguishes his position from that of the classical Reformers. Because our understanding of what it means to be human cannot be restricted to the merely ethico-rational but must as well affirm human choosing, loving, and willing, the "full integration of mind and emotion and unfathomable individuality we call a self," Torah must include all these aspects of being human and being Jewish.[23]

Borowitz, then, seeks to avoid the pitfalls of two extremes. On one hand, his commitment to autonomy and reason is too great for an Orthodox understanding of covenant. "For me, as for many others, today's Judaism cannot be an orthodoxy even in the rather open and flexible form in which the new Orthodox left is speaking. For all its promise, such an interpretation of Judaism still gives the halakah and, more significantly, the interpreters of the law, priority over the individual so that his autonomy becomes a heteronomy. Because I cannot see that heteronomy as the equivalent of a theonomy and thus the fulfillment of my autonomy, I cannot be Orthodox."[24] Borowitz's Torah is not mere halakah. His openness to and affirmation of the basic tenets of the modern world prevent that. On the other hand, however, Borowitz's distance from Orthodoxy does not lead him to embrace what he considers to be an attenuated view of revelation as mere ethics. Nor, for all his debt to Buber's work on relatedness, does he finally concur with the latter's emphasis on individualism. Borowitz is concerned with finding a way for the individual Jew to remain autonomous without necessitating a wholly privatized Torah.

In a highly significant essay, "The Autonomous Self and the Commanding Community," Borowitz defends and explicates his understanding of the basic tenets of modernity. In so doing, he contends that there is a Jewish warrant for the "modern imperative of autonomy." Our autonomy, Borowitz argues, is "more God-oriented than our secular teachers admit. . . . [It derives from] the freedom that God has given us." Autonomy is therefore not a form of "enlightened selfishness." Rather, inasmuch as God is the ground for and creator of all humanity, our *autos*—our selfhood—though not denied, cannot escape its social dimensions, its interrelationships to other human beings.[25]

For individual Jews, this means that to be religiously authentic persons they must see themselves as part of a covenantal community. Relying on both modern social scientific theory of the self-in-culture and the biblical-rabbinic notion of covenantal existence, Borowitz asserts that it is scientifically impossible and Jewishly inauthentic for Jews to view themselves as totally isolated individuals. "Jewish existence," he points out, "is not merely personal but communal and even public." Although the individual remains the ultimate arbiter of God's will, the individual is also indissolubly bound to the larger community: "In responding to God out of the Covenant situation, the relationally autonomous Jewish self acknowledges its essential historicity and sociality. . . .

The Covenanted self acknowledges the need for structure to Jewish existence. Yet, this does not rise to the point of validating law in the traditional sense, for personal autonomy remains the cornerstone of this piety.[26] Autonomy remains secure. Still, Jewish law and the written documents containing that law are sacred to the individual Jew because of his or her attachment to the Jewish people and the values expressed by this people Israel in its classical literary heritage. To ignore these writings would be to deny their significant role in the past and ongoing identity of the Jewish community. They cannot help but influence individual Jews' perceptions of their Jewish and human duties and obligations. "Responding to the Divine presence cannot only be a matter of what is commanded to me personally at this moment," as a Buber might have it. Instead, the Jewish self is commanded and responds to that commandment "as one whose individuality is not to be separated from ... being one of the historic Jewish people."[27] Borowitz views this approach in the following way:

> The individual stands in intimate relationship to God, and from that—or from the tradition or the teachers who authentically articulate the consequences of this relationship—the individual discovers what must be done.
> That is true universally; all mankind shares in the Noahide covenant. The Jewish self, however, does not stand in isolated relationship with God but shares in the people Israel's historic covenant. Jewish duty derives from this and is, therefore, ineluctably particular as it is universal, social as it is personal. Yet it must be individually appropriated and projected. For all that the Jewish self comes before God as one of the Jewish people, the Jew remains a self with the personal right to determine what God now demands of the people of Israel and of any particular member of it.[28]

The halakhic system, in its traditional sense, has been abandoned. Nevertheless, commandment and the enduring importance of Torah are highlighted and taken seriously.

The practical application of this thought to matters of ethical and political import can be seen in representative articles and books Borowitz has written on topics as diverse as the notion of the modern state, the nature of Jewish attachment and response to the State of Israel, and the multilayered issues of human sexuality. In "The Old Woman as Meta-Question: A Religionist's Reflections on Nozick's View of the State," an article both clever and subtle, Borowitz discusses and critiques Robert Nozick's philosophical defense of a "minimalist state" as presented in his famous book *Anarchy, State, and Utopia.* In this book, Nozick argues against the notion that a state bears a "corporate responsibility" toward its citizens. Instead, Nozick contends that a state should do no "more than is strictly necessary to enable citizens to exercise their private rights."[29] To coerce its citizenry in any way in order to act on behalf of the disadvantaged is to violate the state's only legitimate function—the protection of the rights of the individual and the preservation of individual human dignity.

Borowitz notes that such a theory runs counter to the approach of liberalism. For liberalism holds that the state has an equal, if not greater, obligation to promote the well-being of its citizens. The advantage of this approach over Nozick's, in Borowitz's view, is that it ameliorates the worst social effects of "the exploitation and oppression which, in effect, become the consequences of political individualism." In sum, from his liberal perspective, Borowitz feels confident that Nozick's state would protect an "old, senile woman" living in a nursing home and growing physically more debilitated daily from those who might subject her to euthanasia. Nevertheless, "while no one will take away her rights, she is not in a position to exercise them. And she is not unique in that respect.... She and her kind may have the negative liberty of non-infringement but not the positive liberty which, practically, is available only for the vigorous and the determined."[30]

Borowitz's distaste for Nozick's state certainly arises from his own liberal political inclinations. More significant for our purposes, however, it stems directly from his understanding of covenantal obligation. "The Bible believes that we are positively obligated to one another.... It prescribes our substantive obligations to others less well-situated or competent. We must plead the case of the widow and the orphan. We must give food and money to the poor.... We must separate a tithe for the poor. These are not options, warmly recommended to the good-hearted. They are commanded, religious laws." The Bible's view is that the protection of individual rights is not the highest, or only, priority of a government. It is, instead, the notion that "we are responsible for one another." This is why most Jews, Borowitz believes, "see in governmental programs promoting social welfare an extension of their own community values."[31] He is careful to note that other

Jews may not read the tradition with the same emphasis that he does, but there is no doubt that his political liberalism is informed much more by his own sense of Jewish covenantal obligation than it is by secular Enlightenment optimism concerning the innate goodness of humanity and the inevitable march of social progress. Indeed, Borowitz explicitly rejects many of the premises of Enlightenment thought. Instead, he supports a liberal political agenda because of the ethos of Jewish tradition as he reads it. Borowitz sees no conflict between the ambience of a modern liberal political agenda and the tradition's call to covenantal faithfulness.

This same approach directs many of Borowitz's attitudes and stances concerning the State of Israel. Anyone who reads Borowitz's words, "Our people has its homeland back," can sense his devotion and admiration for the state, which he acknowledges as "a glowing reality." What the Israelis "have done with political power ... has been, by comparative standards, extraordinarily just." Israeli culture influences Jews throughout the world and touches their lives "in a way that not even Ahad Ha-am could have imagined." "The State of Israel," Borowitz asserts in a Zionist vein consistent with the thrust of Jewish tradition, "is the center of world Jewry."[32]

Yet for all its significance and importance Israel remains a state and "no state," Borowitz contends, "is the messiah."[33] Jewish existence rests upon the transcendent reality that is God and the covenantal relationship which Jews, as individuals and as part of a community, share with the divine. Precisely because the land of Israel is such an integral part of that covenantal relationship, the religious Jew, out of devotion to Israel and as a result of covenantal obligation, must be prepared, at times, to criticize actions of the government of the State of Israel. The invasion of Lebanon, and the massacre at Sabra and Shatila were such times for Borowitz. "All of us," he wrote in the pages of *Sh'ma* following the massacre, "must share in the shame that has fallen on our people this week." Jews must be prepared, he maintained, if Judaism "is to survive as anything more than tribalism," to protest publically against such Israeli acts and policies. He called upon Jews to assert, out of covenantal loyalty and in the recognition that "service of God [is] unequivocally our highest Jewish priority," that "a State of Israel that can conspire with Phalangist thugs is *not* a proper response to the Holocaust. And we are *not* one people if that means condoning blatantly immoral Israeli acts."[34] Such sentiments concerning Israel have been both condemned and applauded within the community. However one regards them, his views on Israel are consistent with his writings on covenant and autonomy and the Jewish responsibilities that spring from them.

In his 1969 book, *Choosing a Sex Ethic*, Borowitz attempts to define a proper Jewish moral stance concerning sexual intercourse without marriage. He asserts that there are four alternate ethical stances advanced by different groups within American society towards this issue, which he labels as the ethics of healthy orgasm, mutual consent, love, and marriage. The first focuses on the egotistical needs of the individual and asserts that since each person's highest duty is to self, each individual "should strive to have as much and as satisfying sex experience as he enjoys." In contrast, the second alternative demands that both partners bring "free, responsible assent to the act." There is a mutuality here lacking in the first ethical alternative. "Sexual acts that arise from and bespeak a genuine love" that two persons share with one another characterizes the third option. The fourth choice, the "ethic of marriage," reflects not only a genuine sense of love and assent that two persons have for each other but a lifelong commitment as well.[35]

Having outlined these positions and defined the basic rationale for each of them, Borowitz considers the teachings of Jewish tradition on the matter. Turning to the biblical-rabbinic category of *pilegesh* (concubine), Borowitz notes that the tradition, in many places, sanctioned sexual unions between such a woman and the master with whom she lived. Although he explicitly notes the problem of sexism inherent in this category, that is not what he wants to emphasize in this context. Rather, his emphasis is that Jewish sexual ethics concerning nonmarital sexual relationships show more tolerance than one might expect. Nevertheless, the thrust of the tradition is that the community is "committed legally and morally to marriage as the only situation in which sexual intercourse should occur." This knowledge, though not binding, should give modern Jews "a fresh perspective on our ... social situation, on the ... contours it gives our version of the sexual problem, and on the values which are implicit in advocating one or another [modern, ethical] response to it.[36] Covenantal loyalty demands that the liberal Jew consider the wisdom of the tradition and be prepared to be informed by it.

In light of Jewish teachings, Borowitz categorically rejects the "ethic of healthy orgasm" as a legitimate Jewish or personal choice. His reason is because Judaism holds that "all persons are of equal moral worth." The egoism inherent in the healthy orgasm ethic, because it makes "possible the subordination of one person's right to that of the other," must be rejected on both Jewish and moral grounds. It invalidates the moral dignity of the other by its refusal to acknowledge that individual's essential humanity and personhood. Borowitz can identify the "ethic of mutual consent" as an advance over the previous one, but he still finds it ultimately demeaning and dismisses it because it sees persons as nothing more than "glands and will." It fails to affirm persons in their fullness as human beings.[37]

In considering an "ethic of love," Borowitz cedes it more than a modicum of legitimacy. He states, "I do not see how I can deny the ethical quality of sexual acts that arise from and bespeak a genuine love.... For people who truly love, to express that love in sexual relations cannot be called unethical." Yet for all its human decency, Borowitz feels that Jewish tradition and a proper sense of morality call for a more significant level of personal existence. Love outside of marriage, as wonderful as it is, remains an affirmation of the present and perhaps the past. "But a person must live ... not only in the present, but into and through the future as well. [A person]," Borowitz maintains, "is that integrity of self which carries on from birth to death." Marital intercourse, because it occurs within a context in which the partners have pledged themselves to each other for life—the future as well as the present and the past—represents the highest degree of holiness a couple can attain. Borowitz acknowledges that both Judaism and a personalist ethic can countenance pluralistic sexual options. Intercourse within marriage, however, embodies "the highest possible level of ethical behavior." Here, as on the other issues, Borowitz finds no conflict between the ethos of Jewish tradition as he reads it and the demands of an autonomous morality.[38]

In a more recent essay, "On Homosexuality and the Rabbinate, a Covenantal Response," Borowitz confronts such a conflict directly. He not only expands upon the sexual ethic he outlined in his previous volume but reflects systematically upon how a liberal

Jew goes about arriving at an authentically Jewish posture on a contemporary issue of grave moral and religious concern. At the outset Borowitz notes that the liberal Jew, as an heir of the Enlightenment, must consider the matter from the perspective of universal moral concerns. But because the "Jewish self" is, "in full autonomy, inextricably linked to God as part of the Jewish people's historic Covenant relationship," the liberal Jew is also obligated to consider the classical texts of the Jewish tradition in reaching a decision. In affirming the "serious claim" these texts make upon him, Borowitz self-consciously departs from an older style of Reform Jewish thinking which mandated ethical concerns as the sole criterion for arriving at a Jewish stance on a problem and only later sought "confirmation [of that stance] from congenial Jewish texts."[39]

Borowitz begins his investigation by ascertaining what might be labeled the universal moral imperative on this matter. That is, what should a human being, apart from any particularistic concerns, feel his or her moral duty to be? "This ... should enable us to be clear about any move we make beyond it to the obligations that arise from our particular Jewish relationship with God, the Covenant." After a prolonged discussion of various ethical options, Borowitz concludes that it is "ethically compelling" for all persons "to fight discrimination against homosexuals" and to condemn any attitude that would "stigmatize and demean [homosexuals] as less than whole, fully human beings." Hence, "If we still believe that universal ethics over-ride all other considerations of Jewish duty, then homosexuality ought to be given full equality among us." The issue of homosexuality forces the liberal Jew to clarify the relationship between universal moral obligations and particular Jewish duties when there is a conflict between the two. Even if no such conflict exists, Borowitz points out that methodologically authentic covenantal decision making requires the liberal Jew to turn to the tradition, for its attitudes are "equally integral to my deciding what I, a Jew, now need to do to serve God properly."[40]

Borowitz's examination of the pertinent halakhic sources on homosexuality forces him to conclude that Jewish law unequivocally condemns homosexual practices. Moreover, such condemnation is virtually unanimous. Rabbinic writing on the subject displays none of the division that characteristically marks rabbinic

opinion on most matters. The rabbis offered such blanket disapproval, Borowitz opines, for two reasons. First, such practices
were regarded as "incompatible with Covenant-holiness," and,
second, the rabbis "saw in generative, heterosexual marriage a
major, if not the major human embodiment of the Covenant
between God and Israel."[41] The case of homosexuality is
especially illuminating for comprehending how Borowitz understands the "Jewish self" because he clearly sees universal moral
concerns and particular, traditional Jewish attitudes as clashing in
this instance. What is the liberal Jew to do? How can the liberal
Jew adjudicate the competing demands of morality, tradition, and
self in a way that will be faithful to the integrity of Judaism and
personhood?

In an attempt to untie these knotty questions, Borowitz turns to
the covenantal community today—those Jews "who seek to live
under Covenant"—to ascertain their views of God's demands in
this situation. As a liberal, Borowitz concedes that this does not
provide an absolute answer to his dilemma. For even among "the
significant community of Israel in our time"—those who strive to
live in covenantal holiness with God—"some [Jews] will sense
[Jewish obligation] here and others there." For this reason, liberal
Judaism "must welcome pluralism," for different groups of Jews,
each in full Covenantal authenticity, may understand God's
demands and Jewish duty differently.[42]

Borowitz acknowledges that "considerable inroads have been
made in the community's prior, relatively unanimous, negative
attitude toward homosexuality." Nevertheless, traditionalists
within the community remain adamantly opposed to homosexuality as a legitimate Jewish life-style option. Furthermore,
even among liberals, Borowitz contends, there has been relatively
little success "in convincing the majority that homosexuality
ought to be granted fully equivalent status with heterosexuality."
The reason for this liberal Jewish perspective stems from the same
sense of covenantal responsibility, Borowitz asserts, that informed
the rabbis. "In sum," he concludes, "I find our community continues to reflect a Covenantal concern ... in denying the equiv-
alence of the faithful homosexual Jewish family to its heterosexual
counterpart." Leaving aside the issue of whether Borowitz's
description of the community's attitude is accurate, a methodological question remains—what weight ought to be assigned to the

community's attitudes in guiding the "Jewish self" to reach a covenantally faithful decision? In keeping with his attitude toward tradition, Borowitz asserts, "Again, as a liberal Jew I do not feel bound by what the Jewish community is saying on this issue, as best I understand it. But as one who shares the community's Covenant, I give its attitude very serious consideration."[43] The dialectical nature of the dilemma is fully revealed. How is the liberal Jew to reconcile the conflicting demands of universal ethics with the obligations imposed by the tradition and the attitudes advanced by the covenantal community on this, or presumably any other, ethical issue?

Borowitz proceeds by stating that "given a choice, the covenant requires Jews to elect the heterosexual option." But "what of the significant number of persons who could only be asked to undertake [this option] by doing violence to a central, ingrained element of their personality?" The concern for self—its inviolability and holiness—causes Borowitz to modify the tradition's negative attitude toward homosexuality.

> All of us need to serve God as much out of who we personally are as by what our community understands the Covenant to require of us generally. Furthermore, while every Jew has always been precious to our people, after the Holocaust, a special responsibility rests upon us to include in our midst every Jew we can.
>
> Therefore, while maintaining its preference for heterosexuality, out community needs to do all it can to make it possible for homosexual Jews to share in our community life.[44]

As Borowitz admits, "This is not an unproblematic line of action to suggest."[45] Indeed, Borowitz's conclusion—that the Reform movement ought to refrain from ordaining homosexuals as rabbis inasmuch as such persons are unable to serve as models of the community's highest ideal of the generative family—will surely be disappointing to gays and others who would have hoped that he would have reached a different position. On the other hand, his contention that the negative stance of the tradition towards homosexuality needs to be amended as attitudes evolve is not likely to please many traditionalists. Be that as it may, Borowitz's essay constitutes an instructive paradigm of how his thought can be employed to deal with pressing issues confronting Jews who participate in the covenantal community. On this issue, others have used his model to arrive at a substantively different conclusion.[46] All this should underscore the nature, method, and significance of Borowitz's approach to liberal Judaism.

The key point here is that Borowitz's belief in covenant leads him to assert that contemporary American Reform Judaism must correct early Reform's exaggerated emphasis on excessive individualism and autonomy. The pioneers of Reform in the nineteenth century did so, of course, because modernity and the allure it offered demanded such an affirmation of them. In our day, however, the acceptance of the notion of autonomy is so secure that the danger to authentic Judaism comes from overemphasizing rather than stifling individuality. "The Jewish equivalent of this exaggerated individualism," writes Borowitz, "is the radical separation of one's self as person from oneself as a Jew.... Thus what needs attention in the present stage of American Reform Judaism is ... the erosion of our self-identification with the Jewish people as the result of an overblown individualism."[47]

In this sense, Borowitz embraces the idea that Judaism possesses a social base that is essentially ethnic. This means that Jews share a special culture. Borowitz even acknowledges that ethnicity is a "primary medium for the transmission of Jewish values." Yet, Jewishness, he argues, cannot be understood or continued "on a purely secular level."[48] This is because "Jewish ethnicity ... is uniquely religious. It has to do with God. It has not and does not exist in and of itself. [I reject] the notion that ethnicity alone can ever furnish a satisfactory understanding of our people ... [and deny] the validity of all purely secular interpretations of the Jews."[49]

Individual Jews and their values, the Jewish people and their ethos, can come together authentically only when the individual Jew stands as a member of the covenantal community in relationship with God. Borowitz expresses this idea most forcefully and clearly when, near the end of *The Masks Jews Wear*, he contends:

> I think the time is ripe for us to ... establish our Jewish integrity. That will come when we make the Covenant the basis of our existence, when we link our lives with our people, joining in its historic pact with God. This commitment focuses Jewishness in an act of self—not in ideas, or practice, or birth alone; but all of these now will take their significance from an utterly fundamental relationship of self with God and people.... If we will to be Jews, if we make our Jewishness our

means of facing existence, then every part of our lives will be Jewish. Since we are part of a historic tie, we will honor the tradition; and since we affirm this in our being, we will create and innovate so as to express it our way. One cannot know where such personal covenanting may lead us. But I am less afraid of what we may choose in such Jewish integrity than that we will do nothing and by our indolence perpetuate our ... inauthenticity.[50]

There are problems, of course, that mark Borowitz's thought and its application. Despite his honesty in admitting that the tradition and the moral imperative can and do clash, it still remains unclear how one adjudicates the sometimes conflicting demands of tradition, morality, and community. Even the suggestion that Jews consult the attitudes of the present-day covenantal community does not resolve the dilemma. Contrasting Borowitz's conclusion on two specific issues of concern to him illustrates the difficulty.

Borowitz's sensitivity to the homophobia of the community is one reason among others that he will not sanction Reform ordination of homosexual rabbis. Yet he clearly will not tolerate the community's sexism on matters of feminine equality. In *Reform Judaism Today* he writes that although "some Reform Jews are resisting [the] effort to make women's rights in Judaism a reality ... most of our adherents know it is our duty to do so and a sign of our willfulness when we balk at it."[51] It could be argued that the difference between gay rights and women's rights rests in the majority's rejection of the former and acceptance of the latter as Borowitz's language suggests. But it is not likely that Borowitz would find the subordination of women acceptable even if a poll of the present covenantal community supported that view. It seems that Borowitz can legitimately be faulted for methodological inconsistency in these two instances. A clear way to mediate between tradition, community, and conscience remains unresolved. Given the nature of covenantal dialectic, it would appear that it must remain so.

For some, even within the non-Orthodox camp, this is unsettling. The problems inherent in the practical application of Borowitz's system are seen as a reflection of larger problems inherent in the overall structure of his thought. Borowitz's entire theological enterprise has thus been soundly critiqued by persons such as William Kaufman and Arnold Eisen. Eisen, for example, contends that the "idea of covenant is not theologically cogent":

Borowitz's persistent search for a means of acting on divine authority
while nonetheless retaining full human autonomy can only end in the
contradiction with which it begins.... One cannot remain continuous
with a tradition and guarantee "complete freedom of conscience" and
"dissent," hoping that both Judaism as accepted guide and as rejected
standard will call forth the mixture of person and tradition that
should mark the modern Jew.[52]

The critique is a powerful one. Yet to all this, Borowitz would
undoubtedly reply that his thought, in the end, is a human mix of
uncertainty and affirmation, intellectual rigor and religious sensibility. He is aware of this contradiction, acknowledging that what
is clear at one moment becomes murky later; what is accepted at
one time becomes rejected at another. Such "religious hesitancy"
is perhaps endemic to religious liberalism. Yet, "For all I do not
know and cannot make clear and distinct, I do not believe nothing.
And what little I can say I do believe is utterly decisive for how I
understand myself and what I try to do with my life."[53]

That "little" Borowitz has said is decisive for others as well. He
has taught liberal Jews more comprehensively than any other
liberal Jewish theologian to integrate their primal intuition that
they, like other Jews past and present, share in a covenant that is
deep, lasting, and true. Furthermore, he has taught them to do this
while affirming the dignity and worth of self. Such teaching is
marked by the risk of openness, but it is surely not anarchic. It
enables the individual Jew to integrate God, Torah, and Israel
with the self. Such a conception of covenant existence allows the
modern Jew to learn and, perhaps even more significantly, to live
the life of Torah in the contemporary world. Borowitz's identification of the "Conventional Jewish self," as well as his explications of its meaning, mark his most enduring legacy to Jewish
thought and life in our day.

Notes

All works cited are by Borowitz unless otherwise indicated.
1. "Freedom," in Arthur A. Cohen and Paul Mendes-Flohr, eds., *Contemporary Jewish Religious Thought* (New York, 1987), p. 265; and "The Autonomous Jewish Self," *Modern Judaism* 4 (February 1984), pp. 53–54.
2. "Freedom," p. 263.
3. *Choices in Modern Jewish Thought* (New York, 1983), pp. ix and 19.
4. "The Problem of the Form of a Jewish Theology," *Hebrew Union College Annual* 40–41 (1969–70), p. 393.

5. Ibid., pp. 400–403.
6. *Choices*, p. x.
7. Ibid., p. 19.
8. "Freedom," p. 265.
9. "God and Man in Judaism Today: A Reform Perspective," *Judaism* 23 (Summer 1974), p. 300.
10. M. Buher "Revelation and Law," in Nahum Glatzer, ed., *On Jewish Learning* (New York, 1965), p. 111.
11. "God and Man in Judaism Today," p. 303.
12. *Choices*, pp. 267–68.
13. "The Idea of God," in Joseph Blau, ed., *Reform Judaism: A Historical Perspective* (New York, 1973), p. 167.
14. "God and Man in Judaism Today," p. 305.
15. "The Autonomous Self and the Commanding Community," *Theological Studies* 45 (1984), p. 48.
16. "The Idea of God," p. 179.
17. *Contemporary Christologies: A Jewish Response* (New York, 1980), p. 190.
18. "Liberal Jewish Theology in a Time of Uncertainty," *Central Conference of American Rabbis Yearbook* 87 (1977), p. 153.
19. *Choices*, p. 284.
20. "The Idea of God," pp. 182–83.
21. Ibid., p. 170.
22. *Commentary Magazine*, ed., *The Condition of Jewish Belief* (New York, 1966), p. 37.
23. *Reform Judaism Today: What We Believe* (New York, 1977), pp. 148–49.
24. "The Problem of the Form of a Jewish Theology," p. 405.
25. "The Autonomous Self and the Commanding Community," pp. 45–49.
26. "The Autonomous Jewish Self," p. 44.
27. *Choices*, p. 286.
28. "Freedom," p. 266.
29. "The Old Woman as Meta-Question," *Journal of the American Academy of Religion* 44 (September 1976), p. 505.
30. Ibid.
31. Ibid., pp. 507–8.
32. *The Masks Jews Wear: The Self-Deceptions of American Jewry* (New York, 1973), pp. 151, 101, 162.
33. Ibid., p. 173.
34. *Sh'ma* (October 15, 1982), p. 155.
35. *Choosing a Sex Ethic* (New York, 1969), pp. 55, 105, 109, 113.
36. Ibid., p. 50.
37. Ibid., pp. 104–5.
38. Ibid., pp. 109, 114.
39. "On Homosexuality and the Rabbinate, a Covenantal Response," in *Homosexuality, the Rabbinate, and Liberal Judaism: Papers Prepared for the Ad-hoc Committee on Homosexuality and the Rabbinate* (1989), p. 1.
40. Ibid., pp. 2, 6, 7.
41. Ibid., p. 8.
42. Ibid.
43. Ibid., p. 9.
44. Ibid.
45. Ibid.
46. See Yoel H. Kahn, "Judaism and Homosexuality," in *Homosexuality, the Rabbinate, and Liberal Judaism*.

47. *Reform Judaism Today: What We Believe*, pp. 57–58.
48. *The Masks Jews Wear*, p. 135.
49. *Reform Judaism Today: What We Believe*, p. 94.
50. *The Masks Jews Wear*, pp. 207–8.
51. *Reform Judaism Today: Reform in the Process of Change* (New York, 1977), p. 133.
52. Arnold Eisen, *The Chosen People in America* (Bloomington, 1983), p. 158.
53. "The Autonomous Self and the Commanding Community," p. 56.

FOR FURTHER READING

Works by Eugene Borowitz

Borowitz's writings have the singular virtue of being lucid and readily accessible to lay readers. His style is conversational, and the reader often feels that he or she is engaging in direct dialogue with Borowitz on the many issues and questions he raises. His writings clearly embody the relational model he so eloquently evokes and describes in his work. He has authored more than ten books and more than one hundred articles. Nevertheless, several works stand out and should be brought to the attention of the reader interested in pursuing his thought further.

Renewing the Covenant: A Theology for the Postmodern Jew, Philadelphia, 1991. This recently published work is, in many senses, Borowitz's *magnum opus*. A distillation and summary of themes present in his work for over forty years, this work is the premier statement of a mature theologian and presents his seasoned thoughts on God, Israel and Torah.

Reform Judaism Today, New York, 1978. This is a three-volume commentary on the 1976 Centenary Perspective issue by the Reform movement. It lucidly explicates each sentence of the perspective and can be read profitably along with *Liberal Judaism*, New York, 1984, as the premier statements on the condition of Reform Jewish belief today.

Exploring Jewish Ethics, Detroit, 1990. This is a collection of forty of Borowitz's papers on ethics.

Choosing a Sex Ethic, New York, 1969. For those interested in how liberal Judaism applies its beliefs in a practical way to issues of ethical import, this work remains unsurpassed. He surveys the teachings of the tradition on sexual matters and explores the various options open to the liberal Jew struggling to forge a responsible ethic of sexual relationship. Again, the work's import for liberal Jewish ethics extends beyond its subject matter.

Contemporary Christiologies: A Jewish Response, New York, 1980. This work displays Borowitz's openness to dialogue with the non-Jewish world and demonstrates both the limits and the utility of such discourse. It is a remarkable example of how a Jewish theologian is prepared to learn from his Christian counterparts and it displays the authority and Jewish integrity of Borowitz's liberal approach.

Choices in Modern Jewish Thought, New York, 1983. Here, Borowitz reveals a similar readiness to engage in conversation with different figures in the Jewish world. He surveys options in modern Jewish thought that stretches from the Orthodox position of Rabbi J. B. Soloveitchik, to the naturalistic stance of the Reconstructionist Rabbi Mordecai Kaplan. Borowitz indicates what modern Jews might learn from each of them and concludes by outlining his own position.

"Covenant Theology—Another Look," *Worldview*, (March 1973), pp. 21–27. This remains a classic description of Borowitz's understanding of covenantal faith and its dialectic nature.

"The Autonomous Jewish Self," *Modern Judaism* 4 (February, 1984), pp. 39–56; and,

"The Autonomous Self and the Commanding Community," *Theological Studies* 45 (March 1984), pp. 34–56.

These two articles are more technical and theologically demanding than many of Borowitz's other works, but provide clear insights into the nature and development of his approach to Jewish religious belief.

Emil Fackenheim

KENNETH SEESKIN

Emil Fackenheim was born in Halle, Germany, in 1916. His father was a prominent attorney, his mother a descendant of a long line of rabbis. He practised what was then known as Liberal Judaism, which he considers comparable to the Conservative movement in America.[1] As a young man, he took a rabbinical degree at the famous Hochschule für die Wissenschaft des Judentums in Berlin, where he might well have remained had it not been for the events of November 10, 1938: *Kristallnacht*. Finding the doors of the school locked, he returned home to Halle, where he was met by the Gestapo the next morning and sent to the concentration camp at Sachsenhausen. He was released some months later and managed to get a visa to leave Germany and go to Scotland. After a few weeks in Scotland, however, he was sent to Canada and assigned to an internment camp, where he was treated like a prisoner of war for a year and a half.

Upon his release from the camp, Fackenheim entered the University of Toronto, an institution he would call home for much of his life. Despite a five-year stint as a rabbi at a Reform congregation in Hamilton, Ontario, it seems clear that Fackenheim's true love was the academy. He is a prolific writer, the author of nine books and well over a hundred articles, and as author, teacher, and lecturer, he is respected by Jews and gentiles the world over. At present, he is a Fellow of the Institute of Contemporary Jewry at the Hebrew University in Jerusalem.

Although Fackenheim is one of the most significant Jewish thinkers of our time, the word *thinker* does not do him justice if it simply calls to mind an academic philosopher talking to other academic philosophers about esoteric matters. Fackenheim is, of course, an expert on esoteric matters. A lifelong student of German idealism, he is an authority on the philosophy of Kant and Hegel. But important as Fackenheim's technical work is, it is only part of his repertoire. He is also a political commentator, a midrashic expositor, a polemicist for Jewish causes, and an intellectual gadfly.

Reading Fackenheim is often a taxing experience. A typical article might begin with a midrash, move to a point in Kant, go on to social commentary, proceed to Nazi atrocities committed against the Jews, extend discussion of these atrocities to a discussion of Israel and the Six-Day War, and conclude with a deeper understanding of the midrash. In addition to its varied subject matter, Fackenheim's work is taxing for another reason. He is a writer of immense passion, and his words engage the reader at every turn. He is at his best when addressing issues most philosophers prefer to ignore—hope, fear, martyrdom, the demonic. His account of Jewish existence after the Holocaust has generated a still rising tide of controversy. To some, he is a good philosopher who made a wrong turn and allowed the specter of radical evil to overwhelm him; to others, he is the first philosopher with the courage to discuss this evil in an authentic way. No proper study of Jewish thought over the past forty years can ignore him. By any account, he has shaken the foundations of the subject.

Existentialist Roots

To understand Fackenheim's contribution, we must first look at his intellectual heritage, in particular the thought of Martin Buber. Buber stands as one of the great proponents of Jewish existentialism. According to this view, it is a mistake to consider God as part of an abstract system of thought. God is not an idea, or a principle, or a supreme thinker of thoughts. Buber wished to revitalize the notion of a living God, who is present to His followers in an immediate and indubitable way. Rather than finding God at the end of a chain of inferences, we find Him in a personal encounter; rather than demanding greater powers of reflection, God demands response and commitment. Clearly one cannot prove that such a God exists. Buber would say that He can be "heard" only by devoted listeners, people who are open to the possibility of standing before God and allowing His presence to transform their lives.

How does one stand before God? Buber answers with the typology of the *I/Thou* relationship. I encounter God not as a thing—an *It*—but as a person. The two parties do not emerge from the relationship exactly as they were when they entered. Each is transformed to the degree that he opens himself or enters into relation with the other. That is why Buber insists that the human/divine encounter is dialogical. Each person both influences and is influenced by the presence of the other. Each encounter is unique, and each speaks to the religious believer in the privacy of the soul. Any effort to approach God through a system of thought is an attempt to change Him from a *Thou* to an *It*, which is a misguided effort. God is the eternal person—the eternal *Thou*—and can never be found in the world of *It*.

This is an appealing description of religious experience. But in the middle of the twentieth century, it ran into an enormous obstacle: how to reconcile Buber's account of the *I/Thou* relationship with the horrors visited on the Jewish people by the Nazis. Late in life, Buber asked the question: "Can one still speak to God after Oswiecim and Auschwitz? Can one still, as an individual and as a people, enter at all into a dialogue relationship with Him? Dare we recommend to the survivors of Oswiecim, the Jobs of the gas chambers, 'Call to Him, for He is kind, for His mercy endureth forever?'"[2]

Buber admitted that the Nazi experience created a problem for his understanding of the dialogue with God; but he was never able to solve it. In its classic form, the *I/Thou* relationship is a timeless moment in which two individuals respond to each other's presence free from the distractions of the workaday world. In this sense, the *I/Thou* relationship is not part of the flow of history. It is not a public event and cannot be explained with reference to historically conditioned forces such as war, famine, or revolution. Thus it is hard to see how an *I/Thou* relationship can take into account the specific circumstances in which the individuals find themselves, especially circumstances such as those that prevailed at Auschwitz. We can imagine an *I/Thou* relationship between God and Moses on Mt. Sinai, but can we imagine one between God and the nameless dead, a million of whom were children?

Jewish Responses to Catastrophe

Like Buber, Fackenheim is an existentialist. He finds a God who is reached by a series of logical inferences too distant to inspire the depth of feeling found in the prophets. Rather than identifying God with a timeless principle, he follows Buber in urging a return to the living God of Scripture, a God who is involved with His people.[3] On the forms such involvement takes, Fackenheim departs from Buber and proposes a set of categories for describing divine presence in human history.[4]

The first category is called a *root experience*, a formative event that took place in the distant past but continues to influence the present. Although root experience occurs in a specific circumstance, its importance extends far beyond. At the Seder, each Jew is asked to view the Exodus as if he or she personally came forth out of Egypt. The Exodus was a public event involving hundreds of thousands of people. According to Fackenheim, the public character of a root experience is crucial; it is not the reliving of a private encounter between two individuals. When people recall a root experience like the Exodus, they do not view it as something that happened once and is over. The Exodus is experienced as a present reality in the sense that the God who saved Israel continues to act as savior.

We then may think of Judaism as founded on root experiences. Epoch-making events, Fackenheim's second category, are moments of crisis, on catastrophes that test the structure of faith as defined by root experiences through unforeseen circumstances such as the destruction of the Second Temple and the transformation of Jerusalem into a pagan city. Faced with these tragedies, the Jewish people could have adopted either of two convenient solutions. They could have denied the importance of the event and taken refuge in a mystical or otherworldly view of religion. Or they could have admitted the importance of the event but lapsed into despair. Fackenheim asserts that the strength of Judaism is its unwillingness to accept simplistic answers to formidable challenges. In the case of the Second Temple, a solution had to be found which was realistic enough to admit the full force of the catastrophe but still preserve the legitimacy of the root experiences.

In Fackenheim's view, the solution was found within the framework of midrash, though it transformed Judaism's understanding of itself. That God permitted the Temple to be destroyed did not mean that He was no longer concerned with Israel and had decided to conceal His presence. On the contrary, He was just as grieved as His people. If His people went into exile, so, according to Rabbi Akiba, did God. He is still present in history, and in that sense, still commands our attention. To the degree that God Himself is in exile and grieves over the destruction of the Temple, the Jewish people are not cut off from Him. Ultimately the God who is present in history will redeem that history by another saving act analogous to the parting of the Red Sea.

The destruction of the Second Temple was epoch-making because it changed Judaism forever. The rabbis did not opt for the view that God was distant and cut off from His people. But neither did they opt for the standard theological solution: that catastrophe is a punishment for sin. For as Fackenheim points out, the punishment—a pagan Jerusalem under the sway of Rome—was vastly out of proportion to the supposed offense. Instead of a case of retribution, the destruction of the Second Temple is a case of God's self-imposed exile with His people, an exile that will last nearly two millennia.

The Uniqueness of the Holocaust

In Fackenheim's view, the Holocaust is also an epoch-making event and therefore calls into question the basic categories of Jewish self-understanding. An essential part of Fackenheim's argument is that the Holocaust is radically different from other tragedies in Jewish history such as the pogroms, the expulsion from Spain, and even the destruction of the First and Second Temples. In previous centuries, Jews were killed for what they did or did not do. They refused to pay tribute to Rome, or to adopt local customs, or to profess faith in Jesus. In all of these cases, Jews were given a way out: if they changed their behavior, they could go on living. The Holocaust was the first time that Jews were killed not for what they *did* but for what they *were*. The Nazis sent people to the gas chambers for the "crime" of having one or more Jewish grandparents. In short, Hitler did not offer his victims the choice other tyrants had offered: convert or die. Hitler's message was limited to one possibility: die. Even death does not adequately describe the full extent of Nazi atrocities. In many instances, the victims were first humiliated—made to despise themselves for the simple reason that they had Jewish blood.

The Nazi horror is even more incomprehensible because the Jews posed no threat to the Reich. In previous ages, people were slaughtered when they got in the way of imperial expansion. But no such justification can be given for Hitler's "war" on the Jews. On the contrary, there is evidence that the Nazis diverted much needed supplies from the eastern front to keep the gas chambers working. Why did they jeopardize their troops to perpetuate a mindless, senseless act of evil? The problem is not that the Nazis put so little value on human life but that they put so much value on eradicating it. Killing Jews was an ideal for which the Reich was willing to make costly sacrifices. In this respect, evil was not just permitted; to use Fackenheim's word, it was *celebrated.*

Fackenheim insists that the Holocaust is incomprehensible: "To explain an action or event is to show how they were possible. In the case of the Holocaust, however, the mind can accept the possibility of both how and why it was done, in the final analysis, solely because it was done, so that the more the psychologist, historian, or 'psychohistorian' succeeds in explaining the event or action, the more nakedly he comes to confront its ultimate inexplicability."[5] There is no logical explanation for the Nazi death machine. So the question is not, Why did it happen? but What, if anything, is a legitimate Jewish response?

The question of response reraises the question of God's presence in history. If we cannot understand how outwardly rational people could operate the Nazi death camps, we still have to ask how God could be present in a history that includes them. There are three more or less traditional answers to this question. It is instructive that these answers are similar to ones that were rejected after the destruction of the Second Temple.

The first alternative is to go back to the old notion that catastrophe is part of God's plan for the moral education of the human race, either to punish sin or to provide a "chastisement of love." Fackenheim rejects this explanation of the Holocaust on the ground that it is morally reprehensible. What sin could justify 6 million deaths including 1 million children? What God would chastise his people in this way? The concepts of martyrdom, chastisement, and vicarious suffering are as old as the Book of Job.

The problem with applying them to the Holocaust is that they make God an accomplice in Hitler's plan; Hitler attains the status of God's agent, the unwitting vehicle by which divine providence works itself out. This is too horrible to contemplate. The result is that theodicy—the attempt to justify the ways of God to man—is as bankrupt now as it was in A.D. 70.

The second answer is essentially one of despair. If we take the evidence of Nazism seriously, we must reject the basic categories of Jewish religious experience: redemption, chosenness, providence, and saving presence. The Jewish people can continue to exist as a cultural or ethnic group, but any attempt to supply a theological underpinning for their existence runs into the stark reality of the 6 million deaths. Fackenheim rejects this alternative because it implies the end of the Jewish people as they have traditionally understood themselves. Without some theological underpinning, Jewish survival would be no different from the survival of any other group. It would no longer have a sacred dimension. The Jewish people would be cut off from their history and would be unable, for example, to experience the exodus from Egypt as a present reality at the *seder* table. It is significant that as a rule this alternative did not appeal to the victims themselves. Fackenheim often points out that the victims held on to their belief in God as stubbornly as did the rabbis in A.D. 70. So in addition to being theologically unacceptable, the second alternative is untrue to the facts. If there is nothing sacred about Jewish survival, what do we say to the people who gave their lives convinced that there is?

The last alternative might be called the standard Jewish response to tragedy. It agrees with Fackenheim that the destruction of the Second Temple was an epoch-making event but purports that it was the last religiously significant event until the coming of the Messiah. This standard response does not deny that there will be triumphs and tragedies in the meantime; it simply says that there will be no events that significantly alter the character of the religion. According to this view, the Holocaust is no different from the other tragedies that have befallen the Jews since the diaspora. The technology for disposing of human life may have improved, but the victims of one episode deserve no more attention than the victims of another. Judaism regards all human life as sacred, having been made in the image of its creator.

We will never know why God permits innocent human blood to be shed. All we can do is continue to practice the religion and hope for the day when human life is no longer considered expendable.

To this alternative, Fackenheim's reply is that we cannot simply contemplate the 6 million deaths and return to business as usual. Hitler is not just another tyrant, and remembering the Holocaust is not like remembering the Ninth Day of Av. The evil the Nazis perpetrated against the Jews is without historical precedent. Fackenheim insists that unless we recognize the distinctive character of Nazi genocide, we run the risk of ignoring history. Let us recall Fackenheim's understanding of A.D. 70. Faced with a historical event that defied description, the rabbis did not take refuge in the notion of a distant God cut off from human experience. They were realistic. They took seriously the importance of what they had witnessed and clung to the idea that God is present to His people. Fackenheim contends that the memory of the Holocaust deserves no less. If the historical record shows that the death camps are unique, then any authentic Jewish thinker must respond accordingly.

The 614th Commandment

Fackenheim is extremely clear about the form response must take. After Auschwitz, Jewish survival takes on a new dimension. It is not just something to be hoped for but something to which every Jew must dedicate him or herself. It is nothing less than a sacred obligation:

> Jews are forbidden to hand Hitler posthumous victories. They are commanded to survive as Jews, lest the Jewish people perish. They are commanded to remember the victims of Auschwitz lest their memory perish. They are forbidden to despair of man and his world, and to escape into either cynicism or otherworldliness, lest they cooperate in delivering the world over to the forces of Auschwitz. Finally, they are forbidden to despair of the God of Israel, lest Judaism perish. A secularist Jew cannot make himself believe by a mere act of will, nor can he be commanded to do so.... And a religious Jew who has stayed with his God may be forced into new, possibly revolutionary relationships with Him. One possibility, however, is wholly unthinkable. A Jew may not respond to Hitler's attempt to destroy Judaism by himself cooperating in its destruction.

In ancient times, the unthinkable Jewish sin was idolatry. Today, it is to respond to Hitler by doing his work.[6]

It should be understood that by referring to a 614th Commandment, Fackenheim is not claiming that God revealed Himself at Auschwitz in the way He did according to the traditional account of Sinai. The "voice" referred to is not to be taken literally. What Fackenheim means is that this is the only way a modern Jew can respond to the horrors of Auschwitz and still hold fast to the commanding presence of God. Buber argued that all commandments are a human response to the divine presence and therefore shot through with human feeling and interpretation. Fackenheim has added the idea that even amid the ovens and mass graves, the divine presence can be encountered. More important, the encounter issues in a positive course of action: the continued existence of the Jewish people.

If the 614th Commandment is a human response, it is a response to the presence of God, which is why the obligation that issues from it is sacred. Fackenheim is convinced that the Jewish resistance to Hitler and the demons of Auschwitz is *absolute*, which is to say it is not a humanly created ideal. It is a human response, but the One who calls for such a response is decidedly more than human.

It is but a short step from the 614th Commandment to support for the State of Israel. We cannot view the formation of the State of Israel as God's way of appeasing the Jewish people for the outrages suffered under the Nazis. That line of reasoning would take us back to theodicy, which Fackenheim not only rejects but considers a sacrilege. The relation between the Holocaust and the State of Israel is not one of cause and effect but of catastrophe and response. The existence and security of Israel are essential to Jewish survival. Jewish survival is a sacred obligation. Therefore every Jew, whether religious or secular, must take up the cause of Zionism.

In his most recent book, *What Is Judaism?* Fackenheim asks us to imagine a situation in which the Holocaust occurred exactly as it did but no State of Israel arose in its wake. He concludes that although there would be pockets of Judaism here and there, they would be inconsequential:

> In a world with a Holocaust but without a Jewish state, all Jews truly sensitive to what has occurred would surely be in a flight from their Jewish condition that would dwarf anything known as "assimilation"

now. And who could blame them? Not long ago the world was divided into one part bent on the murder of every available Jew, and another that did less than was possible to prevent it, to stop it, or at least to slow the process down. If after that there had been no *radical* change, who would want to be a Jew? Who could be expected to remain one?[7]

The formation of the State of Israel has changed forever our understanding of what it means to live a religious or a secular life. Fackenheim argues that even secular Israelis fulfill a religious obligation by helping keep the state of Israel alive: "The whole Israeli nation is collectively what each survivor is individually: a testimony *in behalf of all mankind* to life against the demons of death; a hope and determination that there must be, shall be, will be no second Auschwitz; and on this hope and this determination every man, woman, and child in Israel stakes his life."[8] Can a modern state facing racial and religious problems of its own live up to this ideal? Can it do whatever needs to be done to protect Jewish life and still claim to be a testimony on behalf of *all* humanity? Only time will tell. Fackenheim, however, resists any attempt to turn ideals into empty rhetoric. Here, as elsewhere, thought must confront the rigors of history.

A standard objection to Fackenheim is that Judaism can get along with the original 613 commandments and does not require amendments, particularly ones that mention Hitler as prominently as he does. Why should Judaism redefine itself in terms of its worst enemy? Is the only explanation for living as a Jew that one is trying to prove something to Hitler? What happened to monotheism and the sense of being a holy people? Surely, the criticism goes, a believing Jew does not need the commanding voice of Auschwitz to continue to practice the religion, and a secular Jew does not believe in commanding voices in the first place. To whom, then, is the 614th Commandment addressed?

Although Fackenheim does not take up this challenge directly, he provides a good indication of what his answer would be. Redefinition in the face of catastrophe is hardly new. In one age, Judaism redefined itself by responding to Pharaoh, in another to Hadrian. Fackenheim is arguing that after Auschwitz, Jews face a similar challenge: to respond to the present at the same time that they retain the root experiences of the past. The purpose of the 614th Commandment is to show that it is still possible to do both.

Fackenheim would answer that if one is a believing Jew, there is no reason why he or she should not go on believing. In fact, there is every reason to do so. One's interpretation of that belief may have to change, and it may no longer be as comforting as it once was, but that is the price one pays for worshiping a God who is involved in human affairs. Still, it is fair to say that the 614th Commandment is intended primarily for the mass of secular Jews whose faith has been shaken and who are prone to despair. To those people, Fackenheim poses a question: In an age with the Jewish people have come so close to extinction, what are the consequences of your attitude? Does it not amount to unwitting support for Hitler and Eichmann? And it if does, how can you live with yourself? Fackenheim believes that a secular life can have religious meaning. The secular Jew who works for the State of Israel is satisfying the 614th Commandment and witnessing to the continued presence of God in history. The real culprit is the person who does nothing. It is clear, then, why Fackenheim's writing on Jewish life after the Holocaust is so passionate: it is a direct call to action, not an attempt to deal with abstractions.

From a philosophic perspective, the problem with the 614th Commandment is its emphasis on survival. No Jew will argue that survival is not a worthy goal; the problem is that it is not an end in itself. At some point, one must address the more fundamental question: for what purpose are we surviving? Unless that question is addressed, the Jewish people run the risk of recognizing no ideal other than the perpetuation of their own existence. And if this should happen, there would be little to separate them from the rest of the peoples of the earth.

To his credit, Fackenheim is aware of these problems. He claims he was once critical of Jewish philosophers who advocated survival for its own sake.[9] But he goes on to suggest that in the present age, Jewish survival is an act of faith, a rejection of evil, and therefore the traditional objections to survival as an end no longer apply. Yet even if one agrees that the Holocaust has no precedent, why should this fact alter a fundamental insight: That any nation which recognizes no end greater than its own existence is morally bankrupt? In another context, Fackenheim allows that Jewish survival, though a duty, is not an ultimate end.[10] But then there is a question of emphasis. If survival is not the ultimate end, what is? What commandment bids us to strive for the ultimate end? Ordinarily one would think that monotheism is the ultimate end and idolatry the ultimate sin. In Fackenheim's presentation of the 614th Commandment, however, this ultimacy is called in question. Without the state of Israel to spearhead Jewish survival, Fackenheim thinks there would be little reason to remain a Jew. Does this mean that the traditional reasons are no longer valid? I believe that for Fackenheim, the answer is yes. To appreciate that answer, we must turn to his magnum opus: *To Mend the World.*

From Past to Future

To Mend the World was published in 1982. The purpose of the book is stated in its subtitle: to offer foundations for future Jewish thought. But once again, Fackenheim does not strive for the usual philosophic detachment. The book is in many ways an intellectual autobiography. It begins with Fackenheim's commitment to revelation as divine presence and his conviction that the Holocaust provides radical "countertestimony" to Judaism and Christianity. Unlike *God's Presence in History, To Mend the World* contains analytical discussion of the philosophers who have had the greatest impact on Fackenheim's development. There are chapters on Baruch Spinoza, Franz Rosenzweig, and G. W. F. Hegel as well as extended treatments of Immanuel Kant, Martin Buber, and Martin Heidegger. Through it all, Fackenheim communicates a growing dissatisfaction with Western philosophy. He finds nothing in the philosophic traditions that prepared the world for the events of 1938–45 and virtually nothing that provides the intellectual apparatus needed to understand them. Worse, the inheritor of the German philosophic tradition, Martin Heidegger, was a committed Nazi. Worse still perhaps, the majority of the philosophic community since 1945 has gone about its business as if the Holocaust never happened. Faced with this record, Fackenheim concludes that thought, that is, philosophy, cannot overcome the horrors of Auschwitz. It cannot subsume these horrors under well-defined categories or rise to a level at which they can be viewed *sub specie aeternitatis.* In Fackenheim's words:

> In an earlier exploration we concluded that thought cannot overcome the Holocaust, that where the Holocaust is overcoming thought is not, and that where overcoming thought is the Holocaust cannot be—a conclusion forcing us to assent to a way of philosophical thought that,

immersed in history, is fully exposed to it. Now that our thought is exposed, and exposed to *that* history, must we not conclude that where the Holocaust is, *no* thought can be, and that where there is thought it is in flight from the event?[11]

In sum, the Holocaust constitutes a rupture. The historical record is so awful that it has torn the philosophic tradition asunder. Yet if this is true, how does a modern intellectual come to terms with it?

Fackenheim's answer is to put away the abstract vocabulary of philosophic discourse and look instead at the testimonies of people who confronted the Holocaust world and resisted it. In this way, Kurt Huber, an obscure German philosopher, is more important than Heidegger for while Heidegger defended the Nazis, Huber lost his life opposing them. And more important than all the philosophers is a Polish woman, Pelagia Lewinska, whose testimony provides a paradigm for how to react to the horrors from which thought is forced to retreat:

> At the outset the living places, the ditches, the mud, the piles of excrement behind the blocks, had appalled me with their horrible filth.... And then I saw the light! I saw that it was not a question of disorder or lack of organization but that, on the contrary, a very thoroughly considered conscious idea was in the back of the camp's existence. They had condemned us to die in our own filth, to drown in mud, in our own excrement. They wished to base us, to destroy our human dignity, to efface every vestige of humanity ... to fill us with horror and contempt toward ourselves and our fellows.... From the instant when I grasped the motivating principle ... it was as if I had been awakened from a dream.... I felt under orders to live.... And if I did die in Auschwitz, it would be as a human being, I would hold on to my dignity. I was not going to become the contemptible, disgusting brute my enemy wished me to be.... And a terrible struggle began which went on day and night.[12]

In a nutshell, if the Holocaust cannot be grasped by thought, at least it can be resisted. An authentic answer to the Holocaust lies not in the realm of abstraction but in what Fackenheim refers to as *"overt, flesh-and-blood action and life."* This is the only "understanding" which is possible—an understanding provided by the victims. According to Fackenheim, the meaning of Auschwitz was grasped when Pelagia Lewinska felt under orders to live. In this sense, resistance to evil becomes a way of being, an ontological category.

It is this resistance without philosophic proofs and in the face of overwhelming odds that justifies Jewish survival after Auschwitz. To the question, "What are we surviving *for*?" Fackenheim would answer, "To continue to be martyrs in the fight against evil." Most thinkers would have ended the book at this point. They would have argued that if Pelagia Lewinska could feel under orders to live, it is possible to reappropriate the notion that human life is sacred and, with it, the religious tradition out of which this notion arises. Fackenheim calls such a reappropriation a *tikkun* or mending. But again Fackenheim is not content with an easy solution. Pelagia Lewinska left testimony which everyone can read. What about the millions of nameless men, women, and children who did not? How do we consider the testimony of those who left no record and lie in mass graves? And if we do find a way to consider it, to "hear" their voices, can there be a *tikkun*? Can we pretend that after examining their plight, everything is back to normal?

It is clear—as he readily admits—that Fackenheim has argued himself into a dilemma.[13] If we emphasize the few who were able to resist Hitler, we can conclude that the rupture has been mended. We can recover the categories of Jewish existence and devote ourselves to the eradication of evil. We may not interpret these categories as our ancestors did, but we can call them our own under the aegis of *tikkun*. If, however, we emphasize the nameless dead, we must despair that any such mending is possible. Apparently there either is no break or no possibility of repair. How do we solve the problem? Both kinds of testimony are authentic. Neither can be discarded without impairing our ability to grasp the events in question. The only solution is to assert both sides of the dilemma and endure the tension of hanging between the extremes, and that brings us back to the idea that Jewish existence after the Holocaust requires a leap of faith.

To some, this will seem to be no solution at all. And in one respect, it is not. There is no logical resolution of the paradox, no way of approaching the historical record with certainty. Fackenheim emphasizes time and again that true religion is never safe or secure. To think about the Holocaust at all is to take a risk. In this case, the risk culminates in a dilemma from which we cannot extricate ourselves. No doubt Fackenheim would respond that *his* dilemma is really *our* dilemma. No future Jewish thought can ignore it, and no intellectually respectable thought can be content with a pat answer. But there is a great gain in seeing that this is the predicament in which Jewish thought, or religious thought in general, finds itself. It is, for Fackenheim, the preeminent issue of our time.

Conclusion

Let us return to Buber's question: Can we still speak to God after Auschwitz? In *What Is Judaism?* Fackenheim reformulates the question: Can we still have an intimate relation with an infinite God?[14] Unless God is infinite, we get idolatry. Unless He is intimate, He is distant or hidden. Fackenheim continues to insist that God has entered into history on at least two occasions: the Exodus from Egypt and Revelation at Sinai. But if God saved the Jewish people from certain death at the Red Sea, why did He not do so at Auschwitz?

Traditional Jewish philosophy would answer that God does not enter into history in the way that a director enters into a play. For the medievals, God affects the world through a series of celestial spheres or intermediaries. For Hermann Cohen, God is a moral ideal which human reason can approach in the way one approaches a mathematical limit. Fackenheim rejects both of these accounts but in so doing saddles himself with an impossible difficulty: If God *can* enter into the world, and did so before, why did He not do so again? Granted God cannot enter human history all the time, but on Fackenheim's own admission, the Holocaust is special. Having rejected the philosophic conception of God as too distant, Fackenheim has little choice but to turn to midrash. In the end of *What Is Judaism?* he uses midrashic materials to try to construct a way of looking at God's failure to act. Although he does not succumb to theodicy, neither does he arrive at a satisfactory conclusion. In the final analysis, he can do nothing but quote a Kabbalistic saying that effort from below calls for a response from above. As a traditional philosopher, I believe that Fackenheim has pushed the midrashic framework further than it can go. As long as we retain the notion that God enters into history in a direct or immediate way, no midrash—indeed, nothing—will explain His silence at Auschwitz. That is why the notion that God enters into history has to be revised. To my way of thinking, it has to be revised along the lines suggested by Cohen and the medievals. Otherwise God's silence becomes totally inexplicable, and the suggestion that we can get around this inexplicability by a leap of faith is an admission of failure.

This essay began by remarking that Fackenheim is a controversial thinker. He is a committed Jew who is willing to test his Judaism by looking at historical events so awful they defy comprehension. He does not regard Judaism as a fixed body of dogma or a way of escaping from the realities of day-to-day life. It could be said, therefore, that his commitment is a precarious one. Rather than run away from countertestimony, he has chosen to confront it. Even if one believes, as I do, that the philosophic foundations of Judaism can survive Fackenheim's efforts to shake them, it must be admitted that they show signs of strain.

Notes

1. Much of the biographical information is taken from an interview of Fackenheim conducted by William Novack first published in 1986. It can be found in an anthology of Fackenheim's works edited by Michael Morgan, *The Jewish Thought of Emil Fackenheim* (Detroit, 1987), pp. 349–56. Morgan's is the best single edition of Fackenheim's work available. Those interested in Fackenheim's life would do well to read "Reflections on *Aliyah*" in the Morgan volume (pp. 369–75).
2. Martin Buber, "Dialogue between Heaven and Earth," in W. Herberg, ed., *Four Existentialist Theologians* (Garden City, N.Y., 1958), p. 203.
3. For Fackenheim's interpretation of the *I/Thou* relationship, see Martin Buber's "Concept of Relevation," in P. Schilpp, ed., *The Philosophy of Martin Buber* (LaSalle, Ill., 1967), pp. 273–96. See also Fackenheim's introduction to his *To Mend the World: Foundations of Future Jewish Thought* (New York, 1982), pp. 5–6.
4. Fackenheim, *God's Presence in History: Jewish Affirmation and Philosophical Reflections* (New York, 1970), chap. 1.
5. Fackenheim, *To Mend the World*, p. 233.
6. Fackenheim, *God's Presence in History*, p. 84.
7. Fackenheim, *What Is Judaism: An Interpretation for the Present Ages* (New York, 1987), p. 38.
8. Fackenheim, *The Jewish Return into History: Reflections in The Age of Auschwitz and a New Jerusalem* (New York, 1978), p. 139.
9. Ibid., p. 21.
10. Ibid., p. 110.
11. Fackenheim, *To Mend the World*, p. 200.
12. Ibid., p. 25.
13. Ibid., pp.309–10.
14. Fackenheim, *What Is Judaism*, pp. 282ff.

FOR FURTHER READING

Works by Emil Fackenheim

Encounters between Judaism and Modern Philosophy: A Preface to Future Jewish Thought, New York, 1973.

God's Presence in History: Jewish Affirmation and Philosophical Reflections, New York, 1970.

The Jewish Return into History: Reflections in the Age of Auschwitz and a New Jerusalem, New York, 1978.

To Mend the World: Foundations of Future Jewish Thought, New York, 1982.

Metaphysics and Historicity, Milwaukee, 1961.

Paths to Jewish Belief: A Systematic Introduction, New York, 1960.

Quest for Past and Future: Essays in Jewish Theology, Bloomington, 1968.

The Religious Dimension in Hegel's Thought, Bloomington, 1968.

What Is Judaism: An Interpretation for the Present Ages, New York, 1987.

Works about Emil Fackenheim

Katz, Steven T., *Post-Holocaust Dialogues*, New York, 1983, pp. 205–47. In this chapter, Katz discusses some of the philosophic problems involved in rethinking Judaism in light of the Holocaust. He is sympathetic with Fackenheim in some respects, critical in others.

Morgan, Michael, "Introduction," *The Jewish Thought of Emil Fackenheim*, Detroit, 1987, pp. 13–18. The introduction to this anthology of Fackenheim's writings was written by one of his best and most devoted students. Morgan argues that Fackenheim is preeminent among contemporary Jewish philosophers.

Wyschogrod, Michael, "Faith and the Holocaust," in *Judaism* 20 (Summer 1971), pp. 286–94. This very critical review of Fackenheim's position takes issue with the idea of a 614th commandment. Wyschogrod accepts a traditional view of Jewish thought and practice.

Irving (Yitzchak) Greenberg

STEVEN T. KATZ

No Jewish thinker has had a greater impact on the American Jewish community in the last two decades than Irving (Yitz) Greenberg. Partly through his writings but still more through his person he has become a central figure in the religious, cultural, and intellectual life of American Jewry. Attuned to the rhythm of modernity and the dilemmas it poses for the individual Jew, as well as for the people of Israel, he has spoken and written on all the main issues of our time: the Holocaust, the State of Israel, Jewish-Christian relations, and the meaning of Jewish tradition and the halakah for contemporary men and women. And in every case his views have found a wide and responsive audience.

Biography

Irving Greenberg was raised in an immigrant, modern Orthodox home whose religious atmosphere was a compound of the elemental piety of his mother and the learning of his father, who was a *mitnaggid* and a student of Rav Chayim Brysker. His father, Eliyahu Chayim Greenberg, was a *shochet* and a rabbi in a *Chevra Shas* in Boro Park. His love of learning and of the Jewish people and his tendency to justify the Jewish people spiritually and to use the power of learning to help the underdog are credited by Greenberg as being the primary shaping influences in his life.

Greenberg's early years were spent in the modern Orthodox day school system and in a religious Zionist youth movement, Hashomer Hadati (later Bnei Akiva). A significant turning point occurred in his college years, when he entered Beth Joseph Rabbinical Seminary, then a refugee yeshiva, whose students were primarily survivors of the concentration camps or had spent the war years in Siberia. To the yeshiva he attributes his exposure and lifetime fascination with Rabbi Israel Salanter and the Mussar movement, an ethical and religious revival movement in nine-teenth-century Eastern European Orthodoxy. The yeshiva's intense focus on character building and ethics as well as its missionary emphasis on educating the masses had a very great effect on his thinking. Greenberg credits the influence of the yeshiva as well as of his father with the lifelong dialectic between activism and reflection that has marked his career. Beth Joseph's intense religious life and models sustained him through the spiritual and intellectual crises that grew out of his direct con-frontation with Western culture in his undergraduate days at Brooklyn College and while doing graduate work in intellectual history at Harvard University.

As an undergraduate he was preoccupied with the challenges of science and religion and of history and society. Since there was little Orthodox Jewish writing dealing with these areas, he found intellectual nourishment and consolation in the work of certain neo-Orthodox Protestant thinkers, most notably Reinhold Niebuhr. Niebuhr's dialectical mode of thought shaped Green-berg's approach to religious and social questions and left a per-manent appreciation for Christianity that is evident in his later theological reflections. In graduate school the challenge of modern critical Jewish studies and of psychology and psycho-analysis were the issues that most affected his thinking. During his time in Boston he came in contact with and fell under the spell of Rabbi Joseph B. Soloveitchik, the premier halakic thinker and philosopher of American modern Orthodoxy. He also began to decide against an academic career, moving instead toward a professional and lifelong commitment to the Jewish community. The intermediate step was a decision to teach American history at Yeshiva University. During the early years at Yeshiva he became involved in the formation of Yavneh, the National Orthodox Students Association, a forerunner of the Jewish student move-ment of the 1960s.

He married Blu Genauer in 1957. They now have five children. In 1961–62 he went to Israel on a Fulbright visiting professorship at Tel Aviv University. He spent the year reading intensively about the Holocaust; the experience was overwhelming, especially in the context of the life of the Greenberg's first child. The Holocaust (and the State of Israel) became the focus of his theological and religious concern and a central strand of his life and work. He returned to the United States and became involved in Holocaust education and theology. There was some resistance at Yeshiva University to introducing Holocaust studies and to his making Jewish studies a primary focus of his career. This friction contributed to his decision to leave academic life and to accept an invitation to become the rabbi at the Riverdale Jewish Center in 1965.

For seven years in the rabbinate Greenberg focused on creating a community and on developing a day school that was an open school with a strong commitment to the integration of secular and religious studies and that included Israel and the Holocaust centrally in the curriculum. He worked with David Hartman in the creation of the Segalls Center for the Study and Advancement of Judaism, which brought together for a summer program rabbis from all Jewish denominations to learn together. In the late 1960s his articulation of the unresolved issues of orthodoxy and of the need to be more open to the other denominations, in light of the Holocaust, began to make him a controversial figure at Yeshiva University and in modern Orthodox circles. By 1972, he concluded that a community synagogue was not the right setting for the work that he wished to accomplish, which included the creation of an educational outreach foundation that would involve all Jewish denominations. Thus he shifted back to academic life, becoming the founding chairman of the Department of Jewish Studies at City College of the City University of New York (CUNY).

Another crucial turn in his intellectual maturation and career came about as a consequence of his involvement with the organized Jewish federations and the United Jewish Appeal starting in the early 1970s. He came to realize that these groups, which, on the surface, were philanthropic rather than religious in their orientation, were a profound expression of the transformational impact of the Holocaust and the rebirth of Israel on Jewish values.

At City College, together with Elie Wiesel and Steven Shaw, he founded the National Jewish Conference Center (NJCC), which eventually evolved into CLAL, the National Jewish Center for Learning and Leadership. The National Jewish Conference Center was separated from City College in 1976. In 1979 Greenberg resigned from his teaching position at CUNY to become the full-time director of the NJCC. In the 1960s and 1970s Greenberg also became involved in the Jewish-Christian dialogue and was moved and influenced by the work of Christian thinkers such as A. Roy Eckardt (and subsequently influenced others such as Franklin Littell and Paul van Buren), who were making an effort to rethink Christianity in light of the Holocaust. More recently, his concern at the failure of the Jewish community to draw religious consequences from the lessons of the *Shoah* and the creation of the State of Israel, particularly what he perceives to be their message of Jewish unity, have occupied a good deal of his time and attention. Reuben Bulka's monograph *The Coming Cataclysm* made him reflect on the subject of growing Jewish divisiveness. His 1985 pamphlet *Will There Be One Jewish People in the Year 2000* addressed this contentious issue and has drawn wide attention. This work, plus his defense of the State of Israel against its critics in, for example, his powerful essay "The Ethics of Jewish Power: Two Views" and his ongoing and maturing theological reflection, most recently exemplified in his monograph *The Jewish Way: Living the Holidays*, all continue to mark his extensive contribution to the intellectual and social vitality of the American Jewish community.

The Holocaust and Its Implications

In a series of five articles[1] to date, Greenberg has sketched (I use this term in its literal meaning) his evolving view of the meaning of the *Shoah* and its consequences. His first[2] and, I believe, still most important statement on the subject was made in the 1973 Symposium on the Holocaust held at St. John of the Divine in New York City. Here he began to articulate his belief that the Holocaust radically challenges the essence of the existing theological frameworks of *both* Judaism and Christianity, that is, it challenges belief in the God of Sinai, the God of redemption. "The cruelty and killing raise the question whether even those who believe after such an event [as the Holocaust] dare talk about [a] God who loves and cares without making a mockery of those who suffered."[3] Moreover, as Greenberg acutely intuits, not only are the traditional theological schemata called to answer, but even more so is modernity itself, that substitute "God" in whose name Europe marched forward from the Enlightenment to the rise of Hitler. "There is the shock of recognition that the humanistic revolt, celebrated as the liberation of humankind in freeing man from centuries of dependence upon God and nature, is now revealed—at the very heart of the enterprise—to sustain a capacity for death and demonic evil."[4]

The consequences of this dual recognition are, as Greenberg contends, (1) that one must respond to this new situation in some direct way for "not to respond is to collaborate in the repetition." (2) "Never Again!"—such a possibility must not be allowed to repeat itself. Every position and group that "failed" the test of the *Shoah* "must be challenged, shaken up, rethought" if it wishes to have any right to survive. (3) "The Holocaust challenges the claims of all the standards that compete for modern man's loyalties." All invented orthodoxies are suspect. "[The Holocaust] does not give simple, clear answers or definitive solutions. To claim that it does is not to take burning children seriously. This would—and should—undercut the ultimate adequacy of any category, unless there were one (religious, political, intellectual) that consistently produced the proper response of resistance and horror at the Holocaust. No such category exists to my knowledge." Thus, Greenberg, concludes, "to use the catastrophe to uphold the univocal validity of any category is to turn it into grist for propaganda mills." (4) "The Holocaust offers us only dialectical mores and understandings." Dialectical here is defined as "moves that stretch our capacity to the limit and torment us with their irresolvable tensions." Moreover, this dialectical response is not one option among others; "it is the only morally tenable way for survivors and those guilty of bystanding to live." This dialectical factor issues forth, accordingly, in the following stark principle of theological meaning and validity: "No statement, theological or otherwise, should be made that would not be credible in the presence of the burning children."[5]

Greenberg understands these imperatives, when translated into a specific theological program, as undermining all security and all dogmatic certitude. Even one's "relationship to the God of the Covenant cannot be unaffected." Out of this ambiguous circumstance the new, post-Holocaust "response," if there is to be one, must arise.

> After Auschwitz, faith means there are times when faith is overcome. Buber has spoken of "moment gods": God is known only at the moment when Presence and awareness are fused in vital life. This knowledge is interspersed with moments when only natural, self-contained, routine existence is present. We now have to speak of "moment faiths," moments when Redeemer and vision of redemption are present, interspersed with times when the flames and smoke of burning children blot out faith—though it flickers again.

And such "moment faith" entails that

> the easy dichotomy of atheist/theist, the confusion of faith with doctrine or demonstration is at an end. It makes clear that faith is a life response of the whole person to the Presence in life and history. Like life, this response ebbs and flows. The differences between the skeptic and the believer is frequency of faith, and not certitude of position. The rejection of the unbeliever by the believer is literally the denial or attempted suppression of what is within oneself. The ability to live with moment faith is the ability to live with pluralism and without the self-flattering, ethnocentric solutions which warp religion, or make it a source of hatred for the other.[6]

Greenberg is quick to recognize that given the horrors of Auschwitz even to speak of "moment faiths" is not self-evident. What makes faith possible at all, even flickering, wavering, uncertain, and anguished faith? "Why is it not a permanent destruction of faith," he rhetorically asks, "to be in the presence of the murdered children?"[7] His reply to this all-important question is given in a series of four arguments, which can be summarized as follows.

First, "There are still moments when the reality of the Exodus is reenacted and present."[8] That is, the original Exodus event is still available to us, especially in its yearly Passover reenactment,[9] and thus reality is not solely one, uninterrupted, unmitigated series of tragic occurrences. The evidence of our life's journey reveals moments of despair as well as moments of redemption.

Second, "The Breakdown of the Secular Absolute," as Greenberg calls the dark side of modern humanistic relativism, demands that we not "jump to a conclusion that retrospectively makes the covenant they [the victims] lived an illusion and their deaths a gigantic travesty." We must be open to at least the possibility of transcendence. Because "the Secular Absolute," modernity, denied God, we must obstinately explore this alternative.[10]

The third argument is a corollary and extension of the second. "It is enough," Greenberg writes, "that this [Western] civilization is the locus of the Holocaust. The Holocaust calls on Jews, Christians, and others to absolutely resist the total authority of this cultural moment." The Holocaust destroyed the belief system of modernity, thus opening up conceptual space for other axiological and normative claims, including "the possibilities of Exodus and Immortality."[11]

Last, and most important, is "The Revelation in the Redemption of Israel." Here Greenberg is willing, as a corollary of his basic and deepest belief that Judaism is a religion of and in history, to posit direct theological weight to the recreation of a Jewish state. He wisely proposes that "if the experience of Auschwitz symbolizes that we are cut off from God and hope, and the covenant may be destroyed, then the experience of Jerusalem symbolizes that God's promises are faithful and His people live on."[12]

If these arguments for belief, especially the last, are convincing, why then only "moment faith"? Here Greenberg's commitment to the provisional, uncertain character of our times, as heirs of *both* Auschwitz and the Western Wall, come again to the fore. "Faith is a moment truth, but there are moments when it is not true."[13]

If this is so, what exactly is to be the substance of our faith commitment, after Auschwitz, after Jerusalem, when each of these *realia* cries out over against the other? Greenberg appeals to three classical theological paradigms for help: Job, the "Suffering Servant" of Isaiah, and what Greenberg calls the model of Lamentations 3—entering into debate with the Almighty. From Job we might learn "the rejection of easy pieties or denials and the dialectical response for looking for, expecting, further revelations of the Presence." For, as Job of old, "when suffering had all but overwhelmed Jews and all but blocked out God's Presence, a sign out of the whirlwind [e.g., the rebirth of Israel] gave us strength to go on, and the right to speak authentically of God's Presence still." From Isaiah we might learn that the "Suffering Servant is a kind of early warning system of the sins intrinsic in the culture but often not seen until later." Thus "the Holocaust was an advance warning system of the demonic potential of modern culture ... a kind of last warning that if man will perceive and overcome the demonism unleashed in modern culture, the world may survive. Otherwise, the next Holocaust will embrace the whole world." From Lamentations 3 we might learn "to justify human beings, not God. It suggests a total and thoroughgoing self-criticism that would purge the emotional dependency and self-abasement of traditional religion and its false crutch of certainty and security."[14]

But these biblical paradigms provide only partial answers in our time and thus Greenberg climaxes the presentation of his view by asserting:

> In the silence of God and of theology, there is one fundamental testimony that can still be given—the testimony of human life itself. This was always the basic evidence, but after Auschwitz its import is incredibly heightened. In fact, it is the only testimony that can still be heard.
>
> The vast number of dead and morally destroyed is the phenomenology of absurdity and radical evil, the continuing statement of human worthlessness and meaninglessness that shouts down all talk of God and human worth. The Holocaust is even model and pedagogy for future generations that genocide can be carried out with impunity—one need fear neither God nor man. There is one response to such overwhelming tragedy: the reaffirmation of meaningfulness, worth, and life—through acts of love and life-giving. The act of creating a life or enhancing its dignity is the counter-testimony to Auschwitz. To talk of love and of a God who cares in the presence of the burning children is obscene and incredible, to leap in and pull a child out of a pit, to clean its face and heal its body, is to make the most powerful statement—the only statement that counts.... Each act of creating a life, each act of enhancing or holding people responsible for human life, becomes multiplied in its resonance, because it contradicts the mass graves of ... Treblinka.[15]

Greenberg here intimates a provocative thesis: we are now responsible for our world as well as for God's "Name" in history. "The religious enterprise after [the Holocaust] must see itself as a desperate attempt to create, save, and heal the image of God wherever it still exists—lest further evidence of meaninglessness finally fill the scale irreversibly. Before this calling, all other 'religious' activity is dwarfed."[16] For the Jewish people this act of life, of affirmation, is first and foremost witnessed to in the reborn

State of Israel. "To fail to grasp that inextricable connection and response is to utterly fail to comprehend the theological significance of Israel."[17] But the command to a new life, even to resurrection, if one likes, goes beyond the facts of the State of Israel, beyond the narrowly Jewish context. It requires that:

> We also face the urgent call to eliminate every stereotype discrimination that reduces—and denies—this image in the other. It was the ability to distinguish some people as human and others as not that enabled the Nazis to segregate and then destroy the "subhumans...." The indivisibility of human dignity and equality becomes an essential bulwark against the repetition of another Holocaust. It is the command rising out of Auschwitz.
>
> This means a vigorous self-criticism, and review of every cultural or religious framework that may sustain some devaluation or denial of the absolute and equal dignity of the other. This is the overriding command and the essential criterion for religious existence, to whoever walks by the light of the flames. Without this testimony and the creation of facts that give it persuasiveness, the act of the religious enterprise simply lacks credibility. To the extent that religion may extend or justify the evils of dignity denied, it becomes the devil's testimony. Whoever joins in the work of creation and rehabilitation of the image of God is, therefore, participating in "restoring to God his scepter and crown." Whoever does not support—or opposes—this process is seeking to complete the attack on God's presence in the world. These must be seen as the central religious acts. They shed a pitiless light on popes who deny birth control to starving millions because of a need to uphold the religious authority of the magisterium; or rabbis who deny women's dignity out of loyalty to divinely given traditions.[18]

Three further lessons are also to be learned from the luciferian reality of the death camps. The first is that the older secular-religious dichotomy must be transcended. "Illumined by the light of the crematoria, these categories are dissolved and not infrequently turned inside out." The second has to do with power. Greenberg puts it succinctly:

> Out of the Holocaust experience comes the demand for redistribution of power. The principle is simple. No one should ever have to depend again on anyone else's goodwill or respect for their basic security and right to exist.... No one should ever be equipped with less power than is necessary to assure one's dignity. To argue dependence on law, or human goodness, or universal equality is to join the ranks of

those who would like to repeat the Holocaust. Anyone who wants to prevent a repetition must support a redistribution of power.[19]

The third deals with Jewish-Christian relations. Here Greenberg asserts that "Jews have not appreciated Christianity enough." He explains:

There is a general Jewish tendency to underestimate Christianity's redemptive contribution to the world, due to the bad experience Jews have had with it. Anger at Christian mistreatment has obscured the ambivalence and importance of Judaism in Christianity, which meant that Christians persecuted, but also kept alive and protected, Jews. Even persecuting Christians gave Jews the option of converting, rather than styling the Jew as intrinsically demonic and beyond the right to exist. Rebuking the widespread, almost stereotyped Jewish identification with secular, liberal modernity and against Christianity, the Holocaust suggests that modern values created a milieu as dangerous as—more dangerous than—Christianity at its worst. Indeed, Jews have a vested interest in Christianity's existence. Russia, the society of secularism triumphant, has demonstrated again that secular absolutism is just as dangerous to Judaism as is an abusive Christianity, unchecked.[20]

This new appreciation of Christianity is not merely based on the relative superiority of Christianity to Nazism and Stalinism. Deeper theological revaluations are now, in light of Auschwitz, both possible and necessary. Greenberg calls upon Jews, as he calls upon Christians, to open an unprecedented dialogue on the spiritual meaning of Christianity (and of Christians on Judaism). Not to do so is to risk indifference to a future Holocaust built upon the old, now recycled, stereotypes. He goes so far as to propose: "Confirmed now in its resumed redemption [State of Israel], shaken by the Holocaust's challenge not to put down others, Judaism can no longer give patronizing answers. It must explore the possibility that the covenant grafted onto it is a way whereby God has called Gentiles to God." At the same time this Jewish response is predicated on a reconsideration of Christian attitudes toward Judaism. Hence Greenberg adds:

Of course, this invokes the principle, "by their fruits, you shall know them." When Jesus' Messianism led to hatred, exclusion, pogrom, it could only be judged false. If it now leads to responsibility, *mitgefuhl*, sharing of risk and love, then its phenomenology becomes radically

different. Suffice it to say—without irony—Christians have an extraordinary opportunity in this age: of showing the power of love and
concern for Jews and the embattled beginnings of Jewish redemption,
the State of Israel. Such a demonstration would give new seriousness
among Jews to Christianity's own perception that it is a vehicle of
divine presence and redemption in the world.[21]

The Dialectic of Jewish History

Having begun with these relatively preliminary and unfinished
remarks, Greenberg recognizes that he has only initiated the
necessary theological task of clarifying the significance of the
Holocaust for contemporary Jewish thought. To proceed further
he must return and reengage, now in a more detailed way, the
meaning of historical experience in Judaism—that is, in what
sense is Judaism a "historical religion" and hence what difference
do historical events (such as the *Shoah* and recreation of the State
of Israel) make to the Jewish view of reality? All of Greenberg's
thought deals, either directly or obliquely, now in one way, now
in another, with this question. History is his main concern. (And
one perhaps ought to add that, for Greenberg, history is never
neutral. It either challenges or confirms covenantal theology.)

The premise of his analysis is that Judaism is a uniquely
historical religion. Since the experiences of the Patriarchs and the
time of the Exodus, Judaism has been shaped by God's actions in
history. History is the primary milieu for the Divine-human
encounter, "at once the scene of human activity and divine
redemption."[22] As such it is also the laboratory of verification, the
test of all theology. One learns of God, His ways, and what
appears to be His absence through the historical experiences of
the Jewish, and other, peoples. Greenberg even allows for the
possibility of the "refutation" of God's existence as a consequence
of historical events. But this affirmation, too, is dialectical. That is,

Faith is not pure abstraction, unaffected or unshaken by contradictory
events; it is subject to "refutation." Yet it is not simply empirical
either. A purely empirical faith would be subject to immediate
refutation, but in fact the people of Israel may continue to testify in
exile and after defeat. It may see or hope beyond the present moment
to the redemption which will inevitably follow. Thereby, it continues
to testify despite the contradiction in the present moment. In fact,
when the redemption comes, it will be all the greater proof of the

assertions of faith and of the reliability of God's promises because it will overcome the present hopeless reality. On the other hand, if redemption never came or if Israel lost hope while waiting for redemption, then the status quo would win and Jewish testimony would come to an end. Thus, faith is neither a simple product of history nor insulated from history. It is testimony anchored in history, in constant tension with it, subject to revision and understanding as well as to fluctuation in credibility due to the unfolding events.[23]

Israel's faith, however, is not groundless. It is rooted in Israel's formative national experience of exodus and covenant. Having known God's redemptive and revelatory acts in times past, it has grounds for hope in their continued reality. And this, Greenberg reemphasizes, is the particularly historical thrust of Judaism. "God's mighty acts of redemption *are* in history. In taking this stand, Jewish tradition promises to move history forward and at the same time leaves itself vulnerable to being shattered on the rock of that very history."[24]

What follows necessarily from this emphasis on the vulnerability of Judaism to historical disconfirmation is the theological significance of national tragedies that seem to be weighty counterevidence to the claims of the Exodus and Sinai. For "unless the facts of suffering and defeat are reconciled with the claims, in fact the ability to make them, is overthrown." Prior to the Holocaust, such a response to national tragedy was to be found particularly in three classic forms. First, the tradition of *mipnei chata'eynu*— "because of our sins we are punished," that is, that such punishment is proof of God's continued concern with even a wayward Israel. This was the primary, though not the only, explanation of the destruction of the First Temple. And, of course, it was connected with a doctrine of the redemption of Israel that was sure because it was grounded in God's promise that the exile was *not* forever. Second, in reaction to national catastrophe, there was a transformation in "the understanding of the nature of God." This, Greenberg contends, is the major feature of the response to the destruction of the Second Temple:

God was no longer going to be as available, as directly or dramatically involved in history, as He had been until then. Rather, God had withdrawn and the human involvement in history, both in tragedy and redemption, was much greater than had been realized before. This is the dynamic behind the triumph of the Halakhic method and the conclusion that prophecy no longer existed. This is the validation of the rejection of heavenly voices as the arbiter in legal disagreements.[25]

Third, there have been Jews like Elisha ben Abuya who have taken Israel's fateful negative experiences as decisive proof that existence is meaningless, "*leth din v'leth dayan*"[26] ("there is no judgment and no judge"), life has no transcendent meaning.

In Greenberg's estimation, consistent with most modern rabbinic scholarship, the second type of response became normative for Judaism after 70 C.E. It is "the one given by Rabbi Yohanan Ben Zakkai and the rabbis. It became the dominant post-Destruction [70 C.E.] form of Judaism.... The crucial development is the shift from the revealed intervening God of the biblical period to the relatively hidden Deity of the exilic period. God is close now as *Presence*, as *Skekhinah*, not as automatic intervenor who brings victory to the deserving."[27] Greenberg goes on to describe this *re*interpretation of God's character in a powerful way. Reflecting on the *aggadic* text in the talmudic treatise *Yoma* 60a, he writes:

Moses had spoken of God as "great, mighty, and awesome." Jeremiah, the prophet of destruction, declined to speak of God's might. If Gentiles cavort in His sanctuary, where is His might? Daniel declined to speak of God as awesome. If Gentiles enslave and oppress his People, where is His awesomeness? The men of the Great Assembly restored this praise by *reinterpretation*. They answered: This is His might—that He controls His urges. When the wicked flourish (for example, the Temple is destroyed). He is patient with them (that is, He gives them time and freedom to act; He does not intervene and stop them). And this is God's awesomeness—were it not for awe of God, how could this one people—the Jewish people—exist among all the other nations that are out to destroy it? How is it known that God is, in fact, present after the Destruction? Only by a radical reinterpretation of His presence in the world: He controls Himself. He is the hidden presence, not the intervening presence. The only other way we know of His presence is that His people continue to exist in defiance of all logic and all force. This proves that behind it all there is a God who keeps the Jewish people alive."[28]

But what of the Holocaust? Can the model of R. Yohanan also be satisfactorily applied to it? Or does it break asunder the rabbinic reformulation of God's presence? Greenberg's answer to this has undergone a two-step development. In the first stage, as given expression in his essay on "Judaism and History," published in 1978, he argued for the radicalizing of the traditional rabbinic response.[29] That is, what was required is the deliberate radicalizing of tendencies already at work within the halakhic tradition. For example, what is characterized as the "secularizing" tendency needs encouragement as well as a new prominence, especially because of the secular, though profoundly religious, character of the State of Israel. Second, and as a corollary of this secularizing tendency, the increasing shift from rabbinic to lay leadership in the contemporary Jewish community is to be welcomed. Third, the redefinition of God's "self-control" in the face of evil, already begun at *Yavneh*, needs further accentuation in the light of God's "silence" at Auschwitz. Fourth, and as a corollary of God's "silence," we need to understand "that the human role in redemption is more central and dramatic than that emphasized in the grandest speculation of rabbinic tradition."[30]

At this juncture Greenberg knew the right question to ask: "Why is this not simply a suggestion that Judaism is entering an atheist or purely natural period?" He answered his own interrogative as follows. The Holocaust has bankrupted humanism, just as radically as it has challenged theism. Second, "Jewish secularism" after Auschwitz is theologically "awesome" in its willingness to continue as an identifiably Jewish phenomenon. Third, "the rebirth of Israel does speak (as Isaiah suggsted) of redemption, purpose and fulfillment in history."[31]

The second, more recent, still more radical stage in Greenberg's theological vision turns not on a deepening of the Yavnean response, but on its dramatic extension (Greenberg would favor more dialectical terms here that still retain certain overtones of the dialectic of continuity and discontinuity), which leads to a transformation through the creation of a new pattern. This new metaphysical configuration speaks explicitly not only of continuity with the past but of a unique beginning, a new era of Jewish covenantal history. Greenberg explicates his meaning in this way. There are three major periods in the covenantal history of Israel. The first is the biblical era, which is characterized by the asymmetry of the relationship between God and Israel. The biblical encounter may be a covenant, but it is clearly a covenant in which "God is the initiator, the senior partner, who punishes, rewards and enforces the partnership if the Jews slacken."[32] This relationship culminated in the crisis engendered by the destruction of the First Temple in 586 B.C.E. To this tragedy Israel, through the Prophets, in keeping with the "logic" of this position, responded primarily with and through the doctrine of self-chastisement. The destruction indicated divine punishment rather than God's rejection of Israel or proof of God's non-existence.[33] The second phase in the transformation of the covenant idea is marked by the destruction of the Second Temple. The meaning adduced from this event, the response of the rabbis, was that now Jews must take a more equal role in the covenant, becoming true partners with the Almighty.[34] "The manifest divine presence and activity was being reduced but the covenant was actually being renewed."[35] For the destruction signaled the initiation of an age in which God would be less manifest though still present. "The Divine Presence becomes more shielded and more present. The Jewish role more active."[36] Moreover, after 70 C.E., the sages began to think again about the meaning of the destruction and God's role in it. According to Greenberg, they now began to recognize

> that explaining the Destruction as divine punishment for sins is not as adequate an explanation as before. Although this remains the dominant explanation—it is also an important defense against the claim that the Destruction is a rejection of Israel as covenant partner. There is significant expansion of an alternate interpretation. The Divine Presence does not so much punish Israel in the Destruction as it suffers alongside Israel. "Since the Temple was destroyed, there is no laughter before the Holy One Blessed Be He" (*Yalkut Shinoni*, Section 454).[37]

And again, and seminally, "that God's might is expressed in allowing human freedom instead of punishing the wicked."[38] The essential thesis that Greenberg is concerned to develop vis-à-vis the rabbis of the mishnah is that they were conscious of *both* their continuity with the inherited tradition and their innovative role in further interpreting the meaning of the covenant.[39] As a consequence, the status of covenantal relationship was reoriented. Previously it had come into being essentially because of God's will and power; now it was reconfirmed "on 'new' terms, knowing that destruction can take place, that the Sea will not be split for them, that the Divine has self-limited and they (Israel) have additional responsibilities."[40] This further "hiding" of the divine

is described by Greenberg as a process of the increasing secularization of history.[41] In such an era it becomes both appropriate
and necessary for human beings to take a more active role in
history, to fill the gap left by the absenting God. In a strikingly
suggestive analysis of the new post–70 C.E. situation Greenberg
proposes that for the mishnaic sages Purim rather than Passover
becomes the "redemptive paradigm."[42] Only through this transformation can covenantal existence continue after 70 C.E.[43]

This brings us to what is decisive and novel in Greenberg's
more recent ruminations, what he has termed the "Third Great
Cycle in Jewish History," which is a consequence of the Holocaust. Whereas previously he saw our contemporary form of
covenantal relationship as a continuous, if extreme stage in the
rabbinic understanding of covenantal partnership, now he
presents it in a new light.[44] The *Shoah* marks a new era in which
the Sinaitic covenant was shattered. Thus if there is to be any
covenantal relationship at all today it must assume new and
unprecedented forms.[45] In this context Greenberg insists that the
covenant always implied further human development. The
natural outcome of the covenant is full human responsibility. "In
retrospect," he suggests, paraphrasing A. Roy Eckardt,

> it is now clear that the divine assignment to the Jews was untenable. In
> the Covenant, Jews were called to witness to the world for God and
> for a final perfection. After the Holocaust, it is obvious that this role
> opened the Jews to a total murderous fury from which there was no
> escape. Yet the divine could not or would not save them from this
> fate.
>
> Therefore, morally speaking, God must repent of the covenant, i.e.,
> do Teshuvah for having given his chosen people a task that was
> unbearably cruel and dangerous without having provided for their
> protection. Morally speaking, then, God can have no claims on the
> Jews by dint of the Covenant.[46]

What this means is that the covenant

> can no longer be commanded and subject to a serious external
> enforcement. It can not be commanded because morally speaking—
> covenantally speaking—one cannot *order* another to step forward to
> die. One can give an order like this to an enemy, but in a moral
> relationship, I cannot demand giving up one's life. I can ask for it or
> plead for it—but I cannot order it. To put it again in Wiesel's words:

when God gave us a mission, that was all right. But God failed to tell us that it was a suicide mission.[47]

Moreover, after the horrors of the *Endlösung*, nothing God could threaten for breach of the covenant would be frightening, hence the Covenant can no longer be enforced by the threat of punishment.[48]

Out of this complex of considerations, Greenberg pronounces the fateful judgment: *The Covenant is now voluntary!* After Auschwitz, Jews have, miraculously, chosen to continue to live Jewish lives and collectively to build a Jewish state, the ultimate symbol of Jewish continuity, but these acts are now the result of the free choice of the Jewish people. "I submit that the covenant was broken but the Jewish people, released from its obligations, chose voluntarily to take it on again and renew it. God was in no position to command anymore but the Jewish people was so in love with the dream of redemption that it volunteered to carry on with its mission." The consequence of this voluntary action transforms the existing covenantal order. First, Israel was a junior partner, then an equal partner, and now after Auschwitz it becomes "the senior partner in action. In effect, God was saying to humans: you stop the Holocaust. You bring the redemption. You act to insure: never again. I will be with you totally in whatever you do, wherever you go, whatever happens but you must do it."[49]

In turn, Israel's voluntary acceptance of the covenant and continued will to survive suggest three corollaries. First, they point, if obliquely, to the continued existence of the God of Israel. By creating the State of Israel and by having Jewish children, Israel shows that "covenantal hope is not in vain."[50] Second, and very important, in an age of voluntarism rather than coercion, living Jewishly under the covenant can no longer be interpreted monolithically, that is, only in strict halakic fashion. A genuine Jewish pluralism,[51] a Judaism of differing options and interpretations, is the only legitimate foundation in the age of Auschwitz. Orthodox observance, no less than Reform, Conservative, or "secular" practices are voluntary—none can claim either automatic authority or exclusive priority in the contemporary Jewish world.[52] Third, and repeating a theme sounded several times in earlier essays, Greenberg offers that the urgency of closing any gap between the covenantal methods and goals is greater in light of the overwhelming countertestimony of evil in this generation. The credibility of the Covenant is so troubled and so hanging in the balance that any internal element that disrupts or contravenes its affirmations must be eliminated. So savage was the attack on the image of God that any models or behavior patterns within the tradition that demean the image of God of people must be cleansed and corrected at once.[53]

A note of caution in pushing this dramatic statement of a "voluntary covenant" too far is required because of Greenberg's further, mediating, remarks on this provocative thesis. He writes: "We are at the opening of a major new transformation of the covenant in which Jewish loyalty and commitment manifests itself by Jews taking action and responsibility for the achievement of its goals. This is not a radical break with the past. In retrospect, this move is intrinsic in the very concept of covenant." And Greenberg goes on: "The Rabbis [of the Talmud] put forth Purim, with its hidden, human agency and flawed redemption, as *the* new redemptive model to which the Jews gave assent in upholding the covenant. *Today we can say that the covenant validated at Purim is also coercive, for then the genocide was foiled, and it is less binding in a world that saw Hitler's murder of six million Jews.*"[54]

The Halakah as a Theology of History

Here a brief description of Greenberg's recent book-length study of the yearly cycle of Jewish festivals, *The Jewish Way*, is in order. Though the overt theme of the book is the character of the Jewish holidays, its real meaning is to vindicate its author's view of the historicity of Judaism, that is, that Judaism sees redemption as occurring within history. In this connection the two stages in the overall drama of redemption are the Exodus and mankind's efforts, first undertaken by the Jewish people in Egypt but ultimately meant as a paradigm for the entire world, to perfect historical existence. In this complex drama humankind is seen as playing an essential role, reinforcing Greenberg's more general thesis regarding the now dominant role that humankind must now assume in the post-Holocaust age. "The ultimate goal," Greenberg writes, "will be achieved through human participation. The whole process of transformation will take place on a human scale.

Human models, not supernatural beings, will instruct and inspire mankind as it works toward the final redemption." And this redemption, the messianic completion, will include, and affect, all peoples. Thus the Jewish task is the universal task, and Israel's redemption is the world's perfection. The cycle of the Jewish year, expressive as it is of the larger halakic *Weltanschauung*, incarnates these repercussive themes and gives them temporal and spatial reality. It provides substance to Jewish theology and the rhythm of Jewish existence. Still more, it offers a perennial history lesson teaching each Jew the record of Israel's past so that "in an annual cycle, every Jew lives through all of Jewish history and makes it his or her personal experience. The holidays generate the sense of community by making the story of all, the possession of each one."[55]

The holidays are of two types, those of biblical origin, Passover, Shavuot, Sukkot, Sabbath, and the Days of Awe, "present a stationary model of Judaism coherent, revealed, structured." Then there are a series of festivals and remembrances, Purim, Chanukah, and Tisha B'av, that emerged because "Judaism opens itself to further historical events that can challenge or confirm its message."[56] Today again Judaism is challenged by the *Shoah* and the recreation of the State of Israel, and as in the past the Jewish people are attempting to find ways to confront the meaning of these extraordinary events without permitting them to destroy the overall character of Jewish faith. Yom Ha-Atzmaut, Israeli Independence Day, and Yom Ha-Shoah, Holocaust Remembrance Day, reflect these struggles in concrete forms. Indeed, it might fairly be said that Greenberg's discussion of these two contemporary events forms the core of *The Jewish Way* for in it such elemental Greenbergian themes as the meaningfulness of life after the Holocaust, the renewal of the covenant essentially through human energy, and the redemption of history microcosmically represented by the "resurrection and redemption"[57] that is the State of Israel find expression. Of the latter he asserts: "The creation of the State was an act of redemption of biblical stature . . . in the 1940's after Auschwitz. The redemption then was nothing less than renewed witness in a world where all transcendence seemed to have collapsed."[58] This event is the source and confirmation of his more general thesis regarding the meaning of a "third era in Jewish history," of the now voluntary covenant and the heroic stature of the Jewish people in carrying on with the work of redemption. Thus he tells us: "In the case of the State of Israel ... the human role is dominant and self-assertive. This secularism should not be confused with atheism or celebration of the death of God.... Rather ... the creation of the State of Israel takes place in the context of a new era in Jewish history. In this new era, God becomes even more hidden, the circumstances even more ambiguous. This ambiguity serves a twofold function: it allows those who prefer to interpret the activity as purely secular to do so, and it permits the religious soul to recognize the divine role out of mature understanding and free will rather than out of 'coerced' yielding to divine *force majeure*."[59] Thus Yom Ha-Atzmaut is the perfect paradigm for Greenberg's new/old vision of Jewish existence.

Critique

The critical remarks I will now offer are meant to be suggestive rather than exhaustive so I shall present them seriatim.

1. In responding to the many genuinely interesting philosophical and theological positions Greenberg has advanced there is, to begin, a certain unease that one has not quite captured his meaning completely. The source of this disquiet lies not only in the limits of one's own understanding but also in Greenberg's imprecise use of essential terms and ideas. Such elemental terms as *revelation, messianic, messianism, history, redemption, real, secular,* and *religious,* are used in a multiplicity of ways, aimed at a spectrum of differently informed listeners, and all are employed (perhaps in part intentionally) without any precise definitions being offered. Then again, his work suffers from a certain lack of logical rigor. This is evident both in the construction of particular arguments and in certain underlying architectonic features of Greenberg's thought as a whole. The most notable of these lapses, which is present so consistently that it should be seen as a structural flaw, is located in his hermeneutical overemployment of the notions *dialectic* and *dialectical* and in his unsatisfactory usage of the interrelated notion of *paradox.* Merely holding, or claiming to believe, two contradictory propositions simultaneously is *not* a fruitful theological procedure.

2. Greenberg offers two seminal criteria of verification for

theological discourse in our time. The first is strikingly powerful in its directness and simplicity: "No statement, theological or otherwise, should be made that would not be credible in the presence of burning children."[60] The second, more philosophically sculpted and no doubt shaped in response to the positivist verificationist challenge, reads as follows:

> Faith is not pure abstraction, unaffected or unshaken by contradictory events; it is subject to "refutation." Yet it is not simply empirical either. A purely empirical faith would be subject to immediate refutation, but in fact the people of Israel may continue to testify in exile and after defeat. It may see or hope beyond the present moment to the redemption which will inevitably follow. Thereby, it continues to testify despite the contradiction in the present moment. In fact, when the redemption comes, it will be all the greater proof of the assertions of faith and of the reliability of God's promises because it will overcome the present hopeless reality. On the other hand, if redemption never came or if Israel lost hope while waiting for redemption, then the status quo would win and Jewish testimony would come to an end. Thus, faith is neither a simple product of history nor insulated from history. It is a testimony anchored in history, in constant tension with it, subject to revision and understanding as well as to fluctuation in credibility due to the unfolding events.[61]

Although modern Jewish philosophers have tended to ignore the all-important challenge raised by requests for verification, here Greenberg, astutely as well as courageously, meets it head-on. The question to be put to him, however, is whether his two formulations are adequate as principles of verification. The first formulation does not set out a straightforward empirical criterion. Empirical evidence will neither simply confirm it nor, as it is phrased in the negative, simply disconfirm it. There is no empirical statement E with which it is incompatible. That is, it is not, finally, a statement of an empirical sort. But this need not matter *decisively*, for it is not put as an empirical criterion; rather, its appeal is to the broader category of "credibility," and many things are credible that are not empirical. Thus the task before us transforms itself into showing that *credible* is not used trivially, but doing so is far more ambiguous and uncertain than at first appears to be the case. Consider, for example, the remarks of the German Protestant Pastor Dean Heinrich Grueber that had such a profound impact on Richard Rubenstein.[62] Grueber honestly held that Jewish children died for the crime of deicide committed by their first-century ancestors. Such "good" Christian theology was obviously credible to him in the face of the Holocaust. Likewise, Satmar Hasidim and other right-wing Orthodox Jews who continue to account for the Holocaust through recourse to the doctrine of "for our sins we are punished" (*mipnei chata'eynu*), remembering, for example, the terrible fate of the children of Jerusalem of old recounted in Lamentations, which is credited to "our sins," also believe that their propositions are credible. It thus becomes evident that *credible* is not a self-explanatory category of judgment. What is credible to Dean Grueber and the Satmar Rebbe is *incredible* to Greenberg—and the dispute between them is not resolved by appeal to the criterion Greenberg has established, as it would be were it a viable criterion. It turns out that credibility depends on one's prior theological commitments, the very issue at stake. Thus the argument becomes circular.

The second, more formal, criterion is attested to be falsifiable, "subject to refutation," yet it is not a "simply empirical" proposition. The two conditions of "refutation" established are (a) "redemption never comes" and (b) "if Israel lost hope while waiting for redemption, then the status quo would win." The first criterion appears, at least in what has been called a "weak" sense, to be empirically verifiable—that is, it states a specific empirical condition under which it would, in principle, be disconfirmed. But the established thesis is inadequate as a criterion because it turns on the temporal notion "never comes." Thus, logically, we could not make any use of this norm until world history ended, in redemption or otherwise. At any time before the end of history an appeal could be made to "wait a minute more," hence putting off the empirical disconformation indefinitely. It certainly is not, *contra* Greenberg, a "testimony anchored in history" in any strong sense, as immediate and available historical evidence such as the obscene reality of the death camps is deflected by appeal to the end that never is.

The second condition offered is of more interest. But it, too, is not sufficient for two reasons. First, the continued and continuing status of Israel's faith *qua* subjective affirmation is not a logical or ontological warrant for any proposition regarding "God's mighty Acts in History," Greenberg's claim to the contrary notwithstanding. What is disconfirmed "if Israel loses hope" is, of course,

Israel's faith—the strength of its commitment—but the ontological content of the commitment is unaffected. Propositions such as "there is a God," or "God Redeems," or "History reveals a loving Providence" are neither confirmed by Israel's faith nor disconfirmed by Israel's apostasy.

Given the weak verification procedures proposed by Greenberg, his advocacy of faith in God after the *Shoah* would seem compatible with any empirical set of conditions. That is, there seems no empirical state of affairs that is incompatible with theism, especially Greenberg's particular exposition of theism.

3. What is the relationship, if any, between the *Shoah* and *halakah?* Does the *Shoah* justify halakic transvaluations? Here one needs to go slowly. As a preliminary conclusion subject to revision it appears to me that the *Shoah* does *not* legitimate either wholesale halakic change or a transformation in the fundamental structures of the halakic *Weltanschauung*.[63] Thus Greenberg's extremely well-intentioned call for widespread and dramatic halakic innovation, for a *voluntary covenant* and the rest, even if made with enormous *ahavat Yisroel*, "love of Israel," may well be misguided. In any case, there seems no certain methodological or metaphysical bridge between Auschwitz and halakah, between Nazis killing Jews and the need for a Jewish redefinition of halakah.

To avoid any misunderstanding, let me repeat that this conclusion is not based on the denial of the uniqueness of the Holocaust as is usually the case with more halakic orientations. Indeed, I am convinced of the historical uniqueness, both in Jewish and in world-historical terms, of the *Shoah*.[64] Having come to this conclusion, however, which I share, for various reasons, with Greenberg and the other post-Holocaust theologians such as Richard Rubenstein and Emil Fackenheim, I do not see any compelling logical or theological reason for equating this historical judgment with a mandate for halakic change. Historical uniqueness is one thing, the legitimating criteria for halakic change is something else, and I am yet to see, or to have been shown, the bridge from one to the other.

4. *Revelation* is a technical and awe/ful term, a term not heard often enough today even in theological circles, yet, ironically, at times overused and almost always employed too loosely and imprecisely in contemporary discourse. These several thoughts are sparked by Greenberg's recurring theological ruminations on

this theme, especially as it becomes decisive in relation to claims made for the putative revelatory character of the *Shoah* and the reborn state of Israel. From a narrowly Jewish theological perspective nothing rivals these assertions in importance for no category is as elemental as revelation. All that Judaism is flows from revelatory claims, is predicated on a specific understanding of what revelation is and is not. The structure as well as the content of Judaism presumes a delimited and defined hermeneutic of the revelatory event as well as of the way the content of revelation is unfolded, expounded, and applied. Because the stakes are so high, insisting, *contra* Greenberg, on a careful employment of this term is required lest the possibility arise that any claim might be advanced as a revelatory one.

5. *God.* The structure of Greenberg's three covenantal eras, his many propositions about a "saving God," his talk of revelation and redemption, and his radical proposition that the Almighty is increasingly a "silent partner" in Jewish and world history cannot be advanced without pondering their consequences for the "God of Abraham, Isaac, and Jacob."

To put it directly, what happens to the God of Judaism in Greenberg's theology? Prima facie the God of all the traditional omnipredicates does not fit easily with a "God" who is a silent partner. This may not be a telling criticism, though I think it is, because Greenberg is free to redefine *God* for the purposes of theological reflection. But having redefined *God* however he feels it appropriate, Greenberg must attend to the myriad metaphysical and theological consequences of such an action. It is thus incumbent to require that whatever Greenberg's "God-idea," its character and implications must be explained fully and carefully. On one hand, this means that the ontological entailments of treating God as a silent partner have to be spelled out. On the other hand, the implication of such a metaphysical principle (God as a silent partner) for such traditional and essential Jewish concerns as covenant, reward and punishment, morality, Torah, mitzvot, redemption, and other eschatological matters has to be attended to. For example, is a God who is a silent partner capable of being the author and guarantor of moral value both in human relations and in history and nature more generally? Or has the axiological role traditionally occupied by God largely been evacuated?[65] Likewise, is there a possibility of sin, in a substantive and not merely a metaphorical sense, in this perspective? Again, is God as a silent partner capable of being the God of salvation both personal and historic? And finally, is God as a silent partner the God to whom we pray on Yom Kippur and to whom we confess our sins and ask forgiveness? If my skepticism regarding the ability of Greenberg's "God-idea" to answer these challenges is misplaced, this has to be demonstrated. For it would appear that though Greenberg's revised "God-idea" allows him to unfold the logic of the "Third Era" as he desires, it generates more theological problems than it solves.

6. This brings us to the most dramatic and most consequential of Greenberg's affirmations—his espousal, in our post-Holocaust era, of a "voluntary covenant." According to Greenberg, as explicated in detail above, the Sinaitic covenant was shattered in the *Shoah*. As a consequence, Greenberg pronounces the fateful judgment: *the covenant is now voluntary!* Jews have, miraculously, chosen after Auschwitz to continue to live Jewish lives and collectively to build a Jewish state, the ultimate symbol of Jewish continuity, but these acts are, post-*Shoah*, the result of the free choice of the Jewish people.

Logically and theologically the key issue that arises at this central juncture, given Greenberg's reconstruction, is this: if there was ever a valid covenant,[66] that is, there is a God who entered into such a relationship with Israel, then can this covenant be "shattered" by a Hitler? Or put the other way round, if Hitler can be said to have shattered the covenant, was there ever such a covenant, despite traditional Jewish pieties, in the first place? The reasons for raising these repercussive questions are metaphysical and are related to the nature of the biblical God and the meaning of His attributes and activities, including His revelations and promises, which are immune, by definition, from destruction by the likes of a Hitler. If Hitler could break God's covenantal promises, God would not be God and Hitler would indeed be central to Jewish belief.

The nature of this essay and the character of my critique reflect the seriousness with which I believe one must take Greenberg's theological position. Its sensitivity to the right issues, its commitment to the Jewish people, its learning and intelligence, its concern with the interfacing of halakah and history, its profound affirmation of the meaning of the State of Israel, are all attributes that recommend it to those truly concerned with the present condition of the people Israel and the viability of Jewish belief in the post-Holocaust age. Though it falls short of being a complete prescriptive account of the current Jewish situation this does not diminish its value as a stimulant to further and still deeper reflection on the rudimentary matters it has the courage to address.

Notes

1. The five articles by Greenberg with which I will be concerned in this section are "Cloud of Smoke, Pillar of Fire: Judaism, Christianity, and Modernity after the Holocaust," in Eva Fleischner, ed., *Auschwitz: Beginning of a Era?* (New York, 1977), pp. 7–55 (hereafter cited as "Cloud"); "Judaism and History: Historical Events and Religious Change," in Jerry V. Dillen, ed., *Ancient Roots and Modern Meanings* (New York, 1978), pp. 43–63 (hereafter cited as "JH"); "New Revelations and New Patterns in the Relationship of Judaism and Christianity," *Journal of Ecumenical Studies* 16 (Spring 1979): pp. 249–67 (hereafter cited as "New Revelations"); "The Transformation of the Covenant" (not yet published); and "The Third Great Cycle of Jewish History," in *Perspective*, printed and circulated by the National Jewish Resource Center (New York, 1981).
2. It is important to add here both for purposes of chronology as well as conceptual clarity that though Greenberg's essay "Cloud of Smoke, Pillar of Fire" is the first essay discussed, it was not his first effort to articulate the meaning of history for Judaism, i.e., the relevance of seeing Judaism as a historical religion. This is clear from his very early publication "Yavneh: Looking Ahead, Values and Goals," *Yavneh Studies* 1 (Fall 1962), pp. 46–55.
3. I will not discuss Greenberg's understanding of the significance and challenge of the Holocaust for Christian theology, most of which I agree with, because my concern here is his account of the way the Holocaust has affected post-1945 Jewish life and thought.
4. Greenberg, "Cloud", p. 11. It should be noted here, however, so as not to distort Greenberg's position by overconcentration on its radical or novel elements, that he begins this powerful essay with the traditional affirmation that "Judaism and Christianity are religions of redemption" (p. 1). Moreover, this element of continuity is more evident in his later essay "Judaism and History" that was, unlike "Cloud," addressed to an internal Jewish audience and is concerned primarily with Jewish historical links between past and present.
5. Greenberg, "Cloud," p. 15.
6. Greenberg, "Cloud," pp. 20–23. I have reversed the order of Greenberg's presentation; my second "consequence" is actually stated first in Greenberg's essay. Already in this early essay, Greenberg was suggesting, however obliquely, that there is something essentially revelatory about the Holocaust and that therefore new theological understandings, by all groups, will be required to understand it and to respond to it appropriately.
7. Ibid., p. 27.
8. Ibid., p. 27.
9. Ibid., p. 28.

10. Spelled out now much more fully in Greenberg, *The Jewish Way: Living the Holidays* (New York, 1988).
11. Ibid., pp. 28–29. Greenberg's full statement of this argument is found in the bottom paragraph on pp. 29–30.
12. Ibid., p. 31. Greenberg defines this postmodernist move: "This new era will not turn its back on many aspects of modernity but clearly will be free to reject some of its elements, and to take from the past (and future) much more fully" (p. 31).
13. Ibid., p. 32.
14. Ibid., p. 33.
15. Ibid., pp. 35, 37, 40.
16. Ibid., pp. 41–42.
17. Ibid., p. 42. In "Cloud," Greenberg was more concerned with people taking political and military power than revising the meaning of power vis-à-vis the covenant. This latter theological notion becomes really important only in his later work. See his further thoughts on this central issue in *The Jewish Way*, pp. 18ff., 127ff., and 370ff.
18. Ibid., p. 43.
19. Ibid., pp. 44, 45, 50.
20. "New Revelations," p. 259.
21. Ibid., p. 265.
22. "JH," p. 47. See also section 1 of Greenberg's "Third Great Cycle in Jewish History."
23. "JH," p. 47.
24. "JH," p. 48.
25. "JH," pp. 49–51.
26. This is the declaration of Elisha ben Abuya, the most famous heretic of the talmudic tradition.
27. "JH," p. 55.
28. "JH,", p. 57.
29. See "JH," pp. 61ff. Greenberg uses the word *projection* for this project. He titles this section of his paper "The Model Projected: The Case of the Holocaust."
30. "JH," p. 62.
31. "JH," p. 62.
32. Greenberg, "Third Great Cycle," p. 6. Greenberg correctly cites the telling prophetic word of *Ezekiel* 20:32–33 in support of this exegesis with which I concur.
33. Greenberg, "Transformation," pp. 7ff. in typescript. See also "Third Great Cycle," pp. 3–6.
34. "Third Great Cycle," p. 7.
35. Ibid., pp. 9ff. in typescript. See also ibid., pp. 6–12, for additional exegesis of this view.
36. "Third Great Cycle," p. 12. See also "Third Great Cycle," p. 8.
37. "Transformation," p. 11.
38. "Third Great Cycle," p. 8. Here Greenberg touches on the theme that Eliezer Berkovits has particularly emphasized in his reflections on the Holocaust. See Berkovits, *Faith after the Holocaust* (New York, 1973). For a discussion of Berkovits' position see my paper "Eliezer Berkovits's Post-Holocaust Jewish Theodicy," in my *Post-Holocaust Dialogues: Critical Studies in Modern Jewish Thought* (New York, 1983), pp. 268–86.
39. In the name of Rav Soloveitchik Greenberg states: "The scholar is the co-creator of the Torah (cf. *Ish Hahalacha* by Rav Soloveitohik)" "Third Great Cycle," p. 14. Whether Rav Soloveitchik would concur with the use of his argument as employed by Greenberg is open to conjecture.
40. Ibid., p. 17. In "Third Great Cycle" Greenberg recalls a teaching of R. Joshua ben Levi that he paraphrases thus: "R. Joshua ben Levi said that God's might, shown in Biblical times by destroying the wicked, is now manifest in self control" (p. 8).

41. See "Third Great Cycle," p. 8. Thus, for example, he correctly calls attention to the fact that "Rabbis were a more secular leadership than priests and prophets" (p. 9). I would, however, prefer a different adjective than *secular*. But in any case, it must be understood that Greenberg's use of the term *secularism* is not equivalent to atheism. He explicitly tells us: "In the Temple, God was manifest. Visible holiness was concentrated in one place. A more hidden God can be encountered everywhere. But one must look and find" (p. 5). And again, and very explicitly, "This secularism must not be confused with atheism or the celebration of the death of God" (p. 10).

42. Ibid., p. 10. See his full explanation of this shift to Purim as the "redemptive paradigm" ibid., p. 10.

43. In "Third Great Cycle" Greenberg makes it clear that he does not want his new position to be understood as representing a wholly discontinuous view of the covenant after Auschwitz. He explicitly states that this view is "not a radical break from the past. In retrospect this move is intrinsic in the very concept of the covenant" (p. 18). This claim is subject to doubt, though the issue is very complex. Greenberg continues to wrestle with the meaning of *voluntary* as in *voluntary covenant* in his ongoing theological work and is, as far as one can tell, not happy with either his original formulation of this idea or any new reading of it.

44. We must, Greenberg recognizes, even take seriously the possibility that the covenant is at an end (ibid., p. 23).

45. Ibid. In this paragraph Greenberg is paraphrasing a remark by A. Roy Eckardt, and there may be some differences between Eckardt's position and Greenberg's over the final understanding of this seminal issue.

46. Ibid.

47. Ibid., pp. 23–24.

48. Ibid., pp. 25, 27. Because of the importance of this doctrine and its apparent radicalness, it is important that we understand Greenberg's position correctly. In further correspondence with this author he has given the following explication, which I quote in full: "It is true that I go on to describe 'the shattering of the Covenant' and 'the Assumption of the Covenant.' However, in the light of this whole essay the human taking charge, i.e. full responsibility for the covenant is God's calling to them. 'If the message of the destruction of the Temple was that the Jews were called to greater partnership and responsibility in the covenant, then the Holocaust was an even more drastic call for total Jewish responsibility for the covenant.' (ibid., p. 36). The more I reflected upon this insight, I grew more and more convinced that this third stage was an inevitable and necessary stage of the covenant. The covenant always intended that humans ultimately must become fully responsible 'In retrospect, the voluntary stage is implicit in the covenantal model from the very beginning. Once God self-limits out of respect for human dignity, once human free will is accepted, the ultimate logic is a voluntary covenant'" (Greenberg to the author, January 3, 1989).

49. "Third Great Cycle," p. 30.

50. See ibid., p. 33. For further adumbration of Greenberg's position on pluralism and its many implications, see also his more recent essay "Toward a Principled Pluralism," *Perspectives* (National Jewish Center for Learning and Leadership, March, 1986).

51. See "Third Great Cycle," pp. 37ff. For Greenberg this means that it is God's will that humans take full responsibility for the outcome of the covenant. Such a grant of autonomy entails that even if the actual policy decisions reached and acted upon are erroneous the error is, in some real sense, legitimate within the broader confines of the covenant rather than a wholly illegitimate form of religious behavior.

52. Ibid., pp. 37–38. See also pp. 16ff.

53. Ibid., p. 18.

54. *The Jewish Way*, pp. 18, 22.
55. Ibid., p. 28–29.
56. Greenberg's title for his treatment of Yom Ha-Atzmaut, ibid., 385.
57. Ibid., pp. 393–94.
58. "Cloud," p. 23.
59. "JH," p. 47.
60. On the details of this encounter see Richard Rubenstein's article in his *After Auschwitz* (Indianapolis, 1966), pp. 47–58.
61. Greenberg replies to my argument as follows: "It is not that Holocaust validates halachic change but that it makes more urgent the accomplishment of the redemptive goals; it calls for a 'messianic' breakthrough in this generation. This expresses itself in coming closer to the ideal norms of the tradition in such areas as women, Gentiles, etc. ... This is not to be confused, however, with faddishness or trying to be on the right side of currently trendy values and issues" (private communication from Greenberg, January 3, 1989).
62. I have made a detailed study of this central issue in my forthcoming three-volume study tentatively entitled *The Holocaust in Historical Context* to be published by Oxford University Press beginning in 1993.
63. Here a further nuance must be noted. Greenberg insists that though God is intentionally more self-limited in the "Third Era" this should not be misunderstood as positing either God's absence or weakness. God is still active, though He is more hidden. In private correspondence Greenberg argued that in his view God is still seen as possessing, at least, the four classical attributes of "calling," "accompanying," "judging," and "sustaining" men and women, as well as of the world as a whole.
64. An open question on independent philosophical grounds.

FOR FURTHER READING

Works by Irving Greenberg

Books

The Jewish Way: Living the Holidays. New York, 1988. This theology of Judaism, interpreted through the holidays, traces Judaism's attempt to transform the world in history and the impact of great events on the unfolding of the religion.

Interpretation of the Holocaust's Significance

"Cloud of Smoke, Pillar of Fire: Judaism, Christianity and Modernity after the Holocaust." In Eva Fleischner, ed. *Auschwitz: Beginning of a New Era?*, pp. 7–55, 441–46. New York, 1977. The initial statement (and the one that has had the greatest influence) of the thesis that the Holocaust challenges Judaism, Christianity, and modernity and that all must be transformed by the impact of the event.

"The End of Emancipation." *Conservative Judaism* 30 (Summer 1976), pp. 47–63. Critiques modernity and the denominational movements, which still reflect the dominance of modernity, in light of the Holocaust.

"The Interaction of Israel and American Jewry after the Holocaust." In Moshe Davis, ed., *World Jewry and the State of Israel*, pp. 259–82. New York, 1977. The argument is that the centrality of Israel in the Jewish world has been achieved demographically and religiously but not yet culturally and spiritually. A prescription is offered as to how centrality can be accomplished in the lagging areas.

New Phase in Thinking about the Holocaust

"The Third Great Cycle of Jewish History." In *Perspectives* (National Jewish Center for Learning and Leadership, September 1981).

"Voluntary Covenant." In *Perspectives* (National Jewish Center for Learning and Leadership, October 1982). In particular, "Voluntary Covenant" reflects a decisive shift in thinking. The "Third Era"/"Third Great Cycle" thesis argues that Judaism has grown by a series of maturations of the covenant in which God self-limited and the Jewish people has come to assume more responsibility. In "Voluntary Covenant" the argument is made that the Holocaust was the occasion, not the cause, of this transformation.

On Christianity

A series of articles has explored the revisions that are needed in Christian thinking about Judaism and Jewish thinking about Christianity in light of the Holocaust and the role of both religions in trying to transform the world. They are listed in sequence.

"The New Encounter of Judaism and Christianity." *Barat Review* 3 (June 1967), pp. 113–25. Mostly focuses on Christian revisions. ("Cloud of Smoke" above develops the thesis somewhat more.)

"New Revelations and New Patterns in the Relationship of Judaism and Christianity." *Journal of Ecumenical Studies* 16 (Spring 1979), pp. 249–67. Argues that the Holocaust is revelatory and develops some other ways in which Christian self-understanding vis-à-vis the world of Judaism must change.

"The Relationship of Judaism and Christianity: Toward a New Organic Model." In Eugene Fisher, James Rudin, and Mark Tanenbaum, eds., *Twenty Years of Jewish/Catholic Relations*, pp. 191–211. New York, 1986. This essay focuses on Jewish rethinking of Christianity and goes beyond Rosenzweig in an attempt to allow Christian self-definition and to sketch a role for each religion in God's redemptive plan.

"Judaism and Christianity as Aspects of the Divine Strategy of Redemption." In James Brashlear and Judith Meltzer, eds., *Interwoven Destinies: Jews and Christians Through the Ages*. New York, 1990.

On Pluralism

"Toward a Principled Pluralism." In *Perspectives* (National Jewish Center for Learning and Leadership, March 1986). Offers paradigms of pluralism that respect the deep philosophical and fundamental differences between the denominations.

"Will There Be One Jewish People by the Year 2000?" In *Perspectives* (National Jewish Center for Learning and Leadership, June 1985). Argues that the breakdown in communication and mutual respect as well as the explosive growth in the number of Jews whose personal status is contested raises the risk of a fundamental split in the Jewish People.

On Modernity

"Adventure in Freedom or Escape from Freedom?: Jewish Identity in America." *American Jewish Historical Quarterly* 55 (Sept. 1965), pp. 5–22. Describes the extraordinary Jewish success in modernity but points to the challenge to Jewish values and continuity implicit in the success.

"Jewish Survival on the College Campus." *Judaism* 17 (Summer 1968), pp. 259–81. Continues the argument by stressing that college is the point of maximum modernization and maximum dissolution of Jewish identity. Some suggestions are given for a strategy of Jewish survival.

"Jewish Values and the Changing American Ethic." *Tradition* 10 (Summer 1968), pp. 40–74. Assesses the impact of modernity on Judaism and on Orthodox Jewish values and compares the strategy of withdrawal as against that which entails greater involvement in Western culture.

On Covenantal Thinking

"The Ethics of Jewish Power." In *Perspectives* (National Jewish Center for Learning and Leadership, May, 1988). Attempts to construct a framework for judging the Israeli exercise of power by the covenantal standard.

"Toward a Covenantal Ethic of Medicine." In Levi Maier, ed., *Jewish Values and Bioethics*, pp. 124–49. New York, 1986. Attempts to sketch a covenantal theory of human power as applied to medicine.

Works about Irving Greenberg

To date there has been little serious study or analysis of Greenberg's work. Some brief comments regarding it can be found in:

Singer, David, "The New Orthodox Theology," *Modern Judaism* 9 (1989), pp. 35–54.

Wyschogrod, Michael, "Auschwitz: Beginning of a New Era? Reflections on the Holocaust," *Tradition* 17 (Fall–Spring 1979), pp. 63–78. A critique of the role the Holocaust should play in Jewish theology.

David Hartman

MOSHE SOKOL

Modernity typically has one of two consequences for committed Jews who seek to understand their Jewish faith. Some thinkers consciously reject all the values and beliefs characteristic of the modern world and articulate a version of Judaism exclusively in categories drawn from earlier times and texts. Others develop some accommodation between modernity and Judaism so that their faith emerges adapted but not wholly transformed. Each of these two approaches constitutes a distinctive response to the challenges of modernity.[1]

In many ways, the accommodationists are especially interesting because they must struggle with the powerful and sometimes conflicting forces of their religious convictions and their modern sensibilities without yielding entirely on either score. David Hartman is an important example of this phenomenon because the currents of modernity and traditionalism flow through his work with great force. On one hand, emerging as he does from a traditionalist Orthodox background, he advocates the centrality of obedience to halakha in leading a Jewish life. On the other hand, he takes with absolute seriousness some of modernity's most important values, such as human autonomy, pluralism, universalism, and freedom. His ongoing struggle to reconcile these two commitments makes for a fascinating and important exercise in contemporary Jewish thought. Hartman raises some of the most important questions a modern Jew can ask and answers them with unusual passion, vigor, and creativity. In so doing he exemplifies the phenomenon of the traditionalist Orthodox Jew who encounters modernity and comes to open himself fully to some of its most important claims.

Biographical Information

David Hartman was born in Brooklyn in 1931. Following an elementary and high school education in traditional Orthodox yeshivot, he enrolled in Yeshiva University, the leading institution of Modern Orthodoxy, where he studied under Rabbi Joseph B. Soloveitchik, the great Talmudist and Jewish thinker. In many ways, Rabbi Soloveitchik shaped Hartman's future development. In Hartman's first book, *Maimonides: Torah and Philosophic Quest*, published in 1976, he asserts:

> The teacher who first introduced me, in depth, to the world of Jewish philosophic and halakhic thought was Rabbi Joseph B. Soloveitchik. He has been for me the paradigm of one who strives to integrate the rigorous discipline of halakhic thought with the study of philosophy. He taught me all that I know and love in halakha; above all, he showed me how halakhic man can be intellectually honest. He was never afraid to raise uncomfortable questions.... He taught me how one can struggle religiously yet remain strongly committed to tradition. It was his example that sustained me throughout my years of encounter with philosophy.[2]

Following nine years of study with Rabbi Soloveitchik, rabbinical ordination, and a master's degree in philosophy at Fordham University, Hartman took a pulpit in Montreal. While at Montreal he completed a doctorate in philosophy at McGill University, his dissertation serving as the basis of his first book. After eleven years in Montreal, in 1971, he and his family moved to Israel, where he became senior lecturer in Jewish thought at the Hebrew University, a position he still maintains. The Six-Day War and his own subsequent move to Israel had a pivotal impact on Hartman's thinking. These two events mark a turning point in Hartman the man and the theologian.

Before the Six-Day War, Hartman says in his introduction to *Joy and Responsibility*, his intellectual concerns were "essentially outside history."[3] The terrifying and then exhilarating reality of the war transformed his consciousness. He could not, he says, "return to his previous way of life."[4] As he tells it, Hartman approached his mentor, Rabbi Soloveitchik, with the request that he proclaim a religious festival. Rabbi Soloveitchik counseled patience, about which Hartman says, "His sobriety and restraint revealed to me, at that moment, the chasm which separated us. I passionately wished to enter history—whereas he chose to be satisfied with history mediated via halakha. My soul was aflame; my thirst for the living God of history was insatiable."[5] If the pre–Six-Day War Hartman was positively shaped by Rabbi Soloveitchik, the post–Six-Day War Hartman was shaped by the break with him.

Hartman's theological writings and activities subsequent to his move to Israel reflect a growing concern with Jewish personal and national adequacy and responsibility. This concern is evident not only in *A Living Covenant*,[6] as we shall see, but also in the work of the Shalom Hartman Institute, which he founded in 1976 and which is devoted to research on important issues facing Israel and the Jewish community. More recently, the institute established an experimental high school and a post–high school program of study, which includes army service and religious studies. Both these educational ventures seek to embody the values reflected in Hartman's theological writings. To round out the picture, Hartman served for many years as an adviser to the Israel Ministry of Education. He lectures widely before North American Jewish leadership audiences and is frequently quoted in the press on matters of current concern. In Hartman, theology and activism form a rare blend.

Hartman's Writings

Hartman's thought shows a clear evolutionary pattern. Many of the themes of his latest major work, *A Living Covenant*, are adumbrated in the early *Maimonides: Torah and Philosophic Quest*. A second work, *Joy and Responsibility*, links the two thematically and chronologically. Nevertheless, a significant shift occurs with the Six-Day War and the move to Israel. In addition to the three major works cited above, Hartman also contributed commentaries to three of Maimonides' epistles, in *Crisis and Leadership: Epistles of Maimonides*.[7] Since the overall theological picture that emerges is unaltered by these commentaries ("discussions," as he calls them), I will focus here on the three major works.

One of the leitmotivs which runs throughout all of Hartman's extended theological writings is a passion for Maimonides. More than any other figure in Jewish intellectual history, Maimonides serves as a role model and guide for Hartman's theological quest. Indeed, a good barometer to the evolution of Hartman's identity as a traditional Jew and the theology that provided intellectual shape to that identity is the evolution of his treatment of Maimonides. In Maimonides Hartman found a thoroughgoing commitment to the philosophical enterprise together with unparalleled halakhic achievements. The erstwhile *yeshiva bokhur* could find no better legitimation of his nascent intellectual stirrings than in the towering figure of Maimonides. It is therefore not at all surprising that Hartman's first sustained effort, his doctoral dissertation, should be devoted to Maimonides.

No one reading the book that emerged from that dissertation, *Maimonides: Torah and Philosophic Quest,* can doubt Hartman's profound identification with Maimonides. Indeed, this is both the book's greatest strength, as well as the source of its weaknesses. Hartman so identifies with his image of Maimonides that the distinction between Hartman and Maimonides is sometimes obscured. This phenomenon occasionally makes the book somewhat less persuasive as an exegesis of Maimonides,[8] while at the same time making it an important statement of a contemporary philosophy of halakha and Judaism grounded in Maimonidean thinking. Given the relative paucity of contemporary Jewish theological efforts, and the relative surfeit of Maimonidean exegeses, this situation is undoubtedly a net gain. Hartman makes obscure medieval texts come alive to the contemporary reader as few others have. He does this by examining them with the passion of a contemporary intellectual struggling with issues similar to those Maimonides himself may have faced. The Maimonidean theological program that emerges is thus of great interest.

If Hartman in his early years might have had difficulty reconciling a growing commitment to the adequacy of human reason with a commitment to a life governed by halakha, he would certainly have seen a resounding echo of that problem in what has always been the greatest puzzle in understanding Maimonides: how can one reconcile the Aristotelianism of the *Guide of the Perplexed* with the strict legalisms of the *Mishneh Torah?* The traditional Orthodox world from which Hartman emerged tended to shove the philosophical Maimonides under the carpet, ignoring him in favor of Maimonides the halakhist. An influential school of interpreters, however, heavily swayed by the late Leo Strauss, had argued that Maimonides was Aristotelian to the core and that his halakhic writings were a politico-religious smoke screen to hide Maimonides' true esoteric philosophical heresies. Neither the Maimonides of the traditional Orthodox world nor the Maimonides of the Straussians would be of much use or interest to Hartman in that phase of his intellectual development. Hence he wrote *Maimonides: Torah and Philosophic Quest*, which is a sustained exercise in proving the traditional Orthodox world and the Straussians wrong and in arguing that Maimonides followed what Hartman calls "the way of integration." In Hartman's own words, his book is an attempt to argue that "Maimonides' ... total philosophical endeavour was an attempt to show how the free search for truth, established through the study of logic, physics and metaphysics, can live harmoniously with a way of life defined by the normative tradition of Judaism."[9]

At this early phase in Hartman's development, his starting point is halakha. Hartman's reaction here—and this is characteristic of many Modern Orthodox thinkers of this period—is more against the antiphilosophical orientation of his youthful education than against the antihalakhism of the Straussians: "Maimonides is not trying to show the Jewish universalist—embarrassed by Jewish particularity—that Judaism is compatible with the universal way of philosophy. Rather, he tries to show pious Jews how their commitment to halakha can be enriched by a philosophical understanding of God.... This goal constitutes the core of his concern as a Jewish philosopher."[10] Hartman, the pious Jew of his early years, discovers through Maimonides the paramount role of reason in Jewish life and thought. What are the affirmations of the power and role of human reason he claims to discover in Maimonides? Hartman argues, first, that universal reason can lead to knowledge of God even without the Jewish tradition. Building on Maimonides' understanding of the pre-Sinaitic achievements of Abraham, Hartman claims that philosophical reflection, for Jew and non-Jew alike, can yield the most important goal that revelation sets out for man: a metaphysical understanding of God.[11]

If reason can achieve so much, Hartman—following Maimonides—goes on to argue, then reason ought not to be fettered:

"The individual within halakhah must have room to cultivate his independent reason; he cannot be asked to submit uncritically to the claims of authority." This is surely a strong statement for the erstwhile *yeshiva bokhur*, who believes in the centrality of obedience to halakha in Jewish life. Indeed, he makes an even stronger claim, that "appeals to authority are justified when it can be shown that demonstrative reason is not able to offer certainty."[12] Here, through his interpretation of Maimonides, Hartman turns things on their head. Instead of the more traditional view, that human reason begins only where religious authority ends, Hartman maintains that authority begins only where reason ends.

Again building on Maimonides, Hartman argues that true love of God is possible only through a philosophical understanding of Him. This understanding in turn will profoundly alter one's orientation to mitzvot and moral behavior. The nonphilosopher will consider divine reward for good deeds and the material and social well-being of the messianic era to be of great religious significance. For the true lover of God, these pale in comparison with the ultimate good of pure intellectual worship of God.[13]

Finally, the great value Hartman places on human reason, freedom, and the lawful workings of nature leads him—again interpreting Maimonides—to conclude that God chooses to limit as much as He possibly can His miraculous intervention in world and human affairs.[14] We human beings are, more or less, on our own.

Even this brief summary of some of the most important themes of the book shows the theological direction Hartman takes. While constantly reminding his readers of the importance of what amounts to an Orthodox commitment to halakha, he makes a powerful case for the role of human reason in the life of a halakhic Jew. His scope, creativity, and extensive knowledge of the Maimonidean corpus, combined with his gift for the apposite citation, makes compelling theology and often interesting Maimonidean exegesis, even if not all of his generalizations are directly justified by the Maimonidean texts in question.

The concluding paragraph of the book reveals a great deal about Hartman's appreciation of Maimonides:

Maimonides, the writer of the *Mishneh Torah* and the *Guide*, remains a lonely figure because he believed that a total commitment to the

Jewish way of life—halakha—can be maintained by one who recognizes that there exists a path to God independent of the Jewish tradition. Maimonides was a witness to the fact that intense love for a particular way of life need not entail intellectual and spiritual indifference to that which is beyond one's own tradition.[15]

For Maimonides here read Hartman. It should be remembered that Hartman's own personal mentor, Rabbi Soloveitchik, wrote a seminal theological essay with a strong autobiographical dimension entitled "Lonely Man of Faith." Like his mentor, Hartman, the contemporary Maimonidean, is lonely, too. His preoccupation with a life of reason and the universalist and pluralistic implications of that life lead to a loneliness quite different from the existential loneliness of Rabbi Soloveitchik. While following in the master's footsteps, he has already begun to chart out new theological territory.

The human reason which the Maimonides book promotes aims primarily at understanding God and His demands of the Jewish people. It operates in the space of theology. The next step Hartman takes—and this is a consequence of his "reentering history" and move to Israel following the Six-Day War—is to apply the adequacy of human reason to the great religious challenge posed by the modern state of Israel. Correlated with this shift toward the practical is an emphasis on the impact of a life of mitzvot on the Jewish personality, what Hartman calls a "religious anthropology." These themes, which culminate in his most recent and theologically systematic work, *A Living Covenant*, are first put forward in *Joy and Responsibility*, a collection of essays published in 1978.

In the introduction to *Joy and Responsibility*, Hartman tells the reader that the book's essays all share a common goal: "to delineate the type of person that emerges from a life grounded in halakha."[16] This arrow could have been lifted directly from the master's quiver; one of Rabbi Soloveitchik's most important essays is "Halakhic Man," which has much the same goal. Similarly, Hartman's halakhic man, like Rabbi Soloveitchik's, is deeply conflicted. The nature of the conflict, however, sharply defines the differences between the two and reflects the diverging trajectory of Hartman's theological program:

On the one hand, the living God of Judaism is revealed in the halakha, i.e., the disciplined religiosity of the legalist and in the confined framework of a story of history. On the other hand, the reality of the present Jewish history mediates the living God of Israel and places Jews within the context of a living community, rather than a community acting in a symbolic domain.... My approach to contemporary images of halakhic man moves between these two options.... [This approach] seeks to be in history and to accept the responsibility of building a total society, yet it wishes to retain the sobriety of the halakhic religious sensibility.... My picture of a genuinely religious person is that of a person who is not averse to getting his hands dirty; who does not await divine intervention but who experiences God's presence in his efforts to discharge the responsibility he feels for the total community.[17]

This picture of the genuinely religious person is, for Hartman, at variance with Rabbi Soloveitchik's quiescence in the face of history. "The tragedy of halakhic man [i.e., Rabbi Soloveitchik and other Orthodox Jews like him] ... is that halakha failed to respond adequately when the Jewish people consciously re-entered history." One of Hartman's goals is to reconceive his master's image of halakha. Instead of Rabbi Soloveitchik's view of halakha as a theoretical model for apprehending the cosmos, halakha is now "best understood through categories of political philosophy."[18]

This thesis provides the framework for Hartman's ongoing focus on the theological significance of the state of Israel, an issue of only limited importance in the overall sweep of Rabbi Soloveitchik's writings:

The difference between Judaism in the land of Israel and Judaism in the diaspora is that Israel demands that Judaism be significant as a way of life for an entire community. Judaism cannot simply offer man a retreat or a moment of protest against an estranged world. Israel deals with spiritual alienation and religious compartmentalization by giving Jews a home where they are responsible for what they do and for the institutions they build. Judaism can no longer remain the prophetic critic in the market place of others.[19]

If halakha is to make a difference in the real world, if it is conceived as an attempt to spiritualize the mundane, then Zionism is, in effect, the ultimate fulfillment of halakha: "The Zionist secular revolution may be described as a rejection of [the] traditional messianic posture which was, in spirit, antithetical to the full realization of the covenantal halakhic ideal." Hartman's revised conception of the halakhic personality is at least in part intended to make this political transformation possible. The first essay of the book, "The Joy of Torah"—the "joy" in *Joy and Responsibility*—provides a good example of how he does this. There Hartman defends halakha against those critics who maintain that obedience to halakha leads to anxiety, insecurity, and a "fixation on submissive obedience to the merciless letter of the law."[20] Rather, Hartman argues,

> The joy of being intellectually engaged in the study of Talmud, the profound intellectual autonomy found in halakhic writings, the feelings of self-respect and dignity that emerges from being commanded and charged with the responsibility of implementing Torah in the daily life of the community are also features that characterize halakhic Judaism. To miss these experiences of joy is to misunderstand the inner spiritual life of a community whose love for God finds expression in a total involvement with details of halakha.[21]

In sum, Hartman seeks to empower the halakhic Jew by arguing for the importance of his autonomy, reason, and responsibility and by urging upon him the significance of community. So empowered, he can take some time from study in the *bet midrash* and create a new national identity embodied in the state of Israel.

These themes are carried forward and developed further in Hartman's most important theological statement to date, *A Living Covenant*, which is a systematic attempt to formulate a theory of Judaism embracing some of modernity's most important values. In *A Living Covenant*, Hartman no longer speaks through the mouthpiece of Maimonides. Indeed, his new appreciation of the role of Maimonides in his thinking reflects the great religious distance he has traveled since his early years. If the early Hartman needed to speak *through* Maimonides to make his theological voice heard, the late Hartman is content, at least in some respects, to leave Maimonides behind: "Although Maimonides has been the major philosophical influence on my reflections on Judaism, the orientation to Judaism reflected in this work represents a serious departure from the way Maimonides believed one should speak about Judaism to the community."[22]

The differences between Hartman and Maimonides are not only a matter of how one speaks to the community. Unlike Maimonides, Hartman now emphasizes the life lived according to the covenant and its consequences for human character, rather than the life of contemplation and knowledge of God. Again unlike Maimonides, Hartman emphasizes the immediate challenges and rewards of the self-contained present, rather than the prospects of divine reward and punishment in the future. The independence Hartman now feels to strike out on his own is sharply expressed in the following passage:

> When Maimonides wrote there was a sociocultural ambience that supported belief in miracle and divine reward and punishment.... This way of experiencing God is not a live and significant option for myself or many other modern Jews.... It therefore would be inauthentic for me to articulate a philosophy of Judaism in the spirit of that [Maimonidean] treatise. I am grateful that the secular spirit of the modern world has made the medieval option of fear of God's punishment spiritually irrelevant.[23]

Although the influence of Maimonides is evident on almost every page of the book, Hartman apparently no longer feels bound to operate under total Maimonidean cover. This new-found independence is reflected as well in his treatment of Rabbi Soloveitchik. Throughout no less than four chapters, Hartman provides an extensive and searching critique of Rabbi Soloveitchik's theological writings on subjects ranging from prayer to the Holocaust to human sufficiency before God. He continues to acknowledge his indebtedness to Rabbi Soloveitchik but he leaves no stone unturned in explicating his many differences with the master. In *A Living Covenant* Hartman has found a theological voice all his own.

Hartman's new-found independence from his mentors is clearly part of a new-found independence from the past as a whole. His theological program begins with his "philosophical appreciation of Judaism," which he says is shaped by the attitude that "one allows the present to surface *without prior legitimization by the past*" (emphasis mine). He takes the modern world, with its particular values, as his starting point and seeks to "provide a framework and religious sensibility from which to chart a new direction for Judaism so that it might become a living reality for a

Jew who takes the modern world with radical seriousness."[24] Hartman here seems to have come full circle. It will be recalled that in *Maimonides: Torah and Philosophic Quest* Hartman, via Maimonides, was attempting "to show pious Jews"—presumably including Hartman himself—"how their commitment to halakha can be enriched by a philosophical understanding of God." Now, however, Hartman is starting from the other side and is "trying to show the Jewish universalist—embarrassed by Jewish particularity—that Judaism is compatible with the universal way of philosophy."[25] Of course, the concern now is not philosophy per se but such modern values as autonomy, pluralism, and, indeed, universalism. The point I wish to emphasize, however, is that the starting point for Hartman is no longer the pious halakhic Jew, but modern man, who assumes many of modernity's values and thus feels estranged from tradition. The difference, it seems clear, is not only in Hartman's audience but in Hartman himself.

The language that Hartman's voice speaks in is the language of covenant. Covenant theology has been a popular motif in modern Jewish thought, but Hartman gives it a distinctive twist of his own. For Hartman, the metaphor that best describes God's covenant with His people and with each individual Jew is the mature love of the husband-wife relationship. This is in opposition to understanding the covenant according to the metaphor of the king-subject, father-child, or master-slave relationships. The fundamental difference between these approaches is twofold: what God expects of the Jew and what the Jew expects of God.

The king-subject model (as well as the others) presupposes an inadequate subject who depends on the king for his self-worth and, indeed, his life. With his fate entirely in the hands of the king, the subject cannot do much more than see to it that the king will duly provide for him. For Hartman, transposing this model to the relationship between God and the Jewish people, as well as between God and each individual Jew, would yield a conception of Jews as unable to take responsibility for their own destiny, as inadequate, dependent people lacking in self-worth and dignity. It would also yield a conception of God as taking unilateral action in dealing with His helpless subjects. The Exodus from Egypt is the classic expression of this form of the God–Jewish people relationship.

If the covenant is modeled after the husband-wife relationship, "the integrity of both partners is recognized, and the human partner is enabled to feel personal dignity and to develop capabilities of responsibility."[26] God and the Jew are mature lovers, so to speak. For the Jew, this means that he feels that God accepts his finite human limitations, that God wants him to achieve his fullest capacities as an autonomous, independent, and free creature. On God's side, it means that He will not act unilaterally in human affairs so as not to undermine the Jew's sense of control and responsibility as a capable partner in the covenant. The covenant at Sinai, where God calls the Jewish people into active participation in the life of miztvot, is the classic expression of this form of the God–Jewish people relationship. Indeed, for Hartman Sinai supplanted Exodus as the controlling model of God's relationship with the Jewish people throughout history. Although Hartman recognizes that there is ample precedent for conceiving the covenant along king-subject lines, he chooses to play this down and to explore how Judaism might look following only the husband-wife model.

The implications Hartman proceeds to draw from this conception of the covenant are striking. Before highlighting some of them, however, it is important to point out that these implications are drawn within a framework that makes obedience to mitzvot the central means of fulfilling the covenant. In this respect Hartman's theology remains unchanged from his earliest days. The Jewish life is the halakhic life. Hartman's new covenantal theology here thus provides no more than a different—and very fruitful—framework for articulating his long-standing commitment to the halakha:

> One who lives within the covenantal framework of halakha understands ... that the multiplying details of the law and the fascination to conceive of every possibility through which halakha may be applied ... reflect[s] the passion of a lover who seeks to be accompanied by the consciousness of the beloved always and everywhere.... If no domain of life is devoid of the possibility of halakhic guidance, then there is no moment or place in reality that is not open to the passion of covenantal theism.[27]

These words could be placed in the mouth of a traditionalist Orthodox rabbi without much strain, yet Hartman's view of what *counts* as halakha is another matter entirely. This question is brought to a head in his consideration of the relation between ethics and halakha. It will be remembered that Hartman's conception of the covenant stresses human autonomy and freedom. "If covenantal mutuality is to be taken seriously," Hartman says, "one's ethical and rational capacities must never be crushed." This leads him to the following conclusion: "The development of halakha must be subjected to the scrutiny of moral categories that are independent of the notion of halakhic authority ... our human ethical sense [must] shape our understanding of what is demanded of us in the mitzvot." Expressions of self-defeat or nonrational submission before God are simply not religious values for Hartman. In this respect Hartman self-consciously veers not only from Rabbi Soloveitchik, his teacher, but from many religious sources and thinkers who emphasize the *akedah*, Abraham's attempted sacrifice of Isaac, as at least one ideal model of Jewish behavior. For Hartman, "covenantal Jews ... move in the direction of religious vitality when they connect with the purpose of the law with truth and rationality."[28] The stress on rationality, so characteristic of the talmudic/halakhic tradition, is taken to serve as an independent criterion for assessing the halakha itself.

This same approach leads to a different conception of the nature of prayer. As traditionally understood, prayer is an expression of dependence on God, a call "from out of the depths" for God's help. For Hartman, however, feelings of dependence on God interfere with one's sense of competence and responsibility for one's own destiny. Thus Hartman is led to a different and novel conception of prayer: "When you discuss your needs in a love relationship you do not necessarily expect your beloved to solve your problems. Reassurance and comfort may be gained simply through knowing your beloved listens to you in your anguish and that you are not alone in your plight. I understand petitional prayer as expressing the need of covenantal lovers of God to share their total human situation with God."[29] The shift from an emphasis on God as unilateral actor on the world stage, characteristic of the biblical worldview, to God as a self-limiting partner in the covenant, is most evident in the period following the destruction of the Temple. The Rabbis were forced to come to terms with a God who had apparently withdrawn from His role as the potent and public protector of the Jewish people. As understood by Hartman, the phenomenon of God's withdrawal is a reflection of His desire to enable us to take full responsibility for our destinies as partners in God's covenant. What, then, of the doctrines of reward and punishment and divine providence, which seem to presuppose unilateral intervention by God in the course of nature?

> The biblical language of reward and punishment need not be understood as a miraculous response by God to human actions, but rather as a description of the sufferings and benefits that are intrinsic to human behavior.... Whoever cheats or steals or lies sets into motion a breakdown of human trust, and as a result human suffering will be inevitable.... If God promises reward for virtuous actions, it is because virtuous actions are contagious.[30]

God, out of respect for the lawful workings of the universe He created, and out of concern for the sense of adequacy He wishes His partners in covenant to develop, chooses to work within nature in carrying out His divine will. "The world pursues its normal course" is the decisive criterion for God's intervention in personal and world history. Miraculous intervention would only subvert the order He created and the character traits He wishes to encourage. Living a life of intense covenantal love, expressed through obedience to the mitzvot, enables the Jew to cope with whatever suffering nature dishes out to him.

In one of the more striking chapters of the book, Hartman carries this argument even further and proposes a noncovenantal way of relating to God which supplements the covenantal:

> When we look at the universe in its impersonal fullness, we know that beside *mitzva* and the covenantal structures of religious relationship with God, there is also a cosmic experience of God that is transethical and transpersonal. This religious reflection on the universe ... points to an awareness that God and creation are not exhausted by the relational intimacy of covenantal speech and *mitzva*. There is also a larger cosmic, ahistorical religious sense, what may be called an aesthetic dimension to religious consciousness.[31]

Hartman goes on to say that once it is recognized that there is an impersonal "divine drama independent of ourselves," then there is no need to believe that there is an ethical pattern to all events in the universe. On this model of understanding God, He is capable of abandoning His universe entirely to its own natural fate, as terrible as that might be. With God thus absconded, there is all the more room for responsible human beings to take charge. It is in this context that Hartman argues that "the vitality of the covenant does not presuppose belief in messianic redemption, the immortality of the soul or the resurrection of the dead."[32]

Such miraculous, unilateral behavior is unwarranted in Hartman's brave world in which people struggle autonomously to achieve hard-won goals. Hartman is, of course, careful to note that he does not mean to suggest that these long-held traditional beliefs are false, naive, or foolish or that God is incapable of such miraculous action. Rather, he means to argue that they are not constitutive of the Sinai covenant, which can therefore retain its vitality even without those beliefs. This is because the covenant reflects a mature love, in which God lovingly accepts human limitations and the Jew can therefore be fulfilled without transcending those limitations through immortality of the soul, the advent of the messiah, or the resurrection of the dead. For the Jew, God's covenantal presence in the world is mediated by Torah and mitzvot rather than by grand eschatological occurrences or by events in nature and history.[33] Of course, understood from the perspective of Hartman's *noncovenantal* way of relating to God, these supernatural events surely have no place.

In the concluding chapters of *A Living Covenant* Hartman stresses the consequences of his covenantal theology for Zionism. Much as he argued in *Joy and Responsibility*, Hartman sees Zionism as the ultimate fulfillment of the covenant: "The normalization of Jewish consciousness that comes from living in the land of Israel is therefore not antithetical to covenantal consciousness, but is a necessary condition for its full realization. The land of Israel is holy from the covenantal perspective because it invites *greater* responsibility and initiative on the part of the community."[34]

Living in the land of Israel, Hartman says, should lead to a greater pluralism and universalism on the part of halakha:

> The spirit of Judaism in exile reflects the concern of a community living in a hostile environment to survive and not be swallowed up by its alien surroundings. Not surprisingly, then, the religious consciousness of exilic Judaism puts great emphasis on the *mitzvot* that separate Jews from their alien environment.... When Jews live in their own environment ... they must also link their covenantal

religious identity to the *mitzvot* through which they share in the universal struggle to uphold human dignity.[35]

Thus the particular covenant between God and the Jewish people leads to a life of renewed political vigor and a concern for universal human values.

Evaluation

David Hartman's significance as a Jewish thinker must be evaluated in two ways. First, there is the theological perspective, the substance of his views. To what extent are his theological claims true, innovative, and of important explanatory force and scope? Second, there are the perspectives of intellectual history and sociology of religion. How does Hartman fit into the overall patterns of the development of modern Jewish thought?

There can be no question that Hartman's overall enterprise, particularly his latest efforts, is of great theological interest. The life of mitzva is usually portrayed as one of profound self-denial and subservience, in which the observant Jew sacrifices his independence and his own needs and interests in unending service to his maker. Hartman, in a Copernican twist, argues that it is precisely the life of mitzvot which empowers the Jew and provides for his dignity, independence, and autonomy. By conceiving the covenant along the husband-wife model he shows how God seeks in countless ways to build rather than sacrifice His loving covenantal partner. The intellectual freedom characteristic of Torah study and halakhic decision making and the joy and satisfaction in freely choosing to serve God contribute to the observant Jew's sense of dignity. Most important, as God's chosen partner in covenant, the observant Jew understands himself to be charged with the responsibility of making the world a better place specifically through the halakhic life. This is a responsibility, Hartman argues, that God Himself will not undertake, preferring instead to leave it in the hands of His competent covenantal partners. More than anything else the self-confidence that must emerge from this consciousness necessarily transforms the regnant picture of the submissive halakhic Jew.

Hartman's theological achievement lies not only in articulating his model of the covenant but in pushing it to its limit, calling upon a wide array of Jewish sources to make his case. The overall sweep of his arguments provide along the way insightful analyses of such perennial concerns as evil, human suffering, covenantal love, and the role of the state of Israel in Jewish life. This latter is of special importance: Hartman provides a fruitful model for appreciating the religious significance of Israel devoid of messianic underpinnings,[36] a much needed corrective to religious reflections about Israel over the past several decades. All of Hartman's writings are suffused with the same passion and richness of insight, and all make compelling and rewarding reading.

Hartman's theological program is thus a considerable achievement, but it has not been without its critics.[37] Several points must be raised in this regard. First, in exploring—indeed advocating—the husband-wife model of the covenant Hartman self-consciously abandons other models such as that of the king-subject or father-child relationships. The question is whether those classical sources, which themselves embrace the husband-wife model, understand that model exclusivistically. Within the rich array of Jewish sources there are also strong tendencies toward understanding the relationship between the Jew and God as a dependent one, as Hartman readily acknowledges. Might it not then be more responsive to the full range of recorded Jewish religious experience to understand the husband-wife model as coexisting alongside the king-subject model and perhaps others? One could well argue that though God wants the Jew to experience himself as independent, autonomous, and dignified, God also wants the Jew to experience himself as in some ultimate way dependent upon Him as well.

Apart from the textual evidence, there are good theological reasons for taking this approach. First, it accurately reflects what seems to be an important part of the religious experience: there are times when the only authentic religious response to some of life's most excruciating physical, emotional, or existential difficulties may well be to throw oneself before an ever-forgiving, ever-helping God. Although Hartman may be right that this response does not typify the Jewish stance, to eliminate it entirely may be to eliminate too much. Second, is the covenant of love a strong enough model alone to account for God's stubborn loyalty to His sinful people? Is it strong enough alone to account for the Jew's stubborn loyalty to the God who stood by during Auschwitz? Two mature lovers may tolerate a good deal of failure on each other's part, but there are limits to what even mature lovers will put up with. Given Jewish sinfulness on one hand and Auschwitz on the other, it is hard to understand why the covenantal love has not snapped—unless, of course, the covenant of love is supplemented by another covenant as well, that characterized by the relationship between a father and child. Failing apparent divine love, the Jew blindly and faithfully throws himself at his Father's feet; failing human love, Father grinds His teeth and sustains His prodigal son.

Related to this point is another: even if one were to accept the husband-wife model as exhaustive of the God-Jew relationship, is it clear that this model never permits feelings of dependence? Even in a healthy love relationship, in which the worth and dignity of each partner is fully affirmed, feelings of dependence are often present. Not all dependence is psychologically or morally unhealthy. Indeed, on occasion absolute love and respect for another may even *require* unilateral and forceful intervention. This would be so, for example, to prevent a beloved from embarking on a self-destructive course of action or to help the partner in desperate need. Transposed to a theological plane, one could argue that even under the controlling metaphor of the husband-wife model, certain feelings of dependence and certain forms of divine unilateral action are appropriate, even in the context of God's concern for autonomy, dignity, and responsibility.

Hartman's response to these suggestions would be—and he makes this point any number of times—that such a dialectic is psychologically untenable. People are simply incapable of experiencing themselves as fully autonomous, competent, and dignified if their religious experience is also characterized by blind submission to God's will. If autonomy is to be valued at all, Hartman argues, it must be embraced at the expense of dependence. Others might claim, however, that people are capable of multidimensional, even conflicting experiences. Even the most competent, secure, and dignified person sometimes feels moments of dependence and need for another, and it is not at all clear that such feelings are inconsistent with a general feeling of autonomy and that they are harmful and to be avoided, even for one wholeheartedly committed to autonomy. This is provided, of course, that these feelings do not predominate.

Hartman's insistence on absolutely inviolable autonomy and

independence grows, at least in part, out of what amounts to an unquestioning acceptance of certain key modern values. Hartman fails to systematically rethink and work through the very *concept* of autonomy from within a Jewish framework, an essential undertaking. Indeed, it would be natural for a philosopher of halakha to consider what the halakha itself has to say about where personal initiative and freedom fit into real-life halakhic behavior. Instead Hartman starts with a broad, contemporary notion of autonomy, conceived in its most unfettered form, and rethinks traditional Judaism accordingly.

This said, however, it is precisely the uncritical embrace of certain modern values which makes Hartman an interesting figure in the overall panorama of modern Jewish intellectual history. Here Hartman's origins are significant. Hartman is not the first yeshiva-educated Jew to confront modernity, but he is distinctive in that his response to modernity has been not only fully to affirm some of its key values and to rethink Judaism accordingly, as others have, but at the same time to maintain a passion for the halakhic life and its centrality so characteristic of his early years. Moreover, not only does he link the two together into an overall theological scheme, but the scheme he develops has profound implications for some of the greatest challenges facing contemporary Jews, most notably the state of Israel.

This distinctive response is part of an important development in Orthodox Judaism as a religious movement.[38] As the historian Jacob Katz points out, *all* forms of Orthodoxy are responses in one way or another to modernity.[39] Traditionalist Orthodox thinkers tend to reject modernity. Modern Orthodox thinkers, however, consciously accommodate their religious beliefs to modern modes of thought. Ever since Rabbi Samson Raphael Hirsch in the nineteenth century, Modern Orthodox thinkers sought what may be called a "synthesis" between their religious convictions and their modernity. It has been suggested, however, that even this synthesis takes as its starting point traditional Orthodox values and beliefs and then attempts in varying, often illuminating ways to interpret those values and beliefs through modern categories of thought. Modern Orthodox literature does indeed make the case for the permissibility—even value—of exposure to the secular sphere. Nevertheless, it typically does not take that sphere as a legitimate starting point in its own right, as a standard by which to measure—and certainly not to reject—values or doctrines long held to be central to Orthodoxy. Hartman, on the other hand, clearly does. In this respect, then, he has taken a critical step beyond the contemporary pale of Modern Orthodox thinking.

The review of Hartman's writings presented here makes it evident just how much his thinking has radicalized over the years, from his early, typically Modern Orthodox perspective in *Maimonides: Torah and Philosophic Quest*, to his more recent *A Living Covenant*. What, then, are the long-term consequences for the Orthodox Jewish thinker in engaging modernity as fully as Hartman has? Hartman is in his intellectual prime, and much more in the way of Jewish theology can be expected of him.[40] It is therefore difficult to predict how it will all turn out. Nevertheless, the process itself is fascinating, not only for the creative theological insights it produces but for what it suggests about the larger drama of the trying encounter between traditionalism and modernity.

Notes

1. This characterization of religious responses to modernity is drawn from Peter Berger's works, most notably *The Homeless Mind* (New York, 1973) and *The Sacred Canopy* (Garden City, N.Y., 1967). See also Jacob Katz, "Orthodoxy in Historical Perspective," in Peter Medding, ed., *Studies in Contemporary Jewry II* (Bloomington, 1986), pp. 3–17.
2. David Hartman, *Maimonides: Torah and Philosophic Quest* (Philadelpha, 1976), p. vii.
3. David Hartman, *Joy and Responsibility* (Jerusalem, 1978), p. 5.
4. Ibid.
5. Ibid., p. 7.
6. David Hartman, *A Living Covenant* (New York, 1985).
7. *Crisis and Leadership: Epistles of Maimonides* (Philadelphia, 1985), with text and notes by Abraham Halkin.
8. See David Blumenthal's review of the book in *Religious Studies Review* 5 (1979): 107–11.
9. *Maimonides*, p. 26.
10. Ibid., p. 66.
11. Ibid., p. 139, and chap. 1 passim.
12. Ibid., pp. 103, 122.
13. Ibid., p. 205 and passim.
14. Ibid., p. 150 and passim.
15. Ibid., p. 214.
16. *Joy and Responsibility*, p. 14.
17. Ibid., pp. 6–8.
18. Ibid., pp. 228, 150.
19. Ibid., p. 68.
20. Ibid., pp. 262, 32.

21. Ibid., pp. 32–33.
22. *A Living Covenant*, p. 300.
23. Ibid., p. 302.
24. Ibid., pp. 13, 18.
25. *Maimonides*, p. 66.
26. *A Living Covenant*, p. 6.
27. Ibid., p. 275.
28. Ibid., pp. 97–98, 90.
29. Ibid., p. 164.
30. Ibid., pp. 238–39.
31. Ibid., p. 266.
32. Ibid., p. 257.
33. Ibid., p. 281.
34. Ibid., p. 284.
35. Ibid., p. 290.
36. In this regard, see also Hartman's recent article "The Challenge of Modern Israel to Traditional Judaism," *Modern Judaism* Vol. 7 (October 1987): pp. 229–52.
37. See Daniel Landes, "A Vision of Finitude: David Hartman's *A Living Covenant*," *Tikkun* 1 1986, pp. 106–11, and Hartman's response to the review together with further comments by Landes, in *Tikkun* 1987, pp. 121–26; Yaakov Elman, "A Humanistic Wolf in Covenantal Clothing: The Covenant as Bill of Divorce," *Judaica Book News* Vol. 17 (Fall–Winter 1986): 20–25 and Hartman's response to the review, together with further comments by Elman, in the Fall–Winter 1987 issue of the same journal; David Blumenthal's review of *A Living Covenant* in *AJS Review* 12 (Fall 1987): 298–305.
38. This perspective is drawn from David Singer's illuminating essay "The New Orthodox Theology," *Modern Judaism* Vol. 9:1, pp. 35–54.
39. Katz, "Orthodoxy in Historical Perspective," pp. 3–17.
40. Hartman's most recent book, *Conflicting Visions* (New York, 1990) appeared after the present essay was submitted to the publisher. In this volume, which includes new and previously published essays, he elaborates on themes pursued earlier, with chapters on several contemporary Jewish thinkers, on the religious significance of Israel and on the consequences of pluralism. While some of the new essays are indeed interesting, *Conflicting Visions* is not a systematic theological statement, and does not break new theological ground.

FOR FURTHER READING

Works by David Hartman

Maimonides: Torah and Philosophic Quest, Philadelphia, 1976. In his first book, Hartman argues that the great medieval Jewish philosopher, Maimonides, synthesized a commitment to philosophy with a commitment to the halakhic life.

Joy and Responsibility, Jerusalem, 1978. A collection of essays in which Hartman discusses the religious challenge of the modern state of Israel, and the impact of the halakhic life on the Jewish personality.

A Living Covenant, New York, 1985. Hartman's most systematic and important theological statement, where he argues for the central role of human autonomy and responsibility for self in Jewish life and thought. He also considers the consequences of these values for the state of Israel.

Crisis and Leadership, with text and notes by Abraham Halkin, Philadelphia, 1985. Here, Hartman provides an extended theological discussion of some of Maimonides' most important letters dealing with Jewish communities in crisis and the challenges of Jewish faith.

"The Challenge of Modern Israel to Traditional Judaism," *Modern Judaism* 7, (October 1987), pp. 229–52. This essay carries forward Hartman's thinking about the theological challenges and opportunities provided by Israel.

Conflicting Visions New York, 1990. A collection of new and previously published essays, rather than a novel systematic theological statement, this volume elaborates on themes pursued earlier by Hartman, including a critique of several Jewish thinkers, and discussions of the religious significance of Israel and pluralism. *Conflicting Visions* appeared after the present essay was submitted to the publisher.

Works about David Hartman

Articles

Singer, David, *Modern Judaism* 9:1, pp. 35–54. "The New Modern Orthodox Theology" includes the most comprehensive and recent discussion of Hartman's work.

Harvey, Warren Zev, "The Return of Maimonideanism," *Jewish Social Studies*, (Summer–Fall 1980). Harvey focuses on Hartman's book on Maimonides.

Book Reviews

Blumenthal, David, *AJS Review*, 12:2, (Fall 1987), pp. 298–305 on *A Living Covenant*.

Gilman, Neil, on *A Living Covenant, Judaism* 39:2, (Spring 1990), pp. 243–48.

Landes, Daniel, "A Vision of Finitude: David Hartman's A Living Covenant," *Tikkun* 1:2 (1986), pp. 106–11.

Shatz, David, "Maimonides: Torah and Philosophic Quest" *Judaism* 28:5, (Spring 1979), pp. 250–56.

Will Herberg

DAVID G. DALIN

When Will Herberg died in March 1977, American Judaism lost one of its most provocative religious thinkers of the post-World War II generation. Like Hermann Cohen and Franz Rosenzweig before him, Herberg came to Judaism from the outside. A Marxist and atheist through much of his young adulthood, with no Jewish education or religious training in his youth, Herberg turned to the study of Judaism only after his romance with Marxism ended. Beginning in the late 1940s, his spiritual journey from Marxism to Judaism was unique in the American Jewish intellectual history of this century. He became a prolific and influential Jewish theologian and sociologist of religion. The only Jewish ex-Marxist to embrace Jewish theology and the study of religion as a full-time vocation, Will Herberg was the quintessential *Ba'al Teshuvah* of his generation.

Herberg was born in the Russian village of Liachovitzi in 1901. His father, Hyman Louis Herberg, who had been born in the same Russian *shtetl*, moved his family to the United States in 1904. When his family arrived in America, his parents, whom he would later describe as "passionate atheists," were already committed to the faith that socialism would bring salvation to mankind and freedom from the restraints that had bound Western societies for centuries. His father died when Herberg was ten, and his mother shared her husband's "contempt" for the American public school system. Although he attended Public School No. 72 in Brooklyn and Boys' High School, Herberg was largely self-taught. A precocious and versatile student from his early youth, Herberg had learned Greek, Latin, French, German, and Russian by the time he was a teenager. He graduated from Boys' High School in 1918 and later attended City College of New York and Columbia University, where he studied philosophy and history but apparently never completed the course work for an academic degree.

Herberg inherited his parents' passionate atheism and equally passionate commitment to the socialist faith. Herberg entered the communist movement while still a teenager, bringing to radical politics a theoretical erudition that helped elevate American Marxism to an intellectual proposition. Although he was less prolific than Max Eastman or the novelist John Dos Passos, Herberg was perhaps the most catholic of Marxist polemicists during the 1920s and early 1930s. He contributed regularly to communist journals such as the *Workers Monthly* and was also a familiar ideologue and polemicist in the *Modern Quarterly*, one of the chief theoretical journals of the Old Left generation. Herberg wrote scores of articles and editorials on an amazingly diverse number of topics, critiquing Edmund Wilson's views on proletarian literature, arguing with Sidney Hook over the textual validity of Marx's ambivalent position on revolution, and explicating the relationship between Freudian psychoanalysis and communist thought. His attachment to communism was no mere affection but reflected intellectual conviction as well as moral ardor. So earnestly did he embrace Marxism that he even sought to reconcile it with Einstein's theory of relativity. Indeed, perhaps his boldest contribution to the radical thought of the period was his effort to reconcile Marxism to the new Einsteinian cosmology, the "second scientific revolution" that had been virtually unnoticed among radical writers in America. Most communists then still condemned Einstein for rejecting Marx's "scientific materialism," but Herberg insisted that both Marxism and the theory of relativity were "scientifically true." As a radical Jew, moreover, Herberg hailed Freud, as he did Marx and Einstein, as a modern prophet. "The world of socialism—to which nothing human is alien and which cherishes every genuine manifestation of the human spirit," he would write during the 1930s, "lays a wreath of homage on the grave of Sigmund Freud."[1]

Herberg's first disenchantment with orthodox Marxism came in the 1920s, when he, Bertram Wolfe, and other young intellectuals and labor organizers joined a group headed by Jay Lovestone, which split off from the main Communist party of the United States, following a struggle for power within the American party leadership. Lovestone, an American supporter of the Soviet Marxist theoretician Nicolai Bukharin, had, like Bukharin, advocated more autonomy from Soviet control for national Communist parties. In 1929, Stalin struck back by demoting Bukharin in the Soviet party and by ousting Lovestone and his followers from leadership of the American movement. After breaking with the official party in 1929, Herberg became a staff member and then editor of the Lovestonite opposition communist paper *Workers Age*, many of whose contributors would later become bitter anti-Stalinists.

As the 1930s progressed, Herberg became increasingly disenchanted with his earlier Marxist faith. The grotesque Stalinist purges, the communist "betrayal" of the Popular Front on the battlefields of Spain during the Spanish civil war, the Russian invasion of Finland, and the Stalin-Hitler Nonaggression Pact of 1939 all contributed to his growing disillusionment. The Moscow trials, Herberg maintained, indicated the extreme barbarous measures to which Stalin would resort to suppress all resistance to his bureaucratic rule within Russia. For Herberg, as for so many former Marxists of his generation, the cynical, opportunistic Molotov-Ribbentrop agreement of 1939 dispelled any remaining belief that "only a socialist government can defeat totalitarianism." His final break with orthodox Marxism, which came in 1939, was no mere change in political loyalties, no mere repudiation of the political radicalism of his youth. As he would confess in recounting his journey from Marxism to Judaism on the pages of *Commentary* in January 1947, Marxism had been, to him and to others like him, "a religion, an ethic and a theology; a vast all-embracing doctrine of man and the universe, a passionate faith endowing life with meaning."[2]

Put to the test, however, this Marxist faith had failed. Reality, as Herberg would later express it, "could not be forever withstood," and by the late 1930s he had begun to recognize that the all-encompassing system of Marxist thought could not sustain the values that had first attracted him to revolutionary activity. "Not that I felt myself any the less firmly committed to the great ideals of freedom and social justice," he would reflect in 1947. Rather: "My discovery was that I could no longer find basis and suppport for these ideals in the materialistic religion of Marxism.... This religion itself, it now became clear to me, was in part illusion, and in part idolatry; in part a delusive utopianism promising heaven on earth in our time, and in part a totalitarian worship of collective man; in part a naive faith in the finality of economics, material production; in part a sentimental optimism as to the goodness of human nature, and in part a hard-boiled amoral cult of power at any price. There could be no question to my mind that as religion, Marxism had proved itself bankrupt." Perceiving Marxism as a "god that failed" rather than as a "mere strategy of political action," Herberg was left with an inner spiritual void, "deprived of the commitment and understanding that alone made life livable."[3]

As the god of Marxism was failing him in the late 1930s, Herberg chanced to read Reinhold Niebuhr's *Moral Man and Immoral Society*, a book that was to profoundly change the course of his life. "Humanly speaking," he would later write, "it converted me, for in some manner I cannot describe, I felt my whole being and not merely my thinking, shifted to a new center.... What impressed me most profoundly was the paradoxical combination of realism and radicalism that Niebuhr's 'prophetic' faith made possible.... Here was a faith that warned against all premature securities, yet called to responsible action. Here, in short, was a 'social idealism' without illusions, in comparison with which even the most 'advanced' Marxism appeared confused, inconsistent, and hopelessly illusion-ridden."[4] More than any other American thinker of the 1930s and 1940s, Niebuhr related theology to politics through a realistic assessment of human nature that seemed inescapably relevant in a time of the breakdown of the Marxist (and liberal) faith in progress and human enlightenment. In the writings of Reinhold Niebuhr, Herberg discovered a compelling theological realism from which to derive and affirm his own post-Marxist religious and political faith.

Some of Herberg's acquaintances would later liken his rejection of communism and return to Judaism to Paul's conversion on the road to Damascus. The comparison may have pleased him, for Herberg always felt that his return to Judaism was the product of events equally unanticipated and dramatic. His memorable road to *teshuvah*, inspired by his first encounter with Niebuhr, was unique in the annals of American Jewish intellectuals of the past generation. In an autobiographical passage in one of his essays,[5] Herberg said that his encounter with Niebuhr's thought in the late 1930s was the "turning point," even before he met Niebuhr personally, who was then teaching at Manhattan's Union Theological Seminary. Like Franz Rosenzweig before him, whose writings he began to read during the early 1940s, Herberg went through a wrenching inner struggle over whether to become a Christian. After several soul-searching meetings with Niebuhr, Herberg declared his intention to embrace Christianity. Niebuhr counseled him instead first to explore his Jewish religious tradition and directed him across the street to the Jewish Theological Seminary, where Herberg went to study. The professors and students at the seminary undertook to instruct Herberg in Hebrew and Jewish thought.

Throughout much of the 1940s, while he was earning a living as the educational director and research analyst of the International Ladies Garment Workers Union, Herberg also devoted much of his time and energy to the study of Jewish sources. Because he had not received a traditional Jewish education in his youth, Herberg was introduced to the classical sources of Judaism through the writings of Solomon Schechter and George Foot Moore and through the instruction of Judaic scholars who became his friends, such as professors Gerson D. Cohen and Seymour Siegel and Rabbi Milton Steinberg. According to Seymour Siegel, Herberg was "extraordinarily moved" by the realistic appraisal of human nature in the rabbinic literature, especially as expounded by Schechter.[6] He was also impressed by the theological writings of Martin Buber and Franz Rosenzweig, who, together with Niebuhr, would shape his evolving views on religious existentialism and biblical faith.

Herberg was inspired and excited by what he learned. In Judaism he found, after years of searching, a faith that encouraged social action without falling into the trap of utopianism. Throughout the 1940s, he met regularly with rabbis and students at the seminary, developing and explicating his emerging theology of Judaism. At the same time, he began to write on Jewish theology for journals such as *Commentary* and the *Jewish Frontier*, and he began lecturing on religious faith and the social philosophy of Judaism to synagogue groups and on college campuses. He was in much demand as a speaker and traveled widely, gaining the reputation of being "the Reinhold Niebuhr of Judaism." He met regularly at his home with rabbinical students and others to discuss his theological ideas. "In those early days," one of these students remembered, "when the naturalistic theology so brilliantly expounded by Professor Mordecai Kaplan was the main intellectual influence in Jewish religious circles, we were fascinated by Herberg's espousal of the orthodox ideas of a supernatural God, Messiah and Torah, expounded with fervor and yet interpreted in a new way."[7]

These intellectual encounters and several essays published in *Commentary* and elsewhere in the late 1940s led to Herberg's first major work, *Judaism and Modern Man*, which appeared in 1951. The book was widely acclaimed as a carefully reasoned and intensely written interpretation of Judaism in the light of the newest existentialist thinking and was highly praised by Jewish scholars. Niebuhr believed that the book "may well become a milestone in the religious thought of America."[8]

Herberg's central theological concern, as he describes it in *Judaism and Modern Man*, is the plight of modern secular man, his spiritual frustration and despair. Herberg examines the various "substitute faiths" in which modern man has placed his hopes and aspirations—Marxism, liberalism, rationalism, science, and psychoanalysis, among others—and finds that each is a way of evading ultimate theological issues. As a religion, as a basis of faith, each of these secular ideologies is found wanting. Modern man, claims Herberg, requires belief in an absolute God. "Man must worship something," Herberg wrote. "If he does not worship God, he will worship an idol made of wood, or of gold, or of ideas."[9] Faith in God, asserts Herberg, is essential to one's being. Moreover, intellectual affirmation is not enough. A "leap of faith" is called for, a return to the living God of Abraham, Isaac, and Jacob and a total commitment to Him.[10]

In presenting his view of God and Judaism, Herberg criticized those theologians of the 1930s and 1940s who espoused a liberal, rational approach to God and, in so doing, reduced God to an idea.[11] For the religious existentialist such as Herberg, who was deeply influenced by the *I-Thou* philosophy of Buber and Rosenzweig, the "idea of God" is meaningless: God is important only if one has a personal relationship to Him. Thus, for Herberg, Jewish faith and theology cannot be predicated upon an abstract idea of

God such as, for example, the Reconstructionist notion of "a power that makes for salvation." Rather, the God of *Judaism and Modern Man* is a personal God to whom we can pray with an expectation of a response, with whom we can enter into a genuine dialogue.[12]

In many respects, as Seymour Siegel has noted, Herberg's theology was traditional. He believed in revelation, covenant, the resurrection of the dead, and the coming of the Messiah.[13] He also affirmed, unequivocally, the traditional theological doctrine of "chosenness." Jewish existence, argued Herberg, "is intrinsically religious and God oriented. Jews may be led to deny, repudiate and reject their 'chosenness' and its responsibilities, but their own Jewishness rises to confront them as refutation and condemnation."[14] At the same time, however, Herberg was not a fundamentalist; he did not view the Bible and the traditional texts as literally God's word. Thus, for example, though he believed in revelation, Herberg did not accept "the fundamentalist conception of revelation as the supernatural communication of information through a body of writings which are immune from error because they are quite literally the writings of God.... The Bible is obviously not simply a transcript from His dictation." Rather, Herberg regarded revelation as "the self-disclosure of God in His dealings with the world" through His active intervention in history, and the Torah as a "humanly mediated record of revelation."[15] In this and other respects, his theology, while traditional, was at variance with Orthodoxy.

Herberg argued, moreover, that a Jewish theology relevant to the postwar period would have to be predicated upon a less optimistic image of man, a sober recognition of human sinfulness and human limitations. The barbarities of Stalinism and, especially, the Nazi Holocaust seemed to Herberg to have destroyed the very foundations of the prevailing liberal faith, shared by Reform and Reconstructionist Judaism alike, in the "natural goodness" of man. Liberal Jewish theology, he maintained, failed to answer the critical question of how evil regimes and institutions could possibly have arisen if man is essentially good. The answer, Herberg wrote, could be found in "Niebuhr's rediscovery of the classical doctrine of 'original sin,' which religious liberalism and secular idealism combined to deride and obscure." Sin, Herberg wrote, "is one of the great facts of human life. It lies at the root of man's existentialist plight." Without an "understanding of the nature of sin," he concluded, "there is no understanding of human life ... or man's relation to God."[16]

Herberg's existentialist approach to Jewish theology struck a responsive chord in the hearts of many within the Jewish community and beyond, who were searching for religious roots and spiritual inspiration. The publication of *Judaism and Modern Man* was greeted with praise and enthusiasm by several respected Jewish reviewers, including Milton Konvitz and Rabbi Milton Steinberg. Indeed, in a prepublication review, Steinberg went so far as to say that Herberg "had written the book of the generation on the Jewish religion."

Some, in the Jewish community, however, found his approach to Jewish theology disturbing, especially in that it seemed more Christian than Jewish. Many of Herberg's Jewish readers complained that he was too pessimistic about human nature, that the doctrine of original sin invoked by Niebuhr was a theological category neither inherent nor central to Judaism. To be sure, neither Herberg nor even Niebuhr posited man's "complete sinfulness." Nevertheless, as critics of Herberg have duly noted, the difference between their emphasis and that of traditional Judaism is unmistakable, even though one may discover, as Herberg does, passages from the Talmud that in isolation convey the impression of a sin-preoccupied culture. Herberg's critics have repeatedly pointed out how much else of his theology derives from Protestant theological sources and categories.[17] The influence of Christian theology, as S. Daniel Breslauer has suggested, is evident in Herberg's calls for "an ethic of perfection," and one is reminded of the Christian exaltation of "an impossible ethics."[18] The influence of Christian theological thinking is also apparent in Herberg's discussion of the concept of salvation: "Salvation is salvation from sin because it is sin ... which alienates us from God, disrupts society and brings chaos to the world ... salvation is by faith and grace alone.... From the pit of sin we can be saved only by God's grace."[19] As Robert Gordis has correctly noted, however, the very concept of salvation is alien to traditional Jewish religious thought: 'The idea of salvation ... is, to be sure, central to Christianity. It is, however, so far from basic to Judaism that no Hebrew term for the concept exists in the vast expanses of Jewish religious literature, from the Bible through the Talmud and Midrash to the medieval philosophers, and even modern writers have yet to find an adequate Hebrew term for the idea."[20]

In formulating his new, existentialist theology of Judaism, Herberg borrowed the thought and terminology of Protestant thinkers such as Niebuhr and Tillich.[21] *Judaism and Modern Man*, in retrospect, seems to be an assessment of Judaism from a Protestant rather than from a Jewish viewpoint. During the two past decades it has had little to say to a new generation of Jewish theologians and laity, for whom a Christian existentialist approach to Jewish faith is no longer relevant.

Herberg's theology was also not "survivalist" enough for many in the Jewish community—traditional and secular alike—who found his views on Zionism and the State of Israel disturbing. Central to Herberg's understanding of the Jewish experience is the assumption that Jewish nationalism is antithetical to the Jewish religious tradition. One may agree with Herberg that "the widely held view that a 'full Jewish life' is possible only in the State of Israel seems ... to be radically false" without accepting his inexplicable claim that Jewish nationalism represented "the most radical perversion of the idea of Israel" and in effect constituted assimilation.[22] Many sensitive Jews of the period might have shared Herberg's belief that the 1947 bombing of the King David Hotel in Jerusalem by "Jewish terrorists" was a denial of the Jewish religious tradition without accepting his unsubstantiated conclusion that "changing our course bit by bit in pursuit of the rising star of nationalism, we have reversed our destiny."[23] Herberg's critique of Zionism is not limited to the more militant views of Ben Hecht, whose "lurid words" he dismisses in the most scornful of terms. Rather, suggests Herberg, all modern varieties of Jewish nationalism—whether the "kind of Zionism" espoused by Martin Buber or the militant revisionism of the Irgun—were not in "full harmony" with Jewish religious tradition.

Ironically, Herberg's denigration of Jewish nationalism seems to have had more in common with the anti-Zionist ideology of the classical Reform Judaism that he so cogently critiqued than with the neo-Orthodox religious thought of Buber and Rosenzweig, to whom Herberg so often paid homage. On the importance of Israel as opposed to the Galut (Diaspora), in the light of modern Jewish theology and religious identity, Herberg cautioned, "what even Buber tends to forget, that there is an 'unperformed task' for the Jew in the *Galut* as well, and will continue to be throughout history," and this "unperformed task" devolving upon every Jew individually is "to 'sanctify the Name' and to help redeem the evil time."[24] Not unlike the more radical ideologues of late nineteenth- and eary twentieth-century Reform Judaism, who claimed that the Jews had a special mission to the nations, Herberg seemed obsessed with the redemptive role of the Jewish people, the "unperformed task" that they are destined to complete. Paradoxically, as Judd Teller noted many years ago, Herberg seems so obsessed despite his otherwise vehement repudiation of the Enlightenment and the religious liberalism it gave rise to, which the Reform movement so "preeminently embodied."[25] Indeed, it is this very liberal Jewish concept of the unperformed task—of the special Jewish "mission" for social justice—which Herberg incorporates into his emerging theology of Judaism that has served (and continues to serve) as the rationale for much of the Jewish political and theological radicalisms of our time that Will Herberg came profoundly to reject.

To admirers of Herberg, his views on Zionism and the State of Israel must seem, at best, a continuing anomaly. The State of Israel never played the prominent role in Herberg's religious thought that it did in the thought of Fackenheim, Heschel, Kaplan, and other postwar theologians. "For the State of Israel, however highly we may regard it," maintained Herberg, "is, after all, but another community of this world." That he did not deem it necessary to revise these views—or at least to publish any such revisions—even after the Six-Day War of 1967 remains one of the more curious facets of his intellectual legacy.

Although *Judaism and Modern Man* made Herberg's reputation as a theologian, it did not immediately secure for him the entrée into academia that he actively sought. Since 1948, his duties with the ILGWU had diminished to the point that his occupation was listed on his income tax return as "writer and lecturer." He offered courses on a part-time basis at the New School for Social Research in 1948 and 1949 and from May 1951 to June 1952 served as editor of the new quarterly journal *Judaism.* Much of his income between 1948 and 1954 came, however, from free-lance writing of numerous articles and book reviews and from lectures on college campuses and to synagogue and church groups. After

1950, he devoted time and energy to the research and writing of *Protestant-Catholic-Jew*, which was published in 1955.

Protestant-Catholic-Jew remains, unquestionably, Will Herberg's most famous book. In its writing Herberg sought to account for the postwar "return to religion," the much-discussed "religious revival" of the late 1940s and 1950s. For Herberg, post–World War II society was marked by a paradox: it was simultaneously religious and pervasively secular. No culture had ever been so thoroughly committed to progressively expanding consumption. America appeared to be the most materialistic of societies, living as if religious teachings and spiritual values were nonexistent. Yet this era also fostered a religious revival, or at least a perception of one that could not have been predicted in the secular 1930s. On a popular level, signs of this return to religion were everywhere: the spectacular rise of Billy Graham, the addition of "under God" to the "Pledge of Allegiance," and the printing of "In God We Trust" on certain postage stamps. President Dwight Eisenhower unexpectedly opened his inaugural address with a prayer and gave a national broadcast speech on the need for religious faith. The best-selling book in America in 1953 and 1954 was *The Power of Positive Thinking* by the Reverend Norman Vincent Peale. Church and synagogue construction was booming, and synagogue and church membership rose dramatically.

American Jews seemed to be participating in this national religious revival. Synagogue building surpassed that of the 1920s and 1930s. New congregations sprang up all over the United States. The American-born children of Jews who had never thought about their Jewishness or who had done so only to reject it suddenly found themselves joining and even organizing synagogues. The expansion of the synagogue, noted Herberg, especially into small towns and suburbia, had become one of the most "striking features" of postwar American Jewish life.[26]

To many observers, the many new synagogues and increasing synagogue affiliation of Jews in postwar suburbia suggested the final transformation of American Jewry into an American religious group for whom religious affiliation, rather than class or ethnicity, had become the primary social determinant. One must be a member of a religious community, argued Herberg, "to belong" in American society. Contrary to established belief, America was not a melting pot but rather a triple melting pot, with individuals finding their place in society through religious, rather than ethnic, identification. To be an American in the 1950s meant to be identified with one of the "three great religions of democracy": Protestantism, Catholicism, or Judaism.

Herberg attributed this change to the coming of age of the third generation, the grandchildren of the immigrants who came to America in the early years of the century. Building on immigration historian Marcus Hansen's "law" of generations, Herberg proposed his "three generation thesis" to explain the return to religion that he observed amid the pervasively secular culture of postwar America: "What the son wishes to forget, the grandson wishes to remember."[27] The third generation, secure and at home in America, sought to reaffirm the religious identities of their grandparents, which their parents had rejected.

Herberg's perceptive analysis and interpretation of the Jewish religious "revival" in postwar America has been both criticized and misunderstood. For example, much has been written about his "three generation thesis."[28] As a *Ba'al Teshuvah*, who found religious meaning and identity in the Judaism that his parents had rejected, Herberg would appear to have personally demonstrated the empirical validity of Hansen's law. And yet Herberg did not demonstrate that the grandchildren of Jewish immigrants, generally, reembraced the same traditional religious faith and practices that their parents had rejected. On the contrary, in "returning" to religion, third-generation American Jews were appropriating and readapting their Judaism in ways their grandparents would never have recognized or understood. They were discarding the older traditional forms of religious expression and developing new, peculiarly American forms that were more secular, albeit in a Jewish context. The empirical evidence from a number of surveys of local Jewish communities since the publication of Herberg's book in 1955[29] supports this often misunderstood dimension of his three generation thesis. Traditional ritual practices such as the observance of *kashrut*, lighting Sabbath candles, fasting on Yom Kippur, and regular synagogue attendance declined steadily from the first generation through the third. Those who voice concern about the future of American Judaism suggest that there was a steady "erosion" of religious commitment among Jews coming of age during the 1960s and 1970s. Traditional Jewish piety as expressed in the observance of ritual is to be found, they lament, only among the smallest minority of American Jews. The same survey data, however, suggest that attendance at Passover Seders and the lighting of Chanukkah candles has increased from the first generation to the third. Nearly nine Jews in ten report that they attend a Seder. As Herberg's analysis so well anticipated, the ritual practices that were retained and emphasized were those which remained functional, from a sociological perspective, within the secular context of American life. Attending a Seder or lighting Channukah candles is a way of affirming Jewish cultural identity, not of obeying God's law. They are cultural rather than religious acts that enjoy popularity in the wider culture. Those traditional ritual practices that have declined, among third-generation Jews are the ones that do not have such social secular orientation.

From the neo-Orthodox religious perspective to which he had moved, Herberg was able to discern how far removed from the "true ends of religion" was the American Jewish religious revival of the 1950s. The revival had been superficial, unmarked by renewed theological commitment or by a widespread return to traditional religious practices. Synagogue growth and expansion had not, as once expected, led to authentic religious belief. Indeed, as Nathan Glazer noted at the time, only the smallest minority of American Jews, if asked about the nature of their religious beliefs, would have responded with "a declaration of faith in the authority of the law, the providence of God, Israel's election, and the coming of the Messiah."[30] Fewer Jews still were familiar with the principles of Jewish faith or even knew there were such principles. The very notion "of being singled out, of standing against the world—that is, of Jewish "chosenness"—was profoundly distasteful to Jewish congregants "for whom well-being means conformity and adjustment." American Jews, Herberg well understood, were increasing their religious affiliation not out of piety but because they regarded it as the socially acceptable thing to do. Herberg pointed to the ways in which weekly synagogue worship served the "other-directedness" that David Riesman had identified in the postwar middle class.[31] One went to temple for business contracts, for the social hours, for the conservative outlook that decorous worship symbolized. The new synagogues of postwar America, secular in both their orientation and interests, no longer represented a "community of believers" for whom prayer and the practice of the most elementary *mitzvot* were existential religious concerns. Rather, complained Herberg, God was made to serve man and his purposes, including material prosperity and peace of mind.[32]

For Herberg, who poignantly lamented the reduction of religious faith in America to church and synagogue membership, the purely institutional religion that so characterized the 1950s began to appear bland and irrelevant, incapable of reaching existential human concerns. Herberg's lament, which so well anticipated an often voiced critique of American religious institutional life in the 1960s and 1970s, continues to have relevance. Three decades after the publication of *Protestant-Catholic-Jew*, the oft-cited "Herbergian paradox" still seems to explain the incongruities of religious behavior in America. Today, as in the 1950s, the same people often appear to be increasingly religious and yet pervasively secular. Most aspects of contemporary religious life continue to reflect this paradox—the strengthening of the institutional religious structure in spite of increasing secularization.

Although there is much to question in Herberg's analysis,[33] *Protestant-Catholic-Jew* remains a work of enduring value to anyone hoping to understand the sociology of American religion. It has become a classic work in American religious sociology, which Nathan Glazer has called "the most satisfying explanation we have been given as to just what is happening to religion in America." The critical and public acclaim that greeted the publication of *Protestant-Catholic-Jew* brought Herberg instantaneous public recognition as one of the country's best-known sociologists of religion, a reputation he would enjoy until the end of his life.

The critical acclaim that greeted the publication of *Protestant-Catholic-Jew* also brought Herberg the academic recognition and position he had long sought. In 1955, he obtained a full-time academic appointment as professor of Judaic studies and social philosophy at Drew University, a Methodist institution in New Jersey, where he would teach until his retirement in 1976, the year before his death.

During the 1950s and 1960s, while teaching at Drew, Herberg also lectured at numerous universities, synagogues, and churches throughout the United States and Europe. He published scholarly anthologies on the works of Martin Buber, Karl Barth, Jacques

Maritain, and other modern existentialist theologians, and a collection of some twenty of his articles on aspects of biblical theology, *Faith Enacted into History*, appeared in 1976.

During the 1950s and 1960s, moreover, Herberg became part of a remarkable group of former communists and former Trotskyists that included James Burnham, Willmore Kendell, Frank Meyer, Max Eastman, and Whittaker Chambers, among others, who transformed the *National Review* into the preeminent intellectual journal of American conservatism. As religion editor of the *National Review*, Herberg emerged as one of the recognized leaders of the post–World War II conservative intellectual movement in America. His new conservatism found its most eloquent expression in his views on religion and state. Earlier than most other American Jewish intellectuals, Herberg called for a reassessment of the prevailing liberal Jewish consensus concerning separation of church and state and the role religion should play in American life. "By and large," he wrote in 1952, those who speak for the American Jewish community "seem to share the basic secularist presupposition that religion is a 'private matter.' ... The American Jew must have sufficient confidence in the capacity of democracy to preserve its pluralistic ... character without any *absolute* wall of separation between religions and public life.... The fear felt by Jewish leaders of the possible consequence of a restoration of religion to a vital place in public life is what throws them into an alliance with the secularists and helps make their own thinking so thoroughly secular."[34] A decade or so later, frustrated by liberal Jewish support for the 1963 Supreme Court decisions banning the Lord's Prayer and Bible reading in the public schools, he entered a plea for a restoration of religion to a place of honor in American public life: "Within the meaning of our political tradition and political practice, the promotion [of religion] has been, and continues to be, a part of the very legitimate 'secular' purpose of the state. Whatever the 'neutrality' of the state in matters of religion may be, it cannot be a neutrality between religion and no-religion, any more than ... it could be a neutrality between morality and no-morality, [both of which] are necessary to 'good government' and 'national prosperity.'"[35] "The traditional symbols of the divine presence in our public life," he warned, "ought not to be tampered with."[36]

Throughout the 1960s, Herberg's warning went generally

unheeded within the American Jewish community. In more recent years, however, his views on church-state relations have gained more adherents. Today, more than a decade after his death, his perceptive critique of a public life devoid of religious values is reflected in the thought of a growing number of Jewish leaders who have come to share Herberg's belief that an American political culture uninformed by religious beliefs and institutions poses a danger to the position and security of America's Jews.

Notes

1. Will Herberg, "Sigmund Freud," *Workers Age*, Vol. VIII (Oct. 7, 1939), p. 4.
2. Will Herberg, "From Marxism to Judaism: Jewish Belief as a Dynamic of Social Action," *Commentary*, Vol. 3 (Jan. 1947), p. 25.
3. Ibid., p. 27.
4. Will Herberg, "Reinhold Niebuhr: Christian Apologist to the Secular World," *Union Seminary Quarterly Review*, Vol. 11 (May 1956), p. 12.
5. Will Herberg, "Reinhold Niebuhr: Christian Apologist to the Secular World," *Union Seminary Quarterly Review*, Vol. 11 (May 1956), p. 12.
6. Seymour Siegel, "Will Herberg (1902–1977): A Ba'al Teshuvah Who Became Theologian, Sociologist, Teacher," *American Jewish Year Book*, Vol. 78 (1978), p. 532.
7. Ibid.
8. Reinhold Niebuhr review of *Judaism and Modern Man* in the *New York Herald Tribune*, Dec. 16, 1951.
9. Janel M. Gnall, "Will Herberg, *Jewish Theologian: A Biblical Existential Approach to Religion*" (Ph.D. dissertation, Drew University, 1983), p. 51.
10. Will Herberg, *Judaism and Modern Man* (New York, 1951), pp. 25–43.
11. Eugene Borowitz, "An Existentialist View of God," *Jewish Heritage*, Vol. 1 (Spring 1958).
12. Gnall, "Will Herberg," p. 54.
13. Siegel, "Will Herberg," p. 533.
14. Will Herberg, "The Chosenness of Israel and the Jews of Today," *Midstream*, Vol. 1 (Autumn 1955), p. 88.
15. Herberg, *Judaism and Modern Man*, pp. 244–46.
16. Will Herberg, "The Theological Problems of the Hour," *Proceedings of the Rabbinical Assembly of America*, Vol. 13 (June 1949), p. 420.
17. Eugene Borowitz, for example, has pointed out the similarities between Herberg's existentialist view of God and that of the Protestant existentialist Paul Tillich (Borowitz, "Existentialist View of God").
18. S. Daniel Breslauer, "Will Herberg: Intuitive Spokesman for American Judaism," *Judaism*, Vol. 27 (Winter 1978), p. 9.
19. Herberg, "Theological Problems of the Hour," pp. 424–25.
20. Quoted in Judd L. Teller, "A Critique of the New Jewish Theology," *Commentary*, Vol. 25 (March 1958), p. 250.
21. Samuel Sandmel has suggested that Herberg "went beyond regarding Niebuhr and Tillich as mentors whose profundity should be emulated, and proceeded to use these men as if they were mentors for Judaism itself." ("Reflections on the Problem of Theology for Jews," *Journal of Bible and Religion*, April 1965, p. 102).
22. Herberg, *Judaism and Modern Man*, p. 277.

23. Herberg, "Assimilation in Militant Dress: Should the Jews be 'Like Unto the Nations'?" *Commentary*, Vol. 4 (July 1947), p. 16.
24. Herberg, *Judaism and Modern Man*, pp. 276–77.
25. Teller, "Critique of the New Jewish Theology," p. 250.
26. Will Herberg, *Protestant-Catholic-Jew: An Essay in American Religious Sociology* (New York, 1955), p. 190.
27. Ibid., pp. 30, 257.
28. See, for example: Stephen Sharot, "The three-generations thesis and the American Jews," *The British Journal of Sociology*, Vol. XXIV (June 1973), pp. 151–64.
29. The empirical evidence, from these local Jewish community surveys, is reviewed in Stephen Sharot, "The three-generations thesis and the American Jews," *Ibid.*
30. Nathan Glazer, *American Judaism* (Chicago, 1957), p. 132.
31. On these points and other aspects of Herberg's critique of the American Jewish religious revival, see Arnold M. Eisen, *The Chosen People in America: A Study in Jewish Religious Ideology* (Bloomington, 1983), pp. 129–30.
32. Ibid., p. 130; Herberg, *Protestant-Catholic-Jew*, pp. 265–69.
33. See, for example, David G. Dalin, "Will Herberg in Retrospect," *Commentary*, July 1988, p. 42.
34. Will Herberg, "The Sectarian Conflict over Church and State: A Divisive Threat to Our Democracy?" *Commentary*, Vol. 14 (Nov. 1952), p. 459.
35. Will Herberg, "Religion and Public Life," *National Review*, August 13, 1963, p. 105.
36. Will Herberg, "Religious Symbols in Public Life," *National Review*, August 28, 1962, p. 162.

FOR FURTHER READING

Works by Will Herberg

Faith Enacted into History: Essays in Biblical Theology. Edited by Bernhard W. Anderson. Philadelphia, 1976. This fine collection of Herberg's essays on theology is edited by a former colleague of Herberg's at Drew University, who also wrote the introductory essay to the volume.

Judaism and Modern Man: An Interpretation of Jewish Religion. New York, 1951. Herberg's major theological work, deeply influenced by the writings of Martin Buber, Franz Rosenzweig, and Reinhold Niebuhr, was an interpretation of Judaism in the light of religious existentialist thought.

Protestant-Catholic-Jew: An Essay in American Religious Sociology. Garden City, N.Y., 1955. Herberg's most famous book has become a classic work in the sociology of American religion, which Nathan Glazer has called "the most satisfying explanation we have been given as to just what is happening to religion in America."

Four Existential Theologians: A Reader from the Works of Jacques Maritain, Nicolas Berdyaev, Martin Buber and Paul Tillich, ed. Garden City, N.Y., 1958. In his introductory essay to this collection of the writings of these four existentialist theologians, Herberg provides a penetrating analysis of their religious thought. Herberg also provides an extensive biographical notes on Maritain, Berdyaev, Buber, and Tillich.

The Writings of Martin Buber, with a Preface and Introductory Essay, ed. New York, 1956. In his important introductory essay to this collection of Buber's writings, Herberg analyzes Buber's theology and assesses the impact of his thought.

Works about Will Herberg

Ausmus, Harry J. *Will Herberg: From Right to Right.* Chapel Hill, 1987. In this detailed yet uncritical review of much of Herberg's writing, the author does not attempt to present an interpretive analysis and evaluation of the development and impact of Herberg's thought.

Breslauer, S. Daniel. "Will Herberg: Intuitive Spokesman for American Judaism." *Judaism* 27 (Winter 1978): pp. 7–12. The author argues that Herberg's fundamental views on Jewish theology and American religion are accurate reflections of the views held, consciously or unconsciously, by the majority of American Jews.

Dalin, David G. "Will Herberg in Retrospect." *Commentary* 86 (July 1988), pp. 38–43. The author examines Herberg's influence and the legacy as a Jewish theologian, sociologist of religion, and analyst of church-state relations in America.

———, ed. *From Marxism to Judaism: The Collected Essays of Will Herberg.* New York, 1989. A collection of Herberg's essays on such topics as socialism, Jewish theology, Zionism, anti-Semitism, the American synagogue, and church-state relations.

Diggins, John P. *Up from Communism: Conservative Odysseys in American Intellectual History.* New York, 1975, chaps. 3 and 7. This excellent study, which examines the thought of several American intellectuals who moved from the political left during the 1920s and 1930s to the political right after World War II, includes two chapters on the evolution of Herberg's political and religious thought.

Siegel, Seymour. "Will Herberg: A Ba'al Teshuvah Who Became a Theologian, Sociologist, Teacher." *American Jewish Year Book*, (1978), pp. 529–37. In this appreciative biographical sketch of Herberg, written shortly after his death, the author provides a useful overview of Herberg's life and thought.

Abraham Joshua Heschel

EDWARD K. KAPLAN

Abraham Heschel's varied writings all strive to convey his certainty of God's concrete involvement in human life. His often lyrical style evokes an intense intimacy with the divine, rare in our modern, post-Holocaust world, and his "depth theology" (as he calls his dynamics of religious thinking) interprets the Bible and rabbinic literature using philosophical categories as points of reference. His work, in its pragmatic aspect, functions as a vast apologetics that aims to help readers recover "pretheological situations," an all-involving awareness of awe, radical amazement, and ultimately faith in the living God—a form of spiritual cognition that precedes, or surpasses, verbal or intellectual constructs. Heschel's ultimate goal is to transform our very consciousness so that we live, think, and pray in ways compatible with God's concern.

Heschel's immense Jewish knowledge, his prophetic radicalism, and his literary genius have led many to consider him the leading exponent of religious Judaism in the twentieth century (as distinguished from Martin Buber, whose background and categories are primarily secular). Yet his insistence on the "ineffable" dimension of metaphysical insight and his apparently unsystematic modes of exposition make some professionals skeptical of his claim to have elaborated a "philosophy of religion."[1] His well-publicized appearances at civil rights marches, his negotiations with the Second Vatican Council, and his militant efforts to stop the war in Vietnam made him an equally unsettling political figure. A review of Abraham Heschel's personal and historical experience should clarify the unity and authenticity of his thinking and his public persona.

From Warsaw to Berlin

Abraham Heschel absorbed the spiritual and intellectual treasures represented by three Jewish capitals of pre–World War II Europe: Warsaw, where he was born and raised in an aristocratic Hassidic family; Vilna, the 'Jerusalem of Lithuania," where he prepared himself for a literary or academic career; and Berlin, where he earned his doctorate in philosophy from the university and decided to become a professor. It could be said that Heschel was, all at once, a Hassidic mystic, emphasizing inner fervor and exaltation; a *mitnagid* (an opponent of Hassidism), emphasizing rigorous talmudic analysis and halakha (Jewish law as God's will revealed); and a German-Jewish intellectual, emphasizing modern scholarship and universality. Heschel's originality and his perceived shortcomings reflect these separate origins of North American Jewry which few of us are capable of integrating.

Born on January 11, 1907, in Warsaw, Abraham Joshua Heschel Heschel (named after his grandfather Abraham Joshua Heschel, the rebbe of Apt) was expected to inherit the Hassidic court presided over by his father, Moshe Mordecai the Peltzovizna rebbe, whose ancestors included Rabbi Dov Baer of Mezeritch (the "great Maggid"), the principal disciple of the Baal Shem Tov, the founder of Hassidism; Rabbi Israel of Rizhyn; and the Apter, who "was buried next to the holy Baal Shem" in 1825. His mother, also of distinguished Hassidic stock, was descended from Rabbi Pinhas of Koretz and Levi Yitchak of Berditchev. Heschel absorbed a mystical world vision: "Every step taken on the way was an answer to a prayer, and every stone was a memory of a marvel." The boy's father died when he was barely ten years old, and he was tutored by a Gerer Hasid who introduced him to the thought of Reb Menachem Mendl of Kotzk, tempering the precocious child's exuberance with an acute sense of human frailty and evil. The Baal Shem and the Kotzker, his "two teachers," represent the two poles of Heschel's energetic personality: "To live both in awe and consternation, in fervor and horror, with my conscience on mercy and my eyes on Auschwitz, wavering between exaltation and dismay."[2]

An authentic prodigy, Heschel had read all the books in his father's library by the time he was ten. His first published writings were brief, clever, though conventional analyses of talmudic passages, published in 1922–23 in a Warsaw journal for Yeshiva students. But by the age of fifteen, he was privately studying Polish and German to prepare his studies at the secular, Yiddish-language *Real-Gymnasium* in Vilna, where he mastered the Polish high school liberal arts curriculum and received a diploma in July 1927. The student also participated in the thriving literary life of this city—40 percent of whose population was Jewish before the war—in a group of writers and painters calling themselves Yung Vilne. He published his first Yiddish poem in the 1926–27 anthology *Warshaver shriftn*.

At age twenty, Heschel was at a crossroads of his career: should he become a poet or a professor? In 1927 he moved to Berlin, where he enrolled simultaneously—as did other Jewish students—at the Friedrich Wilhelm University (now Humboldt University in the former East Berlin) and the Hochschule für die Wissenschaft des Judentums, the liberal rabbinical college devoted to modern research and teaching. The scholars at both these institutions and David Koigen, a sociologist and philosopher of history, provided the context in which Heschel developed his theocentric approach to the arts and to religious studies.

In 1933 he attained two momentous achievements: he defended his doctorate in philosophy with a dissertation on the phenomenology of prophetic consciousness (*Die Prophetie*, published in Cracow in 1936) and his Yiddish poems were published in Warsaw, *Der Shem Ham'forash: Mentsh* (Mankind: God's ineffable name, sixty-six pieces, many of which had already appeared in periodicals). This youthful poetry dramatizes the attachment to God and moral hypersensitivity which underlies Heschel's mature work. During this time of increasingly dominant Nazi power, Heschel devoted himself to Jewish education at several levels; he prepared scholarly monographs on medieval Jewish philosophy, taught Talmud at the Hochschule, lectured at the Berlin Lehrhaus, and edited a series on Jewish subjects for the Eric Reiss Publishing Company. His biography of Maimonides, written in masterful literary German, was published by Eric Reiss in 1935 as part of the commemoration of the sage's eight hundredth anniversary.

"A Brand Plucked from the Fire"

It is impossible to imagine, let alone express, the excruciating pressure Jews experienced in those years of Nazi tyranny. Heschel continued to develop his skills as a teacher and scholar. In 1937, Martin Buber, acknowledged giant of Jewish spiritual resistance, called Heschel to Frankfurt to replace him, after his emigration to Palestine, at the Central Organization for Jewish Adult Education and the Jüdisches Lehrhaus. One of Heschel's many public lectures of that time is "The Meaning of This Hour," given before a Quaker group at Frankfurt on the Main in February 1938.[3] Heschel's well-earned promotion, however, was brutally interrupted. Along with thousands of other Jews with Polish passports, he was awakened at 5 A.M. on October 28, 1938, by two members of the German police who entered his apartment and ordered him to pack two small bags and walk to the railroad station, where he was sent to Zbaszyn (in German, Neu-Bentschen), a border post between Germany and Poland. Just a few days later, on November 9, the *Kristallnacht* pogrom burst forth, after which Jews could no longer deny, as Leo Baeck had perceptively announced in 1933, that "the end of German Judaism has arrived."[4]

After Heschel had spent a short time in the displaced persons camp, which one could leave only with a specific visa, he found a position at the Institute for Jewish Studies in Warsaw where he taught for the academic year. In April 1939 he received an invitation to join the Faculty of the Hebrew Union College, the Reform rabbinical seminary in Cincinnati, Ohio, which had already saved several of his professors from the Berlin Hochschule. So he was able to escape, as he said, "just six weeks before the disaster began."[5] He left in July for London, where his older brother Jacob Heshel (who had taken an anglicized spelling of the family name) had established himself as rabbi of an Orthodox congregation. In London Heschel studied English and founded and taught in an Institute for Jewish Studies, probably similar to the Frankfurt Lehrhaus. On September 1, 1939, the Germans invaded Poland. Two years later, Heschel's mother and two sisters, whom he had been unable to help escape from the Warsaw Ghetto, were murdered by the Nazis.

In America Abraham Heschel mapped out the vision of a civilization redeemed by sacred values. Arriving in the United

States in 1940, he spent five years as associate professor of philosophy and rabbinics at the Hebrew Union College. These were difficult years, for the American Reform movement was hostile to traditional practices and few students had sympathy with Heschel's pietistic sensitivity. Yet the immigrant mastered his new language, and his first English article became the cornerstone of his philosophical opus: "An Analysis of Piety" (*Review of Religion*, 1942) was reprinted as the final chapter of *Man Is Not Alone* (1951), "The Pious Man."[6] At the time of the destruction of European Jewry, of which Heschel was acutely aware after his arrival on our shores, rather than writing about the Holocaust, he chose to portray the ideal religious personality.

Abraham Heschel's career after 1940 developed under the pressure of what I call his intimate havoc. Every word he subsequently wrote challenges Hitler by fostering the biblical spirit among the remaining witnesses. As he himself wrote of the pious person, he turned his pain into song. In 1945 Heschel moved to New York to join the faculty of the Jewish Theological Seminary of America, where he was named professor of Jewish ethics and mysticism, elaborated his mature work, and became nationally known as an activist in the realm of prayer as well as social action. His visiting professorship at the Protestant Union Theological Seminary (1965–66) ratified his tremendous influence on the Christian rediscovery of the Hebrew Bible. The activist fulfilled the promise of his early years.

Scholarship and Depth Theology

Heschel's philosophical writings can be distinguished from his technical scholarship, although they all pulse with the passion of a man of faith. He directed his first essays at American Jews out of touch with traditional piety. *The Earth Is the Lord's: The Inner Life of the Jew in East Europe* (1950), as the subtitle suggests, evokes the ideal shtetl society and the closeness to God and Torah that pervaded his childhood. The essay, written in subtly musical and lucid English, emerged from a Yiddish address he gave in 1945 at the YIVO Institute in New York, and its summary of Kabbalistic theology sketches the system underlying his philosophy.[7] The sanctification of time (as opposed to space) was the approach to observance in *The Sabbath: Its Meaning for Modern Man* (1951), a poetic as well as analytical interpretation of this "palace in time," the heartbeat of Jewish spirituality and culture. These two modest-sized books respond implicitly to the Shoah by translating the Jewish experience of holiness to our minds.

A linguistic and literary genius, Heschel chose to write in the language and idiom appropriate to his subject and its readership. He began by writing in German a series of technical monographs on Solomon Ibn Gabirol and Don Itzchak Abravanel; and in New York he published, in English, "The Quest for Certainty in Saadia's Philosophy" (1943–44). He wrote highly detailed, historical articles on Hassidic masters in Hebrew and Yiddish, abundantly documented with oral and manuscript as well as rare published sources.[8] He wrote the first two volumes of his masterpiece of talmudic interpretation in a beautiful rabbinic Hebrew replete with allusions, *Torah min Ha-Shamayim b'Espaklaryah shel Ha-Darot* (literally Torah from Heaven in the light of the generations, translated as *Theology of Ancient Judaism*, 1962 and 1965); the third volume, still in manuscript at Heschel's death, has just recently appeared. This work, which some scholars consider his fundamental contribution, defines a theological polarity amid the dizzying heterogeneity of rabbinical interpretations: Rabbi Akiba who took Moses' words as God's exact speech and Rabbi Ishmael for whom the Torah's vocabulary is a mixture of divine and human.[9] His final work, two large volumes written in Yiddish, *Kotzk: In gerangle far emesdikeit* (The struggle for integrity), printed right before his death, probes this troubled master obsessed with uncompromising moral truth.

But Heschel's prominence was buttressed by his less technical, sweeping philosophical opus which began, in 1951, with *Man Is Not Alone: A Philosophy of Religion*, which was hailed by Reinhold Niebuhr in a highly influential review: "He will become a commanding and authoritative voice not only in the Jewish community but in the religious life of America."[10] His specifically Jewish magnum opus appeared in 1955, *God In Search of Man: A Philosophy of Judaism*. It makes explicit the scholarly foundation (i.e., footnotes) missing from the previous volume, which it expands and, to the regret of some readers, in several places, repeats. These two germinal volumes expound Heschel's entire system.[11]

Both books are organized according to the same strategy, beginning with evocations of the sense of the ineffable so as to prepare our spiritual awareness of living as objects of God's concern. Heschel analyzes the intense experiences of awe, wonder, and radical amazement that should jar our thinking off the beaten track. The second half of each book reinterprets basic moral and religious concepts in light of transformed consciousness.

Heschel's argument depends upon his ability, as poetic stylist and polemic philosopher, convincingly and seductively to evoke the experiential antecedents of faith, the "pretheological" situation of the modern person inspired by the mystery of being itself. For Heschel, "radical amazement" is a "cognitive insight" into the reality of God, whose presence both pervades and transcends existence. Such intuitions, shared at the outset of reflection by secularists and observant people alike, open the mind to biblical thinking: "The entire range of religious thought and expression is a sublimation of a presymbolic knowledge which the awareness of the ineffable provides.... Philosophy of religion must be an effort to recall and keep alive *the meta-symbolic relevance of religious terms.*"[12]

God in Search of Man is divided into three parts, which summarize the Jewish philosopher's program: Part I, "God," says that spiritual insight can be trained through experiences of the sublime, but contact with God's presence comes through awe and a sense of mystery. Understood in the categories of religious thinking, the world becomes an "allusion" to God; everything bespeaks His question to us. Specifically, it is wrong to think of mankind as seeking God; religious thinking makes us aware of God's search for the children of Israel. This "Copernican revolution" effects what I call a recentering of subjectivity from the person to God and is the fundamental goal of Heschel's apologetics. God is the ultimate Subject of which I am a privileged—and morally responsible—object.

In Part II, "Revelation," Heschel develops his theory of biblical language as "understatement" to justify the truth of the prophets' claim to divine inspiration. We must interpret the Bible responsively, not only literally: "To be able to encounter the spirit within the words, we must learn to crave for an affinity with the pathos of God."[13] Part III, "Response," posits that Jewish piety is living in a way compatible with God's concern for mankind (His pathos) and religious law (halakha) is but one pole of ritual commitment. Regularity must constantly be nourished by spontaneity. The Jews, as all people, are partners with God in the redemption of the world.

Religious Teacher and Role Model

Heschel's other books focus on more specific issues. His luminous study of prayer and symbolism, *Man's Quest for God* (1954, reprinted as *Quest for God*), gathers two controversial encounters into an inspiring testimony to the possibilities of modern worship. In 1953, Heschel addressed the Reform Central Conference of American Rabbis on the importance of halakha, revealed law and codified observance, and the Conservative Rabbinical Assembly on "the spirit of prayer," the inner dimension of ritual behavior. He challenged the conventional ideologies of each audience. The book analyzes verbal prayer as a form of poetry that educates our sensitivity to God, with the ultimate aim of recentering our consciousness: "Prayer takes the mind out of the narrowness of self-interest, and enables us to see the world in a mirror of the holy. For when we betake ourselves to the extreme opposite of the ego, we can behold a situation from the aspect of God."[14] Prayer can effect the recentering of our subjectivity and trains us to live according to divine will. Regular observance can structure our inner life and inspirit it with *kavvanah* (or intention), leading to ethical choices.

The Prophets, an expanded translation of Heschel's German doctoral thesis, defines the theological foundation of his social action. A basic text in many college courses, *The Prophets* etches a vivid portrait of dynamic faith, which the graphic preface, "What Manner of Man Is the Prophet?" evokes in vigorous prose: "The prophet is a man who feels fiercely. God has thrust a burden upon his soul, and he is bowed and stunned by man's fierce greed. Frightful is the agony of man; no human voice can convey its full terror. Prophecy is the voice that God has lent to the silent agony, a voice to the plundered poor, to the profaned riches of the world. It is a form of living, a crossing point of God and man. God is raging in the prophet's words." Scholars have debated the validity of Heschel's central notion that God is emotionally involved in the moral life of individuals. Many find it hard to grasp that Heschel does not use anthropopathic terms literally but more than literally: to suggest what is metaphysically real from God's perspective.[15]

Heschel's decisions derive from his identification with the prophets: "He lives not only in his personal life, but also the life of God. The prophet hears God's voice and feels His heart. He tries to impart the pathos of the message together with its logos. As an imparter his soul overflows, speaking as he does out of the fullness of his sympathy."[16]

Heschel's theology of divine pathos leads to a sacred humanism—perhaps the most universal aspect of his thinking. One does not require a confident faith in God to understand his insistence that each and every individual is infinitely precious. *Who Is Man?* (1965), using an elegant, flowing, though sometimes abstract terminology, condenses the biblical anthropology of his larger developments. Depth theology is thus completed by Heschel's almost visceral conviction that every human being is an image of God. Every person—body and spirit—is sacred, as he wrote elsewhere: "The human is a disclosure of the divine, and all people are one in God's care for man. Many things on earth are precious, some are holy, humanity is holy of holies. To meet a human being is an opportunity to sense the image of God, the *presence* of God."[17]

The public addresses and articles collected in *The Insecurity of Freedom* (1966) apply Heschel's sacred humanism to problems of youth and aging, the ecumenical movement, Israel and the diaspora, Soviet Jewry, racism, and civil rights. Each chapter is a drama of modern prophetic judgment which bristles with bold formulations, for example, "*Racial or religious bigotry* must be recognized for what it is: *satanism, blasphemy.*"[18] Other expressions of his moral passion include his searing contribution to *Vietnam: Crisis of Conscience* (1967), which profoundly moved his Christian partners as a living echo of the Bible: "Though deaf to the distant cry of the orphaned and the maimed, I know that my own integrity is being slashed in that slaughter."[19] We can begin to fathom his complex devotion to Zion in *Israel: An Echo of Eternity* (1969), written after Israel's military victory of June 1967, in cooperation with the Anti-Defamation League of B'nai B'rith, which explains to gentiles why the Holy Land is precious to Jews.

Heschel expressed himself vividly but rarely confessed his own inner turmoil. The exception is his last book written in English,

A Passion for Truth (1973), delivered to the publisher just weeks before his death during the Sabbath night of December 23–24, 1972. Heschel recognizes the anguished side of himself in the Danish philosopher Søren Kierkegaard, the father of existentialism, and the Kotzker rebbe—both radically antisocial spiritual dissidents. His autobiographical preface, cited at the beginning of this essay, defines his personal struggle with despair and exaltation. The Christian and the rebbe bring modern absurdity into the arena of interfaith dialogue, challenging meaninglessness. Finally, Abraham Heschel's engaging presence—his intellectual brilliance, elegance, wit, righteous anger, and compassion—can be sensed from several transcribed dialogues, as yet uncollected in book form.[20]

Criticisms and Controversies

Heschel took flexible positions regarding ritual obligations that many Orthodox Jews considered to be controversial or, at worst, inauthentic. He was too traditional for most Reform Jews and too intent upon inwardness for many adherents to any Jewish denomination. His increased media visibility in the 1960s caused some to question his humility, for the public could be overly impressed by his beard, his flowing white hair, and his lush oratory. Protestants and Catholics saw in Heschel a Hebrew prophet, and some skeptics felt that he derived too much pleasure from being called "Father Abraham," as William Sloane Coffin dubbed him. Some Jews even disapproved of his willingness publically to confront the Second Vatican Council, despite his rigorous defense of Jewish autonomy. His profound involvement with the anti–Vietnam War movement as an active cofounder of Clergy and Laity Concerned, who participated in board meetings as well as demonstrations, aroused the anxiety of some establishment leaders, who felt that his personal stand would hurt U.S. support of Israel—despite Heschel's love song to Zion, *Israel: An Echo of Eternity.*

These objections are worth considering because they represent, in miniature, divisions within modern Jewry. Heschel's social commitments grew from his past experiences, first with bitter poverty in Warsaw and Vilna, which his family endured, and the vicious anti-Semitism that allowed millions of "civilized" people to support Hitler with enthusiasm. His Yiddish poetry of 1926–33 amply attests to his ethical vulnerability and bold social conscience. And his fruitless efforts from 1941 to 1943 to engage American Jewish organizations to help the European victims more than justify his vociferous denunciation of moral "callousness" during the 1960s. Although Heschel claimed that his activism was not awakened until he revised his dissertation on the prophets, his life history demonstrates that, as a private person, he was never insulated from the world.

Most Jewish opposition to Heschel comes from exclusionary interpretations of the tradition, for example, those who revere ritual acts without a concern for emotional involvement; rationalists (in the Lithuanian mode) who find authentic religion only in the Talmud; those who consider theology and philosophy as foreign to Judaism (a variation of the preceding); and of course literalistic readers who debase Heschel's lyrical celebration of God for being irrational, "poetic" fantasy. Practicing Jews of all backgrounds have missed the ethical implications of Heschel's "mysticism" because Kabbalistic scholarship has only recently come into vogue. Objections to his strong personality, with its frailties as well as triumphs, can also be placed into context.

Heschel insists that Jewish existence must include adherence to "three sacred entities: God, Torah, and Israel [that is, the Jewish people]." It is a "grave distortion" to exclude any one dimension.[21] Heschel was thoroughly committed to halakha and accepted and promoted the pluralism of rabbinic Judaism. It is understandable that defenders of what he called "pan-halakhism" would find his preoccupation with spiritual and moral inwardness subversive and that Jewish nationalists—secular or Orthodox— might be threatened by his insistence that God transcends peoplehood and rabbinical authority. Heschel challenged reductionism or fetishism of any kind by appropriately acknowledging the complexities of modern experience. His Jewish learning was impeccable and his commitments utterly sincere. Experts can debate the details.

Some scholars complain that Heschel rarely documents his sources. But the footnotes missing from *Man Is Not Alone* (1951) can easily be found in the germinal essay "The Mystical Element in Judaism" (1949), *God in Search of Man* (1955), and *Torah min Hashamayim* (1962, 1965). It is true that Heschel is reluctant to name opponents—such as Kant, Heidegger, Paul Tillich, Saul Lieberman, Mordecai Kaplan, even Martin Buber—whose basic ideas and phrases he would transform (as an implicit critique) without attributing their specific origin. His goal provides the explanation. Respectful of coworkers with whom he differs, Heschel is an irenic polemicist who seeks both to maintain a dialogical environment and to preserve his own authority as a thinker.[22] At the same time, conscientious professionals might be expected to take offense at some of his judgments such as "Religion declined not because it was refuted, but because it became irrelevant, dull, oppressive, insipid." Such honesty, however, gives confidence to outsiders seeking faith.

Heschel's daughter Susannah, a Judaic scholar, appropriately defines her father as an "edifying philosopher" (to use Richard Rorty's term), who conveys his system through evocation not abstract concepts.[23] More precisely, Heschel consistently uses the phenomenological method, as Lawrence Perlman has demonstrated, to bring our spiritual discernment to the surface of consciousness. His remarkable prose, indeed, is both an entrance and a stumbling block. Heschel's multileveled discourse combines a literary style replete with imagery and elegant aphorisms and lucid manipulation of basic metaphysical, aesthetic, and ethical categories. He must be followed slowly and responsively, with patience, savoring words and phrases to appreciate the tonality as well as the ideas.

Heschel's "philosophy of religion" can be systematized (see my remarks below on Fritz Rothschild), although his procedure is not academically neutral or abstract. Reading Heschel is a situational, dynamic process of "religious thinking." The many chapters of his big books are divided into sections with highly charged subtitles such as "The Ineffable Name," "The Meaning of Awe," "Ultimate Concern Is an Act of Worship," "The Paradox of Prophecy," "All Joy Comes from God." These brief subsections are like prose poems which develop feelings and intuitions, and the conceptual armature of Heschel's argument may become accordingly elusive. Often we must meditatively unpack sentences such as "Who lit the wonder before our eyes and the wonder of our eyes? Who struck the lightning in the minds and scorched us with an imperative of being overawed by the holy as unquenchable as the sight of the stars?"[24]

No Religion Is an Island

Abraham Heschel masterfully articulates our most intimate yearnings. He stresses the universality of religious insights, although he insists on the divine authority of the Hebrew prophets. He most successfully addresses religious moderates (including some neo-Orthodox), Christians and Jews, open-minded people receptive to spirituality, as well as agnostics touched by a hunger for the holy. Heschel's reverence for the Bible and his shameless passion for God can enrich all branches of Judaism in their autonomous development.

The most accurate and practical introduction to Heschel's wide-ranging opus is *Between God and Man: An Interpretation of Judaism*, a comprehensive anthology of Heschel's writings to the date of publication in 1959 (with selections from the manuscript of *The Prophets*) chosen by Fritz A. Rothschild, a close associate of Heschel's at the Jewish Theological Seminary and a gifted philosophical mind. Rothschild was the first to define Heschel's philosophical and theological system; his selections are followed by a biographical essay and complete bibliography (updated most recently in 1976).[25] John C. Merkle, a Catholic theologian, in *The Genesis of Faith: The Depth Theology of Abraham Joshua Heschel* (1985), demonstrates in detail a terminological rigor which many of Heschel's sympathetic readers have not discovered. Accompanying this impressive volume is the publication of the papers from an interdenominational conference—also edited by Merkle—at which leading Jewish, Catholic, and Protestant experts explored Heschel's biblical, philosophical, theological, social, ethical, and ecumenical contributions.

Heschel the person possessed an enormous capacity to inspire individuals. Those who responded to his spirit felt that every fiber of his being proclaimed the "joy of being a Jew" and that explains why so many Christians revered him and treasured his books. He brought countless seekers of all faiths into a living relationship with the holy. Heschel could sit for hours with an individual and help him or her define an urgent problem or commitment. The man is gone, but his energetic prose, which lends itself to quotation but eludes exact definition, maintains that personal presence.

Abraham Joshua Heschel produced dynamic interpretations of the prophets, the Talmud, the experience and theology of prayer, medieval Jewish philosophy, and Hassidism, weaving these traditions into a tapestry of thought, feeling, and devotion. His scholarship and admonitions, however, have yet to be translated into the religious education to which he devoted his life. Whether specialists will excuse the relatively elliptical construction of his major works and apply his erudition and fiery faith to their specific disciplines remains to be seen. But Heschel's witness conveys a richly complex Judaism which responds with prophetic intensity to modern realities. His attachment to God is equaled only by his endless striving to sanctify all humanity.

Notes

1. In his review of *God in Search of Man* Emil Fackenheim first made the fundamental distinction (which some people contest) between "religious thought" (or philosophy) and "religious thinking" (*Conservative Judaism* 15 [Fall 1960]: 50–53). For the most useful recent analyses of Heschel's critics see Arnold Eisen, "Re-Reading Heschel on the Commandments," *Modern Judaism* 9 (February 1989): 1–33; and Lawrence Perlman, *Abraham Heschel's Idea of Revelation* (Atlanta, Ga., 1989).
2. From Heschel's most explicit autobiographical sketch in the preface to *A Passion for Truth* (New York, 1973), p. xiii–xiv.
3. "Versuch einer Deutung" was widely circulated in Germany and then expanded and published in English in the *Hebrew Union College Bulletin* 2 (March 1943) as "The Meaning of This War," and later as an appendix to *Man's Quest for God* (New York, 1954; rpt. as *Quest for God* New York, 1990), as "The Meaning of This Hour."
4. Leo Baeck quoted in the excellent historical biography by Leonard Baker, *Days of Sorrow and Pain: Leo Baeck and the Berlin Jews* (New York, 1978), p. 145.
5. "No Religion Is an Island," *Union Seminary Quarterly* 21 pt. 1 (January 1966): 117. The subhead to this section is a quote from Heschel's inaugural lecture of 1965 as visiting professor at the Union Theological Seminary in New York.
6. See also "The Holy Dimension," *Journal of Religion,* 23 (April 1943), 117–24, and "Faith," *Reconstructionist* 10 (November 13, 1944), 10–15; (November 17, 1944), 12–16. For the complete references, see my chapter in John Merkle, ed., *Abraham Joshua Heschel: Exploring His Life and Thought* (New York, 1985), p. 118, n. 10. The final chapter of *Man Is Not Alone* was purportedly drawn from his uncle, the Novominsker rebbe Alter Yisrael Shimon Perlow (1874–1933), his mother's twin brother, who supervised his education after his father's death. For Heschel's efforts during the war see the interview quoted in Samuel Dresner's important introduction to *The Circle of the Baal Shem Tov* (Chicago, 1985), p. xxv, n. 30.
7. Heschel documents the Kabbalistic sources of his theology in one of his most important articles, "The Mystical Element in Judaism," in Louis Finkelstein, ed., *The Jews: Their History, Culture, and Religion* (New York, 1949), pp. 602–23 (in Vol. 1

of the two-volume edition, and in Vol. 2 of the four-volume edition). See chaps. 10 and 11 of *The Earth Is the Lord's*, "Kabbalah" and "Hasidism."

8. Collected in the posthumous volume edited, translated, with an original biographical introduction by Samuel H. Dresner, *The Circle of the Baal Shem*. See also Steven T. Katz, "Abraham Joshua Heschel and Hasidism," *Journal of Jewish Studies* 31 (Spring 1980): 82–104.
9. See esp. Jacob Neusner, *Conservative Judaism* 20 (Spring 1966): 66–73; Eisen, "Re-Reading Heschel" and Perlman, *Abraham Heschel's Idea of Revelation*.
10. Reinhold Niebuhr, "Masterly Analysis of Faith," *New York Herald Tribune Book Review* 118 (April 1951): 12.
11. Some of the following discussion is taken from my article "Heschel's Poetics of Religious Thinking," in Merkle, ed., *Heschel*, pp. 103–19.
12. Heschel, *God in Search of Man*, p. 116.
13. Ibid., p. 252.
14. Heschel, *Man's Quest for God*, p. 7.
15. Heschel, *The Prophets* (New York, 1962), p. 5. See Edward K. Kaplan, "Language and Reality in Abraham J. Heschel's Philosophy of Religion," *Journal of the American Academy of Religion* 41 (March 1973): esp. pp. 98–99, n. 8.
16. Heschel, *The Prophets*, p. 26.
17. Heschel's "No Religion Is an Island," p. 121.
18. Heschel, *The Insecurity of Freedom: Essays on Human Existence* (New York, 1966), p. 86.
19. *Vietnam: Crisis of Conscience* (New York, 1967), p. 57.
20. See his dialogue with Jewish educators: "Teaching Jewish Theology in the Solomon Schechter Day School," *Synagogue School* 28 (Fall 1969): 4–18; interview with Carl Stern, "The Eternal Light Program" recorded days before his death (mimeographed copy); and Patrick Granfield, *Theologians at Work* (New York, 1967), pp. 69–85.
21. Abraham Joshua Heschel, "God, Torah, and Israel," in Edward L. Long, Jr., and Robert T. Handy, eds., *Theology and Church in Times of Change: Essays in Honor of John Coleman Bennett* (Philadelphia, 1970), pp. 71–90.
22. See Harold Stern, "A. J. Heschel, Irenic Polemicist," *Proceedings of the Rabbinical Assembly* (New York, 1983), pp. 169–77. Heschel added remarks on Maimonides' lack of footnotes to his translation of the final chapter of his biography: see "The Last Days of Maimonides," in *Insecurity of Freedom*, pp. 285–98. The observation at the end of this paragraph is taken from *God in Search of Man* (New York, 1955), p. 3.
23. Susannah Heschel, Preface to *God in Search of Man* (Northvale, N.J., 1987), p. xxxvii.
24. Heschel, *Man Is Not Alone*, p. 68.
25. See also Rothschild's necrology of Heschel, *American Jewish Yearbook* (1973), pp. 533–44; and Perlman, *Abraham Heschel's Idea of Revelation*.

FOR FURTHER READING

Works (in English) by Abraham Joshua Heschel

Maimonides. A Biography. Translated by Joachim Neugroschel. First published in German in 1935, New York, 1982. A spiritual and cultural biography of a complete scholar, medical activist, and man of faith. Heschel's medieval role model completes his self-portrait in *The Prophets*.

The Earth Is the Lord's: The Inner Life of the Jew in East Europe, New York, 1950. A graceful introduction to Hassidic spirituality and Heschel's Kabbalistic theology and ethics.

The Sabbath: Its Meaning for Modern Man, New York, 1951. Philosophical and poetic meditations on Judaism as a religion of sanctified time. The Sabbath is seen as a foretaste of eternity.

Man Is Not Alone: A Philosophy of Religion, New York, 1951. First volume of Heschel's theological system and a profound, lyrical evocation and analysis of religious experience.

Man's Quest for God: Studies in Prayer and Symbolism, New York, 1954; reprinted as *Quest for God*, New York, 1990. Lucid and inspiring analyses of Jewish prayer, language, ritual, and spiritual insight as a harmony of law and spontaneity.

God in Search of Man: A Philosophy of Judaism, New York, 1955. Second volume of Heschel's theology, longer and well documented from Jewish classical and secular philosophical sources.

The Prophets, New York, 1962. A passionate introduction to the Hebrew prophets which combines vision with detailed critiques of other scholarly approaches. It presents the foundation of Heschel's moral and political positions.

Who Is Man?, Stanford, 1965. Lucid and concise summary of Heschel's theology of human being and responsibility. Excellent condensation of the sacred humanism of his two philosophical volumes.

The Insecurity of Freedom: Essays on Human Existence, New York, 1966. Heschel in action. Collection of dynamic and incisive essays and public addresses on civil rights, medical ethics, aging, youth, Israel and the diaspora, depth theology, prayer, Reinhold Niebuhr, ecumenism, Soviet Jewry, and Maimonides.

Israel: An Echo of Eternity, New York, 1969. A fervent, often poetic, and passionately argued defense of the State of Israel, written in response to the June 1967 war. Magnificent prayerful prose.

A Passion for Truth, New York, 1973. Fascinating comparison of Kierkegaard with the Kotzker rebbe, an abrasive spiritual dissident. It is of psychological as well as theological interest.

The Circle of the Baal Shem Tov. Edited by Samuel H. Dresner, Chicago, 1985. Translation of Heschel's scholarly monographs on Hassidic masters previously published separately in Yiddish and in Hebrew. Important biographical introduction by the editor.

Interview with Carl Stern, "The Eternal Light Program" presented by the National Broadcasting Company, February 4, 1973, under the auspices of the Jewish Theological Seminary of America. Videotape and transcript available. A vivid experience of Heschel's personal presence, recorded shortly before his death.

Selected Articles Not Included in Heschel's Books

"The Quest for Certainty in Saadia's Philosophy." *Jewish Quarterly Review* 33 (1943): 263–313; 34 (1944): 391–408. An elegantly written monograph on the problem of faith and doubt in a fundamental medieval philosopher. This is the best of Heschel's German scholarship.

"The Mystical Element in Judaism." In Louis Finkelstein, ed., *The Jews: Their History, Culture, and Religion,* pp. 602–23. New York, 1949 (in Vol. 1 of the two-volume edition and Vol. 2 of the four-volume edition). Richly documented with citations from the Zohar, this systematic exposition identifies the classical Jewish sources of Heschel's ethics and his theology. A basic text.

"No Religion Is an Island." *Union Seminary Quarterly Journal* 21 pt. 1 (January 1966): 117–34. A dramatic statement of Heschel's experience of the Holocaust and its relation to interfaith understanding and dialogue. His sacred humanism appears here at its best.

"From Mission to Dialogue." *Conservative Judaism* 21 (Spring 1967): 1–11. Another crucial definition, this time addressed to rabbis, of the spiritual necessity for Jewish autonomy in any Jewish-Christian relations.

"The Moral Outrage of Vietnam." In *Vietnam: Crisis of Conscience,* by Robert McAfee Brown, A. J. Heschel, and David Novak, pp. 48–61. New York, 1967. Searing biblical oratory in the service of individual conscience and political commitment. *The Prophets* applied.

"The Jewish Notion of God and Christian Renewal." In L. K. Shook, ed., *Renewal of Religious Thought,* pp. 105–29. Montreal, 1968. Conditions for substantive cooperation and its urgency for renewal for both faiths.

"Conversation with Martin Luther King, Jr." *Conservative Judaism* 22 (Spring 1968); 1–19. Heschel sees King as a modern prophet and defines the spiritual basis of a true black-Jewish coalition. The article is a model for race relations.

"Teaching Jewish Theology in the Solomon Schechter Day School." *Synagogue School* 28 (Fall 1969): 4–18. In a dynamic and charming fashion, Heschel speaks to educators whose language and spiritual values he implicitly shares. It is his clearest portrait as pedagogue.

"God, Torah, and Israel." In Edward L. Long, Jr., and Robert Handy, eds., *Theology and Church in Times of Change: Essays in Honor of John Coleman Bennett.* Philadelphia, 1970, pp. 71–90. Important statement on the interrelatedness of religious reality (i.e., God), community, and ritual in Heschel's interpretation of Judaism. Translated from the manuscript of volume 3 of *Torah min Hashamayim.* This article does not appear in volume 3, edited by David Feldman and published in 1991 by the Jewish Theological Seminary of America.

"On Prayer." *Conservative Judaism* 25 (Fall 1970): 1–12. A fervent, dramatic statement of Heschel's spiritual radicalism. Prayer is a commitment to God and to human justice and compassion and a challenge to institutional religion.

Anthologies

Between God and Man: An Interpretation of Judaism. Selected, edited, and introduced by Fritz A. Rothschild. New York, 1959; revised most recently in 1976. The best access to Heschel's varied writings with an authoritative analysis of his philosophical and theological system. It is the most complete bibliography of Heschel's writings and those of his critics. It remains the best research tool and introduction.

I Asked for Wonder: A Spiritual Anthology. Edited by Samuel H. Dresner. Selections organized by topics and subtitles, with an emphasis on the brief formulation. A handy, inspirational introduction.

To Grow in Wisdom. Edited by Jacob Neusner and Noam M. M. Neusner, Lanham, MD, 1989. Important uncollected articles on aging, youth, etc., with a sometimes harsh but informative biographical and scholarly introduction by the editor.

Works about Abraham Joshua Heschel

Books

Conservative Judaism 28 (Fall 1973). Memorial tribute to Heschel with important articles by Avraham Holtz, Fritz A. Rothschild, Edmond La B. Cherbonnier, Edward K. Kaplan, Seymour Siegel, Louis Finkelstein, and others.

Friedman, Maurice. *Abraham Joshua Heschel and Elie Wiesel: You Are My Witnesses.* New York, 1987. A personal as well as scholarly introduction to Heschel's personality and his philosophy.

Kasimow, Harold and Byron and L. Sherwin, eds., *No Religion Is An Island. Abraham Joshua Heschel and Interreligious Dialogue,* New York, 1991. Important collection of essays, including Heschel's inaugural lecture at Union Theological Seminary, representing Jewish, Protestant, Catholic, Hindu, Muslim, and Buddhist responses to Heschel and his works. Among the contributors are the editors, Susannah Heschel, Jacob Y. Teshima, Daniel Berrigan, John C. Merkle, Eugene J. Fisher, John C. Bennett, Johannes Cardinal Willebrands, and Jerzy Kosinski.

Merkle, John C. *The Genesis of Faith: The Depth Theology of Abraham Joshua Heschel.* New York, 1985. A remarkably detailed systematization of Heschel's entire theological system by a Catholic theologian. Merkle refers generously to other scholars and astutely defines the presuppositions of Heschel's critics.

————., ed. *Abraham Joshua Heschel: Exploring His Life and Thought.* New York, 1985. Papers presented at an interreligious conference on Heschel at the College of Saint Benedict, Minnesota. Important papers by Bernard W. Anderson, Robert McAfee Brown, Samuel H. Dresner, Eva Fleischner, Edward K. Kaplan, Wolfe Kelman, John C. Merkle, Ursula M. Niebuhr, and Fritz A. Rothschild. Expert responses to Heschel's many scholarly and public accomplishments.

Moore, Donald J. *The Human and the Holy. The Spirituality of Abraham Joshua Heschel,* New York, 1989. An elegant summary and analysis of Heschel's religious philosophy by a priest and professor at Fordham University.

Perlman, Lawrence. *Abraham Heschel's Idea of Revelation.* Atlanta, Ga., 1989. An important revised doctoral dissertation on Heschel's phenomenological method. Technical study which convincingly demonstrate the consistency of Heschel's philosophy of religion.

Sherman, Franklin. *The Promise of Heschel.* Philadelphia, 1970. A useful elementary introduction.

Major Articles Not Included in Books Cited

I have not annotated this list since the titles are self-explanatory. Rothschild's anthology provides the most complete bibliography.

Cherbonnier, Edmond La B. "Heschel as a Religious Thinker." *Conservative Judaism* 23 (Fall 1968): 25–39.

Borowitz, Eugene B. *A New Jewish Theology in the Making,* pp. 147–60. Philadelphia, 1968.

Dresner, Samuel H. "The Contribution of Abraham Joshua Heschel." *Judaism* 32 (Winter 1983): 57–69.

Eisen, Arnold. "Re-Reading Heschel on the Commandments." *Modern Judaism* 9 (February 1989): 1–33.

Fackenheim, Emil L. Review of *God in Search of Man. Conservative Judaism* 15 (Fall 1960): 50–53.

Fox, Marvin. "Heschel, Intuition, and the Halakhah." *Tradition* 3 (Fall 1960): 5–15.

Kaplan, Edward K. "Language and Reality in Abraham J. Heschel's Philosophy of Religion." *Journal of the American Academy of Religion* 41 (March 1973): 94–113.

———. "Mysticism and Despair in Abraham J. Heschel's Religious Thought." *Journal of Religion* 57 (January 1977): 33–47.

Kasimow, Harold. "Abraham Joshua Heschel and Interreligious Dialogue." *Journal of Ecumenical Studies* 18 (Summer 1981): 423–34.

Katz, Steven T. "Abraham Joshua Heschel and Hasidism." *Journal of Jewish Studies* 31 (Spring 1980): 82–104.

Neusner, Jacob. Review of *Torah min Hashamayim. Conservative Judaism* 20 (Spring 1966): 66–73.

Petuchowski, Jakob J. "Faith as the Leap of Action: The Theology of Abraham Joshua Heschel." *Commentary* 25 (May 1958): 390–97.

Rotenstreich, Nathan. "On Prophetic Consciousness." *Journal of Religion* 54 (July 1974): 185–98.

Rothschild, Fritz A. "Abraham Joshua Heschel." In Thomas E. Bird, ed., *Modern Theologians,* pp. 169–82. Notre Dame, 1967.

———. "Abraham Joshua Heschel (1907–1972): Theologian and Scholar." *American Jewish Yearbook,* pp. 533–44. New York, 1973.

Schachter, Zalman M. "Two Facets of Judaism." *Tradition* 3 (Spring 1961): 191–202.

Siegel, Seymour. "Abraham Heschel's Contribution to Jewish Scholarship." *Proceedings of the Rabbinical Assembly*, vol. 32, New York, 1968, pp. 72–85.

Stern, Harold. "A. J. Heschel, Irenic Polemicist." *Proceedings of the Rabbinical Assembly*, pp. 169–77. New York, 1983.

Tanenzapf, Saul. "Abraham Heschel and His Critics." *Judaism* 23 (Summer 1974): 276–86.

Weborg, John. "Abraham Joshua Heschel: A Study in Anthropopodicy." *Anglican Theological Review* 61 (October 1979): 483–97.

Isaac Hutner

STEVEN SCHWARZSCHILD

By far most Jews are long since not "orthodox." Indeed, they know
so little about "orthodoxy" that their notion of it and the reality
have extremely little in common. (This is even more true of
non-Jewish ideas about it.)

One of the valuable by-products of studying[1] the thought of a
teacher like Rabbi Isaac Hutner (1907–80), who is somewhat off
the beaten track of what is conventionally regarded as typical for
Orthodoxy, is that it will make it clear how greatly differentiated
so-called Orthodoxy is within itself: you can do most anything
within "orthodoxy" that most people think can be done only
beyond it, or, if you cannot do quite everything, you can
certainly think and say most anything. (The "orthodox" themselves have, therefore, long complained that in Judaism, "ortho-
praxis" rather than orthodoxy, "right belief," is the decisive
standard.)

Another valuable by-product will be the demonstration that the
idea of Orthodoxy as an insulated parochialism is far from the
truth: it faces, sometimes to accept and at other times to reject,
most commonly to accept, to reject, and to adapt in different
mixtures, just the same intellectual, scientific, ethical, political,
and even religious forces that the rest of the world tries to cope
with—to be sure, from its own perspective—as everybody does.
Furthermore, to call it fundamentalism, as is being done at the
present time, is foolish, first, because a Christian-Protestant category is being used, and, more important, because "orthodox

Judaism" is first and foremost rabbinic-talmudic, and the Talmud handles the Bible in the most extraordinarily unfundamentalist, unliteralist fashion.

Further yet, the spectrum of Orthodoxy is so wide, and has always been, that almost nothing ever goes or has gone undisputed within it (*pace* the well-known Jewish cultural propensity for argumentativeness, divisiveness, and legalism), and what one may or may not do, certainly what one ought or ought not to believe, depends fully on who and what one's teacher is and how one reacts to him; teachers are, of course, in the long run chosen by their students. As this essay was being written, the squabbling between the various so-called religious parties in Israel, not to speak of Orthodox groups that, contrary to the monolithic impression abroad, arraign themselves in the "peace camp," were displaying Orthodox diversity very visibly for the perceptive spectator. At bottom such differences result from their often subtly distinguished attitudes toward Zionism. (I will consider R. Isaac Hutner's stand on this score below.) A great deal of acrimonious infighting occurs in his life and writings.

One can go so far as to say that in Jewish Orthodoxy belief in the Sinaitic revelation is the passport to total freedom. Orthodoxy requires that the Jew accept the Torah (not "the Bible") as divine revelation. Having done this, he or she is obligated, because it is divine, to pay infinite attention to it, to learn as much about it as possible in the most assiduous manner. In precise proportion to how much one has studied, one is then free—actually, one is then obligated to interpret and to apply not only all of the Torah in accordance with one's best understanding, taking all relevant factors into consideration, but to do this even with respect to the foundational belief in the Sinaitic revelation.

R. Hutner's teaching is one strand in the multicolored garment of traditional Judaism—a particularly interesting one, it will turn out.

Another valuable by-product of this study is to bring us closer to the authentic forms and substance of historic Judaism.

Most Jews nowadays and certainly almost all non-Jews have next to no idea of the real moral and intellectual forces at work in or of the religious, philosophical, and theological foundations of Judaism. One of the most important causes of this state of affairs is that the character of Judaism is so different from the essential natures of other cultures, especially Western-Christian culture, that the categories through which the latter are understood do not fit it. When, as is usually the case, those categories are applied to it, Judaism is either fundamentally missed, distorted, or misunderstood, or a combination of such maltreatments results—as though a bassoon were used to play a violin passage.

With the respective categories go, of course, their own particular genres and vocabularies. Theoretical writings in the Occidental manner (philosophical, theological expositions, and the like) are rare in historic Jewish literature. Usually, when they do occur, whether in medieval or modern times, they tend to be of an apologetic character; that is, they translate the substance of Judaism more or commonly less successfully into the languages of other cultures for the intended benefit of non-Jews or of alienated Jews.

The indigenous language of Jewish culture is halakah (law) and aggadah (homiletics) and, most frequently, an inextricable combination of the two. These two categories, especially when fully and deeply complexified, are next to unfathomable in every non-Jewish setting. Further, they are invariably formulated in a rabbinic Hebrew that has incorporated the technical language and subtle wealth of more than two millennia of literary allusions, and it is no wonder that all but the initiates are almost bound to ignore the existence of—or at best fail to appreciate the authentic substance of—Judaism. This is then commonly given expression to in the complaint that Judaism lacks a properly sophisticated intellectual foundation.

R. Hutner's thought, though fully committed to the centrality of the halakah in Judaism, as is the norm, deals much more than usual in midrash (homiletical exegesis), aggadah, and their product, makhashavah (Jewish thought). Combined with these elements are strong components of Kabbalah (mysticism), lyricism, and poetry—in all a very complex, unusual, productive, and yet completely characteristic synthesis. It would, therefore, be preferable to present his own words here, even if in translation, but because to do so would be inappropriate to the purpose at hand, we hope to convey at least the timbre and the broad melodic line of his Jewish thought and thus to hear the polyphony of Judaism a little more fully than is often the case.

Overview

Rav Hutner was born in Warsaw in 1906 into a family prominently identified with Kotzk Hassidism (a highly intellectualized, rerabbinized, and idiosyncratic form of Hassidism). He was early recognized as so promising a student that he was literally snatched away to the yeshiva in Lithuanian Slobodka, famous for its combination of traditional talmudic studies with the ideas of the pietistic Musar (Morality) movement and with the philological analysis of sacred texts. Here he became a protégé of its head, R. Nathan Tsevi Finkel. In 1926 R. Hutner went to study in Hebron, where in turn he became a protégé not only of R. Avraham Yitzhak Kook, the famous first Ashkenazic chief rabbi of Palestine, mystical thinker, and supporter of Zionism, but also of the non-anti-Zionist R. Joseph Hayyim Sonnenfeld. R. Kook, together with many other acknowledged scholars, endorsed R. Hutner's first book, *Torat ha-Nazir* (Kovno, 1932), on Maimonides' "Laws of the Nazirites." After the riots of 1929 uprooted the Jewish community of Hebron, R. Hutner returned to Warsaw and then studied briefly at the University of Berlin. In 1932 he returned to Palestine, and in 1935 he came to New York. Here he founded and headed the rabbinical academy and seminary Mesivta R. Hayyim Berlin/Bet Midrash Gur Aryeh; eventually he also headed its sister institution in Jerusalem. For the rest of his life he commuted between the two schools, at one time finding himself on a hijacked plane in Jordan.[2] He died in Jerusalem in 1980.

On the practical side R. Hutner was a member of the Council of Torah Greats in Israel. This council, which is part of the Agudat Yisra'el organization, is regarded as the religious authority by so-called ultra-Orthodox institutions and individuals, and it plays a critical role in determining their attitudes toward such issues as Zionism, the legitimacy of the state of Israel, and secular education. Yeshivah R. Hayyim Berlin produces a large number of rabbis, rabbinic scholars, and especially teachers for Jewish schools. R. Hutner presided over Torah u-M'essorah, the Orthodox educational agency. Although for many years Hutner did not publish at all, at least under his own name, he eventually published a considerable body of writing, especially *Pakhad Yitzhak*, 8 volumes (Brooklyn, N.Y., 1951–1982), which is a compilation of his lectures at the academies on special occasions;

Haggahot 'al Perush R. Hillel [of Verona] *'al Sifre* (Jerusalem, 1961) and related studies;[3] a volume of letters and assorted writings, and occasional pieces. In his earlier years he even wrote a good deal of prose and poetry.

R. Hutner's theological and religious posture was formed by his checkered life story. He combined traditional rabbinism with Kabbalah and Hassidism, plus modernistic Jewish cultural and even non-Jewish philosophical concepts (the latter usually by silent implication). The confluence of all these tributaries in his thought results in a striking and both substantively and literarily felicitous body of teachings, which, therefore, together with his very strong personality, has had widespread impact.

In broadest terms, R. Hutner offers the following worldview. The "hidden God" reveals himself in the universe, specifically through the Torah and the people of Israel. The universe is thus dialectically both a product of God and essentially alienated from God, while esoterically the Unity looms beyond phenomenal multiplicity. Every Jew is potentially a fragment of the meta-physical truth within historic reality. History itself is defined by the evils of its distance from God and the manifold nature of this evil, consisting of sin, death, enmity to Israel and its Torah, and so on. Two forces impel history toward the restoration of the pri-mordial unity: the Jewish enactment of the Torah and the inner dialectic of the historic evils themselves. Indeed, the dénouement is imminent. Then the unity of Israel and of mankind in the Jewish truth will presage the restoration of the primordial unity of the hidden God.

Exemplifications

Lecture 21 of the volume of lectures on the Festival of Weeks presents a highly dialectical philosophy of the nature and destiny of man.

The one initial truth is that "man was created single" (viz., Adam). From this initial truth result two supplementary and contradictory truths: first, all mankind, Adam's descendants, are one and, therefore, we must love all other men as we love ourselves; second, each single human individual has absolute, ultimate value. This absoluteness and ultimacy are, however, countermanded by the reality of death, which was subsequently inflicted on the first man, because death overcomes both individual man and mankind. In effect, then, the reality of death falsifies and destroys no fewer than four truths: (1) it destroys the absolute and ultimate value of every human individual; (2) since the absolute value of every human individual stood in dialectical unity with the unity of mankind, the destruction of the former is also the destruction of the latter: (3) since the unity of mankind resulted in the love of fellow man equal with self-love, the destruction of that unity also destroys that love and is replaced by egotism; and (4) God causes only good—but death is clearly not good—and thus death also destroys the unity of God. Conditions 1–4 describe the reality of history. Within history, that is, in human experience, the singularity of man and of God are adumbrated as their extrahistorical, ultimate natures only insofar as they manifest themselves in their "countenances" (i.e., by their respective, unexchangeable uniquenesses). Since death produces all these consequences, only the abolition of death, that is, eschatological resurrection, can and will overcome them all. The belief in the resurrection is the full acknowledgment of the ultimate value of every human being in its total reality, body and soul. In other words, in "the end of days" (really "the after-days"), with the resurrection, the absolute value of every human individual, the real unity of mankind, the love of one another equal with the love of self, and, indeed, the unity of God Himself will be restored. The people of Israel is a historical anticipation of the eschatological kingdom, inasmuch as what one might call "resurrectability," that is, the fundamental inseparability of body and soul, has been built into it through the divine Torah. As R. Hutner expounds at length in other places,[4] the Day of Atonement is the actual enactment of this Jewish anticipation of the resurrection within historical time.

Notice should be taken of this typical unity of Jewish particularism and human universalism: on one hand, Israel is, indeed, the special and sui generis patrimony of God, and, on the other hand, the Jew is at least the potential actualization of the full humanity of all men, who will in the consummation of history share Israel's faith and fate.

Lecture 35 in the volume of lectures on Passover presents a highly dialectical exposition of the metaphysico-historical relations between Israel and Christianity.

R. Hutner is often concerned with the relations between Jews and non-Jews, as is shown by his frequent discussions of Noachitism, that is, Jewish universal law for non-Jews, which is long since an unusual interest in Jewish Orthodoxy. In his attitude toward Gentiles and Christianity in particular, he may fairly be said to pull no punches and to be quite hostile. (This, too, is commonly muted in most circles. R. Hutner's silence about all things Moslem is, however, eloquent.[5]) No doubt the experience of what is called "the Holocaust" has something to do with this.[6]

Several general observations need to be made before we can summarize this lecture. One is that in the text R. Hutner follows the traditional Jewish equation Esau = Edom = Rome = Christianity. Another is that he here deals with the claim that "We are Israel," as put forward by non-Jews, which refers to the classic Christian claim, based on the New Testament—for example, Romans 9, Galatians 6:16—and which underlies the bulk of Christian attitudes toward Jews and Judaism for the last two thousand years, that the church is "the true Israel" (according to the spirit, as the phrase goes). (R. Hutner, who was also quite "traditional" in being extremely wary of all secular, non-Jewish learning, especially for his students, clearly was familiar with Christian texts, as again, is common in that society.) Finally, it should be stressed that R. Hutner's philosophical methodology emphasizes the contradictions that characterize human and Jewish, and even divine, existence within history, toward the end of resolving and overcoming them messianically.

Jacob as the prototype of Israel and Esau as the prototype of Christianity are not only biblical brothers but, on this reading, even identical twins. R. Hutner's dialectical theory of the interconnectedness of similarity and difference, even opposition, arises from total identity. Thus Christianity, sprung from the identical source as Judaism, is the latter's most extreme opponent. When this opposition has been most fully actualized (antithesis), as is the case in the present historical era, then the total consummation of the synthesis must shortly come about. This is, on the basis of the present dominance of Christianity, the immediate triumph of Judaism is in the offing.

This classically dialectical process is actually exemplified in the liturgical gesture of praying with spread hands (as, say, in the priestly benediction in the synagogue to this day): originally a

Jewish posture of attack on idolatry (as in the incident in Moses' life Exod. 17:11), it was, paradoxically, adopted by the idolators and, therefore, abandoned by Jews. In the fast-approaching messianic kingdom and with the triumph of Judaism, however, it will return from its alienation by Christians into Jewish possession.[7]

In this lecture, as in the one previously summarized and in many other places, an extremely urgent messianism, one might almost say adventism, is conspicuous in R. Hutner's faith. The use of a traditional phrase like "soon in our days," extended exegeses of Daniel, and especially a poetic language of passionate chiliasm reveal this characteristic. The attention paid to Noachitism and the purity laws of Nazirites may also be connected with this messianic ambience. It is perhaps noteworthy as well that lecture 35 constitutes the last chapter, and thus in a sense the climax, of the volume of which it is a part, which is concerned with the Feast of Redemption. As was the case in lecture 21, the cleavage between the two metaphysical natures of God and man and their historical conditions is in this fashion transcended—"sublated," in the Hegelian phrase—in the eschatological estate.

As another specific example of R. Hutner's interpretation of classic Jewish texts in an extraordinarily complex and dialectical fashion so as to arrive at teachings that approach what almost all Jews would fear as heresy, we stop to consider his doctrine that on the Day of Atonement Jews attain the status of angels. It is best presented in lecture 5 in the volume on the Day of Atonement. (This matter is so delicate that R. Hutner uses extremely cautious language, and I, too, want to beat around the bush somewhat.)

The four-letter biblical name of God was pronounced as it is spelled by the high priest in the Temple in Jerusalem on the Day of Atonement, but ever since then this usage has been proscribed as exteme heresy. We, therefore, use all sorts of euphemisms for the name of God, even in prayer and in the reading of the Torah. The articulation of the "ineffable Name" is now reserved for the angels and, as far as human beings are concerned, for the messianic fulfillment. But on the Day of Atonement, while we live in almost an immaterial manner (not eating, solely devoted to repentance and prayer), and having cast away our past sins without yet having contracted new ones, "Israel are pure like the angels." Though we may still not actually pronounce the sacred Name, for we are only "like angels," not actual angels, we are at least to think it at the very time that we utter the euphemisms. Thus all Jews come close on this occasion to being high priests, and we bring God into the world not merely as "Lord" (the chief euphemism), who commands that the world be made into what it is supposed to be, but as "Being" (the grammatical root of the tetragrammaton); that is, at such times God and the world are as one. A bit of "the world-to-come" has briefly entered "this world." When we lapse back into normal human existence at the end of the holy day, we are ever more motivated to keep God's law and thus to bring about a universal and perpetual state in which all things are as they ought to be. For all present foretastes of the endtime cause the pious Jew to pursue without rest the full attainment of the end time because the belief in its coming is built into the very essence of the Jewish soul. In the passionate language that characterizes all of R. Hutner's frequent and lengthy eschatological expostulations he defines the endtime, on the basis of Rashi's famous interpreta-tion of the *sh'ma*-sentence (Deut. 6:4: "The Lord, who is our God now but not the God of the nations, will in the future be the one Lord"), as the time when, unlike all historical times, all the nations of the world will believe in and obey the one and only God, that is, "when all the forces of the nations of the world will pour into the treasure of the sanctity of the holy community of Israel."

One must be sensitive to the revolutionary implications of this doctrine. For one thing, in history the pronunciation of the four-letter Name is so identified with pseudo-messianism and heresy that even to talk about it strikes fear and horror in the Jewish heart. (Its use in modern Bible criticism is an entrenched offense.) For another, if and when the world is as it ought to be, it might seem that there will be nothing yet to be done, nor will we need any longer to be commanded to act one way or the other because we already will be such as to do whatever is right. What happens to the Torah under such circumstances (Jer. 31:33–34— "the new covenant," under which we will know God's will instinctively), unless it turns out that even angels and angelic men still have new, though different, tasks to perform?

With its highly unconventional and even dangerous character, this doctrine has considerable precedent in Jewish literature—in some sectors of kabbalistic mysticism and in the small Kotzk-Ishbitz-Radzin school of Hassidism.[8] Here another implication of this outlook is sometimes adumbrated, which appears on the margins of R. Hutner's thought, too. The dialectical march of providential history toward the messianic consummation also embraces evil and sin. Even these perform a function in accordance with God's plan, for how could anything happen that goes counter to divine omnipotence? Sin turns out, then, to be a human misunderstanding of behavior that is determined by God but wrongly intended by its human agent. The messianic perspective will provide the psychological therapy for such doubly misinterpreted past events.

How delicately and yet stunningly the Hassidic tradition of Kotzk is continued by R. Hutner can be illustrated in part of a lecture of his about Chanukkah, which extrapolates further the esotericism of the subject under discussion here.[9]

Perhaps the single most famous doctrine of the Kotzker Rebbe is the virtue and practice of silence: what is not said and cannot be said is at least as important as what is put in words. Says R. Hutner, without explicitly referring to Kotzk, a student who learns also from his teacher's silence is a better student than one who learns only from the teacher's words.[10] For one thing, a sage often has to keep some of his insights to himself, if only because his students might misunderstand him, if not leave him totally uncomprehended. This is also true of God Himself, the ultimate Teacher. His silence is at least as eloquent as His explicit revelations.

Talmudic history has it that the only three attributes we may predicate of the deity, and this only because Moses used them, "great, mighty, and awesome," were excised from the liturgy by Jeremiah and Daniel when they had to witness the destruction of the first Temple. Obviously God, who had at least permitted this event to happen, was not, or did not want to be seen to be, "great and mighty." The so-called "men of the Great Assembly," however, during the Second Jewish Commonwealth, restored those terms to the liturgy, where they remain, even after the destruction of the Second Temple. The rabbis justified their decree that the prophets' ordinance be set aside by basing themselves on the words of the Bible itself, in their willful interpretation: "Who is like unto Thee among the gods (*'elim*). To begin with, the rabbis read *elim* as *ilemin*—*the mute* in place of *the gods*, and then they exclaim: "Who is like unto Thee in keeping silent" and in also otherwise restraining Himself in the face of such provocations, for His own ultimate purposes! Thus God's silence here betokens His "greatness, might, and awesomeness." "Silence is a fence around wisdom" (Eccl. 5:1) also in God.

Indeed R. Hutner goes on, there are also degrees of silence. There is a silence within silence. If the present fate of Israel is worse than it was in past eras, as it is, then God's silence is correspondingly deeper, and He, literally *e silentio*, manifests His greatness the more. Indeed, our ongoing recitation of the three attributes of the deity synthesizes the original thesis of Moses' description of God and the prophetic antithetical silence about Him, in spoken words that also include our stunned silence. (In his early, more literary, writings, R. Hutner had held that thought requires but is also deformed by language and that song and prayer are then the synthesis of silent thought and of speech.)

As our final exemplification of R. Hutner's unusual and yet quintessentially traditional teaching, consider what he entitles "A Tract on Grace" (*kuntress haKhessed*) but what can more conventionally be called his ethics.[11]

The Jewish covenant is a covenant of grace, that is, God bestowing unmerited, gratis, benevolence on Israel. By dint of the Jewish obligation to imitate the deity, we are obligated to engage in gracious behavior toward our fellow men: by enacting moral grace "we create and bring into being the inner world of humanity, i.e., the image of God." "He (on the other hand) who does not practice deeds of loving-kindness (*g'milut khassadeem*) is like one who has no God." (Tr. *Idolatry* 17b). And as the prophet Amos proclaimed, Jews, because of their election, are then punished the harder for any deed less than divine. "There is a grammar of the punishment of the righteous that are in the environs of God."

Political Application

All that I have discussed until now may seem extremely abstract and metaphysical. Let us at least look at one important and controversial extension of such religious thinking—R. Hutner's attitude toward Zionism and the State of Israel.

It is almost universally blocked out these days that the large bulk of Jewish Orthodoxy in Europe, Palestine, the United States, and elsewhere opposed Zionism and the creation of a state until and even beyond 1948. Indeed, to this day there is certainly more anti-Zionist Orthodoxy than Reform or even assimilationist anti-Zionism—some of it extremely radical.

R. Hutner and his immediate followers have always tried to walk a very thin line on this question. His messianic adventism is, of course, the basic posture that, when translated into politics, can result in anti-Zionism: the Jewish people is a religious, not a secular, entity, and the redemption of Israel, including its ingathering in the Holy Land, is believed to be a divine, messianic event that must not be, cannot be, usurped by human, Jewish hands. Extreme Orthodox anti-Zionism (Satmer Hassidism, for example), therefore, combats Israel vehemently. Orthodox Zionism (the Mizrahi) regards the state as "the beginning of the blossoming of our redemption" and, therefore, cooperates with it as much as its religious outlook permits.

R. Hutner tries to take a stand somewhere between these two alternatives. I have noted that in the 1920s he was close to both the Zionist R. Kook and the anti-Zionist R. Sonnenfeld. At the same time, he opposed Zionist behavior in a famous controversy about Arab milk production.[12] In his analysis of the religious meaning of the destruction of European Jewry he pulls no punches in following a widespread anti-Zionist Orthodox view that much of prewar Zionist politics was responsible for the catastrophe that ensued, not to speak of modernist Jewish assimilation. R. Hutner used to like to tell the story that one day the Council of Torah Greats wanted to condemn the Satmer Rebbe for his hostility to the state, whereupon he, R. Hutner, told his colleagues the story of the lion in Noah's ark that bit him; he was tempted to kill the dangerous lion but restrained himself: it is the king of animals, and if you kill it its entire species will be wiped out, which would violate God's purpose in creation—and "the wise will understand." Furthermore, for example, in the lecture on praying with spread hands, R. Hutner reiterates the view widely held in traditional circles that the messianic restoration of the Holy Land to the possession of the Jewish people will and may come about only as the Second Jewish Commonwealth did, through the action not of Jews but of gentile rulers.[13] Redemption happens to those who are in exile.[14]

In another respect the intense "religiosity" of understanding Judaism and Jewish history in this way leads to conclusions that have typically been regarded as liberal or even Reform interpretations in the last two centuries. Thus the belief in the worldwide "mission of Israel" has tended of late to be mocked as supercilious and exaggerated universalism. In fact, R. Hutner teaches that the Jewish people can messianically return to the Holy Land only after it is able to say to God: "I have carried out Thy mission" (*'assitee shlikhutekha*).[15] And that mission consists of, on one hand, instantiating the life of the Torah in the world and, on the other, acting toward and with non-Jews in a manner that exceeds mere reciprocity.[16]

Conclusion

What we have briefly looked at sounds very different from what is usually heard in conventional Jewish pulpits, schools, and publications. There is much more on the same order. It presents a world that is filled with forces and events which probably strike most products of modern Jewish or non-Jewish education, of whatever level, as outlandish. It is, indeed, a mystical world. In it ordinary things and texts assume new meanings and ramifications, "a spiritual significance." The world suddenly is more interesting. Furthermore, this mysticism has at least two special character- istics: it is a highly intellectual mysticism so that it can be translated with relative ease into more conventional terms and usefully compared to standard worldviews; and a vast amount of the accumulated literature and practice of Judaism that has fallen into desuetude is brought back and given a new life. The hard core of millennial Jewish culture has been stated anew—"to perfect the world by means of the kingdom of God" through piety and morality.

Notes

1. I have drawn freely in this essay on previous studies of mine of R. Hutner: "Two Lectures of R. Isaac Hutner," *Tradition* 14 (Fall 1974), pp. 90–109; "Hutner," in M. Eliade, ed., *The Encyclopedia of Religion*, Vol. 6 (New York, 1986), p. 541; and "An Introduction to the Thought of R. I. Hutner," *Modern Judaism* (Fall 1985), pp. 235–77.
2. Now that R. Hutner is deceased I can say publicly that I am glad to have been useful in helping to bring about the release of the hijacked plane on which he and many other Jews were captured at a time when I did not know R. Hutner personally. When I later spent some time with him, this point was never mentioned.
3. See Hillel Goldberg, "Rabbi Isaac Hutner: A Synoptic Interpretive Biography," *Tradition* 22 (Winter 1987), n. 19. This article considers Hutner's life and spiritual development, though not always carefully enough.
4. See "Introduction to the Thought of R. I. Hutner," pp. 235–45.

5. Thus, after he had been in Arab captivity, many people wondered aloud why he never said anything even faintly hostile about his captors. For the Jewish superiority of Islam to Christianity see *Memorial Volume on the Late Author of 'Pakhad Yitzhak'* [Hebrew], ed. J. Buksboim (Brooklyn, N.Y., 1984), p. 271. In "Holocaust," *Jewish Observer*, October 1977, however, he ascribes a great deal of the responsibility for the destruction of European Jewry to the Mufti of Jerusalem and to "Easterners" in general.

6. R. Hutner forbade the use of the term *Holocaust*, and on one famous occasion he had other things of real importance to say on this subject, which immediately caused a furor: see "Holocaust," pp. 3ff., *Jewish Observer*, January 1978, and in the Yiddish and Hebrew press at the time; cf. Goldberg, "Rabbi Isaac Hutner," n. 37, and Irving Greenberg, "Orthodox Judaism and the Holocaust," *Gesher* (Yeshiva University) 7 (1979), pp. 55ff.

7. Lecture 33 in *Pachad Yitzchak* on the Feast of Weeks makes the same point briefly and very pungently. On the hassidic tradition about praying with raised hands see also R. Alexander Suskind of Grodno, *The Foundation of the Root of Worship* [Hebrew] (Nowy Dwor 1782/Jerusalem, 1965), chap. 1, "The Gate of Song—On Raising the Hands in Prayer."

8. For an English introduction to Kotzk Hassidism see Abraham J. Heschel, *A Passion for Truth* (Philadelphia, 1973). More familiarity with this trend in Hassidism is desirable if only to balance the facile popular perception of it, also spread by Martin Buber, as fatuously optimistic and anti-intellectual.

9. *Pachad Yitzchak* lecture 8, pp. 46–53 (1964). On page 49 there is an exposition of why the dispersion of Israel is providentially necessary.

10. Perhaps the repeated and strained use of the Kotzk motto-word *emeth—truth*, page 45, is a hint at the Kotzk connection here.

11. Appropriately enough, the volume for New Year's 1974, lectures 1–4 and section LXII in *Memorial Volume*.

12. See *Memorial Volume*, pp. 62ff., letter XLIII. (I have notes of a long conversation with R. Hutner in Jerusalem in February 1975, which makes his extremely critical stance toward Zionism and the State of Israel very clear. The reference ibid., p. 80, to an anonymous American professor is to me.) S. S. Shragai, "Redemption According to the Teaching of Ishbitz-Radzin," *Hassidism and Zion* (Hebrew), ed. S. Federbush (Jerusalem, 1963), distorts the picture not least for the purpose of co-opting it into Zionism.

13. Volume on Chanukkah (1974), p. 65.

14. Ibid., p. 108.

15. See e.g., volume on New Year's, pp. 47ff., volume on Day of Atonement, sections 7:2, 5, 8:14, 12:8, etc.

16. *Memorial Volume*, letter XLIII.

FOR FURTHER READING

Works by Isaac Hutner

Pachad Yitzchak ... (The Banner of Isaac—Torah Discourses on Matters of Faith and the Duties of the Heart), [Hebrew]. 8 vols. Brooklyn, N.Y., 1965–1982. These volumes contain the chief literary work of R. Hutner. It consists of collected lectures on the law, conceptual significance, and classical texts of the chief holy days one volume each on New Year's, Day of Atonement, Passover, Feast of Weeks, Tabernacles and Sabbath, Purim, and Chanukkah, plus one additional volume of collected letters and essays by him.

Sefer haZikkaron ... (Memorial Volume on the Late Author of 'Pachad Yitzchak'), [Hebrew]. Edited by J. Buksboim, Brooklyn, N.Y., 1984. This volume consists of the following sections: a short biography, legal novellae, letters and themes on Jewish thought, scholarly annotations to historical texts, and annotations to recent rabbinic authorities.

Haggahot ... (Notes on the Commentary by R. Hillel of Verona on 'Sifre'), [Hebrew]. Anonymous when first published. Jerusalem, 1961. This is a text, previously unpublished, by an early medieval authority on an halakic midrash (rabbinic Bible commentary for legal utility), with R. Hutner's explications.

"Holocaust." *Jewish Observer,* October 1977.

Works about Isaac Hutner

Ashkenazi, Léon, "Un enseignement sur le 'Chabat'." In *Tenth Anniversary Souvenir Journal.* Brooklyn, N.Y., 1966. R. Hutner on the Sabbath.

Goldberg, Hillel. *Between Berlin and Slobodka: Jewish Transition Figures from Eastern Europe.* Hoboken, N.J., 1989. Chapter 4, "Rabbi Isaac Hutner," pages 63–87, is an admiring yet critical overview of the life and work of R. Hutner in a sort of "Jewish psychohistorical" mode.

———. "Rabbi Isaac Hutner: A Synoptic Interpretive Biography." *Tradition* 22 (Winter 1987). An intellectual biography, with some interpretive speculation and implied criticism.

Schwarzschild, Steven S. "An Introduction to the Thought of R. Isaac Hutner." *Modern Judaism* 5 (Fall 1985), pp. 235–77. An analysis of R. Hutner's eschatology and its conceptual kinship with the neo-Kantian German-Jewish philosophical rationalist Hermann Cohen and with the present-day French-Jewish postphenomenologist Emmanuel Levinas.

———. "Two Lectures of R. Isaac Hutner." *Tradition* 14 (Fall 1974), pp. 90–109. Two lectures translated from the Hebrew, with an English introduction.

Louis Jacobs

ELLIOT N. DORFF

Synthesizing Tradition with Modernity

Jews face modernity in a variety of ways. Some embrace it so tightly that they let go of any connection with the Jewish tradition. In most cases, this is simply the result of a gradual drift away from Judaism, eventually concretized through intermarriage or other forms of assimilation; in some, though, it flows from a conscious rejection of the faith on ideological grounds. On the other end of the spectrum, some Jews reject as much of modernity as they can, closing off their minds, hearts, and sometimes even their bodies from the modern world. The more moderate members of this group study non-Jewish subjects in universities and work among other Jews and gentiles, albeit with some accommodations in their dress and work schedules; but when it comes to religion, they leave their world behind and think and act as if modernity has nothing worthwhile to say about Judaism. The more extreme members of this group reject the intellectual bifurcation that this accommodation requires and create closed communities in an effort to escape the influence of all people and ideas outside their enclave.

Because these positions are extreme, they are easy to formulate and recognize. One therefore may get the mistaken impression that they are the only alternatives with any ideological integrity. One may live either as a modern or as a Jew; anything else is an inconsistent, intellectually lazy, and perhaps even dishonest compromise. The truth, however, is that in this aspect of life, as in most others, the extremes are neither the only options nor the most intelligent or realistic. Intermediary positions, which take both ends of the spectrum seriously and seek to integrate them, may require more effort to articulate and embody in life, and they certainly demand more tolerance for uncertainty and pluralism; but they have the distinct advantage of facing up to the conflicting truths and values that characterize life, and they thus are more adequate, honest, and wise.

Louis Jacobs espouses such an intermediate interpretation of Judaism. His position is, indeed, a quintessential example of a philosophy of Judaism that combines an ardent commitment to the tradition with an uncompromising quest for truth. He articulates his approach in the very first paragraph of his first book on his own theology in striking language:

> There are three pitfalls to be avoided by Jewish Apologetics in its attempt to grapple with the problems raised by modern thought. It must not refuse to recognize the existence of the problem by rejecting, in the name of tradition, modern thought and all its ways as of the devil. It must not encourage that division of the mind in which incompatible ideas are allowed to exist side by side in water-tight compartments. Nor must it be desperately stampeded into postulating an artificial synthesis, a queer hybrid faith which both the adherents of traditional Judaism and representative modern thinkers would repudiate. A true Jewish Apologetic, eschewing obscurantism, religious schizophrenia, and intellectual dishonesty, will be based on the conviction that all truth, "the seal of the Holy One, blessed be He," is one, and that a synthesis is possible between the permanent values and truth of tradition and the best thought of the day.[1]

Jacobs forthrightly describes the struggles involved in being fully a Jew and fully part of the modern world, the strengths and weaknesses of the various ways of doing so, the uncertainties any thinking human being must entertain, and the epistemological status and value of faith. These discussions occur in works that are written clearly, thoughtfully, and passionately, the products of a master teacher. As one reads them, one appreciates not only Jacobs' broad knowledge of both general and Jewish thought but also his candor and sense of judgment. Indeed, one gets the sense that one is in the presence of someone who is not only learned and committed to Judaism but who is also sophisticated, intelligent, feeling, open, and authentic. One may not agree with everything he says, but Jacobs is clearly an attractive model for how to be Jewish in the modern world.

The Man and His Works

Louis Jacobs is an English rabbi, one of the few European rabbis affiliated with the American Conservative movement. Jacobs was born in Manchester and studied at the yeshivot of Manchester and Gateshead and at London University. After teaching for some time at the Golders Green Beth Hamidrash in London, he served as rabbi of the Central Synagogue in Manchester and, from 1954 to 1959, at the New West End Synagogue in London. From 1959 to 1962 Jacobs was a tutor at Jews' College in London, but he resigned when Rabbi Isidore Epstein retired as principal and Chief Rabbi Israel Brodie, who took over as acting principal, vetoed Jacobs' appointment as principal of the college because of his allegedly heterodox views. Brodie also blocked Jacobs' reappointment to his former post as rabbi of the New West End Synagogue. These events led to a violent controversy within British Jewry, with the *London Jewish Chronicle* strongly supporting Jacobs. Jacobs' followers seceded in 1964 from the United Synagogue, the organization of British Orthodox synagogues, and appointed Jacobs rabbi of the New London Synagogue, which they then founded, a post he has held ever since. In addition, over the years he has lectured at a variety of universities, most recently as a visiting professor at Harvard Divinity School.

Jacobs has published extensively in both theology and rabbinic literature. The theological works that describe his own position are, in chronological order, *We Have Reason to Believe* (London, 1957, 1962, 1965); *Faith* (London and New York, 1968); and *A Jewish Theology* (New York, 1973). In these books he discusses a wide range of topics including God, creation, evil, revelation, the authorship and nature of the Bible, the authority of Jewish law, sin and repentance, the chosen people idea, the attitude of Judaism toward other faiths, Jewish statehood, the messianic hope, and the hereafter.

In addition to these expositions of his own views, Jacobs has written more strictly scholarly works in theology and mysticism, including translations of Moses of Cordovera's *Palm Tree of Deborah* (London, 1960) and Dov Baer of Lubavitch's *Tract on*

Ecstasy (London, 1963); *Principles of the Jewish Faith* (London, 1964), an analytical study of Maimonides' creed; *Seeker of Unity: The Life and Words of Aaron of Starosselje* (London, 1966); *Theology in the Responsa* (London, 1975); *Hasidic Prayer* (New York, 1978); *Jewish Mystical Testimonies* (New York, 1978); and *A Tree of Life* (Oxford, 1984), an extensive analysis of how Jewish law adjusted to new circumstances over the centuries, the justifications given for such changes, and how Jewish law should be applied now. His scholarship extends as well to the area of rabbinics, in which he has written *Studies in Talmudic Logic and Methodology* (London, 1961); *TEYKU: The Unsolved Problem in the Babylonian Talmud* (New York, 1981); and *The Talmudic Argument* (Cambridge, 1984).

As one might expect of a person so learned and prolific, Jacobs has also written numerous articles in scholarly journals and anthologies on topics in the areas of his expertise—theology, mysticism, and rabbinics. What is perhaps more surprising and impressive for a scholar of his rank is the clarity and skill with which he has written books designed for a popular audience, including the five volumes on Jewish law, ethics, philosophy, mysticism, and exegesis in the Behrman House Chain of Tradition Series (1968–76); *Jewish Values* (Chappaqua, N.Y., 1980) and *The Book of Jewish Belief* (New York, 1984). These works demonstrate clearly that Jacobs is as much an educator as he is a scholar.

This chapter will focus on those works of Jacobs in which he articulates his own faith. I will concentrate on his approach to three topics that especially characterize his thought—God, revelation, and the hereafter.

God, Revelation, and Law

The foundation of traditional Judaism is belief in God. As Jacobs points out, during the biblical and rabbinic periods God's existence was taken for granted; only God's involvement in human affairs was subject to doubt. It was in the Middle Ages that rational proofs for the existence of God came into vogue, historically because of the influence of Greek philosophy at that time and philosophically because thinkers in each of the Western religions recognized that although they may differ on which revelation is authoritative, all people share the faculty of reason. Reason could therefore function as a common ground for making and proving religious claims. The claims in dispute, however, were generally not the existence of God, but rather secondary beliefs such as God's providence, attributes, and ability to effecutate miracles. God's existence was as evident to the medievals as to their predecessors.[2]

Later, however, Hume and Kant demonstrated that no argument constructed by a human being could possibly prove God's existence, for no human being can demonstrate that which is beyond human senses and intellect. Jacobs accepts that result openly, but says:

> To say this is not to surrender reason—this would be suicidal, for unreliable as the human reason may be it is the only instrument we have for testing truth—but a recognition, in the name of reason itself, that we must look beyond it for the apprehension of certain truths. In other words, a distinction must be drawn between *proof* and *conviction*—proof is one of the ways to conviction, but there are other ways too. So that the real question is not whether the existence of God can be proven but whether belief in His existence is overwhelmingly convincing.[3]

Other than proof, what are the ways to conviction applicable to God? He answers that question most fully in his book *Faith*, in which he devotes a full chapter each to the way of reason, the leap of faith, the way of experience, and the way of revelation-tradition.[4] In discussing these ways to conviction, we shall come to understand not only the grounds for his belief in God but also what he believes about revelation and its record, the Torah, and how he understands the authority and appropriate methodology of Jewish law. We shall also see a prime characteristic of his thought: rather than argue doggedly for exclusively one way of thinking about an issue, Jacobs learns from the many varied approaches Jewish sources and philosophers have suggested in creating his own synthesis.

The Way of Reason

The rational proofs, Jacobs suggests, have value even if they cannot prove God's existence. They should instead be taken as indications of, or arguments for, God's existence. Although each of them individually is insufficient to prove God, taken together they can provide convincing evidence for God's existence and nature in much the same way as scholars in all the empirical disciplines (including science) amass evidence to support a theory. Invalid proofs do not add credence to each other, but pieces of evidence, though insufficient in themselves, may together produce conviction (although not proof).[5]

Jacobs finds the reasoning in the cosmological and teleological arguments to be convincing.[6] Both the cosmological argument, which flows from the need to find an explanation for why anything exists, and the teleological argument, which stems from the need to explain the order we encounter in our experience of the world, posit a conscious, benevolent, powerful God as the cause of the existence and the order of the universe.

Since we can have "no idea of the nature of God" (or, as I would prefer to put it, no adequate idea), to posit God as the source of both the existence and the order of the universe "does not really enable us to understand how the world came into being" or was ordered, but it at least affirms the principle of explanation—that is, that there is *some* explanation, and that the human quest to seek explanations in the various areas of life is therefore well-founded. In ascribing existence and order to God, according to Jacobs, the theist affirms that mind is the ground of the universe and that all aspects of the universe can be explained, even if human beings do not or cannot know all of the explanations. In contrast, the alternative, which Jacobs variously describes as that of the "sceptic" or the "atheist," denies the existence of any explanation for the existence and order of the universe, and that is "contrary to all our experience, to the way we use our minds, to the constant quest for meaning and the principle of explanation which the sceptic himself shares." The alternative, in other words, is ultimately self-contradictory: "The Theist does, indeed, declare that he cannot understand how the explanation works but he stakes his life on the conviction that there is an explanation. The atheist can only say that he is prepared to live without any explanation, which only means that [he] belies himself. He offers and seeks for explanations for the individual phenomena of the universe while accepting that there is no explanation for the universe as a whole."[7]

Atheists presumably will want to affirm the ultimate rationality of the universe, either because they see no alternative or because their experience in using their minds to analyze, predict, and sometimes control their world has often proved to be successful, which would make no sense if the universe were ultimately irrational, if it followed no rules. Jacobs' argument for the existence of God thus rests on the belief shared by both theist and atheist that the world is rational, a belief that, he claims, is unfounded if one is atheistic. That is, he believes that the phenomenon of rationality itself demands the assumption of a primordial mind to initiate it.

But why cannot the atheist affirm the rationality of the universe without positing a God (mind) behind it? Because, says Jacobs, "how can mindless matter have produced [human] mind unless Mind was there from the beginning directing the whole process?"[8] Jacobs thus assumes a radical mind/body dualism; for him, mind and body are totally disparate entities, and therefore matter cannot, in and of itself, be reasonably expected to produce mind, whether human or divine. In a later work he correctly criticizes Maimonides for building his ethics on a fundamental dichotomy between body and soul, and he carefully warns against misinterpreting the "evil inclination" in rabbinic literature as a denigration of the body; on the contrary, he points out, the Torah was given precisely so that Jews would *not* need to escape from life but would direct their bodily as well as their mental energies toward accomplishing divine purposes.[9] That, of course, is in the ethical sphere, but one wonders why Jacobs does not carry out that view of an integrated body and soul into his metaphysics as well.

If he did, he would see that a similarly minded atheist might strongly assert the rationality of the universe while refusing to affirm the existence of a separate mind called God. Such a person would claim that the substance of the world was always composed of an integration of material and mental charcteristics, from which the material and mental features of the world as we know it sprang. Where that substance came from we do not know, but neither does the theist, who ascribes creation of the world to God without knowing how it was done. Indeed, Jacobs argues forcefully (and correctly) against taking the biblical or rabbinic descriptions of creation literally.[10]

None of the above constitutes an argument for atheism. It is rather a claim that what divides a religious perspective from a nonreligious one is not their respective positions on the rationality of the universe but their attitudes toward it. Atheists and agnostics deduce from the rationality of the universe the possibility to understand and exploit it; that may engender a profound appreciation for, maybe even a worship of, the ability of the human mind, which can accomplish these tasks. Religious people are also interested in analyzing nature and using it for their purposes, but they have an attitude of awe toward it and worship its Creator. In other words, the way of reason does not find God by claiming that God is the only explanation for the rationality of the universe, but rather that God is the only reasonable response to it. Indeed, in my view an important part of what defines a religious person is that he or she acknowledges the awesomeness of the fact of creation and its order and responds by worshiping its Creator. Religious persons are marked not so much by their knowledge as by their piety.

Ironically, Jacobs himself claims something similar in another place, but he does not see this as the outcome of the way of reason:

> The significance of the doctrine of God as Creator—and this is unaffected by any modern scientific theories—is that the whole universe is subordinate to Him, that He exercises control over and manages it, and that human beings hold their possessions in a stewardship deriving from Him. The Rabbinic doctrine of man as co-partner with God in the work of creation is relevant here. God gives man the skills with which to master the world (see Gen. 1:28), but man must not use his powers destructively but to further God's creative purposes. This is the importance of the sabbath in the Jewish scheme ... [and] the duty to procreate.[11]

Moreover, one of the indications of God listed separately from the way of reason in *We Have Reason to Believe* is "the urge to worship in the human breast [which] affords evidence of God's existence."[12] In *Faith*, Jacobs includes this idea in the chapter on the way of reason, but he denotes it as an argument separate from those based on the existence and order of creation, calling it "the argument from religious experience."[13] If one abandons a mind/body dualism, though, the import of the cosmological and teleological arguments reduces to his argument from religious experience, the one which I think is ultimately convincing.

Jacobs also briefly discusses the moral argument, which finds God in moral experience for lack of any other satisfactory basis for moral obligations that transcend societies. Once again, the explanatory value of theism for Jacobs is based on a strict mind/body dualism: "On the atheistic view there can be no standards 'out there' in the universe apart from man because apart from man there is only soulless, mindless matter." Atheists often behave morally, but that they do so indicates that the atheist, too, experiences moral standards "grounded in a reality other than and far greater than himself. And unless this Ground is God, it is difficult to see what else it can be."[14]

For many people, moral experience does indeed afford a road to God, but Jacobs is too quick to dismiss all of the nonreligious attempts to ground morality—particularly because the philosophical problems in religious theories of morality, though somewhat different from those in secular theories, are no less difficult. Jacobs thoroughly discusses one of the most important of those problems, the existence of evil,[15] but there are others. For example, if God is the source and sanction of morality, moral behavior may seem to collapse into pragmatic behavior designed to gain His rewards or avoid His punishments, but we commonly assume a distinction between moral and pragmatic action. Beyond such specific problems of a religious theory of morality, if Jacobs is to affirm the moral argument for the existence of God to the exclusion of all other theories of morality, he must supply a more careful consideration of the alternatives than he has in what he has written so far.

The Leap of Faith

William James, Søren Kierkegaard, and, among Jews, Martin Buber stress that religious faith is never simply a matter of intellectual assent. A living faith involves the totality of one's being; it is a reaching out to God in trust; it is a continuing relationship with God in which one's physical, mental, emotional, and conative faculties come to the fore at various times; it is a passionate affirmation of that which is true for me, even if that which is true for me cannot be objectively demonstrated to be true for all. God, for these people, is to be reached not by thinking about Him and His world but by encountering Him.

These characteristics of faith make it personal. They also make it similar to the relationships human beings have with each other.

To use James' example, we never know all the facts about the person we marry at the time of the wedding. The facts are not all in, and they will not be until the moment the marriage is dissolved, either through divorce or death. If we wait until the facts are all in so that we can make an intellectually certain decision, we have lost the opportunity to have the relationship. Therefore we must take the risk of leaping into a relationship if we are going to have one at all. The same, says James, applies to God.

Jacobs notes that this "existentialist" approach[16] has the strength of reminding us that reason is not enough, that religious conviction must involve not only "faith *that*" God exists and has a specific nature, but also "faith *in*" God.[17] Jacobs emphasizes, however, that the reverse is also true: a leap of faith without rational analysis is blind and can easily lead to credulity, superstition, cultism, and the like. Existentialists to their detriment tend to neglect or even disparage the role of reason in faith; a vibrant, true faith must include both reason and personal commitment.[18]

Jacobs does not explain, however, *how* reason is to interact with the leap of faith. Is reason primary, or is the leap primary? In other words, if reason finds the object to which one has leaped objectionable, does that make any difference? If so, does it simply raise questions, or does reason have veto power, as it were, over what constitutes an appropriate leap? What is the role of tradition in making that decision? Or does this depend on the individual? Jacobs is certainly correct in arguing for an integration of the ways of reason and existentialism, but we need more guidance in how this should take place.

The Way of Experience

Existentialists are opposed to a systematic, rationalist approach to God, but they use reasoned argument to elucidate their position and convince others of it. In contrast, those who adopt the way of experience, according to Jacobs, see faith as nonrational, based on a special kind of experience: "In the way of reason God is to be known in the same way as a proposition is known, through ratiocination. In existentialism God is to be known as a person is known, through encounter. In the way of experience God is to be known as beauty is known, through the use of a special faculty peculiar to itself."[19]

Jacobs describes two forms of experiencing God: apprehending God in the overpowering, awesome aspects of the universe, an approach described by Rudolf Otto in his book *The Idea of the Holy* but anticipated in some measure by the fifteenth-century theologian Joseph Albo; and coming to know God through an inward, mystical contact with Him. The former finds God in the holy, which includes, for Otto, the numinous, the ethical, and the rational. It is an awareness of an objective reality and not a mere feeling. The latter finds God through a variety of techniques of turning inward, away from the allegedly illusory world of concrete objects.

It is unfortunate that Jacobs never evaluates these claims. How, for example, does one know that one is experiencing God and not something else? Jacobs says that the fact that mystics of all traditions report similar experiences lends credence to their claims.[20] Does that mean that all traditions apprehend the same godhead and only describe it and its implications differently, or is the God of Israel unique? Jacobs asserts that God has revealed Himself to people of other religions and that Jews can learn from the classical texts of other faiths and from secular works, but there is more truth in Judaism.[21] How does he know that? Or does the way of experience ultimately reduce to an existential leap of faith—or, perhaps, a personal decision, in the mode of James, to believe in *x* rather than *y*?

In addition to these questions of identifying an experience as one of God, there are questions concerning the character of the experience. For example, since, for Otto, the holy includes the rational, why does Jacobs say that the way of experience is nonrational? More broadly, Jacobs asserts that although it is impossible to comprehend God's nature, "we do know that it is a nature compatible only with goodness, wisdom and power and totally incompatible with evil, folly and weakness."[22] How does he know that? And are there not experiences of God other than the ones he describes? The way of experience to God is a crucial one, but one fraught with questions that need to be addressed.

The Way of Revelation-Tradition

Jews traditionally learned about God primarily through the Torah, that is, the Pentateuch, and, in the more extended meanings of the word *Torah*, the rest of the Hebrew Bible and rabbinic interpretations and amplifications of those texts throughout the ages. Even those medieval Jewish philosophers who stressed the role of reason in religion often claimed that reason itself demanded that the Jew use the Torah as a source of knowledge, for its crucial events (especially Sinai) were, according to its own account, witnessed by more than 2 million people (six hundred thousand households). Modern biblical criticism, however, has cast severe doubts on the traditional belief that the text of the Torah is a verbatim and unique record of God's word at Sinai. Instead, the picture it paints—based on literary analysis, archaeological evidence, and studies of comparative religion, language, and law—is of a text edited together from a variety of sources from different times and places.

Jacobs' problems with Chief Rabbi Brodie in England stemmed chiefly from his endorsement of the methods and results of modern biblical (and Talmudic) criticism. Fundamentalists such as Brodie assume that if the Torah is not believed to be an exact record of the verbal revelation of God, it loses its cognitive and legal authority. Jacobs goes to great lengths to combat this view. He stresses the need to be intellectually honest about the classical texts of the tradition, even if that requires altering our understanding of the way they were composed and became the canon. At the same time, he emphasizes that classical Jewish texts like the Bible, Talmud, Midrash, and codes remain authoritative because Jews and many others continue to hear the word of God in them. The evidence for the divine nature of these texts, then, derives from their ability to engender encounters with God for the people reading and living by them together with the longevity of the Jewish people committed to them:

> What guarantee therefore have we that the tradition is reliable even in its basic contention that there is a God who has revealed Himself to man? The answer ... is not a matter of simply relying on an ancient tradition but of hearing for ourselves the great echoes of the original series of encounters between God and man as recorded in that tradition....
>
> It is exceedingly difficult, if not impossible, to account for the lofty teachings of the Hebrew prophets, the civilizing influence of the great Law of Moses, the history of a small people who found God and brought Him to mankind, the Sinaitic revelation itself and the spiritual power these books continue to exercise over men's souls, unless

Israel really met with God and recorded in immortal language the meaning of that encounter. We can be skeptical of individual details in the Bible. We can dwell on the numerous parallels with Egyptian, Babylonian and Assyrian *mores*. We can point out the striking resemblances between Hebrew poetry in the Bible and Canaanite hymns in praise of the pagan gods. We are forced to recognize, to a degree quite beyond the imagination of our ancestors, the human element in the Biblical record. What cannot be seriously doubted is the 'something else', which has ensured that this and no other collection of books has become the sacred Scripture of a large proportion of mankind; that there are living Jews who regard themselves as the heirs to the Bible and no living Babylonians, Canaanites and Assyrians; that there is a Voice which speaks here in promise of great vision, of dreams of world peace, of holiness, justice and mercy, of freedom and the unique worth of each individual as a child of God....

For all our recognition of the dynamic rather than static quality of the tradition, the basic belief that it is all the work of God in co-operation with the humans who sought Him can reasonably be said to be based on experience, the experience of the prophets and law-makers in the first instance and the later experience of sages, thinkers and undistinguished people who live by the great truths. The existence of the Jews does explain the existence of God. The Jews are the most powerful proof for God's existence. There is still great power in the appeal to tradition.[23]

Just as the Bible remains divine for Jacobs despite literary and historical analysis of it, so too do Jewish observances retain their divine character and authority: "this approach in no way invalidates the observance of Jewish practices. These derive their authority from the undeniable fact that they have provided Jews with 'ladders to heaven' and still have the power of sanctifying Jewish life in accordance with the Jewish ideal; because of this we recognize that it was God who gave them and it is His will that we obey when we submit to the Torah discipline."[24]

These paragraphs are quoted at length because they articulate the foundation of Jacobs' philosophy. They speak to some of the critical question posed earlier concerning the leap of faith and the way of experience. We now see why Jacobs thinks that the Jewish believer has grounds to identify the object of his leap or experience as God: ancient Jews came into contact with God in the ways described in the Bible and rabbinic literature; the contemporary Jew identifies with their experiences and relives them in praying, thinking, and living as a Jew; and this chain of believing Jews would never have survived if it were based on folly or illusion.

Jacobs also differentiates and rank-orders experiences of God in the various philosophical and religious traditions: Judaism is supreme, it appears, because of its widespread influence. Both of these aspects of Jacobs' thought—his faith that the object of Jewish experience is indeed God, and his belief in the epistemological supremacy of Judaism—are based on his judgment concerning the worth of the content of the Jewish, in contrast to other traditions, and the evidence of Judaism's longevity and influence. Jewish commitment, for Jacobs, is thus not simply a matter of accident of birth or individual tastes; it is a function of ultimate value commitments and objective criteria.

One can now also understand that Jacobs is at once committed to the divine authority of Jewish law and to its ongoing development for both historical and theological reasons. Historically, observance of Jewish law has characterized what it has meant to be a Jew perhaps more than anything else, and yet its content has often changed to meet new circumstances and new moral sensitivities, as Jacobs documents thoroughly in his book *A Tree of Life.* Theologically, the experience of God is an ongoing one, and Jews as a people must respond to that experience through continued practice of Jewish law and adjustment of it occasionally when necessary. Jews must seek God through observance and listen for God as they act. Neither behavioristic obedience to the law as formulated in the past nor abandonment of its practice is historically or theologically authentic for a Jew.[25]

Jacobs' discussion of God illustrates a feature of his thought mentioned earlier as one of his chief strengths: he does not rely on one approach alone but learns from many theories in creating his own synthesis. With respect to God, he understands the four ways to Him as not only philosophically complementary but developmentally so. It is not, as he puts it, "as if the would-be believer goes shopping in the market for ways to God." Most believers use several or even all of them at various stages of their lives. In one's early years, religious faith is generally a matter of family and communal tradition. During one's teens and twenties, when one questions many things about one's background, the way of speculation comes to the fore. The existentialist emphasis on involvement or the way of experience eventually supplements and moderates the purely intellectual approach, which, even if convincing, leads to a bare assent to God's existence with little religious vitality and less personal concern. Even so, "the way of reason shows how belief in God affords the most satisfactory explanation of existence. Thus the ways converge to produce complete conviction."[26]

The Hereafter

The aspect of Jacobs' thought that may be the most surprising to modern readers is his firm conviction that human life continues after death, that there is a hereafter. Contemporary Jews tend to think of Judaism as decidedly this-worldly. Jacobs does not deny Judaism's strong commitment to this life; on the contrary, he says that "there is something sublime in the persistent refusal of Jews to turn their back on life, to refuse to give up the struggle to establish the Kingdom of Heaven on earth." He affirms, however, that the doctrine of an afterlife is "inextricably woven into the fabric of Judaism," and "no really spiritual interpretation of Judaism is possible without it."[27]

He goes further: he says that Jews who affirm immortality only in the sense that one's thoughts live on in others or that one's life is continued by one's descendants are engaging in "a complete travesty of any recognizable version of traditional Judaism." He says this although he recognizes that most of the Bible speaks of immortality in those terms.[28] The few biblical sources that do talk about a life after death contradict each other, some affirming and some denying it. Judaism, however, rests on the rabbinic interpretation and expansion of the Bible. The rabbis (Pharisees) most definitely did believe in a world to come, and "by no stretch of the imagination can the persistence of our ideas in the lives of those we leave behind on earth be considered as 'us.'" Consequently, to be a traditional Jew means, in part, to believe in a world to come in one or both of two somewhat conflicting senses entertained by the rabbis: resurrection of the dead person at some future time or the eternal life of the person's soul beyond the death of the body. Jacobs believes the latter.[29]

Jacobs is not satisfied, though, with simply citing tradition; consistent with his general methodology, he opens the issue to question and adduces philosophical reasons to believe in life beyond bodily death. This involves, first, removing two objections to the belief, one moral and the other metaphysical.

Those who deny an afterlife on moral grounds worry that concentration on an afterlife will lead to indifference to the needs of this world. Jacobs concedes that that is logically possible and perhaps true of other religions, but he demonstrates that Judaism has maintained an active commitment to this life while believing in a world to come.[30]

The metaphysical objection concerns the connection between body and soul. In our experience, bodily injury can negatively affect the mind, emotion, and will, but, Jacobs points out, that only indicates that *in this life* the soul depends on the body and interacts with it. It does not prove that the soul cannot exist without the body in some other form of human existence, just as human life on the moon requires a special space suit which is inappropriate on earth. Immortality of the soul is therefore at least possible.[31]

Moreover, says Jacobs, belief in a theistic God should induce one to affirm a life after bodily death. An omnipotent, *benevolent* God would not frustrate human values and hopes by restricting their scope to the brief span of human life: "The strongest argument for immortality is provided for the theist by his basic theistic affirmation. Can it be believed that God has created only to destroy, that all man's hopes and dreams of a higher life are doomed to frustration? ... Surely the idea that man's deeds have eternal significance is not to be treated lightly as a kind of optical belief or pious opinion."[32] God's justice also requires life after death so that the just can get their proper reward and the evil their proper punishment. Jacobs therefore believes that the good soul attains a state of Heaven and the bad is punished by falling into a condition we call Hell—although he is careful to state that Heaven and Hell are not places but conditions of the soul.[33]

Jacobs complains about the "dogmatism" and "frightening certainty" of medieval views of life after death.[34] When describing his own view, he notes that no human being can with reason know what happens in a life after death.[35]

One wonders, though, whether the same must not be said with regard to its very existence. If such a life does exist, God's benevolence and justice can more easily be reconciled with the fact that in this life sometimes the good suffer and the evil prosper, but is philosophical consistency ever enough to affirm a fact? Jacobs himself believes that the problem of evil can only be solved in small measure,[36] and his grounds for believing in a life after death are tightly woven to the need to keep God good and just despite the existence of evil (which, for these purposes, includes the frustration of worthy human desires).

Therefore, the lack of evidence available to human beings concerning a life after death and the need to let the problem of evil go ultimately unresolved suggest that the more plausible course—and the more consistent one for Jacobs—would be to say the same thing with regard to the existence of a life after death as we must say about its nature: we simply do not know. Yet although we may not share the biblical certainty that reward and punishment will be meted out in this life, at least on a communal level, we do have patent evidence of the other elements of the biblical view of the afterlife—specifically, the ongoing influence of one's life, even after death, on others, most especially on one's descendants. The most reasonable position, then, and ironically the one most consistent with some of Jacobs' own positions, would be to affirm these elements of the biblical view and remain agnostic about a personal life after death.

That, of course, would remove much of the assurance we would like to have about the meaningfulness of our efforts for good in a world where we often do not witness their success. It would thus require greater faith, for a Jew would then be called upon to observe God's law without certainty of reward. Rabbinic comments about a life after death would still be meaningful, for they are a vivid assertion of the importance of Jewish values as a part of the very structure not only of this universe, but of the one to come. The existence and nature of a world to come would, however, be kept in abeyance by the modern Jew while he or she remained deeply committed to Judaism for its own inherent worth as a pattern of life and for its ability to link the Jew with God. That could be a very spiritual Judaism, although perhaps not in Jacobs' sense of "spiritual."

These reservations notwithstanding, one cannot help but sympathize with the reasons why Jacobs takes the stand he does. Life certainly does have more meaning, and sacrifices make more sense, if not only our efforts and values but we ourselves in some way last beyond our bodily lifetime. Believing that may also help us to face death—both our own and those of our loved ones. Moreover, the existence of a life after death in which our moral accounts are rectified may not explain the persistence of evil in this life, but it does reconcile evil with the theist's belief in the goodness and justice of God. And finally, one who believes in either resurrection or the eternity of the soul carries on the rabbinic tradition in this matter. Therefore, even if one is too skeptical to affirm a life after death in the literal sense in which Jacobs does, one can readily appreciate Jacobs' forthright defense of the doctrine, and the very fact that he courageously opened up the matter for discussion once again among contemporary Jews.

Tradition and Modernity

Modern philosophers of Judaism often either assume the authority of the tradition and then try to give it a modern cast, or they take the tenets of modernity for granted and adopt whatever parts of the tradition they find to be compatible with it. Jacobs is one of the few who take both tradition and modernity seriously. And he does so with depth of learning in both Jewish and general sources, with clarity of expression, with candor, and with a keen sense of analysis and judgment.

Notes

1. Louis Jacobs, *We Have Reason to Believe* (1957; rpt. London, 1965), p. 9.
2. Jacobs makes this point in *Faith* (New York, 1968), p. 45.
3. *Reason to Believe*, p. 26; cf. pp. 23ff.
4. In *We Have Reason to Believe*, Jacobs lists these and also briefly alludes to the urge to worship, the evidence of heroic people motivated by their belief in God, and the existence of the Jews as evidence for God; see pp. 28, 29, 34.
5. *Reason to Believe*, p. 28; *Faith*, pp. 46, 60. Jacobs, on the first page cited, seems to object to this normal usage of the word *evidence*: "Granted that the proofs carry no weight as *evidence*, they are *indications* and as such have the power of supplementing each other."
6. He does not, however, put much store in the ontological proof, even as an argument. See *Faith*, pp. 46–48.
7. Ibid., pp. 49–50; cf. p. 60.
8. Ibid., p. 50.
9. Louis Jacobs, *A Jewish Theology* (New York, 1973), pp. 238, 244–46.
10. *Reason to Believe*, pp. 82–86; *Jewish Theology*, chap. 7, esp. pp. 91–98.
11. *Jewish Theology*, p. 97.
12. *Reason to Believe*, p. 28.
13. *Faith*, pp. 61–62.
14. Ibid., p. 61.
15. *Reason to Believe*, chap. 5; *Faith*, chap. 7; *Jewish Theology*, chap. 9.
16. James is not usually classified as an existentialist for lack of sufficient personalism and individualism, but this essay is perhaps the most articulate exposition of the individual's right to believe, as Jacobs notes; see *Faith*, p. 66.

17. He discusses this distinction at length in chapter 1 of *Faith.*
18. Ibid., pp. 72–73, 75.
19. Ibid., p. 80.
20. *Reason to Believe*, p. 27.
21. *Jewish Theology*, pp. 289–91.
22. *Faith*, p. 35.
23. Ibid., pp. 107–9. See also *Jewish Theology*, chap. 14.
24. *Reason to Believe*, p. 73.
25. I discuss Jacobs' approach to Jewish law at greater length and in comparison to that of others in my *Conservative Judaism: Our Ancestors to Our Descendants* (New York, 1977), pp. 110–57, esp. pp. 114–15 and 136–43.
26. *Faith*, p. 109.
27. *Reason to Believe*, p. 118.
28. He understands the biblical view as a conscious reaction against the otherworldly emphasis of all other Near Eastern religions, but it may also be motivated by the biblical expectation that reward and punishment would come in this life, at least on a communal level.
29. *Faith*, pp. 191–93; *Jewish Theology*, pp. 307, 319–22, and the rest of chapter 23 for an excellent description of the various forms of Jewish belief in an afterlife through the ages.
30. *Reason to Believe*, p. 120; *Faith*, pp. 126–34.
31. *Faith*, pp. 192–93; cf. *Reason to Believe*, p. 123, where he uses instead an analogy to electricity.
32. *Jewish Theology*, p. 318.
33. Ibid., pp. 318–22.
34. Ibid., p. 312.
35. Ibid., p. 321; *Reason to Believe*, pp. 120–21.
36. *Jewish Theology*, chap. 9; *Faith*, chap. 7.

FOR FURTHER READING

Works by Louis Jacobs

Jacobs' Theology and Philosophy of Jewish Law

Faith, New York, 1968.

A Jewish Theology, New York, 1973. These are Jacobs' most recent expositions of his own beliefs. *Faith*, the more philosophical of the two, describes the grounds for faith, the objections to it, and the life of faith. *A Jewish Theology* is, as the title indicates, more strictly a work in theology rather than philosophy. It describes his own integration of Jewish and modern ideas in his understanding of the attributes of God, worship, revelation, Torah and mitzvot, sin and repentance, reward and punishment, Jewish peoplehood and statehood, and views of the Messiah and the hereafter.

A Tree of Life, Oxford, 1984. In this book, Jacobs articulates his philosophy of Jewish law. Drawing amply from Jewish legal sources, he explains how he understands the origins, methods, and development of Jewish law so as to regain in our time "a non-fundamentalist Halakhah."

Studies in Jewish Mysticism and Theology

Translations, with introductions and notes:
   a. Moses Cordovero, *The Palm Tree of Deborah*, New York, 1960.
   b. Dobh Baer of Lubavitch, *On Ecstasy* Chappaqua, New York, 1963, 1982.
   c. *Seeker of Unity: The Life and Words of Aaron of Starosselje*, New York, 1967.
These books present translations of three key works in classical and modern Jewish mysticism, together with notes and introductions.

Hasidic Prayer, New York, 1973. This is an exploration of the nature of Hasidic prayer, including its methods (preparations, gestures, and melodies), its aims (contemplation, ecstasy, inspiration), and its relationship to more standard, Jewish prayer.

Jewish Mystical Testimonies, New York, 1977. Rabbi Jacobs edited and, in most cases, translated these mystical sources from the Jewish tradition, ranging from Ezekiel to the twentieth century. They provide a good collection in English of primary sources in Jewish mysticism.

Theology in the Responsa, London and Boston, 1975. This is a fascinating study of matters of belief treated in the genre of legal decisions, with all of the clarity and decisiveness that genre requires. Among other people, it demonstrates the strong integration of Jewish belief and practice.

Principles of the Jewish Faith, Northvale, New Jersey, 1964, 1988. A thorough study of Maimonides' Thirteen Principles of Jewish Faith, this book examines the grounds for each belief, the problems associated with each, and a comparison to the ways in which other Jewish theologians have interpreted and defended these beliefs.

Studies in Rabbinic Law

TEYKU: The Unsolved Problem in the Babylonian Tamud, London, 1981. Jacobs explores the use of "Teyku"—the word used in rabbinic literature when a problem is left standing—to determine the circumstances under which the rabbis did not feel the need to resolve an issue. This illuminates the society for which they were functioning as teachers and judges.

The Talmudic Argument, Cambridge, 1984. 220 pages. This is a thorough, but clear, study of the logic used by the sages of the Talmud to arrive at their conclusions.

Books about Judaism designed for a Popular Audience

Jewish Values, Hartford, 1960, 1969; Chappaqua, New York, 1980. A clear exposition of some important Jewish values, with many applications to modern life and without being preachy, this book can profitably be used with teenagers as well as adults.

The Book of Jewish Belief, New York, 1984. This is a clear, brief, but thoughtful description of basic Jewish beliefs, practices, values, institutions, and literature.

The Behrman House "Chain of Tradition" series:
a. *Jewish Law*
b. *Jewish Ethics, Philosophy and Mysticism*
c. *Jewish Thought Today*
d. *Jewish Biblical Exegesis*
e. *Hasidic Thought*

This is a series of books, published by Behrman House, designed for teenagers and adults who want to be exposed to sources of the Jewish tradition directly. In each of these books, Jacobs translates important Jewish sources of the genre and origin indicated in the title and gives explanations, interpolated into the translations, to make the source at hand clear and interesting to the modern reader.

Works about Louis Jacobs

On His Rift with the British Chief Rabbi
Encyclopaedia Judaica, 9:1236–37

Maybaum, Ignaz. *Judaism* 13 (Fall 1964): 471–77.

Sherman, Alfred. *Commentary* 38 (October 1964): pp. 60–64.

Temkin, Sefton. *Conservative Judaism* 18 (Fall 1963): 18–34.

On Jacobs' Philosophy
Dorff, Elliot N. *Conservative Judaism: Our Ancestors to Our Descendants*, pp. 114–15, 136–43. New York, 1977.

Katz, Steven T. *Jewish Philosophers*, p. 249. New York, 1975.

Yeshayahu Leibowitz

DAVID HARTMAN

The Jewish world knows Buber, Rosenzweig, Mordecai Kaplan, Heschel, and Soloveitchik as leading intellectual figures who have shaped modern religious thought. By contrast, little is known about Leibowitz outside of Israel. In Israel itself, however, he may be the best-known Jewish philosopher and religious thinker.

Leibowitz's thinking is indeed deeply anchored in the Israeli context. He does not address himself abstractly to the problems of religion in modern society in general but conducts an ongoing critique both of Israeli society in the light of Judaism and of Judaism in the light of the Jewish revolution constituted by the very creation of Israel. This dual thrust partly explains the paradoxes in his writings. Leibowitz is a Jewish patriot who always despised the Jewish life in exile he saw in Europe. Yet there is hardly a more severe critic of any manifestation of chauvinism by the Israeli establishment. When he denounces trends in Israel, therefore, it is not with the moral pathos of an alienated Jewish universalist intellectual but with the conviction of an unwavering Zionist who fought in Israel's war of independence and is proud of his more than twenty grandchildren all living in the land.

Another paradox is that Leibowitz is a strictly observant Jew who has not greatly influenced the majority of the religious community but who awakens notable interest in secular circles that would otherwise be very averse to hearing moral lessons delivered by anyone wearing a *kippah*. Despite his age, his energy matches the endless demands upon him as a public speaker, not only before his academic colleagues but at every level of society.

From Dan to Beersheba, Leibowitz is invited to speak to all audiences at all times. Although the polemical tone of his statements and ripostes can be biting, he maintains an underlying respect for every group, be it academics, professionals, or laborers, Jewish or Arab.

In his academic pursuits, too, Leibowitz displays a versatility that many can envy. The university knows him for his serious scientific research and as a teacher of the philosophy of science. Thousands listen to his regular radio lectures on *Pirkei Avot*, Maimonides, and other Jewish sources. He has been deeply involved in adult education and was for years the editor of the *Hebrew Encyclopedia.*

Every complexity and ambivalence of Israel, be it the moral and religious problematics of the country, the struggle to write a new chapter in Jewish history, the conflicts between messianists and antimessianists, religious and secular, territorial maximalists and minimalists, the whole dynamism and confusion of Israeli intellectual and spiritual life will be found reflected in the thought of Yeshayahu Leibowitz.

The Challenge to Judaism

Leibowitz is not alone in seeing in the creation of Israel a fundamental challenge to Judaism. His unique formulation of the challenge reflects his view on the nature of Judaism itself. He sees Judaism as fundamentally a communal frame of reference. Its prime concern is not with saving the soul of the individual but with providing a way of life whereby a community can express its total commitment to serve God.

What has made Jews different from other nations, according to Leibowitz, is not their theology. Other religions share basic assumptions of Jewish monotheism, eschatology, and the like. Nor is it their Bible, which has also been adopted by the Christians. What has made them unique was the halakah that governed their traditional way of life.

The essential point for Leibowitz is that the primacy of halakah in Judaism is not a theological judgment but an empirical description of what in fact occurred in Jewish history. He points out that the medieval Jewish community could tolerate sharply conflicting theological tendencies in its midst, but there could be no comparable toleration of conflicting halakic practice. Those who held minority halakic views could at most state them, but must conform to the established majority outlook.

Such was the character of the Jewish community down to the beginning of Jewish emancipation at the end of the eighteenth century. From then on, the Jewish community's self-understanding began to break down, giving rise to what Leibowitz sees as one of the crucial questions for Judaism in the modern world. The invitation to assimilate completely into the surrounding non-Jewish culture provided competition to the traditional self-understanding of the Jew. Some Jews sought to meet that competition by amending or even abandoning much of halakah, though preserving the synagogue as a place of worship. Secular Zionism provided an even more powerful mode of competition because it was an ideology that aimed to redefine the Jewish people in wholly nonreligious terms as a national political community.

The challenge to Judaism in Israel is therefore very different from the challenge in the western Diaspora. In the latter, assimilation threatens to dissolve the Jewish ethnic group, absorbing the Jews in such a way that they are no longer identifiable as Jews. In Israel, that threat does not exist. Instead, there are two competing consciously Jewish frameworks: one revolutionary, which claims to continue Jewish history through a radical transformation of Jewish society and self-definition, the other religious, which maintains that the Jewish community is doomed to disaster if it abandons its religious roots.

Jews in the Diaspora can argue that Judaism is the necessary instrument for maintaining their identity as a particular community. That argument loses its vigor in the Israeli context. Hanging on to religion merely as an instrument for perpetuating Jewish identity makes no sense in a society whose total national political framework already gives Jews an anchorage for their identity.

Leibowitz's constant argument against the secular option for defining the continuity of Jewish history is that it is a distortion of the historical framework of the Jewish people. His argument not only springs from the framework of faith but also rests on empirical fact. To claim continuity with the historical Jewish people and yet abandon halakah is a falsification of what actually happened in Jewish history. Consequently, he disagrees both with the religious

Zionists, who have joined the revolution to build political state-hood, and with the secular Zionists, who claim to continue Jewish history although abandoning the halakic framework.

The Critique of the Religious Zionist Community

For Leibowitz the essential subject of Judaism is not the individual but a community. Judaism is not meant to offer a way in which the individual can overcome the problems of finitude, sin, and death and find eternal salvation; it is a manner whereby a community expresses its unconditional commitment to worship God.

Consequently, Leibowitz well understands the motivation of that sector of the religious community which sees the Zionist decision for political independence as an act of Satan. The laws of Judaism, as they see them, require Jews to live under the rulership of alien powers for as long as the era of exile is not replaced with the era of the Messiah. Unlike those religious conservatives, however, Leibowitz was one of the religious Jews who joined the political revolution to reestablish an autonomous self-governing Jewish community. For him, no event in the last fifteen hundred years can compare with this bold move by Jews to alter their political fate in the darkest period of Jewish history.

Leibowitz is fully aware that this move was not taken out of a religious impulse. The majority of Zionists did not found the state to establish the rule of the Torah in their lives. It was, he believes, a purely natural decision of an oppressed community to abandon the condition of alienation and subservience to foreign political powers. This nationalistic response was legitimate and healthy. It did not have a religious significance because it did not grow from the intention of realizing a religious ideal. Both the observant and the secular Jews who participated in creating Israel did so out of the same natural impulse of patriotism.

Yet this is not the view of most of the religious Zionist community. They see a redemptive process working itself out in the reborn Jewish state. They are prepared to participate in this secular revolution because they can give it a religious meaning. To them, Leibowitz poses the following question: how can you participate religiously in statehood and simultaneously give allegiance to a halakah that in no way authorized or prepared the religious community to assume the role of responsibility for the maintenance of the well-being of a total political community? What religious perspective is needed to give integrity to the decision of the Jewish religious community to embrace political statehood?

Far too many in the Israeli religious establishment, Leibowitz claims, refuse to realize the dishonesty of transferring to Israel the diaspora practice of relying on nonmembers of the observant Jewish community to provide essential services. The laws of the Sabbath as they crystallized in the context of exile make it impossible for observant Jews to maintain a police force in the modern world or to run a foreign service that is available to respond to crisis situations that may occur on the Sabbath. For Sabbath observers to participate in the Israeli community, they have implicitly to hope that the Jewish state will always have a sufficient number of Jews who will violate the laws of Judaism.

This is seen by Leibowitz as a distortion of the intention of Judaism. If maintaining their Judaism requires the religious community to become parasitical upon a majority of the Jews disloyal to Judaism, this Judaism has lost its religious integrity. Essential to Judaism is not only that the individual maintains loyalty to the Sabbath and worships God through a disciplined life as an individual but also the desire that the whole Jewish community remain faithful to Judaism as well.

Consequently, Leibowitz ceaselessly and tirelessly argues against all attempts at making the religious community merely a pressure group that guards the interests of its own particular sector. He argues against freeing yeshivah students and religious girls from service in the army. He opposes attempts to keep religious Jews out of the police force and other life-saving departments which are needed for the maintainance of a total state.

All this is morally obscene and creates among observant and nonobservant Jews alike a distorted understanding of what Judaism should be in the modern world. Leibowitz offers a Jewish categorical imperative for the religious community: act in such a way that you could wish all Jews to act in a similar fashion. Halakah obligates community. The decision how one should live as a Jew must be defined on the basis that all Jews can equally well

194 . Yeshayahu Leibowitz

participate in this framework. The task of religious Zionism is to offer in Israel a total religious option for Jewish political autonomy. It must engage in the cultural battle with the secular option in its totality.

The hope in Leibowitz's early writings was that the religious community would boldly assume responsibility for developing a Judaism capable of functioning in a society wholly controlled by Jews. One cannot but feel the depth of his anger over the timidity of the official rabbinate and the hypocrisy and failure of nerve of the religious Zionist community, as manifested in the pseudo-solutions offered for serious religious problems. He is a halakic existentialist who feels that the new situation demands that we authentically face the fact that our decision to participate in statehood cannot find legitimization from a halakic framework that mirrors the conditions of Jewish exile.

What, then, is the fundamental difference between Leibowitz's call for enormous halakic change and the changes of law made by diaspora Conservative and Reform Jewish communities? Leibowitz thinks that the tendency for change in the Diaspora reflects a desire by Jews to accommodate themselves to a non-Jewish world, to overcome separateness by eliminating the laws of kashrut, to minimize the Sabbath laws so that they can mingle socially and economically with non-Jews. These changes in no way express for Leibowitz an authentic religious impulse. Always in history, the Jewish people was a distinct community. Modernity and the desire for social integration have no normative weight and no serious religious legitimacy to transform the halakah. Conversely, the impulse for change that grows from the reestablishment of a Jewish national political community is indigenous to Judaism and thus can be legitimated without reference to ethical humanistic considerations.

As a result, there is in his attitude to halakah a striking but wholly logical dichotomy. He is conservative and deeply authoritarian on the personal psychological dimension of halakic Judaism, he does not allow personal needs to dictate the direction of Judaism, and he is totally submissive to the disciplines of kashrut and the laws of sexual purity. At the same time, he is boldly revolutionary when it comes to those conditions needed to maintain a social and political entity called the State of Israel.

The Critique of Secular Zionism

Scholem rightly observed that there is a deep dialectical tension within the Zionist secular revolution. On one hand, it casts off tradition, undermines the Jewish religious perspective, and denies the authority of the halakah and the rabbis to define how Jews should live. It proclaims a new Jew with a new spirit, capable of building and becoming responsible for a total society. Yet with all the anger and rejection of the past, there is a profound connection to much that historically shaped the identity of the Jewish people.

There is, therefore, a deep need within secular Zionist ideology to find historical legitimation for their revolution. They cannot find it through the halakah, through the official religious community. The Talmud was viewed as a creation of exile. The early pioneers found their heroic figures not in the talmudic sages but in the early biblical leaders such as Joshua, Gideon, and David.

The Bible also served the Zionist concern to build a new society filled with social and political justice. Citing the prophetic critique of ritual, they claimed that the essentials of Judaism had to be sought not in the disciplined way of life of the halakah but in the prophetic call for justice and social equality.

Early Zionists, therefore, used the Bible to reject the Talmud. Zionism claimed to be able to heal a diseased religious Jewish self-understanding that stemmed from two thousand years of diaspora. There is a deep similarity in spirit between early Zionist ideology and the critique of Judaism found in much traditional Christian theology. Students in Israeli schools know the history of the Bible, but most are ignorant regarding the spiritual process that resulted from the creation of the Talmud. The centuries of exilic Jewish history, it is implied, did not contain great creative achievements. Rather, they are understood by many Israelis as just a series of persecutions and oppressions.

During my first year of aliyah, when the holiday of Chanukah came around, I was profoundly shaken by a television program on the significance of Chanukah for our time. To my astonishment, no rabbi, philosopher, or teacher appeared. Rather, a military analyst spoke with a historian who had studied the wars of Napoleon about the battles of Judah Maccabee. It was a lesson in comparative strategy and in the importance of surprise attack.

I was amazed and unable to explain the profound unease I felt. What had happened to the miracle of the lights? What had happened to the power of Judaism to keep the Jewish people alive and keep the flame of Torah burning under all conditions? Who among my circles in the Diaspora had reacted to Judah Maccabee as a brilliant military strategist?

In his writings, Leibowitz constantly attempts to correct what he believes to be the distortion of making the Maccabees of Chanukah a symbol for contemporary Israeli military courage. Chanukah cannot be used as a paradigm for modern Israel. The Maccabees fought to reestablish the reign of Torah; the Israeli army fights for the reign of secular government. To Leibowitz, the Israeli army is less similar to the Maccabees than to the Hellenists against whom the Maccabees were fighting.

Leibowitz is repelled by what he sees as the attempt of the secular Israeli to distort the tradition so as to legitimize secular nationalist aspirations. Jewish history up to the emancipation testifies to the Jewish community's covenantal identity and loyalty to God as it expressed itself through halakah. To remove God and Judaism from Jewish history is to empty it of any authentic content. Similarly, to make the prophets into social revolutionaries and to make the bible into a historical document legitimating the secular community is to take lightly a literary document that everywhere proclaims its religious purpose. Leibowitz abhorred the attempt of people to turn the *Shema Yisrael* into "Hear, Israel, Israel is our people. Israel is one." The secular Zionist revolutionaries must recognize that there is nothing in preemancipation history that could be used to legitimate the building of a secular Jewish society.

Religion and State

Leibowitz's major accusation against the religious Zionist establishment was that it joined the Israeli government and thus gave religious legitimacy to a secular regime. In his early writings he urged the religious Zionist community to think in communal national terms so that religious thought and legislation would not be for a particular interest group. The religious Zionist community, however, did not listen to Leibowitz. To make things worse, that community joined hands with the secular state. In response,

Leibowitz took up a more difficult challenge: he would expose all attempts to give Jewish religious significance to secular human institutions. In Israel, that meant giving absolute significance to the state. Leibowitz demanded that Judaism with its concern for worship of God must act as a critique of nationalism; it must expose man and all his institutions to judgment. Judaism must make all Jews constantly vigilant against the intrinsic dangers of power.

Because of the centrality of peoplehood and land within Judaism, there is an intrinsic danger in Israel that religion may be used as an instrumental value to legitimate the activities of the state and the policies of the government. For Leibowitz, it is a modern expression of idolatry to make Judaism an instrumental value to serve human purposes. To give secular Zionist institutions a religious veneer is to prostitute Judaism for the sake of the political national aspirations of the Jews.

Leibowitz does not place Jewish nationalism in a unique category of its own. Because there was no specifically religious impulse behind the Zionist revolution, it contains the dangers inherent in all nationalist revolutions. The attempt on the part of the religious community to put a religious label on the creation of Israel, as by calling it the beginning of the messianic redemption, is especially problematic. It creates the illusion that we are doing God's work and are therefore immune from the corruptions inherent in all human activities.

To Leibowitz, the major religious and moral imperative for Jews living in Israel is to keep Jewish nationalism clean from all religious interpretations and legitimation. The religious establishment, however, failed to exercise the critical function demanded by Leibowitz. Instead, it sought political accommodation with the secularists. Worse still, it acquiesced in a chief rabbinate appointed under secular law and subject to government control. Religious Zionists have lost the autonomous power of the religious institutions that they possessed in exile.

Leibowitz sees Judaism and the Jewish people as inseparably connected. The organic connection between peoplehood and faith in Judaism, however, contains the danger that the Jewish faith commitment may be turned into absolute loyalty to the Jewish people. This brings Leibowitz back to the theme of idolatry because it is idolatry to put Jewish peoplehood in the place of

God. The trauma of the Holocaust period has made this problem even more intense. Saving Jewish life has become central to Jewish consciousness.

It would be a mistake, however, to define Leibowitz's religious critique exclusively as a polemical response to the social and political reality of Israel. He has a coherent systematic religious outlook that goes beyond the exigencies of his political critique.

Leibowitz's Religious Philosophy

To Leibowitz, God is not to be understood in personalist theistic terms. All attempts at describing God from the perspective of human concerns is tantamount to idolatry. Leibowitz is religiously very close to the theological position articulated by Maimonides in his negative theology. Maimonides claims that all descriptive language about God is either false or inadequate and possibly close to idolatry because of the radical otherness of God from the human world. One cannot subsume God under any genus or species, and therefore one cannot apply to God categories used to describe human reality. Biblical anthropomorphic descriptions of God are for Maimonides a concession to human beings who cannot think about the divine reality in noncorporeal terms. In Leibowitz's theology, one cannot talk about God but can only act in the presence of God. Judaism does not give a description of the reality of God, nor should one attempt to establish ways of making sense of the existence of God. Rather, religious language is prescriptive—it tries to direct man in his worship of God.

Maimonides bases his theology on logical considerations in insisting upon the transcendence of God, inasmuch as all attempts at descriptions of God violate the uniqueness and unity of God. For example, thinking of God in corporeal terms would violate the notion of unity. In the case of Leibowitz, however, the reason for insisting on radical divine transcendence is not logical but religious. It is not that human descriptions of God are false; rather, they are religiously inappropriate. To think of God as a way of satisfying human needs, as a way of legitimizing ethical categories, as a way of enhancing and securing political structures so as to give order and coherence to human society is to make God subservient to the needs of man.

Certainly, Leibowitz recognizes the importance of social and ethical actions within a religious framework. What he rejects is the primacy of the ethical as an autonomous category. In the framework of Judaism, it is not "Love thy neighbor as thyself" but "Love they neighbor as thyself: I am the Lord." Your love for your neighbor takes place within the context of worship and service of God.

Even an atheistic society, Leibowitz claims, can create a very serious ethical personality. One chooses a religious worldview not to discover rules for ethics but because one recognizes that God is the ultimate principle in reality and that the meaning of life is expressed in acts of worship of God. For Judaism, the act of worship of God is expressed through the framework of halakah.

The centrality of *mitzvah* (divine commandment) in Judaism implies that God is a source of demand, not a guarantor of success and meaning in history. Here is where Leibowitz distinguishes Judaism from Christianity, the latter being a religion in which God redeems man and liberates him from finitude and sin. Judaism offers no promise of resolution and redemption; it does not offer solace, peace, security, meaning, and happiness. Whereas Christianity promises to serve man's needs, Judaism calls man to strive to worship God within the world as it is given.

The given world, just as it is and without needing promises of redemption, expresses the will and wisdom of God. Nature and the conditions of human behavior which create history are all willed by God in the sense that whatever exists does so because of the ultimate reality of God. The principle of divine transcendence is what makes man, nature, and history intelligible and possible. Judaism does not offer man a way of explaining the facts of the universe; it is a way of explaining what man does with those facts within the world. It is therefore a constant striving to realize God's commands in the world, although in essence the gap between God's demands and human action remains permanent.

The religious seriousness with which the Jew strives to worship God is what gives significance and purpose to reality. It violates Leibowitz's sense of worship to think of God as manipulating the world to move in a specific direction for the worshiper's benefit. To think of God as one who provides for my wealth and health is to reduce Him, to use a Leibowitzian metaphor, to being the superadministrator of the Kupat Holim sick fund. To think of

God as making good the failures of man, to think of Him as a crutch on which one can rely when human efforts fail, is to make Him the grand administrator of the world and robs Judaism of its essential thrust of worship.

Leibowitz sees two approaches to prayer within the Jewish religious tradition. One treats prayer as growing from human crisis and human needs; it expresses the longing to have God look on my suffering and aid me in my tragedies. In the other approach to prayer, it is not personal need and the existential human condition that cry out for divine attentiveness but rather the disciplined commitment to obey the commandment to stand before God in worship. Leibowitz rejects spontaneous prayer; he is wholly content to regard prayer as a regime and discipline that obligates man to stand before God irrespective of his present psychological or social condition. The irrelevance of that condition is shown for Leibowitz by the fact that the mourner who has just buried his child and the groom who has just married his beloved are called upon to recite the same prayers.

Leibowitz, consequently, has no problem regarding petitional prayer in the modern world because the essence of Judaic prayer is *not* to ask God to respond to human needs but simply to accept the obligation to stand in worship of God. Therefore, by tautology, all prayer is answered because the very meaning of prayer is simply the willingness to accept the discipline of standing in worship of God. No matter what is thrown at us in history, no matter what nature reveals, no matter what we discover in the world, the ability to worship remains permanent.

The paradigm of the Judaic religious life for Leibowitz, the model of genuine worship of God, is Abraham's readiness to sacrifice his son Isaac. Abraham's ability to submit to God's commands, although doing so violated all his natural impulses of love for his child, although it contradicted all his dreams for building a religious community in history, created a moment in which Abraham's worship transcended all human strivings, longings, and aspirations for the world.

Leibowitz therefore has serious religious difficulty with the personal theistic framework found in the Judaic tradition. The source that defines his religious consciousness is not the Bible but the religious community that emerges out of the talmudic tradition. In the classical tradition of Judaism, the oral tradition of the

Talmud defines how one is to respond to the biblical tradition. Leibowitz takes this approach to its extreme in which the Bible no longer has any autonomous validity. For him, the revelatory movement of God in history present in the Bible has been replaced by the prayerful movement of man toward God found in the talmudic tradition. When in the talmudic world descriptions of revelation and miracles cease to be an essential part of the story, claims Leibowitz, we notice a strengthening of the Jewish people as a covenantal religious community.

An example for Leibowitz is the power of talmudic Judaism to combat idolatry. In the biblical world, God is described as very active and constantly interfering in human history, yet the community repeatedly reacts by turning to idolatry. After the miraculous liberation from Egypt comes the story of rebellion. Even after the great spectacle of revelation at Sinai, the story is told of the golden calf. The biblical narrative teaches us that miracles and direct revelation do not create a religious community. The Jewish people became resolutely monotheistic only when the discipline of the talmudic halakah was internalized and institutionalized in Jewish life.

When the Jews became a prayer community, when they adopted a life disciplined by the normative framework of halakah, they at last succeeded in becoming a committed religious community. This living religious community shapes Leibowitz's perception of Judaism. He is not interested in the theology of the Bible but is drawn to make religious sense of Judaism mediated by a living people. *Mitzvah* and its concretization in halakah constitute the community's way of expressing its commitment to God.

This viewpoint also enables Leibowitz to dismiss all arguments about the factual accuracy of the Bible. The biblical descriptions of the exodus from Egypt and the miraculous interventions in the desert are interpreted by the Judaic community, he claims, within the conceptual frameworks of the legal tradition rather than as factual historical accounts. The sanctity of the Bible in Jewish life is not a result of the fact of revelation but results from the halakic decision of the authoritative teachers of the Talmud to endow the twenty-four books of the Bible with sanctity. The canon was established by the normative authority of the Talmud and not by divine intervention in history. One who regards the Bible as authoritative only in the framework of the legal authority of

Jewish tradition is not forced to regard the Bible as a source of factual information but only as a source of normative direction—that is, as Torah and *mitzvah*.

The theistic vision found in the Bible does not need to be seen as factual truth. Rather, it reflects a specific stage in the community's normative religious development. Before the community of Israel can truly enter a theocentric framework, it is portrayed in the Bible as having an anthropocentric vision of God. This is what is called in the Talmud *she-lo li-shemah*, the service of God not for its own sake, since it is motivated by human psychological concerns and needs. This *she-lo li-shemah* was accepted and legitimated by the Judaic tradition but only as a stage on the path to *li-shemah*, service of God for its own sake. Although the authentic paradigm of Judaism is Abraham's readiness to sacrifice Isaac at God's command, there is a great distance separating normal human beings from the ideal archetype found in Abraham. One must strive for a theocentric consciousness, but Judaism accepts as a preliminary stage in man's religious life actions that mirror an anthropocentric frame of worship.

This is how Leibowitz understands the general communal approach to petitional prayer, the biblical descriptions of God, and the stories that deal with God's promises of reward and punishment. All these personalist descriptions mirror the anthropocentric focus, the *she-lo li-shemah* level of religious life. Ultimately, however, the tendency of Judaism and the essence of its religious power lie in its demand to love God unconditionally and to perform *mitzvot* motivated by pure disinterested love of God.

For philosophical reasons of this kind, Leibowitz cannot use concepts drawn from biblical anthropocentrism or from messianism and eschatology to ascribe religious significance to the mere historical fact that Israel has been reborn as an independent polity. Reborn Israel will be significant religiously only if this community demonstrates how all of life in an autonomous Jewish society is dedicated to the worship of God.

Although Jewish commitment to the *mitzvot* must be unconditional, the halakic concretization of the *mitzvot* can change. Indeed, Leibowitz calls for bold, innovative halakic changes in Israel. If these changes come, if the religious community shows to the people of Israel how the halakic theocentric passion can have vital significance in the modern world, then Judaism has a future,

If, however, the religious community cannot offer that vision, or if it fails to persuade the larger community to shift its focus from a secular humanistic framework to a covenantal halakic perspective, Leibowitz does not see much hope for the continued existence of Judaism.

Will religious Zionism uproot the incipient idolatry in its midst? Will its followers have the courage to build a society that mirrors the new spirit needed for the renewal of halakah? Will the Jewish community awaken to the internal dangers of assimilation and spiritual decadence? Leibowitz offers us no automatic hope, no promise, and no prayer. He offers only the voice of an honest critical thinker who lives daily in Israel with great trepidation regarding the future but nevertheless continues with great passion and sincerity to march across the country with the dedication of a young man, speaking to all who are willing to listen and learn.

FOR FURTHER READING

Works by Yeshayahu Leibowitz

In addition to scientific papers, which include more than forty-five articles on organic chemistry, biochemistry, and biology, as well as books on the chemistry of carbohydrates and enzymology, Yeshayahu Leibowitz has written and lectured extensively on philosophy, Jewish studies, and current affairs.

Encyclopedia Hebraica, entries titled "Brian," "Chemistry," "Darwinism," "Development," and "Life," as well as many shorter articles on philosophy and Jewish studies.

ha-Torasha Mahi (What is heredity), Tel Aviv, 1945 [Hebrew].

Torah u-Mitzvot ha-Zman ha-Zeh (Torah and Mitzvot today), Tel Aviv, 1946 [Hebrew].

Yahadut, Am Yehudi u-Medinat Israel (Judaism, the Jewish people and the State of Israel), Tel Aviv, 1975, [Hebrew]. (English translation Harvard University Press, Cambridge, Ma., 1992, selections have also appeared in Italian translation in 1980 and in French translation in 1985.)

Yesodot ha-Beaiah ha-Psichofizit (Foundations of the psychophysical problem), Tel Aviv, 1974 [Hebrew].

Sichot al Pirke Avot (Talks on the ethics of the fathers), Tel Aviv 1979 [Hebrew]. (German translation, 1984.)

Emunah, Historiah ve-Arachim (Faith, history and values), Jerusalem, 1982 [Hebrew]. (Selections in English translation.)

Hitpatchut ve-Torasha (Development and heredity), Tel Aviv, 1978 [Hebrew].

Guf va-Nefesh: ha-Baaiah ha-Pshicofizit (Body and soul: The psychophysical problem), Tel Aviv, 1983 [Hebrew].

Emunato shel ha-Rambam (Maimonides faith), Tel Aviv, 1984 [Hebrew].

Sichot al Mada ve-Arachim (Talks on science and values), Tel Aviv, 1985 [Hebrew].

Bein Mada le-filosofia (Between science and philosophy), Jerusalem, 1985 [Hebrew].

Sichot al shmone Prakim la-Rambam (Talks on Maimonides' eight chapters), Jerusalem, 1986 [Hebrew].

Al Olum u-Meloo: Sichot im Michael Shashar (On everything: Talks with Michael Shashar), Jerusalem, 1987 [Hebrew].

Hearot le-Parashiot ha-Shavua (Comments on the weekly Torah portions), Jerusalem, 1988 [Hebrew].

Sefer Yeshayahu Leibowitz (The Yeshayahu Leibowitz book), Edited by Asa Kasher and Yaakov Lavinger, Tel Aviv, 1977 [Hebrew].

Shelilian Lishmah klaoel Yeshayahu Leibowitz, Edited by H. Ben-Yeruham and H. A. Kolitz, Jerusalem, 1983 [Hebrew].

Emmanuel Levinas

RICHARD A. COHEN

Biography

Emmanuel Levinas was born on January 12, 1906, in Kovno, Lithuania, where his father owned a small bookshop and stationery store. Kovno was the district center, with a population of about one hundred thousand people, more than a quarter of them Jews. Though second to Vilna in fame, in Kovno traditional, self-absorbed, yeshiva-oriented Lithuanian Judaism flourished. Here it also encountered modern European influences. The Levinas home, the life, and finally the ethical philosophy of Emmanuel Levinas are a manifestation of this fateful encounter of Judaism and modern Europe. Two examples from his childhood reveal this combination of old and new. From the age of six Levinas was tutored in Hebrew, but his tutor used Hebrew-language textbooks rather than the traditional Jewish sources. When he was able, Levinas read the Bible in Hebrew, but his text was not a *Makraot Gedolot*, an "expanded Scripture" containing the authoritative rabbinical commentaries which he later came to see as essential.

In May 1915 the Jews of the Kovno district were expelled by order of the czarist government. By 1916 Levinas's family had settled in Karkhov in the Ukraine. At age eleven, Emmanuel was admitted, with great family celebration, as one of the five Jewish children permitted, by competitive examination, to enter the czarist high school in Karkhov. By now Levinas was reading the great Russian authors, Pushkin, Lermontov, Gogol, Turgeniev,

Dostoyevsky, and Tolstoy, in Russian. They provided the first stimulation for his philosophical thinking.

His first year in high school coincided with the final months of the czarist regime and the first months of the Russian Revolution. In the disruptions of the Russian Civil War, Ukrainian anti-Semitism broke out in all its unspeakable horror. In 1919–20 alone, more than one hundred thousand Jews were murdered under the "socialist" government of S. Petlyura. Levinas's family survived, but as Jews and petite bourgeois they suffered harassment that made them decide to leave the Ukraine at the earliest possible opportunity, which came in July 1920, when they returned to Kovno. In comparison with the Ukrainian interlude, Levinas remembers his days in the Kovno Jewish community as ones of "happiness and harmony."

The Judaism of Levinas's childhood was not a religion or an ideology or a system of beliefs, it was a way of life, a manner of living and thinking that permeated every aspect of a Jew's life, like the very air one breathes. Trying to describe this Judaism of his boyhood days in Kovno, seventy years later Levinas said: "The spiritual essence—and this remains a quite 'Lithuanian Judaism'—rested for me not in mystical modes but in a tremendous curiosity for books."[1]

Levinas's second stay in Lithuania lasted only three years. In 1923, at the age of seventeen, he set out with his family's blessings for France to obtain a university education. At that time for Jews everywhere France was the land of Captain Alfred Dreyfus. True, it was France—its ruling elite, its military, the church—that had conspired to make of Dreyfus a scapegoat, falsely to accuse and convict him of treason, to send him to Devil's Island. But France was also the land of liberty, equality, and fraternity, where the clarion call of Emile Zola was heard and where after much travail and suffering Dreyfus was finally exonerated—in the very year of Levinas's birth, 1906.

Levinas enrolled at the University of Strasbourg, geographically the closest French university to Kovno. His first year he studied Latin. Independently he learned French and German. Beginning his second year, Levinas turned to philosophy. In all his published recollections of this period Levinas singles out four of his Strasbourg teachers for special appreciation: Maurice Pradines, professor of general philosophy; Charles Blondel, professor of psychology ("very anti-Freudian"); Maurice Halbwachs, sociologist (martyred in deportation to Buchenwald); and Henri Carteron, professor of ancient philosophy. Levinas was impressed by these four men, by their characters as well as by their knowledge, seeing in them the embodiment of Western learning and humanism. He became personally close to Professor Blondel, "a man to whom I could say everything."[2]

In addition to the study of the established philosophical curriculum, Levinas was drawn to contemporary philosophy. He was especially attracted to the thought of Henri Bergson and Edmund Husserl, both of whom were still teaching at the time. The influence of these two philosophers, both born Jews, both assimilated, both making significant contributions to the highest intellectual levels of European culture, Bergson in France and Husserl in Germany, is unmistakable in Levinas's own thought. From Husserl Levinas learned a scientific method, phenomenology, and through this method a philosophical appreciation for the existential conditions of intellectual life; from Bergson he learned a variety of profound philosophical insights, especially regarding time and existence. In Strasbourg Levinas also began his lifelong friendship with Maurice Blanchot, a fellow student who would later become what he is still today, one of France's leading literary critics.

The 1928–29 academic year was a special one for Levinas. Like the many German students who would travel from university to university to attend the classes of the greatest professors of their day, Levinas traveled to Freiburg to learn phenomenology at its source, from Husserl. In this brief time he became close to the almost legendary founder of phenomenology, who had just the year before retired from his university professorship but who still directed students and was still reviewing and reformulating his own thought. Levinas became Mrs. Husserl's French tutor, an employment that was one of Professor Husserl's discreet ways of providing support for his less affluent students. Levinas quickly entered into the circle of phenomenology's elite students, and as early as the next year he published articles in France reviewing Husserl's latest ideas and those of his leading students.

During the same 1928–29 academic year Levinas attended the lectures of Husserl's successor at the University of Freiburg, Martin Heidegger. Heidegger's reputation in German academic circles had already begun to surpass Husserl's. Just two years earlier, in 1927, Heidegger's *Being and Time* was published. This book, more than any other, not only redirected phenomenology but altered the course of twentieth-century thought. Forty years later, after having worked out and published his own original (and anti-Heideggerian) philosophy, Levinas did not hesitate to write, in a now famous passage, that henceforth "all philosophy must pass through" Heidegger's *Being and Time*. We must not forget that these carefully considered words of praise for Heidegger's philosophy were said in the teeth of Levinas's fundamental and uncompromising criticism of Heidegger's personal commitment to Nazism. To this day Levinas rigorously maintains this separation between Heidegger's thought and Heidegger's life, speaking at conferences on the former and refusing all invitations to celebrate the latter. In his Freiburg days Levinas learned from Heidegger's penetrating phenomenological studies without becoming a Heideggerian, unlike so many of Heidegger's other students. Levinas was one of the privileged few to attend the now famous Kant seminar held in Davos in 1929, where Ernst Cassirer, philosopher of science, disciple of Hermann Cohen, and editor of Kant's complete works, debated Heidegger on Kant. It was during this period too that Levinas began his study of the rabbinic texts, a study he continues to the present day.

After his year in Freiburg, Levinas moved to Paris. He quickly completed his doctoral dissertation under Professor Jean Wahl. In 1930, when Levinas was only twenty-four years old, his thesis was published as *The Theory of Intuition in Husserl's Phenomenology*. It won the Prix de l'Institut from the University of Strasbourg and is still in print today after four French editions. The first book in French entirely devoted to phenomenology, according to Simone de Beauvoir's published account it inspired the young Jean-Paul Sartre to leave Paris for Freiburg to learn the new phenomenological philosophy. It was also the first of Levinas's books to be translated into English, appearing in 1973.

Levinas obtained his French citizenship and married a girlfriend from his earliest Kovno days. In 1931 his translation (along with Gabrielle Pfeiffer) of Husserl's *Cartesian Meditations* appeared. At the same time, Levinas began working as an administrator at the Alliance Israelite Universelle, a French Jewish organization dedicated to increasing the political rights and education of Jews throughout the Mediterranean basin. During the prewar years Levinas continued to study philosophy and to publish articles on Husserl and Heidegger. He also began publishing essays in Jewish thought and on Jewish current events. In 1934, for example, he published an article entitled "Some Reflections on the Philosophy of Hitlerism" in *Esprit*. It warned the French of the dangerous "awakening of primitive feelings" across the German border, subtly linking this movement to Nietzschean and Heideggerian reflections. In the early 1930s Levinas attended the celebrated Saturday night gatherings of the philosophical avant-garde at the home of the philosopher Gabriel Marcel, where he met Jean-Paul Sartre and Jacques Maritain among others. During this period he also met another future leading French philosopher, Paul Ricoeur.

In 1939, as a French citizen, Levinas was drafted into the French army. Shortly thereafter, along with the entire French Tenth Army, he was captured at Rennes and made a Germany prisoner of war. After a few months' detention in France, he was transported to a prisoner-of-war camp near Hanover, Germany, for Jewish French soldiers. Here, like other prisoners of war elsewhere, he was forced to do manual labor, chopping wood in a nearby forest. Again the meeting of Judaism and modern Europe was fateful: Levinas's Jewish life was saved by his French uniform. It is a little-known fact that Hitler adhered to the provisions of the Geneva Conventions regarding prisoners of war for signatory nations such as France. Levinas's wife and daughter survived the war hidden at the Saint Vincent de Paul monastery near Orleans. In their escape from Paris they were aided by Maurice Blanchot. Though imprisoned and cut off from the awful and awesome social, political, and military events of the day, Levinas found time to read some of the prison library books, notably works by Hegel, Diderot, Rousseau, and Proust, and "many things which I had not had the time to read otherwise."[3]

After the war Levinas rejoined his family in Paris. He was appointed director of the Oriental Israelite Normal School, a position he retained until 1961, when he took his first academic post as lecturer in philosophy at the University of Poitiers. In the 1946–7 academic year, Levinas gave a series of four lectures at the Philosophical College of Paris set up by Jean Wahl in the lively and bohemian postwar Latin Quarter. These lectures, which form the first outline of Levinas's own thought, were published under the title *Time and the Other* in 1947 (English translation, 1987). The same year also saw the publication of another book-length expression of Levinas's own thought, *Existence and Existents* (English translation, 1978). These two relatively short books, whose theses were for the most part developed in isolation from the rest of contemporary French intellectual life, represent the first sustained articulation of Levinas's distinctive philosophy. Then and henceforth Levinas would propound an ethical and dialogical metaphysics grounded in a careful phenomenological description of the human situation in both its individual and its social moments. From the pain, horror, and confusion of political, social, and ethical upheavals on a scale unprecedented in European history, Levinas would forge a philosophy grounded in the highest demands of personal ethics and social justice. From the unparalleled extremity and incongruous juxtaposition of this historical and historic contrast of good and evil, war and peace, culture and barbarism, justice and injustice, Levinas created a philosophy infused with the highest moral teachings of Judaism.

From 1947 to 1951, Levinas entered into an intensive study of the Talmud under the firm guidance of the brilliant, demanding, and mysterious R. Mordachai Chouchani. Independently and unknown to each other, Elie Wiesel was at that time also in Paris learning from this same extraordinary talmudist. (For more on R. Chouchani see *The Wandering Jew* in Elie Wiesel's *Legends of Our Time.*) Though in his many "talmudic" lectures and publications Levinas has never named this teacher, to this day he speaks of R. Chouchani with only the highest of high praise, indeed, with reverence.

From the late 1940s to the present, Levinas published a great many articles, most of which have been republished in various collections. Based in part on these later collections, one can roughly divide Levinas's articles into four categories. First, there are articles developing and deepening his own philosophical thought, his ethical and dialogical metaphysics. The articles in this category can be further subdivided into two groups: those which, with revisions, come from or make up Levinas's two major works, *Totality and Infinity* (1961; English translation, 1969) and *Otherwise Than Being or Beyond Essence* (1974; English translation, 1981), and the rest. These latter do not link up to form integral books like *Totality and Infinity* and *Otherwise Than Being or Beyond Essence* but are gathered into four collections: *Humanism of the Other Man* (1972), *Of God Who Comes to the Idea* (1982), *Transcendence and Intelligibility* (1984), and *Between Us* (1991). There are also two short volumes, each containing one important essay: *Of Evasion* (1982), reproducing one of Levinas's earliest articles, first published in 1935, and *Transcendance and Intelligibility* (1984). In the second category are the many essays and secondary articles that analyze and comment on the work of various modern and contemporary philosophers, critics, writers, and poets, confronting perspectives more or less close to Levinas's own thought and concerns: Agnon, Blanchot, Buber, Celan, Derrida, Heidegger, Husserl, Kierkegaard, Rosenzweig, et al. These sorts of articles are now collected into four volumes: *Discovering Existence with Husserl and Heidegger* (1949, 2nd ed. 1967), *Proper Names* (1975), *On Maurice Blanchot* (1975), and *Outside the Subject* (1987). In the third category are the more than twenty "Talmudic Readings," Levinasian commentaries on talmudic *aggadah*, given as invited lectures since 1957 at the annual colloquia of French- Speaking Jewish Intellectuals, sponsored by the World Jewish Congress. Nineteen of these pieces have been collected into four volumes: *Four Talmudic Readings* (1968), *From the Sacred to the Holy* (1977), *Beyond the Verse* (1982), and *In the Time of Nations* (1988). In the fourth category are the many brief and occasional pieces on topics of general Jewish and religious interest such as Israel, Jewish-Christian relations, monotheism, assimilation, and the Bible (plus Levinas's three earliest talmudic readings), which have been gathered together into the two editions of *Difficult Freedom* (1963, 2d ed. 1976).

One can see that despite his duties as director of the Oriental Israelite Normal School (1946–62) and despite the teaching responsibilities of his academic posts at the University of Poitiers (1961–62), the University of Paris at Nanterres (1962–73), and the University of Paris-Sorbonne (1973–76), Levinas has been a prolific, an engaged, and, in my estimation, a profound writer.

Before moving on to Levinas's philosophy, there are some further words, simple but important words, that must be said about the man. Levinas has lived through interesting times, and he has been spiritually productive. He has tasted some rewards for his efforts, concluding his career as a distinguished and now an emeritus professor of philosophy at the Sorbonne. But through all this objective history and beyond the brilliance of Levinas's works, one still wants to know more about him. What is his character? How does he treat those near to him, his family, friends, colleagues and students? Perhaps these questions are too personal and can only be answered by those persons who have known Levinas according to their own unique experiences. But if I may venture an answer that I think those who have known Levinas would endorse overwhelmingly, I would put it as follows: Levinas is and has been a good person, an exceptionally good person. Goodness, of course, does not only mean avoiding evil, it means positively doing good, reaching out to others, helping. Levinas's is not at all the case of an "abstract" intellectual, whose creative works have been purchased at the price of hypocrisy, pain, and hurt for those "behind the scenes." Quite the contrary. Beyond the generosity and probity of Levinas's public work, his book reviews, secondary articles, prefaces, contributions to Jewish causes, direction of an important Jewish educational and cultural institution, university teaching, dissertation supervision, a global correspondence, lectures every Sabbath morning in the synagogue, and the like, not to mention raising a family, there shines Levinas the man, his outgoing friendliness, his real concern for others, his genuine modesty and personal dignity, and always a warm and ready sense of humor. The ethics of Levinas the man and the ethics of Levinas the thinker are, in a word, at one. This too is in the oldest and best tradition of Judaism's spiritual leaders.

Philosophy

Levinas's major achievement is to have created an original, profound, and comprehensive philosophy, a dialogical ethics. Two basic moves characterize his thought, one negative or critical and the other positive. Negatively, he opposes the primacy which philosophy quite naturally accords to ontological and epistemological interests, the hegemony to which it raises the quest for truth. Positively, he proposes the higher priorities of ethics, the obligations and responsibilities that one person has for another person encountered face-to-face and that ultimately each person has for all humanity. For Levinas the absolute alterity of goodness takes precedence over the relative alterities of the true and the beautiful. Those who are familiar with the many layers and the long history of Jewish thought will see in Levinas's philosophy not only a thought in dialogue with the whole history of philosophy but a thought at the same time thoroughly consonant with many of Judaism's most significant beliefs and practices. There are few if any other philosophies about which the same can be said.

The titles of Levinas's two major works offer clues to his criticism of traditional philosophy: *Totality and Infinity* and *Otherwise Than Being or Beyond Essence*. Both titles are striking in their wide range and dramatic contrasts. In one, infinity is contrasted with totality, in the other, being and essence are contested by an "otherwise" and a "beyond." Although Levinas's ethics is concrete, elaborating the significance of flesh-and-blood human encounters, influenced by the descriptive analyses of phenomenology and existentialism, these titles are abstract. More than just abstract, they contain an essential and deep enigma: the alternatives contested are fundamentally incontestable.

Totality, being, and essence do not constitute a "side." In the Western philosophical tradition they are terms used to express the whole, the all—the whole of reality, all that is. Such terms are meant to be immune to opposition in principle. Does it even make sense, then, to speak of an *otherwise* than being? Anything that is, anything that is a "what" in any sense whatsoever, has being, is. Just *saying* "being" already affirms being, however nominal. As for totality, it means everything. How can everything have an alternative, an other, an exteriority? "Totality" and "being" are as all-encompassing as terms can be, which is precisely their value for philosophers. If Levinas's titles make sense, then, that sense is enigmatic, paradoxical and challenging.

The titles are indeed paradoxical and enigmatic. Levinas's critical aim is to disturb and challenge rational thought. His terms and locutions are carefully chosen to upset reason at its most rational. They aim to upset reason *in the way that the obligations of ethics upset the telos of reason—from outside and above*. The issue is not one of titles, of course, but of thought and life. To appreciate what is at stake in Levinas's oppositions, one must appreciate the nature of reason and the role it plays in the West.

Basically "the West" is a will to truth, the quest for universal knowledge of the real, reason. This determination is what unites "being," "totality," and "essence." That Levinas sees in the West the will to universal truth is hardly a new insight. Hegel saw this and then saw himself fulfilling the Western telos. Nietzsche saw it and then strove to reverse or disperse it. Levinas, however, wants neither to fulfill nor to reverse or disperse the Western telos. Without disparaging the genuine achievements of reason, he wants to reorient the West to an "essentially" higher vocation. Above the will to truth Levinas discerns the call of goodness, a call whose appeal is not that of another truth but of a height that makes truth possible.

Attentive to the links between thought and temporality uncovered by contemporary philosophy, especially by Bergson, Husserl, and Heidegger, Levinas understands the Western telos in a yet more precise way. Its distinctive characteristic, its will to truth, is founded upon the equation of being and being-present. It is because being is first determined as what must be-present that the truth of being is then determined in terms of totality and essence. What is is what is true, justified. But what is true and justified is what is based on evidence that can be brought to the presence of mind, however broadly or "existentially" one conceives mind. The rational quest for being *qua* totality and essence, the very project of reason, science, is the ongoing quest for complete presence of mind, absolute knowledge. There is a great deal at stake, then, in Levinas's philosophical criticisms, for his oppositions strike at the core of the Western spiritual adventure begun by the ancient Greeks: the love of wisdom *qua* reason, science, objectivity, universality, absolute knowledge, total self-presence. Levinas attacks this core at its core, by upsetting the self-presence of reason.

There is an enormous if not insuperable difficulty, however. Because the West is essentially a scientific civilization, is determined by the will to truth, it leaves no room, as it were, for a criticism that strikes at the roots of critical thought. One cannot challenge the comprehensiveness of being, the totality of what is, the absolute, in other words, when there is no vantage point or place from which to make the challenge. From the point of view of reason, Levinas's oppositions are then not even false, they are *less* than false. Neither are they possible, because "possibility" is itself an integral part of the totality Levinas claims to oppose. If Levinas's oppositions were possible, so reason reasons, then they would be impossible, encompassed by what they claim to exceed. By the same token, so reason must also reason, Levinas's oppositions cannot be impossible either, because "impossibility" is also included within the unity of being, totality, and essence. Neither possible nor impossible, outside the excluded middle, neither contradictory nor noncontradictory, such is the conundrum, the impasse, the exasperation, but also precisely the transcending inspiration that motivates and is activated by Levinas's thought—*otherwise* than being, *beyond* essence. It escapes a thought that it astutely recognizes as having no exits.

Levinas's opposition to the circumspection of reason is not, however, only a negative enterprise; it is neither a "negative dialectics," to use Adorno's expression, nor a "deconstruction" to use Derrida's. There is a completely positive side to Levinas's criticism: the positivity of the good. The positivity of goodness, however, is precisely what exceeds the positivity of positive science. The peculiarity and exasperation of Levinas's challenge to reason, then, is the sign of the entry of another dimension, the ethical, which remains other while yet intervening in what is not itself. The ethical orientation, its up and down, cannot be directly stated, said, explained, articulated, thematized, because know-ledge is not its proper arena. If the good is to be thought in its goodness, and not thought as the thought of goodness, then it must be "thought" beyond thought itself.

The positivity of goodness is recalcitrant to thematization not because of some lack but because its positivity is too extreme, *too exigent* for reason alone. The good is both *farther* and *closer* than presence, hence invisible to reason. It is farther because the good remains transcendent, irreducibly other. Reason can reason as far as the transcendental but not as far as the transcendent. It is closer because its exigency is greater than the circuits of self-presence, imposing demands more pressing than the self could ever impose on itself by itself. The way of goodness is, in a word, *better* than the thematization of being, more glorious. This "better" is emphati-cally more important and serious than being; its "more" is immeasurable because its force lies outside the calculus of making-present. Not truer, of course, but better. Everything lies in an *emphasis* that breaks through the confines of a language and a reasoning unavoidably self-obsessed.

But all the above is still too abstract to capture the heart of Levinas's ethical philosophy. For Levinas the excess of ethics is anything but abstract, indeed it is an excessive immediacy and concreteness. It is the excessive immediacy and contreteness of human relationship, the face-to-face encounter. Levinas is careful not to say that humans first relate to one another and *then* can relate to one another ethically. Ethics is not a gloss on a prior reality, is not a second order experience. What Levinas is saying, to the contrary, is that the *human* first emerges in the ethical face-to-face. The human emerges not as a genus or the specification of a genus, but as responsibility for the other. Only in the ethical relation does one encounter the other person as *other* and not as a role or mask in an historical play of behaviors. Thus the *real* also emerges from the ethical relation. The distinction so dear to philosophy between reality and appearance emerges not as philosophy supposes from the distinction between truth and opinion but rather from the source of this distinction, from the more primitive difference between sincerity and ceremony, between ethics and the refusal of alterity. The otherness that constitutes the other person as an other person is, for Levinas, not something true or false or beautiful or ugly, but a moral force, an obligation, a putting of the self into question.

Ethics exceeds reason, then, without being deduced from the limitations of reason. Ethics is not a consolation for reason's failure. Rather, ethics comes first, to the point that reason's capacities derive from the ethical relation. In this perspective Levinas has only admiration for the accomplishments of reason, that is, for an ethically responsible Western civilization. The priority of ethics does not come from choosing the right theory or from choosing to be good. Rather, ethics comes first because *the other person comes first.* The priority of the other person, putting the other before the self, is what constitutes ethics in the first place. Here is the positivity of Levinas's ethical philosophy. One does not know ethics, one undergoes it. And one only undergoes it in the first person singular, in the face-to-face relation with the other person, responsibly.

In linking ethics to the I-Thou of interpersonal relations Levinas is following in Buber's path. But there is an important difference. Levinas felt that Buber did not fully appreciate the fundamental asymmetry of the intersubjective relation. It is not the mutuality of the self and the other person but the priority of the other that makes for the *height* proper to ethics. Unless the rectitude of the other's alterity is maintained in its absoluteness, in its ireducible exteriority, the height of ethics will sooner or later be sacrificed, Levinas believes, to the horizons of ontology and aesthetics. For Levinas the face of the other person is from the first a moral height and destitution, imposing obligations on the self, disturbing its equilibrium.

Although Levinas's ethics prolong certain Kantian themes, especially by locating ethical relations outside the historical totality, they do not begin with a self freely legislating its moral obligations and responsibilities. Against Kant, Levinas argues that precisely the autonomy of choice is what makes it inadequate to the transcendence of moral demands. All decisions of the self remain precisely that, the self's. Levinas's philosophy is oriented by a different direction: from the other to the self. Only in the face of the other does the self come to feel its own natural capacities as potentially murderous. Animality is truly surpassed and a genuine humanity arises in the experience of shame, an experience coming out of the face-to-face. "Thou shalt not murder" is not for Levinas a command written on tablets of stone, it is the very apparition of the other as other, the epiphany of the other's face and the beginning of the self as moral agent. Moral agency is higher than will to power.

Nothing could be more serious, then, than the ethical relation, though no scale can measure the weight of the responsibilities it imposes. Responsibility, for Levinas, extends all the way to the other's death, which is to say, to a responsibility for the other's life. For Levinas the self is its brother's keeper; the other's material requirements are the self's spiritual requirements. Responsibilities, unlike ideas, increase in the "measure" that they are assumed ... to infinity. Precisely this structure escapes reason, being better than the calculations of rationality.

Justice, for Levinas, grows out of ethics and remains bound to it. Responsibility for the other leads to responsibility for all others. Ethics and justice are nonetheless distinct for Levinas. Ethics comes from the inequality of the other's priority over the self, whereas justice requires equality before the law and the establishment of this equality through enduring institutions. For Levinas the call for equal treatment before the law derives from the inequality of the face-to-face relation, from responsibility for the other; without this connection justice itself becomes tyrannical. Just as the ethical self is not the specification of a genus but the uniqueness and exigency of an irreplaceable responsibility for the other, humanity for Levinas is not the genus of which individual human beings are the specification. Humanity is precisely the exigency for justice which shines in the face of the other person, for the other who faces is also the other of others who do not face. Thus in the face of the other, beyond its absolute transcendence, as it were, lies the transcendence of all humanity, of all others.

Moral life transpires not in the reference of word to thing or word to word but in the infinite rectitude of each face and every face. All of Levinas's published works attempt to express, by means of careful, nuanced descriptions, the ethical trace of movements recalcitrant to the light of reason, hidden to knowing, yet higher. They show the transcendence of moral force in all the registers of human life: in the warmth of the home, in shared work, in the voluptuousness of eros, in the face's expressiveness, in language, in the priority of peace over war, in the suffering of a humanity that demands justice. In each case Levinas shows the movement and priority of a superlative transcendence breaking up the seamless unity—and complacency—of being's presence.

Judaism

Levinas draws on many Jewish sources for his thought. But Jewish sources can be found for almost any thought, especially when the thinker is Jewish. Levinas's thought is deeply rooted in Judaism, but it is important to remember that what is basic about his creative work is its philosophical character. Despite his radical criticisms of the hubris of knowledge, Levinas's work remains philosophical. Philosophy is, of course, "Greek" rather than Jewish. *As a philosophy* the work of Levinas stands or falls independently of its relation to Judaism and Jewish thought. In this sense, Levinas's work is not vital to Judaism. But Levinas has throughout his work (and life) remained true to his Judaism. His work shows, then, to what extent Jewish sources can be made vital to global "Western" civilization.

One way to characterize the "Jewishness" of Levinas's thought at the broadest level is to see its opposition to philosophy as the most recent avatar of the ancient and perhaps eternal opposition between Jerusalem and Athens, Bible and Homer, Jew versus Greek. Jews are reminded of this conflict every year on the holiday of Hanukah, celebrating the origin of their continual and miraculous triumph over the universalism which is Hellenic. Levinas's revival of this struggle occurs on a refined intellectual plane, in the most advanced terms of contemporary continental philosophy. In his work, as we have seen, it takes the form of an opposition between the absolute transcendence of the other person encountered ethically and the relative transcendence of the truth of being determined as presence, especially as found in the phenomenologies of Husserl and Heidegger. Opposing the primacy of knowledge, Levinas opposes all that is Greek. Against intellectual history's various formulations of the Socratic dictum that "one must know the good to do the good," the ethical priorities of Levinas's thought recall the altogether different priority expressed in the famous response of the Jewish people at Mount Sinai: "We will do and we will listen." Thus Levinas's entire philosophy can be understood as but another layer of meaning attached to Sinai, another interpretation—the priority of the other, conscientiousness before consciousness, ethics before reason—exalting and penetrating to the heart of one of the greatest moments in the religious history of the world.

But Levinas willingly concedes much to the genius of Greece in his contest with Greek hubris. Indeed, as a philosopher his very medium, his basic vocabulary, is Greek. The "Jewish" side of Levinas's thought is "enlightened," that is, it is a Judaism made universal, though not universal in the way of Greek science. Levinas opposes philosophy with an externality, to be sure, but not with the ethnic externality of a Jewish particularism. Rather, he opposes philosophy externally with the absolute or pure exteriority of ethical transcendence—philosophy can undergo opposition this far and no farther. But even if this opposition is not exclusively Jewish, it leaves room for Jews in their difference.

The Judaism that Levinas taps, then, is one that speaks to Jews, opens the space of their difference, but does not speak only to Jews because as a philosophy it can at best open the space of a pure difference and not only the space of Jewish difference. It is a Judaism, then, that speaks to all humanity, that teaches humanity its humanism, the absolute transcendence that opens up between people united ethically.

Whether a dialogical ethics expressed in the language of philosophy is Levinas's vision of all that Judaism is and can offer, equating Judaism and universality as did the early German Reformers, or whether this ethics is just what Levinas has to say as a Jew speaking in the forum of European intellectual life, is a question that cannot be decided on the basis of texts alone. The "Judaism" Levinas invokes in his publications, in any event, is one that teaches the whole world. The extent to which Levinas's ethics is "Jewish," then, is that wherein the Jewish message is a message for all mankind. "Whenever one sees 'Israel'" in the sacred texts, Levinas writes, "one can substitute 'humanity'." And, let us add in fidelity to Levinas's thought, in substituting "humanity" one need not erase "Israel." Perhaps one can say of Levinas what Levinas says of Moses Mendelssohn: "He did not forget in his universalism the singularity of the Jewish people and its universal meaning, which results from that very singularity."

The Holocaust is, of course, a unique historical event, the Nazis' resolute and systematic attempt to exterminate European Jewry from 1933 to 1945. Its meaning for Jews and Judaism is just beginning to be grasped, more than half a century afterward. But however Jewish the Holocaust is and however much it is a specific historical event, its meaning, for Levinas, is not just Jewish or for Jews alone. And this is the case not simply because non-Jews were also murdered, or because all historical events are open to public scrutiny and evaluation, but because this specific violence against Jews, like all things in Jewish history, has implications and lessons extending to the whole of humanity for all times. The Holocaust teaches in detail the real workings of totalitarian politics, the empirical horror that results from ideology dominating man. People are often heard to express their ignorance about the nature of evil. Henceforth one can point to the Holocaust, in all its gruesome detail, as the "textbook" par excellence of how evil acts in the world. It also teaches the end of naive theodicy.

Interpreting the Holocaust this way, through universalization, recalls the traditional Jewish reading of Amalek. The rabbis understood that Amalek was not just a desert tribe that once viciously made war on the Jews long ago when they left Egypt. Rather, Amalek's war, so the rabbis taught, teaches Jews how all radical evil operates, shows concretely the extreme, virulent, active, unprovoked hatred of Jews, an evil that recurs again and again in Jewish history, as Haman in Persia and as Hitler in Germany. Thus for the rabbis a particular event in Jewish history becomes paradigmatic for Jewish experience eternally. For Levinas all the particulars of Judaism and Jewish history are paradigmatic not just for Jews as Jews but for all humanity.

Everything in Judaism, right up to the most Jewish elements so seemingly "for Jews only," the discussions in the Talmud about details of Jewish observance, the fringes of prayer shawls, the donning of tefillin, Hebrew prayers tacked onto doorways, all teach universal and not merely Jewish lessons.

What makes the Bible and the Talmud important to Levinas is not their divine origin—about which he says little and in whose defense he says nothing against higher criticism—but the unity and concreteness of their moral lessons. "I have always thought," Levinas said in 1981, "that the great miracle of the Bible lies not at all in the common literary origin, but, inversely, in the confluence of different literatures toward the same essential content. The miracle of this confluence is greater than the miracle of the unique author. Now the pole of this confluence is the ethical, which incontestably dominates this whole book."[4]

The discourses and activities of the sages, personages, and rabbis of the Bible and Talmud are not quaint but expendable "examples" or "illustrations" subordinate to an abstract moral theorizing, as they would be for philosophy. Nor do they offer "proofs" in a rigorous philosophical sense. They are the sources to which humanity is turned and turns to learn its ideals in the first place. This perspective permits Levinas his talmudic readings, where, for example, he enters into a meticulous study of *Bava Mesi'a* 83a–b, of the Babylonian Talmud, to discover a lesson on modern revolution. Or, in the same tractate, he finds that in the words of R. Simeon ben Lakish (Resh Lakish) "the notion of an American or industrial society is thought out to the end." The ethics Levinas finds in the Jewish texts is, of course, the face-to-face dialogical metaphysics that he elaborates in his properly philosophical works. The question as to whether he finds this ethics or introduces it is not Levinas's question. Levinas says very little directly about method. The meaning, the ethics, however, is at once thoroughly and authentically Jewish and given to all humanity.

Even if this be put into question, one thing remains certain: it is the same ethics—the face-to-face, the priority of the other, the obligation to respond—that is found in both Levinas's philosophical works and in his Jewish works.

It is not a simple matter, then, to separate the philosophical from the religious in Levinas's work. Properly religious or Jewish terms—"revelation," "election," "glory," "God"—are found throughout his writings, though always cast in an ethical light.

Levinas does not deny the idea of election, for example, but in his hands it becomes the individual's election to moral agency. The irreplaceability of the self confronted by the other, put into question by the other, made responsible for others, is the elected self.

Revelation, for Levinas, is not understood as a specific event with specific commands, oral and written, given to Moses at Mount Sinai in the year 2448. Rather, revelation is the epiphany of the face, the face of the other person, a bursting through being, a nakedness greater than bare skin.

Prophecy is not the words of the major and minor prophets recorded in nineteen books of the Bible, once and for all, sealed. These words are prophetic for Levinas, and he often quotes the biblical prophets, especially Isaiah, but so too is all speech that calls forth the interlocutor's responsibility to respond. Levinas finds prophetic speech in Dostoyevsky, in Shakespeare, and in his contemporaries.

Levinas does not deny the holy, he interprets it ethically. Holiness is neither an attenuated or otherworldly sanctity nor an adherence to ancient laws. It is precisely and concretely love for the neighbor, food for the hungry, shelter for the unsheltered, a kind word, a door held open, an "after you." The material needs of the other are my spiritual needs—such is holiness.

And God? Levinas does not deny God, to be sure, but he does deny that the issue regarding God is one of affirmation or denial, belief or disbelief. It is the presence and not the existence of God that concerns Levinas. And for Levinas, as one might guess by now, God Himself appears in the ethics and justice of the relation of one person to another, in the one for the other. "A You," Levinas writes, "is inserted between the I and the absolute He."

In the face of this ethically and socially responsible linking of Jewish specificity and humanist universalism, as well as in the face of his appreciation for the advances of scientific knowledge, not to mention his omnipresent high intellectualism, what does Levinas say about Judaism's traditional religious observances? Nothing in his philosophy makes ceremonial and ritual observance necessary, but neither does anything rule it out. Indeed, his own practice of delivering a lecture at his Paris synagogue every Sabbath morning and remarks like the one that follows indicate that like most religious Jews outside of the United States, Levinas's sympathies lie with maintaining traditional Jewish observances. In his preface to the 1982 French translation of Mendelssohn's *Jerusalem*, on the question of assimilation, Levinas writes:

> Without doubt one still finds in Judaism today the unwavering minority of strict observance where—is there need to recall it?—the ceremonial and ritual law is not only a conduit intended to uphold, without distortion, certain representations of rational theology. It is, to the contrary, the very mode according to which the thought of the believer is dedicated to a God whose will is expressed through this law. Here the practice of the law, like its study, are not a simple expression of faith, but the ultimate closeness to a God who is revealed in History. Through all the ventures of dejudaization, it is in these groups, indifferent to the variations of the epochs and as if cut off from every relation to History, which have preserved the energy of the tradition and its invisible influence.

Here is perhaps the place to name Rabbi Hayyim of Volozhyn and the high regard that Levinas has for his work, *The Soul of Life* (first published posthumously in 1824; translated into French in 1986 with a preface by Levinas). What attracts Levinas to this text are not the many Kabbalistic references, since Levinas eschews overt mysticism. Rather, it is Rabbi Hayyim of Volozhyn's basic thought that the Above and the Below, the divine and the human, are linked through human ethical behavior. Human ethical behavior has cosmic implications. What humans do, according to Rabbi Hayyim, is both divinely caused, insofar as humans learn how to behave by having been made in the image of God, *imitatio dei*, and has divine effects, having unlimited consequences that reverberate throughout all creation, from the lowest to the highest realms. Thus, as in the philosophy of Levinas, the good takes priority over the real, and God Himself, who created humans in His image, requires human goodness—ethics and justice—for His own redemption.

Levinas thus takes up the intense ethics of Judaism. His readings of the Talmud are not traditional or rabbinic for they do not conclude with halachic rulings. And if his readings are only scientific or literary, then we cannot understand why he so favors the sacred Jewish texts. Levinas characterizes his readings as "aggadic," teaching ethical lessons. Perhaps one must say that he is engaged in a double task: teaching Jewish ethics to the non-Jewish world and teaching non-Jewish philosophy to the Jewish world. For Levinas Judaism is a "religion for adults." This means that it is a religion committed to interpretation, intellection, discussion, understanding, and commentary, where alternative and divergent views are expected, taken seriously, and have their respected place within the unifying and personalizing frame of an absolute transcendence present in the exigencies of ethics and justice. It is perhaps this vision that allows Levinas to speak as both a philosopher and a Jew, as a Jew to philosophers and as a philosopher to Jews.

Critical Appraisal

Levinas has created a philosophy of the first rank. It is therefore difficult to subject it to critique, at least at the present time. Were Levinas's thought rent with the contradictions, errors, omissions, exclusions, deceptions, and other internal weaknesses that provide the usual fodder for critique, it would not be a philosophy of the first rank. Nor would it deserve extended attention.

Still, because Levinas's work has influenced two generations of European thinkers, it has inevitably attracted its share of criticism. The criticisms of Levinas that have been articulated, however, have either not been sufficiently attentive to the actual contents of his philosophy, such as, for example, Simone de Beauvoir's early and passing criticism in *The Second Sex*, or like most criticism they reduce to the expression of fundamentally different commitments. These differences are especially evident in the dimensions of religion, where Levinas's thought has been both admired and disputed by Christian theologians; ontology, where Levinas's ethics upsets the reigning mystique of Heidegger's *Seinfrage*; and epistemology, where Levinas's priorities challenge the hegemony of scientific discipline. To these and other alternatives, to their actual and implied criticisms, Levinas has conscientiously responded in his work.

Although Levinas's main opponent is without question Heidegger, there is another contemporary thinker who merits special consideration, both because of his intellectual stature and because he has grappled at closest quarters with Levinas's thought. This thinker is Jacques Derrida, founder of the philosophical-literary school known as deconstruction.

On one hand, Derrida acknowledges a great indebtedness to Levinas: the derivation of the decisive if not central deconstructive notion of the "trace" from Levinas's 1963 article "The Trace of the Other." On the other hand, in two long articles published in 1964 and 1980, Derrida radically challenges the ethical and metaphysical priority Levinas attributes to the irreducible otherness of the other person. Derrida attempts to show that more compelling than an ethical characterization of alterity is a semiotic reading. According to this account, meaning derives not from a relationship with the other person qua ethical other, but from the alterity of a differential and ever marginal field of linguistic signifiers. For Derrida Levinas has ultimately only masked the alterity of this deeper slippage of meaning with an updated version of an essentially outmoded negative theology.

Levinas, of course, rejects Derrida's assessment. Against the semantic ambivalencies that result from a preoccupation with the internal dynamics of language and are, in addition, exalted by deconstructive analysis, Levinas returns again and again to the concrete straightforwardness, the extralinguistic significance of the dative. Language must ultimately be spoken by someone and to someone. Deference to the other person precedes the Derridaian deferrals of sense generated by the play of language. Or, to use Levinas's formula, "saying precedes the said." The ethical positivity of the difference that separates and joins interlocutors—nonrepresentable, asymmetrical, irrecuperable—precedes, with an ethical precedence, and conditions, without establishing an ontological foundation, the deconstructive *différance* that plays in all language.

Though Levinas has replied time and again to Derrida, most followers of the deconstructive school remain unmoved or unconvinced by his efforts (or perhaps unaware of them). Derrida himself, in contrast, seems to have come around, or come back to Levinas's ethical claims. This change was evident in Derrida's address to a plenary session of the Eastern Division of the American Philosophical Association on December 30, 1988. Speaking on the topic of the politics of friendship, Derrida's discourse was Levinasian more than anything else. Using the language of *Totality and Infinity*, Derrida attacked the "Greek model" of relationality in the name of friendship, which he conceived in terms of "heterology, asymmetry, and infinity," where "one *answers* first *to* the Other."

Only time will tell to what extent Derrida has taken up Levinas's ethics and what this appropriation will mean in his own idiom and for the deconstructive enterprise. Whatever the outcome, this recent public address by one of Levinas's most brilliant and persistent "critics" testifies to the resilience and appeal—under fire, as it were—of Levinas's metaphysical ethics.

Although his thought has already exerted an extensive influence in continental European intellectual circles, in America, even though all his major works have been translated into English, Levinas's impact has been minimal. This is true in academic philosophy departments as well as in Jewish intellectual circles. In professional philosophy the neglect of Levinas is doubtless another symptom of more than half a century of Anglo-American attention to entirely diffferent matters. Perhaps recent shifts to new concerns by professional Anglo-American philosophers will lead to a greater interest in Levinas.

In American Jewish intellectual circles Levinas's name is known, to be sure, but his work rarely is, or is rarely known in depth. There are a variety of explanations for this neglect. Eugene Borowitz attributes it to a more general neglect of rationalism. Beyond that, he continues, "Levinas's lack of followers may be due to the difficulties many thinkers find with this uncommon form of rationality."[5] Another stumbling block may be that Levinas's work does not fit neatly into one or another of American Jewry's competing denominational alignments. Of course, these explanations for neglect—rationalism, difficulty, and nondenominationalism—certainly do not amount to a justification. They probably reveal more about the contemporary American Jewish intellectual scene than about problems in Levinas.

Notes

1. Interview with Levinas, March 1986, in Francois Poirie, *Emmanuel Levinas: Qui êtes-vous* (Lyon, 1987), p. 67. [My translation.]
2. Poirie, *Levinas*, p. 70.
3. Poirie, *Levinas*, p. 86.

4. Interview with Levinas, February, 1981, in Emmanuel Levinas, *Ethics and Infinity*, translated by Richard A. Cohen (Pittsburgh, 1985), p. 115.

5. Eugene Borowitz, "Reason," in *Contemporary Jewish Religious Thought*, edited by Arthur A. Cohen and Paul Mendes-Flohr (New York, 1987), p. 752.

FOR FURTHER READING

Works by Emmanuel Levinas

La theorie de l'intuition dans la phenomenologie de Husserl. Paris, 1930; Paris, 1962, 1970, 1984. *The Theory of Intuition in Husserl's Phenomenology.* Translated by Andre Orianne. Evanston, 1973.

De l'evasion (1935). Montpellier: Fata Morgana, 1982.

De l'existent a l'existence. Paris, 1947; Paris, 1973, 1978. *Existence and Existents.* Translated by Alphonso Lingis. The Hague, 1978.

Le temps et l'autre. In J. Wahl, *Le Choix, Le Monde, L'Existence.* Grenoble, 1948, pp. 125–196; with new preface, Montepellier, 1979. *Time and the Other, and Other Essays.* Translated by Richard A. Cohen. Pittsburgh, 1987.

En decouvrant l'existence avec Husserl et Heidegger. Paris, 1949; 2d ed., 1967, 1974.

Totalite et infini: Essai sur l'exteriorite. The Hague, 1961, 1965, 1968, 1971, 1974, 1980. *Totality and Infinity: An Essay on Exteriority.* Translated by Alphonso Lingis. The Hague, 1969; Pittsburgh, 1969, 1979.

Difficile liberte: Esais sur le judaisme. Paris, 1963; 2d ed., 1976. *Difficult Freedom: Essays on Judaism.* Translated by Sean Hand. Baltimore, 1990.

Humanisme de l'autre homme. Montpellier, 1972.

Autrement qu'etre ou au-dela de l'essence. The Hague, 1974, 1978. *Otherwise than Being or Beyond Essence.* Translated by Alphonso Lingis. The Hague, 1981.

Sur Maurice Blanchot. Montpellier, 1975.

Noms propres. Montpellier, 1975.

La mort et le temps (1975–76). Paris, 1991. Edited by Jacques Rolland.

Quatre lectures talmudiques. Paris, 1968.

Du sacre au saint: cinq nouvelles lectures talmudiques. Paris, 1977. *Nine Talmudic Readings.* Translated by Annette Aronowitz. Bloomington, 1990.

L'au-dela du verset. Paris, 1982.

De Dieu qui vient a l'idee. Paris, 1982.

Ethique et infini. Paris, 1982. *Ethics and Infinity.* Translated by Richard A. Cohen, Pittsburgh, 1985.

Transcendance et intelligibilite. Geneve, 1984.

Hors sujet. Montpellier, 1987. *Outside the Subject.* Translated by Michael B. Smith. London, 1993.

A l'heure des nations. Paris, 1988. *In the Time of the Nations.* Translated by Michael B. Smith. London, forthcoming.

Entre nous: Essais sur le penser-a-l'autre. Paris, 1991.

Collected Philosophical Papers. Edited and translated by Alphonso Lingis. Dordrecht, 1987.

The Levinas Reader. Edited by Sean Hand. Cambridge, 1989.

Discovering Existence with Husserl. Edited and translated by Richard A. Cohen. Bloomington, forthcoming.

For the most complete Levinas bibliography, see Roger Burggraeve, *Emmanuel Levinas: Une bibliographie primaire et secondaire (1929–1989).* Leuven: Peeters, 1990.

Works about Emmanuel Levinas

Edith Wyschogrod, *Emmanuel Levinas: The Problem of Ethical Metaphysics.* The Hague, 1974.

Steven G. Smith, *The Argument to the Other: Reason beyond Reason in the Thought of Karl Barth and E. Levinas.* Chico, California, 1983.

Face to Face with Emmanuel Levinas. Edited by Richard A. Cohen. Albany, 1986.

The Provocation of Levinas: Rethinking the Other. Edited by Robert Bernasconi and David Wood. London, 1988.

Re-Reading Levinas. Edited by Robert Bernasconi and Simon Critchley. Bloomington, 1991.

Richard A. Cohen, *Elevations: The Height of the Good in Levinas and Rosenzweig.* Forthcoming.

Nathan Rotenstreich

A. ZVIE BAR-ON

I.

Professor Nathan Rotenstreich, one of the most prominent Jewish thinkers of our time, was born in 1914, in Sambor (then Galicia, Austria, afterwards Poland, now the Ukraine). His father, Fishel Rotenstreich, was one of the leaders of Polish Jewry between the two World Wars. Some time after the establishment of the Polish government he was nominated as a member of the Polish Senate and a few years later made his début on one of the benches of the Sejm (the elected Polish House of Commons). He was active in the General Zionist Party, which was the right wing of the Zionist movement in Poland at that time. In 1935 he was elected by his party as its delegate to the 18th Zionist Congress, and by the Congress as a member of the Jewish Agency. He then made aliyah, shortly after which he gained the position of the Chairman of the Jewish Agency's Department of Commerce and Industry, a post which he held until his death in 1938.

Nathan emigrated to Palestine three years before his father in order to enroll at the Hebrew University where he studied philosophy and related subjects. In 1936 he received his Masters degree and two years later his Ph.D. In 1949 he was nominated Senior Lecturer in his *Alma Mater*. In the years 1957–61 he acted as the Dean of the University's Faculty of Humanities, and in the period between 1965 and 1969 as its Rector. He has also taught in a number of universities outside of Israel as a visiting professor. Several prestigious awards have been conferred on him, including the Tchernichowsky Prize for Literary Translation (1954), and the Israel Prize (1963).

His first article on a philosophical topic, "Place and Time in A. D. Gordon's Doctrine," was published a year after his arrival in Palestine in *Hapoel Hazair*, the journal of the Jewish Labor Movement in Palestine. His first philosophical book, *The Problem of Substance in Philosophy from Kant to Hegel*, a revised version of his Ph.D. dissertation, appeared six years later (published by Reuven Mass, Jerusalem, 1939). Rotenstreich soon became known as an original and independent thinker and as a very prolific author. The bibliography of his publications, compiled by one of his former students, A. Gilead, and published in the 1984 volume of the Hebrew Philosophical Quarterly *Iyyun*, contained some 430 items to that date, including more than 40 books.

Rotenstreich's massive literary production exposes the enormous range of his thought. Even if we take into account only philosophy proper, his work encompasses an impressive range of subjects: Theory of Knowledge, Ontology, Philosophical Anthropology, The Philosophy of History, Ethics, Political Philosophy and more. Rotenstreich, however, has never merely enclosed himself in the ivory tower, and since his youth has shown an intense interest in problems of the Jewish people, as well as in problematic issues to be found within the international arena. His extra-mural political and socio-cultural activities have drawn much public attention.

The Israeli public remembers in particular his involvement in the so-called Lavon affair. Pinchas Lavon, one of the outstanding and sharp-witted leaders of the Israeli Labor Movement in the forties and fifties, became entangled, or so it was assumed, in a strange and infamous affair having to do with an Israeli Intelligence miscarriage in Egypt. Most of his colleagues abandoned him in his stubborn and pathetic fight for rehabilitation, but Rotenstreich, Lavon's friend for years and once very close to him ideologically, stood firmly at his side and defended him vigorously. This caused a serious breach between him and the establishment of the Labor Movement that lasted for many years.

In his writing on political subjects we always find Rotenstreich going down to the roots of the problems which are on the public agenda. he has his special way of calling the political leaders to order, urging them to forsake their narrow personal and/or factional interests and requiring that they listen to their national conscience and pay attention to the ethical aspects of politics. He is also one of the last Jewish thinkers, especially among those who live permanently in Israel, that still pays close attention to the Zionist dimension of Jewish existence, whether in Israel or in the Diaspora. His important scholarship on the history of Jewish thought in modern times provides an excellent basis for this part of his activity. In this historical work not only individual Jewish thinkers are dealt with, but the entire canvas of Jewish spiritual life in the modern period is set out and analyzed.

Within the limited framework of this essay it is impossible to discuss all the fields of Rotenstreich's thought. Instead I shall focus on his contribution to Jewish and general philosophy, his conception of Zionist ideology, and his treatment of some of the major problems confronting the State of Israel.

II.

Rotenstreich opens his *History of Modern Jewish Thought* with a short but penetrating analysis of the great changes that have occurred in Jewish thought since the beginning of the modern era.[1]

To begin with, modern rationalism caused an important change in the evaluation of cultural creativity in general. It became common to accept a plurality of cultures and to assign only relative value to each of them. It was not easy for Judaism to accept this idea but it was finally absorbed, and it eventually led to the secularization of Jewish thought and customs, as well as to the emergence of a basically secular Jewish national movement.

Moreover, the idea of religious relativity became connected with the concept of historicity in the way that Judaism grasped itself. It was no longer possible to ignore the fact—metaphysical in nature—that Judaism, as one among many religions, and as a part of the general record of human creativity, is subject to changes and reflects certain features of a temporal process.

Does such a concept contradict the very notion of revelation as an absolute, eternal value? Not necessarily, Rotenstreich argues. Logically, you may retain the idea of an eternally valid content of revelation, and at the same time assume that the way people conceive of this content, i.e., their religious consciousness undergoes changes in time and is of an historical character. Now, however, while such might have been the situation in theory, in practice the consequences of the encounter of Jewish thought with the modern world has entailed a crisis for Judaism the focus of which has been the relation between what is asserted to be Judaism's essence and its actual historical character.

The new movements that emerged in Judaism in modern times, and that matured in the nineteenth century, deviating from the traditional conservative establishment, were the outcome of this historical and conceptual crisis. The most important of these new changes were the Reform movement and Zionism.

This brings us to Rotenstreich's interpretation of Zionist ideology. In an essay published in 1980 Rotenstreich discerns three main aspects of Zionist ideology: (1) Zionism as the renaissance of the Jewish people and of Jewish culture in modern times; (2) Zionism as the striving for the normalization of "Jewish existence;" and (3) Zionism as the shift "from Messianism to modern historical aspirations." The argument that Rotenstreich advances in support of this characterization of Zionism starts with the following consideration"

> "[T]raditional Jewish culture involved [a] synthesis of its *Weltanschauung* (articles or belief, codes of behavior) and the subject or carrier of that *Weltanschauung* (i.e. the Jewish people itself), since a view of the position of the Jewish people in the world was part and parcel of that *Weltanschauung.* Its position as thus conceived, served to some extent as [a] barrier between Judaism and those universalist religions which regarded themselves as successors to Judaism and which denied the position of the Jewish people as the basic subject and carrier of the religion.[2]

In this relationship between the Judaic world-outlook and the Jewish people as the social carrier of that outlook Rotenstreich detects a paradox: Jewish religion has a universalistic character; it relates to the Universe as a whole, and it believes in a God who is said to have created that Universe and kept control of it. Yet this very same religion assigns to the Jewish people, out of all the nations on the Earth, a special role; it is a religion of one chosen people exclusively. Universalism and particularism are hence joined together, not altogether without difficulty, in it.

In Rotenstreich's view, Zionist ideology retains the above

mentioned basic relationship between its *Weltanschauung* and the whole Jewish people as its carrier. It tries, however, to overcome the paradoxical feature of this conjunction by assimilating what Rotenstreich calls "the modern, national awareness" and by interpreting that awareness in the Jewish case as "the drive towards normalization." In this way Zionism function on the one hand as a reformulation of traditional Jewish concepts and on the other as an adjustment to the modern, general (or, more appropriately European) world-outlook.

The shift from messianic eschatology to the Zionist aspiration within the framework of a sovereign Jewish state is in Rotenstreich's view another such modernizing reformulation. In this respect we should look at Zionist thinking as "a major change in the Judaic conception of time." He writes:

> Zionism is on the one hand a continuation of Jewish attempts towards redemption through the ingathering of the Jewish people in the land of Israel and on the other hand Zionism *neutralizes* that redemptive aspect by shifting the endeavour from future eschatological expectations to present historical and thus empirical acts.[3]

With this interpretation, Rotenstreich implies, Zionist ideology is an appropriate response to the Jewish condition that prevailed since the nineteenth century in both Central and Eastern Europe, as well as in Western countries. In the former case (to be referred to as Con$_1$), Zionism was a reaction to the unhappy state of a community that was for ages subject to cruel discrimination and persecution, a community whose members were deprived of their basic human rights, and which was also deprived as a whole of its fundamental national right, i.e., the right to exist as a national entity shaping its own collective destiny. In the latter case (Con$_2$) the Jewish condition was determined by the Emancipation of the Jews which bestowed on every Jew, as an individual, equal human rights, but denied national rights to the Jewish community as a whole.

The Zionist solution for Con$_2$ seems to entail logically its solution for Con$_1$. The Jew from any Central or Eastern European country, as an individual, was supposed to gain the status of a free person endowed with all the basic human rights, i.e., to reach emancipation *through* auto-emancipation of the Herzlian variety: the status as a free citizen of an independent, sovereign Jewish state.

III.

This solution, however, turned out to be a mixed blessing. The Zionist goal was to be achieved by two parallel processes: 1) the establishment of a Jewish sovereign state with its own government, army, legal system, culture and educational institutions, etc.; and 2) the ingathering of all, or almost all, Jews of the Diaspora in that sovereign state, i.e., the liquidation of the Diaspora.

The first of these two processes can be considered completed, or almost completed. "Almost," because as soon as Israel was formally established the neighboring countries launched a war against it which is still going on (with the exception of Egypt that signed a peace treaty with Israel).

The other process, however, is far from completed. True, immediately after the establishment of the state and in the first decades of its existence the process gained impressive momentum in the form of large waves of massive immigration of Jews from all parts of the globe. After that, however, the tempo of immigration slowed significantly. And now we witness the breathtaking phenomenon of a renewed massive influx of Jews, this time mainly from the Soviet Union. Many Soviet Jews, however, would readily prefer changing one Diaspora for another as thousands of them did in the seventies and early eighties. They did everything possible to reach the shores of America instead of the country which they called their homeland when they sought to escape from the Soviet Union.

But is America still Diaspora?

Rotenstreich raises this question in the context of a discussion of the relevance and justification of the Zionist movement in our time.[4] He criticizes the contention of many Jews in the West, particularly intellectuals, successful businessmen, and those engaged in local politics, that Western democracies, are no longer Diaspora. These Jews do not deny that in many other countries such as the Arab states, the formerly communist states of Eastern Europe, including the Soviet Union, and some countries of the so-called Third World, Jews are still fighting for their elementary rights. These countries can be classified as Diaspora. However, the affluent democracies, led by the U.S.A., where Jews enjoy complete equality and freedom to choose their way of life are, or so it is contended, are not Diaspora.

Rotenstreich replies to this claim as follows: There is indeed no precedent in the history of Diaspora for such a situation. Nevertheless, the strict definition of the Diaspora concept also applies to the modern democracies of the West. Even in these countries the Jewish people is not recognized as an entity entitled to shape its *collective* existence without outside interference. Such a status belongs only to the Jews of Israel, and in this respect Israel is unique in the contemporary world.

The obvious conclusion therefore, predicated on these considerations, is that at least "half" of the Zionist goal has not yet been achieved. And in consequence Zionism is still a relevant response to the Jewish condition in the present era.

Is it more morally justified? The first impression is that Rotenstreich tries to avoid this question by a somewhat cryptic statement: "Moral justification of Zionism is not a Zionist issue."[5] It soon becomes clear, however, that there is no mystery in this contention. What it means is that the justification of Zionism lies in its very nature as a national liberation movement. So that on this level the question of justification does not arise. If it arises at all, it arises only in the context of the Jewish-Arab conflict. The realization of the goal of Zionism creates a real conflict with another national liberation movement, morally justified in equal measure.

On that issue, much discussed in the last few years, both in Israel and in the Diaspora, Rotenstreich's position is quite clear. There is only one possible way of solving the problem and bestowing moral justification on Zionism: the way of mutuality and compromise.

It is worth noticing that Rotenstreich has no doubt about the Zionist movement (we should perhaps say: the central trend of this movement) having chosen such a compromise policy from its beginning. You do not need, he suggests, a better proof of this than the acceptance by the Zionist establishment of the Partition Plan of the Palestine territory in 1947 (to which, for the sake of consistency one should perhaps mention here another partition accepted willy-nilly by the Zionists, that of 1922 as a result of which the Kingdom of Jordan was created). The position of the Arabs was entirely different:

> Their line was from the beginning a total denial of recognition of Zionism. Today the Arabs still deliberately misrepresent the desire of

the Jewish people to preserve its uniqueness; they portray it as a desire to lower the status of others and therefore as racism.[6]

Obviously, Rotenstreich categorically rejects this kind of accusation as a distortion of the essence of Zionist ideology, strongly supporting instead the thesis of mutuality:

> [T]here can be no genuine solution of the Arab-Israeli conflict without the mutual recognition by Zionism and Arab nationalism of each other's right to exist. This means, on our part, that we should declare that we accept the basic right of the Arabs to decide their own fate.[7]

Such a position puts Rotenstreich somewhere to the left of the center politically as far as the main issue of Israeli politics goes. In the context of our discussion, however, it may be more appropriate to bring out Rotenstreich's approach to the Israeli reality on a still more fundamental level. We can do so by presenting three of his observations on the nature of the State of Israel and the main dilemmas it faces.

Under the subtitle "The Jewish horizon of Israel" Rotenstreich writes:

> As a rule, a state compromises three main elements: the physical element, i.e. the *territorial* basis to which the authority of the state applies and on which its citizens (and other residents) live; the human element, namely, the *human population* of the space delineated by the territorial basis; and third, the authority, or the element of sovereignty (...). Those three elements exist and operate in the structure of the State of Israel, of course, and because of them it is a state. At the same time the State of Israel, when considered in terms of its Jewish significance, is characterized by a fourth component by virtue of which its overall character differs from that of other states. The fourth component is what may be called its "horizon" ... The horizon of Israel comprises, in the first place, the generations of Jews who adhered religiously, emotionally or otherwise to the notion of organized, collective Jewish existence. Within the horizon are those Jews of today's world who view themselves as attached to Israel, whether because of their own personal ideological decision or simply because Israel exists and is present in their day-to-day consciousness.[8]

This is a far reaching thesis about the bond—or it you wish, the covenant—between Israel and the Jews of the Diaspora, which is not only a matter of common origin or of political expediency, but an intrinsic part, and unique feature, of Israeli statehood.

Rotenstreich's second observation concerns the conflict between "old" and "new" in Israeli life, between the active force of tradition, both religious and otherwise, on the one hand, and the new outlook derived from science and technology, as well as from socialism and modern democratic values, on the other. This conflict takes various forms. The most stormy and perhaps dangerous is that between the religious and the secular parts of the society. In Rotenstreich's view, some kind of synthesis and compromise between these central factors is necessary to keep Israel a viable, creative society.

The last observation by Rotenstreich worth emphasizing relates to still another conflict that can be detected in Israeli reality, though less visible. This collision is economic. In order to grasp its nature we should keep in mind the distinction between two kinds of economic growth, the first sees economic growth as leading to "the strengthening of the society and enhancement of its security," the second sees economic growth as a process of "raising the standard of living of the individual." Only the first variety fits smoothly together, Rotenstreich argues, with the Zionist principle of auto-emancipation. The second kind of economic growth does not. It is bound to cause inequality within the population, first in the economic and then subsequently in many other fields of activity. Rotenstreich calls attention to this issue as one of the gravest dilemmas presently facing Israeli society.

IV.

Before we embark on an analysis of Rotenstreich's purely philosophical views let us say a few words about his *mode* of philosophizing, his *method*. As I see it, Rotenstreich makes use of an approach that is very close to Husserl's phenomenological method but he has enriched it with typically Kantian insights. However, elements of other traditions can be discerned in his philosophizing as well: the aporetic method of Aristotle; and Hegel's dialectic, especially as it was developed and amplified by Bradley, Collingwood and others. Also, he lavishly employs the device known since pre-Socratic times—the paradox. All these components are combined in his work producing an original technique of theorization that has enriched the contemporary philosophical scene.

The heart of Rotenstreich's philosophical system is his conception of man, i.e., his philosophical anthropology. This conception he applies to various domains of human activity. What is of a particular interest is that this is done in confrontation with an alternative scheme of ideas, that of the Anglo-American philosopher Alfred North Whitehead. The question that Rotenstreich is primarily concerned with is: what should be required of an anthropological scheme in order to enable us to explicate in its terms the concept of moral responsibility? It is presupposed here, and in my view justifiably, that moral responsibility is one of those "stubborn data" of human activity that requires a philosophical explanation. It is a fundamental challenge to any anthropological scheme. In Rotenstreich's philosophy this issue is of particular importance since it concerns the problem of deciding between the primacy of the individual or of the community. Rotenstreich argues that were we to adopt Whitehead's notion of the "superject," intended to replace that of the "subject," the meaning of the very concept of moral responsibility would be destroyed. This would happen, according to Rotenstreich, since moral responsibility presupposes the self-consciousness of the ego *which endures in its identity.* How, that is to say, shall we make S responsible at time t_2 for the action S performed at t_1, if we are not allowed, as Whitehead's concept of the superject suggests, to maintain that S-in-t_2 is identical to S-in-t_1, i.e. that it was a common self, S, who performed both actions?

This is not the first time that Whitehead has been attacked in this context. It seems to me, however, that all this criticism rests on a mistaken interpretation of the concept of responsibility. I do not think that it follows from the concept of responsibility that the person made (or who considers themself) responsible for A must be the agent who literally performed A. Is it not in certain circumstances a matter of course to make parents responsible for their child's doings, for the director of some enterprise to be made responsible for an action of its employees, or for the commander of a military operation to be made responsible for the action of his troops? We have to distinguish, then, between the case in which responsibility for an action is attributed to its performer and the case in which somebody is made responsible for an action though he did not perform it personally. Moreover, from a purely logical point of view, there is nothing to prevent us from considering the case of making the agent who performed an action responsible for it a particular instance of the case of making responsible for it *either* that agent *or* a person who is related to him in a way that can be unequivocally defined. We can derive from this distinction a terminological rule to the effect that the sort of responsibility attributed to the performer of A will be called "direct responsibility," while the other type will be called "indirect responsibility." We can now see that the difference between the approaches of Whitehead and Rotenstreich consists in the decision as to where to put the dividing line between these two kinds of responsibility. According to Rotenstreich's conception, every case of making me responsible for an action that I performed in the past, do in the present, or will do in the future, refers to *direct responsibility*. By contrast, any case of making me responsible for actions done by others, no matter what has prompted such a judgment, refers to *indirect responsibility*.

Now, within Whitehead's conception, the responsibility that can be attributed to the agent, and only here and now while the action is being performed, would count as direct responsibility. The responsibility for actions which "I" performed in the past or which "I" will perform in the future count as a type of indirect responsibility for actions performed by somebody else.

We have in front of us two readings of the concept of moral responsibility. The choice between them should be the consequence of choosing between two different anthropological (or perhaps ontological) conceptual schemes, and not *vice versa*. On this point I disagree with Professor Rotenstreich who makes the choice between the schemes dependent on one's concept of moral responsibility.

V.

The point at issue in Rotenstreich's inquiry into historicity and what he calls "the historical dimension of human existence" is the Hegelian distinction between the subjective and objective "poles of history", i.e., between history as the real process of events and history as a science, as historiography. Rotenstreich's treatment

reveals the relationship between the two as abounding in paradoxes. The main problem appears to be of a transcendental
nature, now, not in the Husserlian sense, but this time according
to its original Kantian meanings. That is, the problem of historicity poses itself in the following form: how is history at all possible?

The set of relations between the two domains of history is
approached by Rotenstreich from the point of view of historical
knowledge, rather than from that of the real historical process, the
object of historical knowledge. History in this sense is usually
acknowledged as a discipline whose object of inquiry is the past
—an event or a series of events that happened in times gone by.
The aim of the inquiry is assumed to be the description and
explanation of that particular past by means of data available at
present. However, if we want to think of history as an essentially
empirical study rather than as an enterprise of a speculative nature
we have, according to Rotenstreich, to reverse the order. The
direct object of history is rather the datum available at present: the
document, the institution, the political movement active now. *We
look into the past for an explanation of the datum existing at present.* In
other words, in the basic act of historical cognition the *explanan-
dum*, i.e., what needs to be explained, is a datum available at
present while the means of explanation, the *explanans*, is the event
in the past. When it occurred the event was multiform, moulded,
concrete. Out of this moulded structure the historical inquiry
chooses only those layers that explain the datum. It can thus be
seen that from the perspective of the historical consciousness,
personified by the historian, the event in the past became a
conceptual construction. The historical consciousness did not
actually intend to construct or to constitute it, i.e., it wanted to
*re*construct the real event in its individuality; this, however, turns
out to be impossible.

This is only one of the paradoxes that emerges from the
encounter of historical reality and historical cognition. Another
aporia takes shape with the demonstration that the historical
science with its constitutive function gets absorbed, swallowed up,
by the historical event. For example, Heinrich Graetz's *History of
the Jews* was, at the time of its writing (the second half of the
nineteenth century), a typical expression of the historical
consciousness in its cognitive function, a bridge built in order to
connect the past with the present. However, as soon as the work

reached its readers' eyes, it became a powerful factor in shaping the event or process called the "renaissance of the Jewish people in modern times."

Does this mean that the difference between history as cognition and history as reality has disappeared, that what remains is the all-swallowing historical process as the historicists argue? No, says Rotenstreich, who considers the refutation of historicism one of the most fascinating modern conceptual challenges. The event may perhaps swallow up the *content* of the historical consciousness but this consciousness retains its independent metaphysical status. Thus, the absorption of Graetz's *History* into the historical reality does not prevent the historical consciousness from using it time and again in contemplative activity, both as a means of reconstructing events from the past, as described by Graetz, and as a historical datum explained by Graetz's personality, his surroundings, time, etc.

Nor should we forget, Rotenstreich argues, that an event, a single brick in the mansion of history, is itself consciousness-dependent. A historical occurrence is not a fact of nature. It is entirely a human action performed by beings whose consciousness is characterized by acts of deliberation, evaluation, decision, planning, and anticipation of the future. Whatever its functions it is still consciousness.

As in the theories of Croce and Collingwood who tried to defend the thesis of the identity between subject and object in history here too there is some danger of confusion. Rotenstreich suggests a transformation of this thesis. Granted, he argues, that from the ontological point of view, such an identity is the case, there is also a clear difference between the two *in their functions*. On the one hand, there is contemplation transcending "the sacred ground of the present" towards the past, but on the other we have the praxis standing on that very "sacred ground," but directed towards the future.

This marks out the multifariousness of man's creative power, different manifestations of which are science and technology, the political realm, language, literature, art, religion, etc. Each of these manifestations has its historical dimension but this historical dimension does not exhaust the specific contents of human creativity. Equally, history is not reducible to only one of the various fields of human activity.

VI.

Lastly, we shall consider one particular manifestation of human creativity, the political realm and the place of the individual within it.

One of the central propositions of Rotenstreich's philosophy of history is that history does not create man but, rather, man creates history. In order to become a historical being man has to be a conscious being. His relation towards the world is that of understanding which is of course impossible without consciousness. A parallel proposition is paramount is his political philosophy: the state, or society, does not create the man; on the contrary, man creates society and the state. The reason is again that in order to become a political being man has to be a conscious, understanding being. Compare from this point of view the following two passages:

> ... man is a historical being because he is *homo sapiens*, but homo sapiens is not an essence created by history. Home sapiens is the presupposition of history and not in himself an upshot of it. The emergence of homo sapiens may be considered as an event in the evolution of the cosmos, but not as an event in the historical process itself. Man is historical precisely because he is more than historical.[9]

and

> ... the existence of the political order presupposes the existence of men who understand it and relate themselves to it on the basis of their understanding. (...) Understanding always points to a relatedness founded in discernment and alertness, and whose nucleus is theoretical. Being practical, political activity within a network of relations controlled by the political order, does not exhaust the essence of human activity. (...) Man's nature, as his essence, is not to be equated with his character as a political creature.[10]

In the first passage the phrase "homo sapiens" is used, in the second one—"men who understand." The idea conveyed is the same. Both in history and in the political realm the human essence actualizes itself. However, this human essence derives neither from the historical process as the historians submit nor from political institutions as some sociopolitical philosophers maintain. Moreover, while history and society are expressions of the actualized human essence, they are not the only possible expressions of it.

Rotenstreich begins his analysis of political reality with an observation that order and power are the essential features of the polis. He ends it by establishing the principles that shape political activity, the last of which is the *principle of rights and duties.* I, however, shall proceed the other way round. That is, I shall start my analysis with the concepts of right and duty, and using Rotenstreich's argument, try to arrive at a reasonable explication of the essential features of political power in its several ramifications.

Rights and duties are, in Rotenstreich's conception, a concrete expression, perhaps the most concrete expression, of the relationship between an individual and the state. The right to live where one does or to settle elsewhere and be active there economically, culturally, and otherwise, the right to protect one's existence and property, the right to bear children and rear them, the duty to obey local custom and norm, the duty to pay part of one's earnings to the state as tax, the duty to serve in the army or otherwise contribute to the community defense—these and other similar functions constitute a very real, though invisible network into which we are born and through which we live our lives. We "use" rights, or "enjoy" their realization; we "fulfill" duties or "dodge" them. We also think about them and take stands regarding them. Sometimes we fight for our rights, for their extension or alteration. Quite often we appraise systems of rights and duties other than the one in which we are living (which may take the form of so-called revolutionary activity). We never question, however (except perhaps for some extreme anarchists), the very structure of rights and duties as an expression of the specific relationship between ourselves and the state.

The questions asked about specific rights and duties or specific system abide in the field of inquiry of an ideologist or a political scientist. The questions that can be raised about the very structure of rights and duties are dealt with by the political philosopher. Some such philosophers argue that the status of rights is *essentially political,* i.e., that it is only within the political framework, the state, that rights and duties of man have any meaning. The individual as such has no rights or duties at all. The status of rights *presupposes* in principle the political framework.

This view may be considered as derived from the Hegelian conception of the essence of the state and of the individual's position within it. It can also be regarded as a variety of the "sociological fallacy" alluded to above.

Objecting to this view, Rotenstreich argues that the status of rights is of an *extrapolitical* nature in spite of the fact that rights are deeply enmeshed within the political and social reality and have received a highly sophisticated judicial articulation. In Rotenstreich's view three parts of the structure of rights and duties may be distinguished: (a) the *definition* of the concept of a right; (b) *principles* by which its status can be justified; and (c) various *strata* in which this status evolves.

The definition of a right Rotenstreich suggests is this:

> By the rights of man we mean the justifiable demands made by men for such consideration as will guarantee them a place in human reality, an ensured field of activity, and an opportunity to partake of the possessions which civilization has to offer.[11]

Rights are defined in terms of *demands*. Accordingly, Rotenstreich sees the status of rights as based on *the principle of freedom*. It is freedom in its elementary, primordial form characteristic of man as an "understanding creature." The fact that men make demands reveals a fundamental presupposition about the existence of the "distance" between them and the circumstances under which they live and act. The necessary condition of human rights, as demands, is the status of man as a free being.[12] But the definition does not speak simply of demands. The basic demand is that he who makes the demand is to be respected. Accordingly, the status of rights is interpreted as based also on *the principle of equality*. The demander is entitled to respect because he is a being who participates in the human essence. Note, however, that each person is able to realize the human essence only partially and in his individual way. Taking him into consideration, respecting him, means therefore acknowledging his individuality, his needs, the particular way in which the human essence is in his case actualized. This is alluded to in Rotenstreich's definition by the expressions "place in reality" and "partaking of the possession," and accordingly Rotenstreich envisages the status of rights as rooted in *the principle of justice*.

It must not be forgotten that on Rotenstreich's account each of the specific principles *transcends the political realm.* They are all implied by man's place in the universe and derived from meta-physical assumptions. This part of Rotenstreich's thought is elaborated upon, as mentioned above, in his important study *Spirit and Man.*

Having discussed the status of rights let us review their specific realizations in life. Rotenstreich lists a number of strata through which rights find their articulation: (a) rights of a human being in relation to himself (like to right to abide by the imperatives of his conscience, the right to evaluate phenomena by his own standards etc.); (b) the rights of an individual with respect to free expression (e.g., his opinion about some other person); (c) the rights of man with respect to the state (here belongs one's right to participate in the establishment of the political entity, as well as the justified demand that the state must keep intact all the other rights of the individual); (d) the rights relevant to civilization and history (basically, the right to an appropriate standard of living in terms of the prevailing state).

Let us return to (c) where the status of rights finds its expression in man's basic political right of constituting and maintaining the political entity. We here touch upon one of the central tenets of Rotenstreich's political philosophy. An ordinary man is not inclined to think that *he* constitutes and maintains the state. In his approach to the state the decisive fact, already alluded to, is that he was born *into* a given political order, and in a certain, quite important sense, *by* that order; a truth so tellingly described in the famous dispute between Socrates and the laws of Athens in Plato's *Crito.* Affected by it, the common man tends to treat the political order as prevailing independently of him or anyone like him. this, argues Rotenstreich, is a naive and mistaken view. There is no political order he writes:

> without acts of directness and intentionality, none in the acknow-ledgement of order as a certain meaning, or even as an idea. Man must live and act in concert for the expression to exist. The existence of political order is rooted in human reality; if it has the status of reality, it is only because the human beings who constitute and maintain it are real.[13]

It has not been said, to be precise, that men altogether create the structure by intentionality and acknowledgement. Even without

246 . *Nathan Rotenstreich*

these the social reality as such is a fact. But it is not yet a state. For the social circumstance to become a political order it must be elevated to the rank of a permanent, explicit order, which can on occasion be enforced over or against the people who live within it. A specific factor must be added to the merely social order for it to become a political one. This factor is power. By intending the formal arrangement and acknowledging it, men endow it with might; they thus constitute the political order day after day, hour after hour. Without this intentionality the political structure degenerates and finally disintegrates. The state depends then upon the special combination of order and might. The most important expression of this combination is the *law*. The law is that factor which enables the state to enforce its will on those, who, in the first instance, have established and maintained it—its citizens.

Conclusion

Professor Rotenstreich's philosophy is an open system. His theoretical equipment is sufficient to permit its further development and extension in any number of addition directions. But even as it stands, his work is a significant contribution to the contemporary philosophical scene. And even more important, his work constitutes a major element within the political and cultural renaissance of the Jewish people in the State of Israel.

Notes

1. *Jewish Thought in Modern Times* (Tel Aviv, 1945), p. 9ff [in Hebrew]. cf. *Jewish Philosophy in Modern Times* (New York, 1968), p. 6.
2. *Essays in Zionism and the Contemporary Jewish Condition* (New York, 1980), p. 58.
3. *Ibid.*, p. 60.
4. *Ibid.*, p. 48ff.
5. *Essays in Zionism*, p. 54.
6. *Ibid.*, p. 54f.
7. *Ibid.*, p. 56.
8. *Ibid.*, p. 87f.
9. *Between Past and Present* (New Haven, 1958), pp. 322f.
10. *Order and Might* (New York, 1988), p. 14.
11. *Ibid.*, p. 269.
12. *Ibid.*, pp. 135f.
13. *Ibid.*, p. 11.

FOR FURTHER READING

Works by Nathan Rotenstreich

Jewish Thought in Modern Times, Tel Aviv, 1945 [in Hebrew]. This is Rotenstreich's major work on the history of Jewish philosophy. It deals with the development of Jewish thought from the second half of the eighteenth century till the second World War. In the first volume of the book the main *trends* in Jewish modern thought are described and evaluated; in the second—the teachings of the prominent *thinkers* of that period are critically analysed.

Between Past and Present: An Essay on History, New Haven, 1958. In this work man is discussed as in one sense creating history, and in another, as being shaped by it.

Spirit and Man: An Essay on Being and Value, The Hague, 1963. In this volume Rotenstreich investigates the essence of man by analysing those features which in his view constitute the basis of human life, culture and political activity (language and learning, historicity, tools, etc.).

On the Human Subject: Studies in the Phenomenology of Ethics and Politics, Springfield, 1966. In this study Rotenstreich attempts to establish the irreducibility of mind and the special status of man as a subject and as a moral agent. In this last respect, the chapters on lying and on being ashamed are especially noteworthy as they are topics that have rarely been dealt with by philosophers.

Jewish Philosophy in Modern Times: From Mendelssohn to Rosenzweig, New York, 1968. This is a condensed treatment of the topics dealt with in *Jewish Thought in Modern Times*, as well as a second look, from a more mature philosophical standpoint, at the problems of the essence of Judaism and its historical transformations.

Tradition and Reality, New York, 1972. This is a further analysis of a variety of Jewish theological and philosophical themes.

Essays in Zionism and the Contemporary Jewish Condition, New York, 1980. In this volume Rotenstreich offers his conception of Zionist ideology, the solutions he proposed on several occasions to problems facing the State of Israel and its struggle for co-existence with the Arab world, and his understanding of the meaning of the relationship between Israel and the Diaspora.

Man and his Dignity, Jerusalem, 1983. This work may be considered the consummation of Rotenstreich's reflections on man. It is a penetrating analysis of the concept of human dignity and of the value of the human person as a free, autonomous, self-interpreting and self-determining entity. It concludes with a discussion on principle of the sanctity of (human) life.

Order and Might, New York, 1988. Here Rotenstreich provides an analysis of the political dimension of human existence. Concepts like justice, freedom, equality, rights and duties, as well as the relationship between politics and history, are considered in detail.

Works about Nathan Rotenstreich

This is the first major synthetic essay on Professor Rotenstreich's large body of work in English.

Richard L. Rubenstein

JOCELYN HELLIG

Richard L. Rubenstein is the only Jewish exponent in the predominantly Christian "Death of God" movement that developed in America during the mid-1960s. He worked independently from yet simultaneously with his Christian counterparts. Unlike their pronouncements, in which there was an air of liberation and celebration, Rubenstein mourned God's death with a cry of agony. He arrived at his theological position in direct response to the Holocaust. Initially embarrassed by the concept of the death of God, as he saw the metaphor as lying within a Christian and not a Jewish context, he could find no other way of expressing the void where God once stood.

Seldom is a theolgian's life and work more closely related than in the case of Rubenstein. Because of the personal and subjective nature of his theology, an exposition of it in isolation from his life circumstances would tend to falsify his statements. He has stated that there can be no substitute for "the agonizing crucible of life's experiences for meaningful theological statement."[1] Similarly, there can be no theology that is out of contact with the actual life of the Jewish people. The decisive moments as lived in the Jewish present, or *kairoi*, assume great significance in his thought. There have been two such moments in the twentieth century, the Holocaust and the reestablishment of the State of Israel.[2]

He was born in York City in 1924 to parents who were deracinated from their Jewish tradition and later were impoverished by the Great Depression. The poverty of his youth and his outsider status in Judaism were to play a considerable role in the formulation of his theological position. Of vital importance is that, owing to his family circumstances, he was denied a proper ritual bar mitzvah. He felt cheated that he was neither confirmed in his identity as a man nor as a Jew at a crucial turning point in his adolescence. He was later to insist on the incomparable power of religious ritual to mark the crises of life. Nothing could perform the emotional work the rite automatically accomplishes.

After suffering a brutal and humiliating anti-Semitic attack on his person while he was a teenager, he saw his beating as an analogue to the worldwide condition of Jewish powerlessness. He regarded Jewishness as an "incurable hereditary disease" from which he had to escape at all costs. Desiring a "vocation for the summit" and wanting the power of the priest to compensate for the marginality and poverty of his youth, he determined to become a minister. He turned to Unitarianism. While he was preparing to become a Unitarian minister, a friend suggested that he change his name to one less Jewish than Rubenstein. This was a demand for ultimate self-falsification, a price too high to pay for an escape from Judaism,[3] and he began his path back towards Judaism.

Attracted to Reform Judaism, which he perceived as "a kind of Jewish Unitarianism," he enrolled at the Hebrew Union College in the hope of becoming a Reform rabbi. The Judaism he came to know was classical Reform Judaism with its characteristic anti-Zionism and optimism. When the horrors of the death camps were disclosed, he was repulsed by Reform Judaism's anti-Zionist stance and its emphasis on the goodness of humanity. Only the most traditional form of Judaism could cope realistically with humankind's anarchic nature and inner lawlessness. Owing to lack of an intimate Jewish education and to insufficient time, he studied to become a Conservative rabbi, but in his personal life he became more observant in the style of Lithuanian Jewish piety. He was ordained as a Conservative rabbi in 1952 at the Jewish Theological Seminary. He attained his doctorate at Harvard in 1960. His thesis dealt with a Freudian analysis of rabbinic Aggadah.[4]

The death of his infant son Nathaniel on the day before Yom Kippur in 1950 intensified his already developing question concerning the existence of a just and powerful God. Since Yom Kippur is associated with guilt and punishment and the child was too young to have offended either his earthly or his heavenly father, the tragedy inaugurated a conversion that was to take seventeen years to mature. In 1966 Rubenstein published *After Auschwitz* in which he formulated his death-of-God theology. In response, he was "bureaucratically excommunicated" from the Jewish world and found it increasingly impossible to find employment in any institution funded by Jews.[5] He attributes his estrangement from the Jewish community as much to his own personality as to the community's response to his theological ideas.

In 1970 he was offered an academic position at Florida State University, which he still holds. In this setting he was forced to continue the study of the traditions of his people in exile from them. In 1977 he was selected by the University as Distinguished Professor. In 1987, at its centennial convocation, the Jewish Theological Seminary conferred upon him the degree of Doctor of Hebrew Letters, *honoris causa.*

Rubenstein is a man with a single problem rather than a single discipline. That problem is the Holocaust. He has spent his life trying to comprehend the tragedy, initially in its implications for Jewish theology and the problem of theodicy, but more recently as it relates to radical secularity, the modernization process, and the problem of population redundancy and programs of massive population riddance. This shift in his thinking from the 1960s to the present is marked by his book *The Cunning of History* (1975) in which he moves from consideration of the Jewish implications of the Holocaust to what can be learned from it in the wider world.

His primary assertion was that *we are living in the time of the death of God.* The statement that God is dead exceeds human knowledge. It reveals nothing about God and is significant only in what it reveals about the maker of the statement. There was no possibility for Rubenstein to reconcile the omnipotent, benevolent God of the covenant with the fact of the death camps. If, indeed, God chose Israel, and God is ruler of history, there had to be a purpose in the annihilation of 6 million of his chosen people. Using the logic of normative Jewish theology, Hitler, like Nebuchadnezzar, could be seen as a rod of God's anger. This idea was too obscene for Rubenstein to accept so he rejected not God, but covenant and chosenness.

He rejected the God-who-acts-in-history and in his stead posited God, the Holy Nothingness, the Faceless Abyss, the Cannibal mother, who gives birth to all only to consume all. This represents the state of quiescence to which all humans return and to which they desire to return. In this respect it is similar to Freud's Thanatos and bears some resemblance to the concept of Nirvana in Theravada Buddhism.[6] As a corollary to this God-concept there is no eschatology and no Messiah. Death is the Messiah. There is no afterlife. Life is "bracketed between two oblivions." Thus there is an urgency to live this life to the full in that it is the only life we may ever have.[7] We may already be living in the "last of days" in that, with our high technology and mutual hostility, we live in the reality of an impending global cataclysm and may be closer than ever to exploding our universe.

Despite his early obedience to the God of the covenant, it is clear that Rubenstein never believed in this God, whom, inded, he "had invented." Submission to the God of the covenant was his way of controlling the horror of the Auschwitz world, which he believed to be regnant in contemporary history and which he feared might explode in the depths of his own soul. The violence and destructiveness in the larger world mirrored a potential for anger, violence, and destructiveness in himself.[8] Strict observance of Jewish law would control his urges, but he was soon to find observance of the law problematic. In this respect he identified with the dilemma of Paul of Tarsus. The more observant he was, the more he felt that there were areas of ritual law that he was neglecting. He became guilty of selecting which laws to observe and which to neglect, thereby acting as God's judge and committing the ultimate act of hubris.

Rubenstein's attitude to religion during the 1960s was heavily Freudian. He saw religion as having the capacity to deal with the darker aspects of humanity on an unconscious level. Judaism's function was to supply meaning in a state of marginality and powerlessness. Rabbinic wisdom lay in the imposition of behavioral restraints and interpreting them as deriving from a heavenly Father God. God was a projection of biblical and rabbinic man and thus an illusion. Rubenstein's personal commitment to the psychoanalytic process helped him find the trauma that had caused the "dis-ease" in his own life, and he began to search for the trauma that had caused the dis-ease in the life of his community.[9] He found this in the "holocaust of ancient times," the defeat of the Jews by the Romans in 70 C.E.

This defeat was of decisive importance for all subsequent Jewish history as the Jewish people entered a two-thousand-year period of powerlessness. Jews were always unwanted guests at the mercy of their host nations. Diaspora Judaism is an adaptation to a situation of powerlessness in that compliance has been the predominant mode of Jewish response to the outside world. Furthermore, the behavioral restraints imposed by the rabbis imbued Jews with a servile consciousness that accepted limited life as better than no life at all. Misfortune was seen as deserved punishment meted out by an angry Father God. Ingrained Jewish responses to suffering and attack aided the Nazis. Thus the Holocaust is the culmination of Jewish powerlessness.

If God has never existed, how can He die? Rubenstein seems to be asserting that the biblical Father-God—an illusion—is dead. It was functional, giving meaning and hope, for two thousand years. In the wake of the Holocaust, the illusion of the biblical God is not only dysfunctional but positively damaging. Divinity has always existed and will continue to exist, and Rubenstein displays an acute awareness of divinity, but God is maternal and the world is characterized by cyclic repetitiveness. Rubenstein proposes an insightful paganism in which humankind celebrates the glory and bounty of the earth.

In subjecting the rabbinic aggadah to Freudian analysis, Rubenstein finds that its stories reveal the rabbis' deepest fears and aspirations. There is much guilt associated with Judaism. The punishment feared by the rabbis was projected onto biblical characters. By elaborating the various punishments that would befall biblical sinners, the rabbis revealed that their deepest fear was of incorporation by such means as drowning, fire, or leprosy.[10] Such "swallowing-up" would indicate a fear of the great Earth Mother rather than of the Father God. While paying outward homage to the norms of the Father-God, the rabbis reflected an unconscious terror of the Mother Goddess. The punishments of the Father God were preferable because they were measurable. The talion principle was operative. The retaliatory punishments of the Cannibal Mother were terrifying, precisely because they were all-consuming and beyond measure.[11]

Consequent to his declaration of the death of God, he saw it as his task as a Jewish theologian to speak of religion in the time of the death of God. He emphasized the need for community. "If all we have is one another, then assuredly we need one another more than ever."[12] In accordance with the conviction that arose out of his failure to have a bar mitzvah, he placed great emphasis on performance of appropriate ritual to mark the crises of life in a community context. The more archaic the ritual, the more effective its psychological function. He also emphasized the need to maintain the prayer book in its traditional form. Rites and prayers that may be embarrassing and seem outmoded to members of our generation may not be so to future generations, and each generation has the right to receive the tradition intact.

Rubenstein has no faith in the rational aspects of religion in the shadow of the death camps and stresses the force of the irrational to move people. Accordingly, he emphasizes the priestly and sacrificial aspect of religion rather than prophetic moral exhort-ation, believing that people are not open to moral exhortation. Sacrifice, even if only verbal, channels aggression and admits the basic sinfulness of all humanity. It is because of its sacrificial nature and the communal confession made by the whole commu-nity during the Yom Kippur ritual that it retains its immense psychological force. One is not cut off as a sinner in isolation, but the darker side of human nature is confessed communally.

Rubenstein developed a highly functional approach to religion which had a predominantly psychological function. The Jewish way is not better or more effective than any other. It is simply the way Jews contend with the ultimate questions and crises of life. People are thrown into their religious traditions by circumstance and birth rather than by choice. As part of this *Geworfenheit,* Jews and Christians have inherited their own mythic traditions, the Christian one based on the Jewish mythic structure. Because both communities lay claim to the Hebrew Bible, Jews and Christians have been locked into a battle of neither's making. There is something in the logic of Christian theology that, when pushed to an extreme, ends with the justification of the incitement to murder Jews. The Nazis were profoundly anti-Christian, but they took Christianity seriously in the one sphere that designated the Jews as the deicide people. A people who kills God is not beyond the most heinous of crimes. The Jews were thus systematically demonized by the church as being beyond all law. Here Rubenstein suggests that a universal human desire, that of killing God as an end to moral restraint, has been projected upon the Jews.[13]

The doctrine of chosenness is also a potent factor operative in anti-Semitism, and Rubenstein believes that Jews should de-mythologize it. First, it results in a rivalry, not unlike sibling rivalry, as to which community, Jewish or Christian, is the Father's favorite son. More important, it places the Jews in a very special category of abnormal demands and decisive hatreds. Jews are perceived either as the best of saints or the worst of sinners. Christianity must take the separate and special character of Judaism very seriously. Jews have been condemned to the domain of the sacred. "Unless the Jews have a supernatural vocation the Christ makes absolutely no theological difference."[14] Chosenness has other negatives. Far from being a doctrine of racial superiority, it has been the cause of millennia of unrealistic self-blame. Jews have never thought their performance was good enough. All catastrophe has been viewed as punitive. Some even see the Holocaust as a divine punishment.

A decisive encounter with a Christian was to influence Rubenstein's theology profoundly. In 1961 he met with Dean Heinrich Grueber of the Evangelical Church of Berlin. Dean Grueber insisted that Auschwitz was part of God's plan. He likened Hitler to Nebuchadnezzar and other "rods of God's anger." His conviction was *not* that of an anti-Semite. He had almost lost his life at Dachau and was the only German voluntarily to go to Jerusalem to testify at the Eichmann trial. Because Rubenstein regarded him as a man of impeccable integrity and religious faith (and because several Orthodox Jews do not shy away from Grueber's conclusion), his unambiguous declaration that God had sent Hitler to exterminate the Jews unified the intellectual and experiential roots of Rubenstein's growing collapse of faith and led finally to his declaration of the death of God. "If indeed such a God holds the destiny of mankind in his power," he said, "his resort to the death camps to bring about his ends is so obscene that I would rather spend my life in perpetual revolt than render him even the slightest homage."[15]

Dean Grueber's insistence that Hitler was God's tool is a manifestation of the incredible extremes to which people are driven when they try to make sense of the surrealistic world of the twentieth century. This encounter led Rubenstein to abandon the concept of God acting meaningfully in history. He opted for a meaningless cosmos in which people suffer unavoidable rather than for the view that suffering is *deserved* and dispensed by an angry creator God. Most individuals find meaninglessness intolerable. Rabbinic Judaism gave meaning in the face of political defeat. The rabbinic response to the holocaust of ancient times was realistic for its time. In the post-Holocaust world such meaning is dead.[16]

Rubenstein has formulated the rabbinic position in what he calls "Yochanan's bargain." With the imminent fall of Jerusalem, Rabbi Yochanan ben Zakkai made a bargain with the Roman authorities forswearing all resort to political power and asking only for Yavneh and its scholars. The bargain rested on the assumption that Caesar (and all subsequent overlords) would be trustworthy and protect the Jews from annihilation. The price Jews had to pay was a religious one: they had to keep faithfulness to the God of the covenant. Yochanan displayed the opposite tactic to that of Eleazar ben Yair, defender of Massada. Yochanan was prepared to settle for limited existence, subjugating his community to the power of others. Eleazar preferred death to subjugation. Rubenstein thus accuses rabbinic Judaism of having inspired a "servile consciousness" in Jews. He opts for the "lordly consciousness" of the defenders of Massada. Yochanan's bargain was kept, more or less, until Hitler broke the rules. Having become accustomed to the limited nature of previous attacks on them, the Jews were totally unprepared for Hitler's vicious onslaught. Trusting their old ways of response, they unwittingly played into his hands. Theirs was the most profound misreading of any enemy in the whole of Jewish history.

The Holocaust led Rubenstein to question the ongoing validity of Yochanan's bargain, certainly with regard to its applicability to his own life. He refuses to be bound by a bargain that was made so long ago and under such different circumstances. It must be emphasized, however, that he denies no Jew the right to live by rabbinic norms. He seems to suggest that to remain Jewish is very risky and that Jews should count the potential cost. In the final analysis only the most traditional Judaism may be worth the risk.

Rubenstein has always exhibited an extreme distaste for powerlessness of any kind. Although he could accept the value of Yochanan's plan for the reconstruction of the community and his program, which endowed existence with hope, he could do so only because of Yochanan's honest religious faith. He realizes that the rabbinic response was the only viable one and that all Jews are indebted to it for their present existence, but he is insistent that it has had negative entailments in Jewish behavior. Focus was changed from the earthly and sensuous to the abstract and intellectual. In place of an altar of stone on which bloody offerings were slain, Jewish religious life focused on bloodless worship and a bloodless book.[17] A messianic hope became predominant in which the inequities of the present would be rectified in a future age.

Rabbinic Judaism, as a response to powerlessness, addressed itself to a situation very different from that which obtained during biblical times. The reestablishment of the State of Israel is the most profound response of the Jewish people to powerlessness. Zionism is a reversal of powerlessness and a closure of a particular type of Jewish existence in that it has turned the intervening two thousand years into a parenthesis. It renders the messianic hope for the future futile and demands that Jews exercise power in a sovereign state unafraid. Zionism is a return to power. It is also a return to the earth and its divinities. The paganism Rubenstein advocates is already in evidence in Israel with its dance, song, and bacchanalian appreciation of the earth.

The ongoing existence of the State of Israel is of great importance to the survival of Judaism. There is, however, a different form of Judaism in evidence in Israel, one very different from rabbinic Judaism.[18] As long as there is the option of Massada, there can never be another Auschwitz. Jewish life in Israel must be normalized, and Israel must resort to tactics used by any other sovereign state to ensure its survival in a brutal world. It cannot be governed by unrealistic ideals and values foisted upon it by the outside world.[19]

In his most recent works, Rubenstein is concerned with the problem of radical secularity, its implications and causes. When he speaks of the death of God, he speaks of the death of a particular image of God on one hand and the radical secularity of our times on the other. He perceives it as a fact that God has disappeared from the affairs of human beings. The world is functionally godless. Radical secularity implies the removal of ever more areas of human thought and behavior from religious contol, particularly in the public decision-making areas. This process is accompanied by an increasing tendency to rationalize behavior and consciousness. Having moved to consideration of the historical, political, economic, and sociological significance of the Holocaust in a secular world, his work retains theological import only insofar as he continues to probe the godless world in which we live.

Whereas in his earlier thought he emphasized the irrational nature of the Holocaust, he has now come to see it as the ultimate expression of the triumph of calculating rationality, a bureau-cratically administered act of problem solving in the face of one of the modern world's most intractable problems, surplus population and consequent population redundancy.[20] He is intent on explor-ing the full implications of the destruction of European Jewry for the understanding of our contemporary civilization. The Holo-caust is not an accidental aberration of modern civilization but an intrinsic expression of its problem-solving methods. In turn, modern civilization is an unintended consequence, or "night side," of biblical monotheism and its values.

Rubenstein, like Harvey Cox, affirms the biblical roots of secularization, but he finds no reason to rejoice at its effects.[21] The disenchantment of nature, necessary for the calculating rationality of the modern period, has had disastrous effects, resulting in the complete dehumanization of people. Unlike Cox, who views secularization as liberating, Rubenstein sees it as an illness result-ing from and inherent in the Judaeo-Christian tradition. He sees no "cure" for the illness save total worldwide catastrophe in which civilization as we know it will disappear.

The Holocaust was a strictly modern enterprise. It could have taken place only in the twentieth century with the consciousness that has culminated in it. Rubenstein argues that one cannot explain the Holocaust primarily as a reflection of anti-Semitism. Although that was an important feature, it is essential to remem-ber that the church, though harsh with the Jews, had never been genocidal. Other factors must be examined to understand more fully the reasons for the Holocaust. Modernization and the related movement of secularization are both essential prerequisites. Taken together, technological progress, radical secularity, bureaucracy, and the triumph of functional rationality are all part of the modernization process. With the Holocaust, a hitherto unbreachable moral barrier was successfully overcome, and its success invites its repetition. Auschwitz has enlarged our understanding of the state's capacity to do violence, and henceforth the elimination of millions of people will forever be one of the capacities and temptations of government, especially under conditions of extreme stress. The destruction of Europe's Jews is regarded by Rubenstein as one of a series of modern historical occurrences involving the elimination of millions of people from their home communities. It is also the most dramatic of such occurrences.[22]

The biblical tradition contributed to the process of radical secularization in that it demystified the world of nature. It also contributed by dividing the world into the "elect" and the "preterite."[23] Biblical man had a corrective in that he was fully aware of his costewardship over the earth and was always under the judgment of a supreme and righteous God. With the increasing transcendence of God, which took place under Protestantism, more and more areas of human thought and behavior have been released from religious control. The result has been radical secularization in which people arrogate to themselves godlike status in making the ultimate decisions as to who shall live and who shall die. Radical secularization and the triumph of calculating rationality had to become culturally predominant before the Holocaust could take place.

Calculating rationality involves the rationality of means rather than ends. The value of all things, including human beings, is calculated in monetary terms. There is no recourse to human dignity or appeal to the sanctity of human life when decision-making elites decide the fate of the inarticulate masses. This results in total dehumanization and renders mass population riddance programs feasible. There is no point in turning back to the Judaeo-Christian tradition for the solution because the Bible is the very cause of the problem. Humankind may yet be destined to render full account for having accepted a religious ideology "that denies the mystery and magic of the natural order and divides the human order into the elect and the damned."[24]

A suitable aphorism for our times is "The dreams of reason bring forth monsters." Rubenstein implies that somehow we can defeat the monster we have created when he states that "every thinker who has ever seriously reflected on the 'death of God' has awaited the moment of divine rebirth."[25] There is an explosive element in his theology. He feels the need to break out of the meaninglessness of radical secularization and the death of God. The world of the death of God "is an impossibility. One way or another, the death of God cannot be the final answer."[26]

The shift in Rubenstein's thinking is problematic. In his earlier thought the Holocaust was an irrational explosion of violence against the Jews; he now sees it as a highly rational exercise carried out by a well-organized bureaucracy and as the outcome and expression of the triumph of calculating rationality. Although there is a progression, there is also a radical break. It is simply not possible to regard the Holocaust as both irrational and as the product of calculating rationality. Rubenstein regards *The Cunning of History* as his most important work. I find *After Auschwitz* more relevant for specifically Jewish theology.

His theology of the 1960s, despite the tension involved in maintaining authentic ritual traditionally addressed to the Father God, offered a meaningful program for Jewish life. Since Judaism is orthoprax and not orthodox, he did not attack it at its roots. In the crisis of faith of the post-Holocaust world, it offered a viable alternative for Jews who could no longer maintain faith. Certainly it can be argued that with subjective freedom to select which rituals to observe, Jewish practice could ultimately disappear. But Rubenstein emphasized the need for maintaining the Jewish tradition intact. By underscoring the sacrificial aspects of Passover, for example, and placing no stress whatsoever on the doctrrine of Jewish chosenness, Jews could still retain meaningful performance of the ritual. His psychoanalytic rationale for the maintenance of *kashruth*, a method of coming to terms with orality, gives it a meaning outside of that which is divinely ordained.

To be sure, there were problems with his theology of the 1960s in that he had a selective and narrow view of Jewish history, looking at it solely through the prism of the Holocaust. It has also been argued that he asserts the death of God as a result of the Holocaust without giving consideration to God's role in the reestablishment of the State of Israel.[27] A correct understanding of Rubenstein's view would imply that God was absent both during the Holocaust and during the establishment of the state. God was a functional illusion for most of Jewish history. Since there is no vertical transcendence, and the Jew is alone, having only his community upon which to depend, just as the Holocaust was a man-made event, the return to Israel was a profoundly human, Jewish response to powerlessness. Rubenstein cuts the Gordian knot with regard to the existence of the biblical God who acts in history.

Rubenstein's present work, for all the insight it gives into our world, supplies no ongoing program for Jewish life. He has moved away from concern with Judaism and the Jewish theological implications of the Holocaust. He sees diaspora Judaism as doomed. Although he wishes Israel well, he has lost his fiery commitment to Zionism. In this sense, it is debatable whether he continues to speak meaningfully to Jews. It seems that today, rather than being categorized as a Jewish theologian, he should be classified as a social theorist.

One of the most serious implications of his present philosophy is the loss of the Holocaust as a unique event. If the Holocaust is one, albeit the most dramatic, of a series of bureaucratically administered programs of mass murder, it must ultimately be drowned in the general category of human evil. Although he has not argued explicitly for the uniqueness of the Holocaust, his stance in the 1960s, was motivated by this very conviction, and it was this uniqueness of the event in Jewish history that led to his declaration of the death of God. In a sense, therefore, his present work would tend to cancel out much of what he said in the 1960s, and that period was his most productive, at least from the aspect of Jewish theology.

His recommendation of an "insightful paganism" has always been somewhat obscure. It arose out of the demystification of nature that has resulted in the dehumanization of people. Biblical history's cunning is that it has led us to a situation of redundancy. What Rubenstein seems to be saying when he asks Jews to abandon history and turn to paganism is that biblical monotheism has entailed far too great a cost. He wants to put the spirits back into nature so that it commands our awe and respect once again.

Rubenstein is a man of tremendous courage and honesty. He was one of the first Jewish theologians to take seriously the Holocaust and the reestablishment of the State of Israel. His forthright pronouncement of the death of God led to his alienation from the Jewish community.[28] There seem to be encouraging signs of reacceptance and recognition, but he has been hounded out of Jewish life. Ironically, the anger of the Jewish community may serve to corroborate his position.[29]

Rubenstein is in mid-career and may yet iron out the incongruencies in his thought. He is clearly groping beyond the confines of the death of God. He has also had an important encounter with Asia, and much of his present work is concerned with Japan. It is difficult to know in which direction he will move, although the likelihood is that he will affirm his present mold of thinking and elaborate it. His theology of the 1960s was honest, passionate, and valuable. His current work gives insight into our world. Although it is not easy to hold the work of the two periods together logically, and his present position is pessimistic and gives no problem for ongoing Jewish life, his work has been of great value in giving an understanding of both the dynamics of Judaism in a post-Holocaust era and of the developments in our world that made the Holocaust possible.

Notes

1. Richard L. Rubenstein, *After Auschwitz: Radical Theology and Contemporary Judaism* (Indianapolis, 1966), p. 177. A new edition of *After Auschwitz*, containing a number of new essays not included in the first edition, was published by Johns Hopkins University Press, Baltimore, Md., in 1992. Unfortunately, this new edition appeared too late to be considered in the present article.
2. Since his life circumstances and theology are so intimately intertwined, some biographical details are given at the beginning of this essay, but the progress of his life and the development of his thought are, of necessity, treated together.
3. Richard L. Rubenstein, *Power Struggle: An Autobiographical Confession* (New York, 1974), pp. 214–15. See *Power Struggle* and the chapter entitled "The Making of a Rabbi" in *After Auschwitz* for his confessions concerning his fears and strivings.
4. This thesis was later published as *The Religious Imagination: A Study in Psychoanalysis and Jewish Theology* (Indianapolis, 1968).
5. See Rubenstein, *Power Struggle*, p. 15.
6. The God-concept which he proposed in the 1960s has remained undeveloped.
7. The concept that we are forced to live a responsible life in the absence of God-given norms motivates his book *Morality and Eros* (New York, 1970).
8. Rubenstein, *Power Struggle*, pp. 90, 85.
9. See ibid., p. 71. In *The Religious Imagination*, p. 183, he suggests that there is much sickness in the rabbinic Aggadah, but because the rabbis objectified their fears and strivings in the Aggadah, it becomes a sickness on the way to health.
10. Since the skin is attacked in leprosy, the individual loses his discrete boundary. There is a consequent experience of incorporation into the atmosphere.
11. A similar study on Paul of Tarsus uncovers some of the deepest meaning that can be derived from Pauline theology. Rubenstein reveals the immense power of

Christianity to come to terms with the negativities of human existence, particularly with death. Much of his own life was motivated by his fear of death. When his innocent infant son died, Rubenstein knew that, no matter how well he performed, he would ultimately die. Paul's similar fears were overcome by faith in the risen Christ. Rubenstein had no such boon. "Had I lived in his time, I might have followed him. Once I realized that I had no escape from dying, I had to learn to live life as if I were newly born.... My analyst was midwife to my rebirth." See *My Brother Paul* (New York, 1972), pp. 17–18.

12. Rubenstein, *After Auschwitz.* p. 119.
13. Rubenstein points out that although responsible theologians try to spread the blame for the killing of Christ to all people, the New Testament leaves no doubt as to who the culprits were. Matthew 27:25 designates Jewish guilt for all posterity. See ibid., p. 12.
14. Ibid., p. 186.
15. Rubenstein, *Power Struggle*, p. 11.
16. Rubenstein saw the book of Job as giving a meaningful answer to the question of suffering before the Holocaust, but he now finds it totally inadequate. Job was restored after his afflictions and, at all times, retained his human integrity. The Jews were totally dehumanized by the Nazis before being killed. They were stripped of all human dignity. His contention is that the author(s) of Job could not, even in their wildest nightmares, have predicted a world in which Auschwitz could take place. See Rubenstein, "Job and Auschwitz," in Martin Marty and J. Peerman, eds., *New Theology No. 8* (New York, 1971).
17. Rubenstein, *Power Struggle*, p. 174.
18. Manfred H. Vogel, in "Dilemma of Identity for the Emancipated Jew," in Marty and Peerman, eds., *New Theology No. 4* (New York, 1967), suggests a similar view. He points out that the Jew's mode of witnessing has changed from biblical times, when he was rooted in power afforded in the concrete world, to the rabbinic mode of witnessing when, bereft of power, the law became the normative mode of witnessing. In Israel, with a return to power, there may emerge a new mode of witnessing which bears similarities to that of biblical Israel. This indicates a possible evolution of a new type of Judaism in Israel.
19. With his emphasis on power and on the normalization of the state of Israel, Rubenstein was in favor of Menachem Begin's incursion into Lebanon in 1982. It seems that in the present crisis, he would be unlikely to favor any but the most practical solution and would be opposed to any resort to special pleading concerning Israel's superior morality or to any romantic and unrealistic notions about what Israel "should" do in the eyes of the world.
20. Surplus population is defined by Rubenstein as one that for any reason has no viable role in the society in which it domiciled. He points out that Jews did not constitute a useless or redundant sector of the German population, but, using the traditional negative stereotype of the Jew, hatred against them could be incited, they could be eliminated, and their positions could be made available to those less alien in German society.
21. See Harvey Cox, *The Secular City* (London, 1965).
22. Richard L. Rubenstein, *The Age of Triage: Fear and Hope in an Over-crowded World* (Boston, 1983), marks the movement from consideration of the Holocaust per se to a consideration of what can be learned from it in the wider world.
23. Preterition means passed over or nonelect. This issue is closely argued in Richard Rubenstein, "The Elect and the Preterite," *Soundings*, Winter 1976, pp. 357–73.
24. Ibid., p. 371.
25. Richard Rubenstein "Plenary Address to the College Theology Society" (personal correspondence).

264 . *Richard L. Rubenstein*

26. Rubenstein to the author, August 21, 1981.
27. See, for example, Steven T. Katz, *Post-Holocaust Dialogues: Critical Studies in Modern Jewish Thought* (New York, 1983), pp. 176–79.
28. He is a man committed to truth. He has stated that he will pursue his research in whatever directions it may lead him, no matter which individuals may be offended or which institutions threatened (letter to the author, April 30, 1980). Ironically, it has been his own career that has been threatened.
29. Jacob Neusner has affirmed that the torrent of abuse to which Rubenstein has been subjected may constitute "the highest possible tribute on the part of his enemies to the compelling importance of his contribution" (*Understanding Jewish Theology* [New York, 1973], p. 184).

FOR FURTHER READING

Works by Richard L. Rubenstein

After Auschwitz: Radical Theology and Contemporary Judaism, Indianapolis, 1966. Second edition, Baltimore, Md., 1992. In a collection of fifteen papers Rubenstein discusses the theological implications of the Holocaust for Judaism. He makes his first formal statement concerning the death of God. This book initiated the ongoing debate on the theological implications of the Holocaust.

The Religious Imagination: A Study in Psychoanalysis and Jewish Theology, Indianapolis, 1968. This is an edited version of Rubenstein's Harvard Ph.D. dissertation. It deals with the rabbinic responses to the holocaust of ancient times, the catastrophic defeat of the Jewish people by the Romans in the wars of 66–70 C.E., and 132–135 C.E., and the subsequent rootlessness and powerlessness of the Jewish community. Through a psychoanalytical interpretation of the rabbinic Aggadah, Rubenstein reveals the unconscious fears and strivings of the rabbis who were forced to interpret Judaism and retain its meaning in a situation of powerlessness.

Morality and Eros, New York, 1970. Rubenstein explores the question of values in a world in which ethical norms can no longer be derived from the revealed will of God.

My Brother Paul, New York, 1972. This is a psychoanalytical study of Paul of Tarsus. Rubenstein turns explicitly to the exploration of New Testament literature as a possible source of the anti-Semitism that contributed to the Holocaust. He concludes that St. Paul was not an anti-Semite, but rather that his theology had the unintended consequence of fostering the permanent alienation between Christianity and Judaism.

Power Struggle: An Autobiographical Confesion, New York, 1974. In this work, Rubenstein explores the overwhelming impact of the Holocaust on his life and thought. Although written in the form of an autobiography, it is an essay in contemporary religious thought. The author is used as a vehicle for the expression of his theological and historical concerns.

Gershom Scholem

DAVID BIALE

For nearly two centuries, the history of the Jews has been subjected to intensive scrutiny by a dazzling line of scholars, from
Leopold Zunz, Moritz Steinschneider, and Heinrich Graetz in the
nineteenth century, to Simon Dubnow, Julius Guttmann, Saul
Lieberman, and Salo Baron in our own. Yet none made as radical a
contribution as Gershom Scholem, whose studies of Jewish mysticism not only created a previously neglected discipline but also
transformed our perception of the "essence" of Judaism. Scholem
showed that Judaism, which had previously been considered a
rational and legal religion, also contained important mystical and
mythical elements. Scholem's historiography is important not
only for specialists in Jewish history; his historical work was
informed by a definite philosophy of history and theology, and, as
such, it constitutes a signal contribution to modern Jewish
thought. Seen in this light, Scholem must be considered one of the
great modern Jewish thinkers alongside Hermann Cohen, Franz
Rosenzweig, and Martin Buber.

The fundamental argument of Scholem's historiography is that
Judaism has never been a monolithic tradition but, rather, a
pluralistic one. This pluralism consists in a range of frequently
contradictory opinions—rational and irrational, philosophical
and mystical, legal and antinomian—all of which are equally
legitimate. Only by understanding this tradition in its anarchistic
entirety can one grasp the "essence" of Judaism, an essence which
is distinguished by its lack of one single definition.[1]

In rejecting a dogmatic view of Jewish history, Scholem also attacked the scholars of the nineteenth-century *Wissenschaft des Judentums*, the school of scientific study of Judaism. He castigated these rationalist, bourgeois scholars for wanting to "remove the irrational stinger and banish the demonic enthusiasm for Jewish history.... This terrifying giant, our history ... full of destructive power, made up of vitality, evil and perfection, must contract itself, stunt its growth and declare that it has no substance. The demonic giant is nothing but a simple fool who fulfills the duties of a solid citizen and every decent Jewish bourgeois could unashamedly bid him good-day in the streets of the city, the immaculate city of the nineteenth century."[2]

German-Jewish Origins

In both his academic work and his political choices, Scholem was profoundly motivated by a sense of *epater les bourgeois*. This anarchistic impulse went back to his childhood in Germany.[3] Born in Berlin in 1897 to a family of printers already two generations removed from traditional Judaism, he was raised in a largely secular, assimilated environment. Most German Jews of this time regarded Judaism as entirely compatible with bourgeois German culture, a position articulated philosophically by the neo-Kantian philosopher Hermann Cohen. At the same time, a growing number of young German Jews, inspired by the mystical thinker Martin Buber, rejected rationalism and liberalism in favor of Jewish nationalism and mystical renewal.

In his youth Scholem was attracted to the Zionist youth movement Jung-Juda and to a Jewish identity. He seems to have been motivated by a desire to revolt against his parents' lifestyle, much like his brother Werner, who chose communism as his form of rebellion. Following his brother, the young Scholem opposed World War I from the moment the war broke out and identified with the small pacifist camp led by the anarchist Gustav Landauer. Scholem's pacifism was based on radical Zionist principles: the Jews had no part in Europe's war and should emigrate to Palestine. This opposition to the war, which was exceedingly rare among German Jews, brought him into conflict with his father, who eventually expelled him from the family house.

Scholem also became critical of the German-Jewish youth

movement for its prowar stance, and he broke with Martin Buber, who supported the war at least until about 1917. As a result of this political disagreement, Scholem came to reject Buber's mystical approach to Judaism and turned to a historical study of Jewish sources. Conflict between the two was to resurface years later in a dispute with Buber over how best to interpret Hasidic sources.[4]

During the war Scholem came to know Walter Benjamin, the brilliant young literary critic, who also opposed the war. Benjamin had a profound influence on Scholem's theological and philosophical views, and Scholem tried with little success to win his friend back from Marxism to Zionism and Judaism. The story of Scholem's relationship with Benjamin, who committed suicide while trying to escape the Nazis, is one of the most poignant accounts of the different paths European Jewish intellectuals took in the decades before the Holocaust.[5]

Following the war, Scholem shifted his university studies from mathematics to Jewish mysticism. He chose as his subject the early Kabbalistic text *Sefer ha-Bahir* and received his doctorate from the University of Munich in 1923. Following the completion of his dissertation, Scholem emigrated to Palestine, one of the few German Jews of this period to do so. He was hired as the Judaica librarian of the nascent Hebrew University, and when the university opened in 1925, he was appointed lecturer (later professor) of Jewish mysticism. Scholem served in this capacity until his retirement in 1965 and continued to be active in university affairs until the time of his death in 1982. His career therefore overlapped with the history of the Hebrew University to whose development he made a central contribution.

Although Scholem did not train a large number of students, his disciples, including Isaiah Tishby, Joseph Weiss, Joseph Dan, and Rivka Schatz, went on to solidify and extend his work, spreading the study of Jewish mysticism. Beyond the specialists he trained, however, Scholem had a profound impact on students in other fields at the Hebrew University and at universities where he lectured and taught around the world. Many studied Jewish mysticism with him for the first time and came to accept it as a legitimate, even central, discipline in the field of Judaica.

Scholem's History of Jewish Mysticism

It is impossible to summarize in a few pages the fruits of Scholem's scholarship, which included nearly six hundred articles and books.[6] The main outlines of his history of Jewish mysticism can be discerned best in *Major Trends in Jewish Mysticism*, which was first delivered as series of lectures in 1938 and published in 1941. Here Scholem developed the idea that the history of religions has three stages: the mystical period of immediacy with God, the legal and philosophical period in which the revelation of the first period is institutionalized, and the third period of mysticism in which an attempt is made to recover the immediacy of the religion's origins. The dialectical structure of this theory is characteristic of Scholem's thought and reflects his German intellectual heritage. Mysticism, he argues, comes to revitalize a religion in danger of losing its mythic forces.

In this work, Scholem also proposed a solution to one of the outstanding problems of Jewish historiography: the dating of the *Zohar*, the classical work of Kabbalah. Although he had argued in the 1920s that the *Zohar* was an ancient work (as it itself claims to be), in *Major Trends* he proved definitively that it dated from the late thirteenth century and was the work of Moses de Leon. He was therefore able to show that the magnum opus of the Kabbalah came from medieval Jewish history—the third stage in the development of the Jewish religion. It was thirteenth-century Kabbalah, Scholem argued, that saved Judaism from the sterility of law and philosophy.

At the heart of Scholem's historiography is the belief that myth is crucial to the vitality of a religious tradition, an idea that betrays the influence of German romantic thinkers such as Franz von Baader. He identified the central myth of the Kabbalah with gnosticism. He argued that by late antiquity, Jewish mystics had developed a monotheistic version of Gnostic dualism. This Jewish gnosticism persisted in underground traditions and made its way from Babylonia via Italy and Germany to southern France, where it surfaced in the *Sefer Bahir* and thence to the Kabbalah of Provence and Spain.[7]

Beyond its careful attention to the dating and authorship of manuscripts, Scholem's history of the Kabbalah is therefore a tracing of this Gnostic myth throughout medieval Jewish history.

Gnostic themes could be found later in sixteenth-century Lurianic Kabbalah and in the heretical messianic Sabbatian movement of the seventeenth century. Indeed, it was the very heretical potential of the Gnostic myth in Judaism that made the *Kabbalah* at once a force of vitality and a source of danger. It pushed monotheism to its limits and thus kept it in touch with elemental psychological forces. In Sabbatianism, the Gnostic myth exploded and caused an outburst of antinomian heresy.

Scholem's studies of Sabbatianism and its mystical theology were among his most pioneering and they complement his intensive work on the origins of thirteenth-century Kabbalah. He regarded this movement, which had previously been considered marginal, as central to any understanding of Jewish history. He argued that Sabbatianism captured the imagination of much of the Jewish world and profoundly shook the hegemony of the rabbis. It was therefore the great watershed between the Middle Ages and modernity, foreshadowing the rise of antinomian secularism. Scholem held that subsequent Jewish movements, including Hasidism and the Enlightenment, were all reactions to Sabbatianism. Hasidism tried to "neutralize" the messianic energies of Sabbatianism, and the early followers of the Jewish Enlightenment were frequently themselves secret Sabbatians. Thus the rise of modern Judaism was a consequence of a catastrophe within the Jewish religious tradition and not primarily the result of outside influence.

Scholem connected his studies of Sabbatianism with his work on earlier Kabbalah through the theme of the Gnostic myth. He dismissed persecution and other external factors as the causes of Sabbatianism and argued instead that it was ideas—primarily the ideas of the Gnostic Kabbalah—that were responsible for the great messianic outburst. The dissemination of the Lurianic Kabbalah, he suggested, with its emphasis on redemption and its apocalyptic overtones, set the stage for antinomian messianism. Nowhere is Scholem's commitment to intellectual history more apparent than in this etiology of Sabbatianism. Although he rejected the nineteenth-century rationalist bias, Scholem wrote a similar *Geistesgeschichte* (history of ideas). He held that Jewish history is driven by the dialectic of ideas developed by intellectual elites, and he generally ignored the role of mass social forces. Similarly, he was more interested in the theoretical Kabbalah than in its folkloristic or popular side.

Scholem's Zionism

Although Scholem was no Kabbalist, he believed firmly that the mythic and mystical impulses that inform the Kabbalah remain hidden forces in Jewish history into the twentieth century. He suggested frequently that Zionism may have taken its vital energies from the same sources.[8] Yet he also made clear his personal ambivalence about these forces. The mystical messianism of the Sabbatian movement led to disaster in the wake of Sabbetai Sevi's failure as a messiah. Zionism, too, might be endangered if these same forces were not properly "neutralized," that is, redirected toward constructive purposes.

Scholem's own political activities were informed by these concerns. In the 1920s, he was active in the Brit Shalom movement, which sought to balance the "apocalyptic" nationalism of Jabotinsky's Revisionists with a policy of compromise with the Arabs. In 1929, following the Arab riots in Jerusalem and Hebron, he wrote:

> I absolutely deny that Zionism is a messianic movement and that it has the right to employ religious terminology for political goals. The redemption of the Jewish people, which as a Zionist I desire, is in no way identical with the religious redemption I hope for in the future.... The Zionist ideal is one thing and the messianic ideal another, and the two do not meet except in the pompous phraseology of mass rallies which often infuse our youth with a spirit of new Sabbatianism which must inevitably fail. The Zionist movement has nothing in common with Sabbatianism.[9]

Much later, in the years before his death, he warned again of the dangers of Zionist messianism and spoke of the messianists of the religious Zionist "Gush Emunim" settlement movement as "latter-day Sabbatians."[10]

Scholem's Theology and Philosophy of Jewish History

Scholem never wrote a systematic or extensive theological treatise; indeed, he was opposed in principle to the discipline of theology and held that the only way to approach Judaism was through historiography. His belief in historiography was based on an original theological position that can be found in a number of places in Scholem's oeuvre.[11] Scholem's position must be considered an important contribution to modern Jewish theology as an alternative to the existentialism of recognized theologians such as Martin Buber and Franz Rosenzweig.

From the beginning of his career, when he planned to write a dissertation on the Kabbalah's philosophy of language, Scholem was attracted to the Kabbalistic treatment of philosophical and theological issues, which have a contemporary resonance. Although it would be a mistake to claim that he imposed his own views on his treatment of the Kabbalah, one might say that a productive symbiosis developed between Scholem's theological speculations and the views of the Kabbalah.

The central theological problem for Scholem concerned the ability of the religious tradition to communicate with the modern Jew who no longer considers himself in touch with the sources of revelation. Since the possibility of communication with a religious tradition ultimately depends on one's view of the nature and efficacy of language to transmit divine revelation, the focus of Scholem's theology was on philosophy of language.

Scholem developed his philosophical position in opposition to that of Martin Buber, in particular in opposition to Buber's *Erlebnismystik* (mysticism of experience), his mystical philosophy of the pre–World War I period.[12] Although Buber's better-known dialogic philosophy contained some of the same ideas, Scholem was most influenced in his formative period by Buber's earlier thought. Buber essentially argued that language has an inferior status to revelation and is unable to communicate more than a pale shadow of the original experience. In the face of revelation, man is literally dumbstruck and only later tries to translate divine silence into inadequate human speech. The essence of the mystical experience is silence; there is no intrinsic relationship between it and the language used to describe it.[13]

Revelation for Buber was an event outside of history. History and time are human creations. For God's perspective, revelation is always in the "here and now," whereas from a human perspective, it occurs in time. Buber implied that he who is truly open to revelation transcends man-made history and appropriates the divine perspective of the here and now.[14] Buber's mysticism therefore disparaged history and tradition. Tradition cannot convey the essence of revelation, which remains personal and individual.

In his earliest attacks on Buber's *Erlebnismystik*, Scholem sought to affirm the validity of history and tradition for the secular Jew.[15] To do so, he adopted a much more positive attitude than Buber toward language as the vehicle for the transmission of tradition. Against Buber's "mysticism of silence," Scholem developed a theology in which revelation and tradition were linguistic experiences: he grounded the authenticity of tradition in the efficacy of language. Revelation is not a silent *Erlebnis* but an auditory experience that can be expressed in language.

Scholem argues that the defining characteristic of Jewish mysticism as commentary on a secret tradition has its origin in a unique and explicitly positive attitude toward language. Commentary is not only the proper mode of Jewish mystsicism but is required because of the divine origin of traditional texts. An essential connection exists between commentator and text because of the divine character of language: "Language in its purest form, that is, Hebrew ... reflects the fundamental spiritual nature of the world.... Speech reaches God because it comes from God.... All that lives is an expression of God's language—and what is it that Revelation can reveal in the last resort if not the name of God?"[16] In the process of creation and revelation, God's hidden name becomes an explicit, communicable word. The divine name, which has no concrete meaning, becomes dialectically the source of all meaning.

The Kabbalists believed, according to Scholem, that there is no pure experience of revelation but only a tradition of interpretations of revelation to which one can refer. The immediate reality of revelation cannot be recaptured without recourse to the mediation of tradition: "This voice which calls forth incessantly from Sinai is given its human articulation and translation in Tradition, which passes on the inexhaustible word of Revelation at any time and through every 'scholar' who subjects himself to its continuity."[17]

When Scholem refers to the "scholar" here, does he have in mind only the Kabbalist or traditional commentator, or does he mean also the modern historian of Judaism? From a variety of sources, it is possible to establish that he identified personally with this Kabbalistic theology of revelation and tradition.[18] In a little-known review of a work of Jewish theology by Hans Joachim Schoeps, the German-Jewish historian of religion and follower of the Protestant theologian Karl Barth, Scholem wrote in his own theological voice and not as a historian of the Kabbalah. Scholem rejected Schoeps's desire to substitute an ahistorical faith for the Jewish tradition. Against the Barthian idea of the "concrete word of God," he wrote, "Revelation is, despite its uniqueness, still a *medium*. It is [the] absolute, meaning-bestowing, but itself meaningless that becomes explicable only through the continuing relation to time, to the Tradition. The word of God in its absolute symbolic fullness would be destructive if it were at the same time meaningful in an unmediated (undialectical) way. Nothing in historical time requires concretization more than the 'absolute concreteness' of the word of revelation."[19] Against Schoeps's ahistorical, dogmatic theology of faith, Scholem called for a return to historical consciousness.

Scholem's critique of Schoeps must be read as an attack on all the ahistorical existentialist Jewish theologies of his time, including those of Martin Buber and Franz Rosenzweig. Not the suprahistorical *Erlebnis* of Martin Buber but concrete historical experience (*Erfahrung*) must be the basis for a revitalized Judaism. In his affirmation of the centrality of history, Scholem argues that "meaningless" revelation is the source of all meaningful language, and language is the means for mediating revelation. Revelation can be known only through its mediation, which is historical tradition.

Scholem's understanding of tradition has the same pluralistic freedom as he finds in the Kabbalah: "Tradition as a living force produces in its unfolding another problem. What had originally been believed to be consistent, unified and self-enclosed now becomes diversified, multifold and full of contradictions. It is precisely the wealth of contradictions, of differing views, which is encompassed and unqualifiedly affirmed by tradition."[20] When Scholem called himself a "religious anarchist"[21] he meant that the historical tradition, which is the only source of knowledge we have of revelation, contains no one authoritative voice. All that can be learned from the study of history is that struggle for absolute values between conflicting voices of authority.

Scholem's transformation of the traditional Jewish notion of commentary into historiography suggests that he viewed historical science, no matter how secular, as the modern form of Judaism. In Scholem we have the fulfillment of the desire of the nineteenth-century *Wissenschaft des Judentums* to find a secular substitute for religion in historical study.[22] But as opposed to the nineteenth-century rationalist historians, Scholem argues that a plurality of contradictory interpretations, and not just rationalism, must characterize historical Judaism.

A Contemporary Critique of Scholem

After his death in 1982, the legacy of Gershom Scholem rapidly became an object of contention in the very university in which he played such a central role. Joseph Dan, who now occupies the Gershom Scholem Chair in Jewish Mysticism, asserted that Scholem should be evaluated primarily, if not exclusively, for his textual studies.[23] Dan wished to isolate Scholem's historical work from his philosophy of Jewish history, fearing perhaps that if one rejected Scholem's Jewish philosophy, it might cast doubt on the validity of his historiography.

Eliezer Schweid, a scholar of Jewish philosophy at the Hebrew University, subjected Scholem's general philosophy of Judaism to just such a wide-ranging critique.[24] According to Schweid, Scholem had ignored biblical religion because particularly the religion of the prophets did not fit into his schema of the development of religions: as a self-reflective attempt to seek a God who is no longer present, prophetic religion belongs properly to Scholem's third stage, yet it is not mystical. Had Scholem confronted the meaning of the prophetic religion, he would have had to reject his belief in mysticism as the only possible religion of the "self-reflective" third stage of Judaism.

Scholem was also wrong in arguing that mysticism influenced the popular religion of the Middle Ages. Up to the sixteenth century, the mystics kept their teachings esoteric so it is hard to understand Scholem's contention that their beliefs were central for the Jewish community as a whole. Moreover, Schweid rejects the dichotomy between a "normative" religion of law and a popular religion, stating that the popular religion was the same as the normative.

Schweid goes on to challenge Scholem's argument about the centrality of the Sabbatian movement in ushering in the subsequent movements of the modern period. For Schweid, Sabbatianism was a barren catastrophe that produced nothing positive in its wake.

Finally, Schweid rejects Scholem's attack on both medieval and modern Jewish philosophy. Philosophy was much more effective in responding to external challenges such as Aristotelianism than was mysticism. Similarly, the nineteenth-century philosophers, as well as the historians of the *Wissenschaft des Judentums* whom Scholem regarded as arid rationalists intent only on giving Judaism a "decent burial," were concerned with meeting the challenge of modernity, and the philological method of the historians became the basis for Scholem's own achievement, a debt Schweid incorrectly claims Scholem did not recognize. For Schweid, not mysticism but philosophy will provide the tools for rejuvenating Judaism in our time.

What lies at the heart of these criticisms is an explicitly stated view that mysticism was not an integral part of the internal dialectic of Judaism, as Scholem believed, but rather entirely marginal to its development. Mysticism was not a "necessary" product of the fossilization of rabbinic Judaism, for not only did the latter never turn into a fossil, but there were other movements of renewal such as philosophy and *musar*, which were much more organically linked to the halakhah than mysticism. In this way, Schweid turns the clock back to nineteenth-century historians such as Heinrich Graetz and resurrects something akin to their philosophical position.

Many of these arguments against Scholem are entirely valid: Scholem undoubtedly exaggerated the importance of mysticism and denigrated the vital impulses in the halakhah; his account of the influence of Sabbatianism goes far beyond the evidence; his attack on the *Wissenschaft des Judentums* turned that school into something of a caricature of what it actually was.

Some of Schweid's criticisms, however, are based on a distortion of Scholem's views. Scholem never claimed that mysticism was a logically necessary result of the second stage of religions, only that mysticism historically emerges at a late stage in a religion's development in an attempt to recapture the immediacy of original revelation. Scholem's argument still seems valid as a phenomenological statement describing at least the three monotheistic Western religions. Moreover, Scholem did not limit the third stage to mysticism: all attempts to recover the immediacy of an absent God, including philosophy, fit into this period. Finally, Scholem never called either philosophy or halakhah "inauthentic," as Schweid repeatedly asserts. Rather, he saw them as inadequate to address fully the religious needs of medieval Judaism.

In part, the argument between Schweid and Scholem rests on the very different set of questions each poses. For Schweid, the key question is how Judaism should respond to external challenges, and he finds the most effective answers in the prophetic, ethical, and philosophical traditions rather than in the mystical. For Scholem, the key question is one of religious psychology: which Jewish discipline (law, philosophy, or mysticism) answers most satisfactorily the internal theological needs of the people? Only mysticism provides a real attempt to address the eternal questions about the inner nature of God and the meaning or evil, questions that arise regardless of external challenges.

But the difference between the two can also be understood historically. Scholem's philosophy of Judaism emerged from the context of the Judaism of early twentieth-century Germany, and his insistence on the importance of mysticism was an act of rebellion against what he perceived as a rationalist, bourgeois culture. Schweid's defense of a continuous prophetic tradition, culminating in an existentialist neo-orthodoxy has its context in the Israel of the 1980s, where secular Zionism is under attack for failing to provide an adequate Jewish identity for the Jewish state. Yet Schweid, like Scholem, does not advocate a return to halakhic orthodoxy per se, but rather to his own interpretation of the mainstream Jewish tradition. Might it be that one reason that the Kabbalah remained seductive for Scholem as a German Jew, although a passionate Zionist, was because it was largely a diaspora creation, whereas for Schweid, a product of the Yishuv and the state of Israel, only a tradition rooted in the Bible can serve as a source of Jewish renewal?

All religious philosphies are children of their time and reflect the historical contexts in which they emerge; arguments that appear convincing in one setting may seem less persuasive in others. Schweid was correct in warning against the tendency, sometimes noticeable today, to turn Scholem's thought into the "truth" about Judaism, just as Scholem himself attacked the dogmatic positions of both the orthodox and the rationalists. Yet the very argument between Scholem and Schweid demonstrates once again that Scholem was right about the fundamental pluralism of the Jewish tradition which is able to encompass a host of contradictory interpretations, from the mystical to the rational, and from the secular to the orthodox.

Notes

1. For a full discussion of Scholem's philosophy of history, see my *Gershom Scholem: Kabbalah and Counter-History* (Cambridge, Mass., 1979). Other interpretations of Scholem have appeared in a collection edited by Harold Bloom, *Gershom Scholem: Modern Critical Views* (New York, 1987).
2. "Reflections on the Science of Judaism," *Luah ha-Aretz* (1944–45), [Hebrew] reprinted in *Devarim be-Go* (Tel Aviv, 1975), p. 396.
3. For Scholem's memoirs of the years up to his emigration to Palestine, see his *Berlin to Jerusalem*, English trans. by Harry Zohn (New York, 1980).
4. See my *Gershom Scholem*, pp. 165–69.
5. Scholem recounted the history of his friendship with Benjamin in *Walter Benjamin: The History of a Friendship*, English trans. by Harry Zohn (Philadelphia, 1982).
6. A comprehensive review can be found in Joseph Dan, *Gershom Scholem and the Mystical Dimension of Jewish History* (New York, 1987).
7. Scholem's most comprehesive treatment of the thirteenth-century Kabbalah, *Origins of the Kabbalah*, is now available in English, trans. Alan Arkush, ed. Zwi Werblowsky (Philadelphia, 1987).
8. Scholem was criticized severely by Baruch Kruzweil for identifying too closely with Sabbatianism. See the references to this debate and an evaluation in my *Gershom Scholem*, chap. 7. The charges have been repeated in a new form by Eliezer Schweid, *Judaism and Mysticism According to Gershom Scholem*, trans. David Wiener (Atlanta, Ga., 1985).
9. "Three Sins of Brit Shalom," *Davar*, December 12, 1929, p. 2 [Hebrew].
10. See my interview with Scholem, "The Threat of Messianism: An Interview with Gershom Scholem," *New York Review of Books*, August 14, 1980, p. 22.
11. See especially, "Jewish Theology in Our Time," *Center Magazine* 7 (March–April 1974): 58–71; "Offener Brief an den Verfasser der Schrift 'Juedischer Glaube in dieser Zeit,'" *Bayerische Israelitische Gemeindezeitung*, August 15, 1932, pp. 241–44; and "Zehn unhistorische Saetze ueber Kabbala," *Judaica 3: Studien zur juedischen Mystik* (Frankfurt, 1973), pp. 264–71. For some treatments of Scholem's theology, see my *Gershom Scholem*, chap. 4 and my "Gershom Scholem's Ten Unhistorical Aphorisms on Kabbalah: Text and Commentary," *Modern Judaism* 4 (February 1985), pp. 67–93; see further Ernst Simon, "Ueber einige Theologische Saetze von Gershom Scholem," *Mitteilungsblatt des Irgun Olej Merkaz Europa*, December 8, 1972, pp. 3ff. and December 15, 1972, pp. 4ff.; and Gerson Weiler, "On the Theology of Gershom Scholem" [Hebrew] *Keshet* 71 (1976), pp. 121–28.
12. Paul Mendes-Flohr, *From Mysticism to Dialogue: Martin Buber's Transformation of German Social Thought* (Detroit, 1989).
13. See in particular Buber's introduction to his *Ekstatische Konfessionen* (Jena, 1909; English trans. by Esther Cameron, San Francisco, 1985).
14. Martin Buber, "Religion as Gegenwart," lectures given at Juedisches Lehrhaus, Frankfurt, from January 15 to March 12, 1922, Buber Archive MS B/29, VIII, 10–12. For a full discussion, see my *Gershom Scholem*, pp. 81–86.
15. See, for example, his letters to Buber criticizing the Buber-Rosenzweig Bible translation in Buber, *Briefwechsel*, ed. Grete Schaeder (Heidelberg, 1972–75), April 27, 1926, 2: pp. 251–53; April 10, 1930, 2: pp. 371–73; May 22, 1920, 2: pp. 380–81; see also

his critical review of Meier Wiener's *Lyrik der Kabbala*, which was inspired by Buber's categories, *Der Jude* 6 (1921–22), pp. 55–69.

16. Gershom Scholem, *Major Trends in Jewish Mysticism*, 3d ed. (New York, 1961), p. 17. See also Scholem "The Name of God and the Linguistic Theory of the Kabbalah," in *Diogenes* 79 (1972): 59–80 and 80 (1972), pp. 164–94.

17. "Jewish Theology in Our Time," in Werner Dannhauser, ed., *Jews and Judaism in Crisis* (New York, 1976), p. 271.

18. An excellent example in which Scholem compares the Kabbalist and the historian of the Kabbalah can be found in the first of his ten aphorisms on Kabbalah. See the text and a commentary in "Gershom Scholem's Ten Unhistorical Aphorisms," pp. 70–72.

19. "Offener Brief," p. 243. In "Revelation and Tradition as Religious Categories in Judaism," in Scholem, *Messianic Idea in Judaism and Other Essays in Jewish Spirituality* (New York, 1971), p. 296, Scholem uses almost exactly the same language.

20. "Revelation and Tradition," p. 290.

21. For a discussion of what Scholem means by this term, see my article, "Gershom Scholem and Anarchism as a Jewish Philosophy," *Judaism* 32 (Winter 1983), pp. 70–76.

22. See Eduard Gans's three presidential addresses to the Verein, the first organization for the Science of Judaism in Hebrew translation in Zalman Shazar, *Ore Dorot* (Jerusalem, 1971), pp. 351–85.

23. See Dan's review of my *Gershom Scholem* in *Kiryat Sefer* 52 (1979), pp. 358–62. More recently, see his *Gershom Scholem and the Mystical Dimension of Jewish History*, chap. 1.

24. Schweid, *Judaism and Mysticism According to Gershom Scholem*.

FOR FURTHER READING

Works by Gershom Scholem
(in English)

Major Trends in Jewish Mysticism, New York, 1961. Scholem's most comprehensive work, covering Merkavah, Zohar, Lurianic Kabbalah, Sabbatianism and Hasidism.

The Messianic Idea in Judaism and Other Essays on Jewish Spirituality, New York, 1971. A variety of Scholem's most important essays on messianism, revelation and Hasidism, including his seminal "Holiness of Sin."

On Jews and Judaism in Crisis. Edited by Werner J. Dannhauser, New York, 1976. Some of Scholem's major essays on issues of contemporary revelance.

Origins of the Kabbalah. Edited by R. J. Zwi Werblowsky and translated by Alan Arkush, Philadelphia, 1987. An expanded translation of Scholem's earlier German work on the thirteenth-century Kabbalah.

Sabbatai Sevi. The Mystical Messiah. Translated by R. J. Zwi Werblowsky, Princeton, 1973. Scholem's magisterial biography of the seventeenth-century false Messiah.

Works about Gershom Scholem

Biale, David, *Gershom Scholem: Kabbalah and Counter-History*, Cambridge, 1979. An examination of Scholem's historiography and philosophy of history in the context of modern Jewish thought.

Dan, Joseph, *Gershom Scholem and the Mystical Dimension of Jewish History*, New York, 1987. A summary of Scholem's historiographical work and its contribution to the history of Kabbalah by the first holder of the Scholem chair of Jewish mysticism at the Hebrew University.

Schweid, Eliezer, *Judaism and Mysticism According to Gershom Scholem: A Critical Analysis and Programmatic Discussion*, translated by David Weiner, Atlanta, 1985. A polemical attack on Scholem's philosophy of Judaism.

Steven Schwarzschild

MENACHEM KELLNER

Steven Schwarzschild was both the last of the major medieval Jewish philosophers and the most modern. Before I explain and defend these statements, a few biographical comments are in order.

Schwarzschild was born in Frankfurt on Main in 1924 but grew up in Berlin, emigrating with his parents and brother in January of 1939. He was educated in the United States at the City College of New York, the Jewish Theological Seminary, the University of Cinicinnati, and the Hebrew Union College, where he was ordained and earned a DHL degree. His dissertation was on philosophy of history in Nachman Krochmal and Hermann Cohen. After ordination Schwarzschild served as rabbi of the reconsituted Jewish community in Berlin, ministering to Jews in all parts of the divided city, from 1948 to 1950. He filled rabbinical posts in Fargo, North Dakota, and Lynn, Massachusetts, before turning to an academic career spent almost entirely at Washington University in St. Louis which ended with his sudden passing in 1989.

Schwarzschild characterized himself as a self-conscious German Jew ("Yekke"), a socialist humanist, an opponent of political Zionism on Jewish, socialist, and ethical grounds, and a "quintessential example of the 'symbiosis' of classical Jewish and classical humanist cultures."[1]

Schwarzschild edited *Judaism—A Quarterly Journal* for eight years (1961–69), turning it into the liveliest and at the same time most serious journal of opinion and scholarship in the Jewish world. He was for many years the only active rabbi to hold joint membership in two rabbinical associations, the Reform Central Conference of American Rabbis and the Conservative Rabbinical Assembly. He has had a vast influence on his contemporaries among scholars, rabbis, and Jewish activists although he is relatively little known in the broader Jewish community. Aside from the obvious impact of his career as editor of *Judaism*, he had important influence as a Hebrew Union College-educated rabbi who took messianism and halakhah seriously. His oft-reprinted and widely cited essay "The Personal Messiah—Towards the Restoration of a Discarded Doctrine"[2] may be noted in this regard. In addition, Schwarzschild has always been ahead of his time in a variety of central developments and insights in Jewish intellectual life. This, for example, his book on Franz Rosenzweig and his pioneering studies on Samson Raphael Hirsch and Hermann Cohen were the earliest serious attention these thinkers had received in English and helped spark the ever-growing interest in them.[3] Schwarzschild's prescience and sensitivity are marked by his unusually sensitive antennae for anti-Semitism and political conservatism[4] and evidence by his warning—as long ago as 1956—of the dangers inherent in triumphalist, messianic Zionism.[5] As a profoundly committed and deeply learned Jew who was also a pacifist, a socialist, and a trenchant critic of Zionism, he has been important to many Jews seeking a way to unite such commitments with their Zionism.

Schwarzschild's two hundred-odd publications—historical, philosophical, and theological studies, essays, reviews, polemics —are studded with insights both brilliant and profound. Here follow a few examples, even though they can be fully appreciated only in context. Take, for example, this brief, cutting, and trenchant critique of orthodox Marxism: "Indeed, except by philosophic sleights of hand, Marxist dialectics have never been able to get around this dilemma of historical necessity which they posit versus social betterment to which they aspire."[6] Moving from Marxism to Christianity one finds the following:

> In Christianity, it is true, God and the world have been so completely separated that they constitute an exclusive alternative: you either choose the world, or any part of it, or you choose God; you cannot have both. This accounts for the well-known otherworldliness of Christianity, its asceticism, its fundamental indifference to social

goals, its rejection of reason in favor of 'faith,' ... Some modern Christians ... have of course been committed to the world. It can, however, be shown that these have followed 'Judaizing' tendencies, or that their social concerns have been of a deceptive nature.[7]

Schwarzschild's deep understanding of figures in the history of philosophy is exemplified by the following comment on Hegel: "Generally it can be said that Hegel simply stretched out on an horizontal plane, i.e., through history, the originally metaphysical vertical ladder of emanations of the neo-Platonists." Further insights worthy of note include the explication of the intimate connection between natural law theory and political conservatism (which might explain the force with which Schwarzschild criticizes scholars who seek to impute natural law positions to thinkers like Maimonides), the definition of the halakhic expression *lifnin meshurat ha-din* as "going beyond—actually into the inner recesses—of the letter of the law," the explication of Maimonides' strange codification of *imitati Dei* in terms of imitating the rabbis by pointing out that the masses imitate the sages, "the men of philosophical understanding, who in turn emulate God directly," and his argument that pantheism must lead to the identity of *is* and *ought*, thus making it impossible for Judaism to be pantheistic.[8]

I stated at the outset that Schwarzschild was the latest of the major medieval Jewish philosophers. It is now time to explain that claim. In the first place, *medieval* does not mean outmoded or old-fashioned. Rather, it places Schwarzschild in the tradition of Jewish thinking which opened with Sa'adia Gaon and reached its highest expression in Maimonides. The common denominator shared by all the medieval Jewish philosophers was their understanding that we could speak intelligibly of a datum called Judaism that had clearly defined, normative, and authoritative features and that this Judaism had to be confronted by and shown to be consistent with some systematic and overarching view of the universe. Sa'adia did this with Kalam, ibn Gabirol with neo-platonism, and Maimonides with what he took to be Aristotelianism. Schwarzschild does it with neo-Kantianism.

Schwarzschild is absolutely convinced that Judaism is a consistent, rational system, possessed of authoritative, normative character, and susceptible of clear-cut exposition. His work is studded with expressions like "the original, traditional position of

Judaism," "it is established Jewish doctrine that ... ," "authoritative Jewish doctrine holds ... ," "the authentic substance of
Judaism," "normative Jewish views," "issues that are Jewish con-
ceptually," "that quintessential Jew ... ," "the differentiating characteristics of Jewish culture," and the like.

What is this essential Judaism? In the first place, it involves "an
absolute belief in and dependence on the historic revelation at
Sinai." Thus "the most fundamental virtue of the Jew" is take the
Torah seriously.[9] The single most important teaching of the
Torah that must be taken seriously is that "truth is above
reality—truth is an Ought, not an Is." In other words, the most
important characteristic of truth is not its description of the
universe as it is but of how it ought to be. This is a reflection of the
neo-Kantian view that the world in and of itself, the world of the
ding an sich, of the noumenon, is beyond our ken; the role of
science and philosophy is regulative, not descriptive. The "outstanding philosophic exemplars" of this view are, "of course,
Judaism on the one hand, which awaits the Messiah and teaches
that 'God is the place of the world; the world is not the place of
God'; and Kant-Cohen, on the other, who have demonstrated that
even the cognition of reality is an ethical imperative."[10] I will
return to the issue of the Kantian nature of Judaism or the Jewish
nature of Kant below.

One must not view the relationship of God and the world in
spatial terms. Judaism adopts the model "of *the will* in trying to
conceptualize the relationship between God and the world ... the
explication of the will of God for man we call 'law' or *Halakhah*."[11]
Viewing the relationship of God to the world in spatial terms is a
pagan or Christian heresy. The cornerstone of Judaism is "the
primacy of practical [ethical] reason."[12] This emphasis on volitionalism, and ethics (which for Schwarzschild are really the
same thing) is what Schwarzschild has called the "Jewish twist,"
which "literally every single Jewish thinker has felt constrained to
introduce ... into the non-Jewish philosophic system which he
happened to work." Because of this emphasis on ethics "Judaism
always advocated, in the name of God absolutely concerned with
the world, the greatest possible human, religious attention to the
welfare and progress of the world ... [and] it teaches convincingly
that this can be done only under the aegis of a Law put forward by
a transcendent God."[13] Schwarzschild summarizes his view of

what in an earlier age would have been called "ethical monotheism" as follows: "Classical Jewish thought is committed to the
belief in the absolutely transcendent God, who is related to the
human world only through his imperatives, and history is, therefore, the enactment of that body of imperatives, to the end of the
messianic achievement, in the inter-action of God and Israel, of
the Kingdom of God on earth."[14] Schwarzschild's ethical monotheism is thus hardly that of the classical Reform Judaism because
of its emphasis on halakhah as the body of divine imperatives.

Since Judaism has a clear-cut philosophical view of the world,
it can be contrasted with other views, notably Christianity on one
hand and a Christianizing philosophical tendency which
Schwarzschild traces from Spinoza through Hegel to Marx on the
other. Before turning to these critiques, however, it is important to
note that if Judaism is defined in terms of its philosophical
perspective on the world, then ideas, movements, individuals, and
concerns that grow out of or express that perspective can, in an
important sense, be called Jewish, whatever their historical, bio-
logical, or confessional status. Schwarzschild does not shrink from
this conclusion; on the contrary, he enthusiastically embraces it.
Many individuals who "do Judaism" are "themselves Jews not by
birth or by conversion but by what might be called 'spiritual
assimilation.'"[15] these "Jewish non-Jews" (as opposed to Deutch-
er's "non-Jewish Jews") include Immanuel Kant ("the real Kant
hailing not from Koenigsburg but from Marburg [the home of
Hermann Cohen's—quintessentially Jewish, according to
Schwarzschild—neo-Kantianism]"), J.-P. Sartre, who "ended as a
Jew *honoris causa*," and such alienated Jews as Ludwig Wittgenstein.
This view also allows Schwarzschild to speak of "doing philosophy Jewishly," to speak of "issues that are Jewish ... concep-
tually," to look for Marx's Jewish theory of usury, and to adum-
brate a Jewish aesthetics ("not the aesthetics of Jewish art, but the
Jewish aesthetics of art").[16]

Judaism, then, has a clear-cut philosophical view of its own.
This, for Schwarzschild, means that underlying the "blooming,
buzzing, mass of confusion," in William James' terms, that is
ordinarily taken for Jewish theological teaching there must be a
continuity, systematicity, and consistency to be found by those
willing to take the trouble to look.[17] Thus, in an important study
on rabbinic views of the messiah, Schwarzschild says that the

crystallization of a systematic, consistent conception of the ideal, messianic society out of rabbinic sources "needs to be done not only with this aspect as well as the rest of rabbinic eschatology, but with all of Jewish-Rabbinic theology."[18] He goes on to criticize the generally accepted view of the Talmud "as a welter of unsystematic thought": "How unsystematic thought is supposed to underly, or result from, what is conceded to be an extraordinarily systematic legal system is incomprehensible." This last comment is important not only for exemplifying Schwarzschild's view that talmudic thought is susceptible of systematization but for what it reveals about Schwarzschild's view of the core of talmudic thought out of which systematic theology is to be spun: halakah. Schwarzschild, on the basis of his views on the primacy of practical (ethical) reason as the defining characteristic of Judaism and of the impossibility of ethics without law, has argued for the primacy of halakah in the elucidation of Jewish theology and has convincingly demonstrated how to do it in several important studies.[19]

One of the consequences of Schwarzschild's view that there is a normative and systematic Jewish philosophical perspective is that Judaism can be clearly distinguished from competing religions and, no less important, competing philosophies. Schwarzschild takes great pains to distinguish Judaism from Christianity:

> The doctrine at issue, be it noted, is not the doctrine of sin, original or otherwise. Man's sinfulness is biblical doctrine.... The doctrine at issue is a basic Christian dualism (Hellenistic and gnostic in origin), between body and spirit, this world and the other world, the kingdoms of the former and the latter. This doctrine leads to Paul's condemnation of the flesh and all that goes with it—to the transfer of God's kingdom from this world to the other and into the heart of man—and to 'Render unto Caesar what is Caesar's and unto God what is God's'.... It resulted ... in the divorce of German Lutherans from all political matters, leaving the road open to the princes' ruthless suppression of the peasants' revolt in Luther's time and to the principled indifference of the German Church as a whole to the rise of Hitler. In such a world, separated from God's direct sovereignty, it is, indeed, true that God's law is ultimately inapplicable. To try to apply it is really hubris.... Judaism, on the other hand, has never abandoned this world to the devil. This is God's world, created by Him, and His law is specifically and even exclusively meant for it.... Sin is not a matter of materiality but of errant spirit.... Furthermore, whatever the total conception of the eschatological state may be in

Judaism, none can doubt that the messianic kingdom is awaited *on this earth*. And thus it follows that, from the Jewish point of view, such matters as foreign policy, like everything else, are directly—not "proximately"—under divine command. Judaism is not only mono-theistic but also, in this sense, monistic.[20]

Christianity is intrinsically conservative, surely an "original sin" in Schwarzschild's eyes. This political conservatism is basic to Christianity, and progressive Christians either are not truly pro-gressive or are unconscious Judaizers:

> The reason for this built-in Christian conservatism is ... the doctrine of the Incarnation. What this doctrine minimally means is that at least one person, at one time and in one place, has been divine. That is to say, the world as it now is, and indeed as it once was, has been at least partly redeemed—and therefore the whole world as it now is is in principle capable of redemption. Cox's only argument with the reactionaries is that they think the entire world is already completely redeemed. The issue between them is one of degree, not of prin-ciple.[22]

Schwarzschild criticizes Spinoza, Hegel, and Marx on similar grounds:

> Hegel's basic error consists of having assumed that theoretical reason, rather than volitional ethics, governs history ... history thus becomes part of nature ... this is Hegel's version of *Deus sive natura*. This in turn leads to the logical conclusion, which neither Spinoza nor Hegel shirked, that everything that is is necessary and rational and, there-fore, in its time and place, is also good. And that, of course, constitutes intellectual and ethical acquiescence to every historical reality, be it good or bad, just or unjust.[23]

Marx failed to free himself of the necessitarian and materialist underpinnings of Spinoza and Hegel. Moses Hess was therefore forced to break "with Marx on ethical grounds, i.e., by holding that socialism was to be the result of the moral will rather than of the inevitable laws of history. Little wonder that he ended as a committed Jew."[24]

The point of all this is that since Judaism equals ethical volitionalism (as has been shown) and since Jewish messianism equals revolution (as will be seen below) and since Judaism insists on God's transcendence, thus refusing to make the real or material world divine (and thus already in theory perfected), Judaism though surely socialist and progressive, must reject the (false) socialism and progressivism of Marx, just as it must reject the politically conservative consequence of Christian immanentism.

It was said above that the defining characteristic of medieval Jewish philosophy was a view of Judaism as normative, consistent, and systematic and the felt need to confront that Judaism with a systematic, architectonically overarching philosophic view of the cosmos. So far I have shown that Schwarzschild's view of Judaism fully satisfies the first part of this criterion. For Schwarzschild there is also a systematic philosophy with which Judaism must be confronted and which can be shown to be consistent with Judaism. Indeed, for Schwarzschild, this philosophical system is not only consistent with Judaism but for all intents and purposes identical with it. This philosophical system, of course, is Kantianism as canonically interpreted by Hermann Cohen, the founder of the Marburg School of Neo-Kantianism.

Schwarzschild clearly and explicitly identifies himself over and over again as a disciple of Cohen's. "Speaking as a Marburg neo-Kantian,"[25] he says in one place, but speaks as such in almost every place. Perhaps the clearest summary of Cohen's and Schwarzschild's Kant is found in the following critique of Hegel:

> The principle underlying Cohen's rejection of Hegelianism in its original form as well as in its transformed state of socialist materialism is the refutation of the pantheistic doctrine that "everything that is is rational, and that everything rational is," on the grounds that, philosophically speaking, this constitutes a confusion of the ideal with the real, of the hypothetical with the empirical, and that, ethically speaking it amounts to a vicious justification of any given *status quo* in history and society. Hegelianism and socialist materialism, in short, are the denial of voluntarism in favor of quietism. Cohen is amazingly radical and consistent in the application of this criterion to all cultural and historical realities.[26]

Kant teaches that reality is never given but must be constructed. The real must not be accepted as the ideal; rather, the ideal, the regulative, must guide our construction of reality. In Jewish terms, this is called messianism and in Kantian terms, critical idealism. The Spinoza/Hegel/Marx denial of volitionalism (and thus of ethics) must be rejected: "Ethical idealism, *Judaism as well as Kant*, must and does answer this pernicious doctrine with the counter proposition that the rational is never real and that it is man's task on earth to realize it ever more."[27]

Having described Schwarzschild's basic Jewish/philosophic position, we may now turn to an examination of the way he expresses that basic philosophic/religious orientation on some specific issues. Among matters that have consistently attracted his attention are messianism, Zionism, pacifism, and socialism. Before analyzing his positions on these questions, however, several introductory observations are in order.

First, Schwarzschild presents himself as a disciple of Hermann Cohen. This is important because, accepting Cohen's "philosophy of origins," we must look for the "essential Schwarzschild" in the "early Schwarzschild." He is not, however, an uncritical disciple. "The live Jew," he wrote at the beginning of his ground-breaking study of Rosenzweig, "never stands still in his Jewishness. If he ever did stand still he would be Jewishly dead; even if he were an extremely pious and learned Jew, standing still he would be an extremely pious and learned dead Jew."[28] Schwarzschild is an extremely pious (not, however, in the terms by which piety is all too often measured today) and extremely learned Jew; but he is by no means a dead Jew. He is constantly growing in his Judaism, whether in his personal life-style, with regard to his teachers (he counts himself as a disciple not only of Hermann Cohen but of Samuel Atlas,[29] R. Joseph Soloveitchik, and R. Isaac Hutner), and, most especially, in his theological explorations.

This growth, however, is organic, never haphazard. Speaking of Sartre, he says that "truly perspicuous philosophers ... tend to begin with a unifying vision, or conceptuality, and this original conception, through sometimes fundamental revisions ... retains its basic philosophical integrity."[30] Schwarzschild is certainly a perspicuous philosopher, and although his thought has undergone some fundamental revisions (particularly with respect to messianism), it expresses a unifying vision and has throughout his career retained its basic philosophical integrity.

This point leads to a second observation. I have just described Schwarzschild in terms he used to describe two other thinkers, Rosenzweig and Sartre. While meticulously adhering to the strictest canons of scholarship in his historical studies, Schwarzschild is so *engaged* a scholar that he is often as revealing about himself as he is about his subjects. For example, Schwarzschild has produced a

large number of truly important studies in the history of philosophy and of Jewish thought; but he has done so, not as a
historian but as a theologian. In Schwarzschild's able hands,
historical works always subserve (but are never corrupted by)
theological ends. This may explain, in part, which his historical
studies, even clothed in all the trappings of academic scholarship,
make such lively reading.

Messianism is absolutely central to Judaism: "the messianic
kingdom is what all of Judaism is for and about;" "messianic
expectation is thus literally the daily and even hourly posture of
the Jew;" "the Messianic vocation of Israel."[31] No person halfway
literate in the sources of Judaism could deny the truth of these
characterizations. For Schwarzschild, however, messianism is also
absolutely central to Kantianism, to reason, to halakah, and to
political and personal ethics. In fact, without too much over-
statement we can say that for Schwarzschild, Messianism *is*
Judaism, which *is* Kantianism, which *is* reason, which *is* halakah,
which *is* personal and political ethics.

Here we have Schwarzschild on Kant and messianism:

> It is noteworthy that the two truths which we have hitherto attempted
> to crystallize have one feature in common: they define the beginning
> and the middle by the end; i.e., death defines the possibility of life,
> ultimate divine peace defines the possibility of peace in our time; or,
> in other words yet, the future defines the past and the present, not the
> reverse as is usually thought. We are not saying anything new. Kant
> highlighted this when he distinguished between the reactionary,
> stand-pattism of the "is" and the revolutionary ethical "ought". And
> even Kant did not, of course, invent anything; he merely put in
> philosophical language what biblical religion had always called "the
> kingdom of God" or the "reign of the Messiah".[32]

As soon as we make ethics a matter of realizing ideals, of always
judging the *is* by the *ought*, of constructing the world in which we
live not in terms of its present nature but of its future possibilities,
when we make ethics a matter of reading the future back into the
present—and Schwarzschild's Kant does all of this—we are in
messianic territory.

Since Kantianism is messianic, so must reason be: "Reason is
thus, I hope to have shown, the companion of faith in all its ways.
Reason, in a sense, prepares the path on which faith can walk;
reason clears the path once faith has begun to walk it and writes an

intelligible record of the distance covered; and when faith has reached its destination, reason embraces faith, and the two companions unite in the kiss of the Messiah."[33]

Halakah both subserves and is defined by its messianic end:

> It would not be difficult to show how literally all of the Halakhah is either the law of society as it should be—and thus whoever fulfills it in fact establishes, as it were, a small forward bastion of the ultimate future in the present—or the law by which the present society is moved forward toward the messianic. I.e. whenever a Jew acts according to the Halakhah he either hastens the coming of the Kingdom or actually institutes it at the moment and in the place where he happens to be.[34]

Schwarzschild's view here is entrenched and established Jewish doctrine; perhaps its best-known expression is in the Lurianic concept of *tikkun*.

If halakah is messianic, then it can come as no surprise that ethics is as well, since Schwarzschild consistently identifies the two.[35] Speaking of political ethics we find the following claim:

> And since the means must be appropriate to the end, the road to the goal, it follows that peaceful action—not war, just and decent action—not exploitation and depersonalization, *Mitzvot*—and not hobbies, timewasters, and flippancies—are the ways in which man must strive to approach his individual and social destination. The opposite or any other action removes us further from the goal and that, therefore, quite literally, must be regarded as reactionary. Contrary to Goethe's dictum, destiny is destination, not character.[36]

We have here a kind of "messianic imperative" by which messianic expectation guides our actions in this world.[37] If we wish to bring about the coming of the Messiah, we must behave in ways consistent with that end. In effect, to make the Messiah's coming possible we must act now as if the Messiah has already come.[38]

Just as our political and social ethics must be defined by the messianic end, so must our personal ethics:

> But men do play a significant part in the drama of salvation, and they can affect its *denoument* by their lives. Thereupon various Messianic courses of action are followed: vegetarianism, socialism, pacifism—the characteristics of the Messianic kingdom are regarded as com-

mandments for daily living; they, as it were, anticipate the world-to-come in this world and try radically and piously to "transform the world in the image of the kingdom of heaven."[39]

It is no surprise that Schwarzschild, the messianic Jew par excellence, is a vegetarian, socialist, and pacifist.

One of the issues related to messianism for which Schwarzschild's contribution is best known is the question of the personal nature of the Messiah. In 1956, using Rosenzweig against Cohen, Schwarzschild argued both for the actual coming of the Messiah and for his personal character is an essay addressed first and foremost to Reform Jews. He was, of course, arguing against one of the important teachings of classical Reform Judaism, which replaced belief in the coming of the Messiah with belief in the advent of a messianic age. Schwarzschild posited an "intimate connection between the belief in the personality of the Messiah and belief in the personality of God." Although Schwarzschild makes an important philosophical argument in this essay, my purposes here may be served by citing the ethical argument he makes for the personhood of the Messiah: "We have learned from religious as well as nonreligious existentialism, that all moral reality, as distinguished from nature and mathematics, is the reality of persons. Man, the person, is the *locus* of ethics, not ages, ideas, or forces. The Messianic age is a Utopia; the Messiah is a concrete, though, future reality."[40] Since the messianic idea is first and foremost an *ethical* idea, and since humanity in all its concreteness must be the focus of ethics, to depersonalize the Messiah is, in effect, to argue against the ethical focus of Jewish messianism. And this would be to empty it of its fundamental content, rendering it vacuous.

Precisely thirty years after the publication of this essay Schwarzschild explicitly reversed part of his position in a study that argues on *ethical* (as well as historical and theological) grounds that to preserve the ideal, regulative character of messianic belief we must side with Cohen against Rosenzweig and see the advent of the Messiah as something for which we must work and toward which we can move ever closer, but as an event that will never actually occur.[41] Schwarzschild uses all his brilliance and insight to show that this admittedly unusual position is actually the teaching of rabbinic Judaism.

It is hard to refrain from suggesting that Schwarzschild's position here might reflect not only a revision of philosophical and theological views (bringing him closer to his mentor, Cohen) but also his growing disillusionment with messianic Zionism. To my mind, this is to throw the baby out with the bathwater, but that must be the subject of another study.

This observation brings us to the next topic I want to discuss, namely, Steven Schwarzschild's views on Zionism. Schwarzschild is well known, in fact notorious, for being the only Jewish theologian of stature in our day to maintain a consistent, radical, and *Jewish* critique of Zionism. In light of some of the unfortunate realities in the Jewish world today and some of the truly ignoble vilification to which he has been subjected, several comments must immediately be made. First, Schwarzschild is a Jewish critic of Zionism; that does not make him an enemy of the State of Israel. Second, because he is not an enemy of the State of Israel, Schwarzschild has been extremely careful not to wash Jewish laundry in public, keeping his criticisms muted and in the family. Given the strength of his feelings on the subject and the provocations (in his eyes) of Israel and the Zionist establishment, this has often involved great self-restraint. Third, Schwarzschild's critique of Zionism is not based on ignorance but on a thorough and deep acquaintance with Zionist theory, literature, and history. Fourth, Schwarzschild's critique of Zionism grows directly out of his *Jewish* concerns. Zionism, he is convinced, is bad for Judaism and thus bad for the Jews. Last, Schwarzschild is not and for all intents and purposes has never been a Zionist. But that does not mean that he has never felt the pull of the amazing events of 1948. He, too, like most other Jews, has occasionally "espied the outlines of the figure of the Messiah in the faintest wisps of smoke over the chimneys of Auschwitz and on the skyline of Jerusalem rebuilding." He, too, like many other religious Jews, has been tempted to see the *athalta d'geulah* (beginning of the redemption), but never the redemption itself, in the establishment of the State of Israel.[42]

Why is Schwarzschild not a Zionst? In this connection it is perhaps apposite to quite the famous remark attributed to Hermann Cohen about Zionists: "Those fools want to be happy!" By this Cohen seemed to mean that Zionists wanted to feel at home in the world, comfortable, not alienated. But the Jew, and here Schwarzschild paraphrases Franz Rosenzweig, must "always and everywhere [be] a stranger except in Judaism and with God and that, as a matter of fact, our commitment to the eventual Messianic kingdom perforce estrange us from the existing conditions of the world at all stages prior to that of the Messiah."[43] Our commitment to ultimate perfection and the regulative character of the messianic utopia forbids us comfort in this dispensation. To feel at home in the present world is to idealize that world and to be guilty of confusing the world of *is* with the world of *ought.*

Not only does Zionism lead to the confusion of *is* with *ought,* but it is also guilty of the materialist immanentism that, as was shown in our discussion of Schwarzschild's rejection of the Spinoza-Hegel-Marx "heresy," is antithetical to Judaism:

> I argue that Judaism and Jewish culture have paradigmatically and throughout history operated with a fundamental dichotomy between nature ("what is") and ethics (i.e., God and man—"what ought to be"). Pagan ontologism on the other hand, and the Christian synthesis of biblical transcendentalism and Greek incarnationism result in human and historical submission to what are acclaimed as "natural forces." Although in the history of Jewish culture such a heretical, quasi-pantheistic tendency asserted itself, first in medieval kabbalism and then in modern Zionism, from a traditionally Jewish standpoint nature remains subject to humanly enacted ends."

A Jew can never feel fully at home in nature, the ultimate *is.* Zionism ignores this fundamental fact of Judaism.[44]

If Jews are not to return to history, does that mean that we have no task in the world? Hardly! "Our task is to be *mentshen* and thus—and thus only—to hasten the Messiah's coming, not by force or by magic or by supererogation." This is so because "the Torah is our business, Israel's survival is God's."[45] This may seem like a recipe for quietism, but is is not. Zionism may not be the proper expression of true Jewish messianism, but that certainly does not mean (and cannot mean, given the unbreakable tie between messianism and ethics) that it has no proper, active, concrete expression in this world. This leads to the last two points in my exposition of Steven Schwarzschild's thought, pacifism and socialism.

Schwarzschild must be a pacifist because of his messianism: if the messianic era will be characterized by peace, the only way to actualize the era (to the extent that it can be actualized) is to act peacefully now. Schwarzschild is also a pacifist because of his belief in God: "Therefore, when God, the Radical, demands that we seek peace, He demands radically that we radically seek radical peace. . . . Because the God of the religious man is the root of all radicalism, the religious man himself is bound to be radical in every respect, including his insistence on peace."[46]

This interpretation of God also underlies Schwarzschild's socialism: "God is the root of all things. He is *the* radical. Faith is, therefore, by definition radical. Whatever is not radical is not faith. God hates comfortable superficialities. He loves all radicalisms—even His own radical opponents. I am sure He prefers these to His facile believers."[47] Socialism, which seeks to change the world in light of the messianic ideals of Judaism, is one of those radical things loved by God and therefore adopted as program and goal by Schwarzschild.

In the preceding survey the broad outlines of the thought—as it has developed and been expressed to date—of one of contemporary Jewry's most important theologians have been delineated. I have suggested that Schwarzschild may be best understood within the framework of the great Jewish philosophers of the past, all of whom had a clear-cut vision of what Judaism is and sought to show that that Judaism could and must be successfully confronted with a comprehensive philosophy held by the Jewish philosopher to be substantially true. Schwarzschild is convinced that normative, authoritative, halakhic Judaism is a consistent, rational system primarily characterized by the primacy it gives to ethical concerns. This system, he maintains, can be shown to have been given its canonical "secular" interpretation in the philosophy of Immanuel Kant as exposited by Hermann Cohen. Among the consequences of this position are that Judaism is systematizable, that non-Jews can, in effect, be "spiritually assimilated" into Judaism, and that there are religious and philosophical positions (Christianity on one hand and Spinoza/Hegel/Marx on the other) absolutely antithetical to Judaism.

Having set forth Schwarzschild's theology to this point, I set out four issues—messianism, Zionism, pacifism, and socialism—on which Schwarzschild has taken important Jewish positions to show how his position on each of these issues grows directly out of his basic philosophical orientation to Judaism.

Steven Schwarzschild has successfully transplanted to America the best of a long tradition of messianic and philosophical reasoning rooted in Europe, immeasurably enriching American and world Judaism thereby.

Steven Schwarzschild died in September 1989 at the age of 65.

Notes

All works cited in the notes are by Steven S. Schwarzschild unless otherwise indicated.

1. "Remembering Erich Fromm," *Jewish Spectator*, Fall 1980, pp. 29–33 (quotation on p. 29).
2. "The Personal Messiah—Towards the Restoration of a Discarded Doctrine," *Judaism* 5 (1956), pp. 123–35.
3. *Franz Rosenzweig (1886–1929)—Guide to Reversioners* (London, 1960); "Franz Rosenzweig and Existentialism," *Central Conference of American Rabbis Yearbook* 62 (1952), pp. 410–29; "F. Rosenzweig on Judaism and Christianity," *Conservative Judaism*, Winter 1956, pp. 41–48; "Samson Raphael Hirsch—The Man and His Thought," *Conservative Judaism*, Winter 1959, pp. 26–45; "The Democratic Socialism of Hermann Cohen, *Hebrew Union College Annual* 27 (1956), pp. 417–38; "Hermann Cohen Today," *Sh'ma* 2, no. 31 (April 21, 1972), pp. 84–87; "The Tenability of H. Cohen's Construction of the Self," *Journal of the History of Philosophy* 13 (1975), pp. 361–84; and many others.
4. See, for one example, "The *Commentary-Monat* Axis," *Menorah Journal* 41 (1953), pp. 87–105.
5. See "Personal Messiah."
6. See "Democratic Socialism," p. 421.
7. "Torah for Our Time," in Ira Eisenstein, ed., *Varieties of Jewish Belief* (New York, 1966), p. 246.
8. "The Lure of Immanence—The Crisis in Contemporary Religious Thought," *Tradition*, Spring–Summer 1967, p. 77; "Do Noachites Have to Believe in Revelation?" *Jewish Quarterly Review* 53 (July 1962): p. 55; the notes in "Moral Radicalism and 'Middlingness' in the Ethics of Maimonides," *Studies in Medieval Culture* 11 (1977), pp. 65–94, esp. pp. 66, 74 "A Critique of M. Buber's Political Philosophy—An Affectionate Reappraisal," *Leo Baeck Institute Yearbook* 31 (1986), p. 361.
9. "Samson Raphael Hirsch," pp. 32, 44.
10. "To Recast Rationalism," *Judaism* 11 (1962), p. 209.
11. "The Lure of Immanence," p. 73.
12. "An Agenda for Jewish Philosophy in the 1980's," *Studies in Jewish Philosophy* 1 (1981), p. 61.
13. "The Lure of Immanence," pp. 73, 87.
14. "An Introduction to the Thought of R. Isaac Hutner," *Modern Judaism* 5 (Fall 1985), p. 260.
15. "Marrano Professors of Jewish Studies," *Association for Jewish Studies Newsletter* 2, no. 2 (April 1971), p. 6.
16. "Agenda for Jewish Philosophy," pp. 62, 57; "J.-P. Sartre as Jew," *Modern Judaism* 3 (1983), p. 59; "Wittgenstein as Alienated Jew," *Telos*, Summer 1979, pp. 160–65. "Authority and 'Revelation," *Studies in Jewish Philosophy* 2 (1982), p. 47; "Karl Marx's

Jewish Theory of Usury," *Gesher*, 7 (1978), pp. 7–40. "The Legal Foundations of Jewish Aesthetics," *Journal of Aesthetic Education* 19 (1975), p. 30.

17. See Schwarzschild's comments on Sartre in "J.-P, Sartre as Jew," p. 60.
18. "A Note on the Nature of Ideal Society—A Rabbinic Study," in H. Strauss and G. Reissner, eds., *Curt Silberman Festschrift* (New York, 1969), p. 105.
19. See, for example, "The Lure of Immanence," p. 86; "A Philosophy of Mitzvot," *Journal of Biblical Literature* 95 (1976), pp. 519–20; "Karl Marx's Jewish Theory"; "Legal Foundations of Jewish Aesthetics"; and "The Question of Jewish Ethics Today," *Sh'ma* 7, no. 124 (December 24, 1976), pp. 29–36, and 7 no. 134 (May 13, 1977), pp. 118–24. Schwarzschild has done more halakhic-based philosophy than any self-proclaimed spokesman of Jewish Orthodoxy other than Rabbi Joseph Soloveitchik.
20. "A Jewish Perspective on International Relations," in Arnold Jacob Wolf, ed., *Rediscovering Judaism* (Chicago, 1965), pp. 258–59.
21. See "Torah for Our Time."
22. "A Little Bit of Revolution?" in Daniel Callahan, ed., *The Secular City Debate* (New York, 1966), p. 146.
23. See "Democratic Socialism," p. 421.
24. "Lure of Immanence," p. 81. For further criticisms of Marxism, see "Jewish Perspective on International Relations" "The Messianic Doctrine in Contemporary Jewish History," in *Great Jewish Ideas* (Washington, 1964), pp. 237–59; "The New Left Meets the Real Thing," *Dissent*, January–February, 1968; and "On Jewish Eschatology," in F. Greenspahn, ed., *The Human Condition in the Jewish and Christian Traditions* (New York, 1986), pp. 171–211.
25. "Authority and Revelation," p. 47.
26. "Democratic Socialism," p. 424.
27. Ibid., p. 422; emphasis added.
28. *Franz Rosenzweig*, p. 5.
29. For Atlas see the dedication of "Democratic Socialism," for Soloveitchik see Schwarzschild's contribution to "The Sixth Annual American-Israel Dialogue," *Congress Bi-Weekly*, February 24, 1969, p. 83; for Hutner see "Two Lectures of Rabbi Isaac Hutner," *Tradition* 14 (1974), pp. 90–109; "Introduction to the Thought of R. Isaac Hutner"; and *Encyclopedia of Religion* (New York, 1986), 6, p. 544.
30. See "J.-P. Sartre as Jew," p. 61.
31. "Lure of Immanence," p. 88, "Messianic Doctrine," pp. 244, 250.
32. "The Necessity of the Lone Man," *Fellowship*, May 1965, p. 16.
33. "The Role and Limits of Reason in Contemporary Jewish Theology," *Central Conference of American Rabbis Yearbook* 73 (1963), p. 214.
34. "Lure of Immanence," p. 88.
35. See, for example, "Torah for Our Time," pp. 250–51, and "Do Noachites Have to Believe in Revelation?" p. 45.
36. "The Necessity of the Lone Man," p. 16.
37. On this subject generally see Menachem Kellner, "Messianic Postures in Israel Today," *Modern Judaism* 6 (1986), pp. 197–209.
38. In the passage just cited Schwarzschild identifies mizvot with just and decent actions. Compare with "Role and Limits of Reason."
39. "Messianic Doctrine," p. 256.
40. "Personal Messiah," pp. 533, 535.
41. "On Jewish Eschatology."
42. "Messianic Doctrine," pp. 240–41.
43. *Franz Rosenzweig*, p. 14.
44. "The Unnatural Jew," *Environmental Ethics* 6 (1984): p. 347.

45. "On the Theology of Jewish Survival," *Central Conference of American Rabbis Journal,* Fall 1968, pp. 19, 21.
46. "The Religious Demand for Peace," *Judaism* 15 (1966): p. 1.
47. "Role and Limits of Reason," p. 200. Compare "On Power in Judaism," *Worldview,* February 1964, pp. 6–10.

FOR FURTHER READING

Works by Steven Schwarzschild

The Pursuit of the Ideal: Jewish Writings of Steven Schwarzschild, Albany, 1990. Edited by M. M. Kellner. This volume collects together thirteen of Schwarzschild's essays on Jewish themes, with a new afterword written by Schwarzschild for the volume and a complete list of his publications. Essays marked with an asterisk below appear in the volume.

"An Agenda for Jewish Philosophy in the 1980's," *Studies in Jewish Philosophy* 1 (1981), pp. 55–71.

"Authority and Revelation," *Studies in Jewish Philosophy* 2 (1982), pp. 45–63.

"The *Commentary-Monat* Axis," *Menorah Journal* 41 (1953), pp. 87–105. A very early attack on the nascent "neo-conservatism."

* "A Critique of M. Buber's Political Philosophy—An Affectionate Reappraisal," *Leo Baeck Institute Yearbook* 31 (1986), pp. 355–88. A detailed demonstration that Buber's socio-political posture, however well-intentioned usually, was inherently foredoomed to failure.

"The Democratic Socialism of Hermann Cohen," *Hebrew Union College Annual* 27 (1956), pp. 417–38.

* "Do Noachites Have to Believe in Revelation?" *Jewish Quarterly Review* 52 (April 1962), pp. 297–308, and 53 (July 1962), pp. 30–65. An historical survey of the subject coming to the conclusion that Maimonides' famous addition to the definition of "Noachite" had partial philosophical justification—a view that Schwarzschild later rescinded.

"Franz Rosenzweig" and Existentialism," *Central Conference on American Rabbis Yearbook* 62 (1952), pp. 410–29.

Franz Rosenzweig (1886–1929)—Guide to Reversioners, London, 1960. Perhaps the earliest full-fledged, though brief treatment of Rosenzweig in English.

"F. Rosenzweig on Judaism and Christianity," *Conservative Judaism,* (Winter 1956), pp. 41–48. A much-disputed thesis that, contrary to the widespread claim, Rosenzweig put Judaism much higher than, not on an equal level with, Christianity.

"Hermann Cohen Today," *Sh'ma* 2, no. 31 (April 21, 1972), pp. 84–87.

"Hutner, R. Isaac," *Encyclopedia of Religion,* 6, p. 544, New York, 1986.

"An Introduction to the Thought of R. Isaac Hutner," *Modern Judaism* 5, (Fall, 1985), pp. 237–77. A rather technical introduction to the thought of this influential "Orthodox" teacher of the last generation and a substantive analogy of it with that of E. Levinas and even of Hermann Cohen—the "mystic" and the radical rationalist brought together!

* "J.-P. Sartre as Jew," *Modern Judaism* 3 (1983), pp. 39–73. A philosophical demonstration that Sartre was more of a Kantian than even he thought and that he wanted to think of himself as an "honorary Jew."

"A Jewish Perspective on International Relations," in Arnold Jacob Wolf, ed., *Rediscovering Judaism*, Chicago, 1965, pp. 245–85.

"Karl Marx's Jewish Theory of Usury," *Gesher*, 1978, pp. 7–40. A technical comparison of Jewish law on monetary interest and Marx's view on it. (Published in a journal at Yeshiva University).

* "The Legal Foundations of Jewish Aesthetics," *Journal of Aesthetic Education* 19 (1975), pp. 29–42. A universal aesthetic as based on Jewish law.

"A Little Bit of Revolution?" in Daniel Callahan, ed., *The Secular City Debate*, New York, 1966, pp. 145–55.

* "The Lure of Immanence—The Crisis in Contemporary Religious Thought," *Tradition*, Spring-Summer, 1967, pp. 70–99. Shows historically that Jewish thinkers always do and have to introduce "The Jewish Twist," the primacy of the ethical, into philosophy.

"Marrano Professors of Jewish Studies," *Association for Jewish Studies Newsletter* 2:2 (April 1971), p. 6.

The Messianic Doctrine in Contemporary Jewish History," in *Great Jewish Ideas*, pp. 237–59, Washington, 1964. (Re-issed as *Concepts that Distinguish Judaism* in 1985).

* "Moral Radicalism, and 'Middlingness' in the Ethics of Maimonides," *Studies in Medieval Culture* 11 (1977), pp. 65–94. In technical detail shows that Maimonides was ultimately not an Aristotelian intellectualist but a Jewish ethicist.

"The Necessity of the Lone Man," *Fellowship*, May, 1965, p. 16.

"The New Left Meets the Real Thing," *Dissent*, January-February 1968.

* "A Note on the Nature of Ideal Society—A Rabbinic Study," H. Strauss and G. Reissner, eds., *Curt Silberman Festschrift*, New York, 1969, pp. 86–105. An attempt to draw a general picture of the Rabbinic/Talmudic notion of the content of an ideal messianic society.

* "On Jewish Eschatology," In F. Geeenspahn, ed., *The Human Condition in the Jewish and Christian Traditions*, pp. 171–211, New York, 1986. An exposition of a particular sort of classical Jewish eschatology.

* "On the Theology of Jewish Survival," *Central Conference of American Rabbis Journal*, Fall, 1968, pp. 2–21.

* "The Personal Messiah—Towards the Restoration of a Discarded Doctrine," *Judaism* 5 (1956), pp. 123–35.

"A Philosophy of Mitzvot," *Journal of Biblical Literature* 95 (1976), pp. 519–20.

* "The Question of Jewish Ethics Today," Sh'ma 7, no. 124 (December 24, 1976), pp. 29–36, and 7, no. 134 (May 13, 1977), pp. 118–24.

"The Religious Demand for Peace," Judaism 15 (1966), pp. 1–6.

"Remembering Erich Fromm," Jewish Spectator, Fall 1980, pp. 29–33.

"The Role and Limits of Reason in Contemporary Jewish Theology," Central Conference of American Rabbis Yearbook, 73 (1963), pp. 199–214.

"Samson Raphael Hirsch—The Man and His Thought," Conservative Judaism, Winter, 1959, pp. 26–45.

"The Tenability of H. Cohen's Reconstruction of the Self," Journal of the History of Philosophy 13 (1975), pp. 361–84. A technical study of the named topic in H. Cohen's philosophy.

"Torah for Our Time," in Ira Eisenstein, ed., Varieties of Jewish Belief, New York, 1966, pp. 243–55.

"To Recast Rationalism," Judaism 11 (1962), pp. 205–9.

Eliezer Schweid

MICHAEL OPPENHEIM

The return of the Jewish people to the land of Israel in the twentieth century represents a revolutionary challenge to Jewish thought. Confrontation with the meaning of being a Jew, of having a Jewish state, and of creating a Jewish culture is now inescapable. Further, these questions must be addressed in light of concrete social, political, and even economic realities of a modern nation. Modern Jewish philosophy is called to seek a reorientation toward the Jewish tradition that can begin to provide direction for an authentic continuity with the past, a fullness to individual and communal life in the present, and a viable foundation for future cultural creations. In the face of this challenge, the depth, maturity, and honesty of this enterprise is being tested.

The writings of Eliezer Schweid represent the initial attempt of native Israeli philosophers to understand and respond to the full meaning of the return of the Jewish people to its old-new land. The strength and integrity of Schweid's response will come to light through this introduction to the philosophical and educational aims as well as the central themes of his works.

Eliezer Schweid was born in Jerusalem in 1929 and served in the Hagana in 1947 and 1948. He was a member of Kibbutz Zoraah until 1953 and received his doctorate in Jewish philosophy in 1961 from the Hebrew University. He is now a professor of philosophy at that university.

The extensive writings of Schweid attest to his understanding of the essential interrelationship between the two facets of his dual vocation as philosopher and educator. He has found that the

Jewish philosopher who feels responsible to his people cannot separate his endeavor to confront the past from the need to teach, to enlighten, and to heal. Since the 1960s, Schweid has published articles and books on Hebrew literature, medieval and modern Jewish thought, and current issues that confront Israel. Particularly during the last two decades, instead of systematic treatments of a historical or philosophical nature, he has produced single essays and groups of essays. He believes that in our time the Jewish philosopher who lives in Israel is not permitted to take the time to stand back, reflect, and make systems because the destiny of the Jewish people and its state is at stake.[1]

Schweid's books of the last twenty years deal with specific issues and crises that confront the Israeli population. This element of timeliness, as well as his dual voices of philosopher and educator, is exemplified in a few works that will be briefly examined. *The Solitary Jew and His Judaism* (1974)[2] was a "hygiene of return"—using Franz Rosenzweig's words about his major work[3]—that sought systematically to explore the nature of the alienation from Judaism that many modern individuals experience and to sketch a path of return. The book was Schweid's major attempt to converse with secular Jews, particularly Israelis, who believed that there was no possibility of finding meaningful contact with Judaism as a religious tradition. Schweid maintained that continuity with the culture and religious sources of the past was a prerequisite for the individual's having an integrated identity. Further, he demonstrated that although a full encounter with Torah as God's address to the Jewish people must come at the end of the individual's return, the beginning of that return consisted in steps as easy as accepting oneself as a member of the family and people out of which one was born.

In two works of 1977, *A History of Modern Jewish Thought*[4] and *Between Orthodoxy and Religious Humanism,*[5] the author chronicled the historical events, as well as political, social, and intellectual processes that have challenged Jewish communities since the time of the Spanish Expulsion. He also diagrammed the responses of Jewish philosophers and religious leaders to these unprecedented changes. These books, as well as a plethora of essays on Zionist thinkers, were not intended to be mere historical inquiries. They examined the past in an effort to recognize the ways the present crystallized. Schweid sought to illuminate the options to the

present secular-religious stalemate in Israel, which were sub-
merged by the tide of history. The goal of his effort to uncover or
rediscover creative expressions of past Jewish thought was to
allow Jews in the present to rethink their positions and to choose
again.

The Introduction to *The Land of Israel: National Home or Land of
Destiny* (1979)[6] situates the work and explains Schweid's motive in
writing it. All of Schweid's writings are permeated with a love of
the land of Israel, *Eretz Israel,* but here Schweid saw himself
responding to a specific situation that had been intensified by the
Six-day War and the Yom Kippur War: the haunting void in the
self-understanding of young Israelis concerning the meaning of
the land of Israel for the Jewish people. Schweid felt that the void
had led to a crisis of purpose. In the face of the moral and spiritual
trials of today, Israelis lack the national memories concerning the
land of Israel which would be the source of the needed confidence,
direction, and even life of individual sacrifice. The book teaches
of the ways the land constituted one of the central pillars of Jewish
religious life, thought, and hope.

The Land of Israel is deeply influenced by Schweid's view that
only an individual who has a basis wider than his or her own
experiences, in a tie to a full and living culture, can experience
authenticity and meaning. There is an enchanting statement at the
beginning of the book that eloquently voices Schweid's perspective: "A Jew who has come to live in his land, or even one born
and raised in it, has still not yet entered the land of Israel until he
has erected a palace of memories there and lives in it through the
symbols around which a way of life can take shape."[7]

The Cycle of Appointed Times: The Meaning of Jewish Holidays
(1984),[8] constituted the second phase, following the book on the
land of Israel, of Schweid's educational endeavor to make the past
sources of Jewish culture accessible to his contemporaries. As do
his other writings, it presents a philosophical argument directed to
a particular internal controversy. Schweid argued with determination that intellectual inquiry into the meaning of Jewish life,
and not just the doing of holy deeds, was and remains a fundamental concern in Judaism. This argument for the relevance of
inquiry into religious. meaning was issued into a climate where
such a plea was anything but taken for granted, by either secular
or religious Israelis.

In this work Schweid explored the Jewish calendar, much as Franz Rosenzweig had done at the beginning of the century, as a key to understanding the wholeness of Jewish culture, both as Weltanschauung and as concrete way of life. Schweid held that the calendar is one of the supreme expressions of a people's historical life, encompassing its values, hopes, goals, and purposes. Through the calendar Jews learn to embrace their communal, familial, and individual obligations.

Finally, a short monograph appeared in 1983, *Mysticism and Judaism According to Gershom G. Scholem*,[9] that is pivotal to understanding Schweid's overall corpus. Other dimensions of Schweid's investigation of Scholem's work will be taken up below, but two features of Schweid's philosophical argument will be briefly mentioned here. Schweid was compelled to respond to Scholem's contentions that Jewish mysticism was a core element in Jewish history and that it represented the only legitimate vehicle of religious renewal in the modern period. These contentions called into question Schweid's entire philosophical enterprise because he saw them as undermining the role of halakah in Jewish history and denigrating the possibilities for a contemporary religious renewal that took the challenges of modernity seriously. Schweid has continually insisted that individual identity and communal life must be built upon some concrete obligations from the past and that for the Jewish people, halakah is the medium for those obligations. Further, all of his writings testify to his belief that the life of Torah is accessible to modern Jews who ask about meaning, are concerned with the direction of the modern secular world, and feel responsible to the entire Jewish people. A discussion of these views will bring us to explore Schweid's treatments of the path of return, the life of faith, and Zionism and the Jewish state today.

The Path of Return

An analysis of the history, dynamics, and challenges that resulted from the encounter of the Jewish people and Judaism with modernity drew much of Schweid's attention over the three decades of his philosophic activity. The goal of his analysis was to explore the possibilities of authentic individual and communal replies to this unique meeting. Within this context, Schweid fashioned a philosophy of return for the individual Jew who seeks a path that will lead from a life of isolation and alienation from the Jewish people and culture to a Jewish life of continuity, wholeness, and creativity.

A number of recurring themes punctuate Schweid's discussion of the individual's return. He begins with the realization that all Jews have been deeply affected by the events and processes of the last three centuries, particularly the emergence of secular culture. Therefore, it is impossible merely to repeat or copy some past Jewish model of individual or communal life without sacrificing the unity and comprehensiveness that Jewish life promises. Every individual solution to this situation requires a communal foundation and must include the feeling of being tied to and responsible for the whole Jewish people. Further, the unique character of the Jewish people is indissolubly tied to its distinct culture, and at the core of that culture lie religious patterns of thought and action. Thus a reappropriation of the religious traditions of the Jewish past, including particular norms or obligations from the past, is required to ground authentic individual and communal return. Finally, Schweid insists that the requisite resources for a full and vibrant Jewish life can be found only in the state of Israel.

In a symposium in 1978 that focused on his works, Schweid reflected on his central effort to understand the relationships between religion and secular culture. In particular, he spoke of his interest in finding out "how a positively secular man can find and re-establish his relations with the religious sources of his culture."[10] Thus, for Schweid, the analysis of the possibilities for the individual Jew to reappropriate his or her past begins with an understanding of the nature of secular culture.

The process of secularization and the concept of secularism are nova in the Jewish experience that demarcate the boundary between medieval and modern. The revolutionary secular spirit that celebrated human autonomy, power, and creativity overturned the previously dominant religious values and institutions. Secularism asserted that humans have the right and the power to decide between truth and falsity, to enrich their lives through material and spiritual creations, and to use nature and to fashion social and political life in accordance with their own goals.

Part of the appeal of Schweid's call to secular Jews resides in his views that the many features of the secular world should be positively evaluated and that Jewish life does not stand contraposed to all of the values of secular culture. Thus he holds that though the quest for an authentic Jewish identity requires a reorientation toward secular culture, that is, a recognition of its limits, the secular individual is not asked to repudiate his or her entire earlier identity.

Just as there is no single recipe or complete answer to the secular Jew's quest for Jewish renewal, according to Schweid, not all of these Jews share the same initial viewpoint. He diagrams two different starting points: one for the person who begins with few existing ties to the Jewish community and tradition and the other for the individual who already maintains an active Jewish life but who affirms a "cultural" definition of Judaism.

There is an existentialist flavor to much of Schweid's discussion of the issue of Jewish return, particularly in the major essay in the book *The Solitary Jew and His Judaism*. He wrestles with situations of alienation, feelings of meaninglessness and lack of direction, contradictions and paradoxes in life, the difficulties of living with freedom and concretely in time, as well as the need for decision and commitment. Schweid proposes a direction that, though remaining true to many of these proper existentialist sentiments, is truly revolutionary. He asserts that the response to the question, "Who am I?" is another question, "From where do I come?" He bases the duty to know the past upon the imperative to know the self.[11] The individual's life does not acquire authenticity and meaning through self-isolation, but through the life of commitment based on an understanding that people are essentially linked to one another. These others, further, are not mere dialogical partners in the present but persons who have formed and continue to form one's family, community, and people.

Schweid contends that the desire to educate their children motivates many people to inaugurate a process of self-examination. One is led to understand that raising children entails the teaching of specific values, relationships, and obligations that transcend the self and the present time. Continuity between a parent and his or her child necessitates a continuity between oneself and one's parents. As Schweid comments, "It is simple. It is impossible to be a father in the full sense of the concept—one who gives birth to his son not only physically but also spiritually—without, being a son in the full sense and correct sense of the word—one who receives a heritage of the life of the spirit."[12]

The relationship to the family is the starting point as well as the paradigm for the ever-widening circle of people, values, and ways of life that provides the context for the individual's identity. Schweid believes that even the most alienated Jew retains some powerful impressions of his or her family and that placing oneself in the context of one's family as well as exploring the nature of the family in Judaism constitutes a significant, but not overly difficult, first step. What uniquely informs the Jewish family is the teaching that relationships of love are also defined in terms of obligations that have been formulated from the Jewish tradition.

The next stage is decisive. Schweid argues that the family is nourished by the values, patterns of thought and action, and history of a specific people. Yet he acknowledges that this argument is not adequate to make a Jew desire to be part of the Jewish people. Choosing to be a member of the Jewish people is a destiny-laden decision about the essence of oneself as a person. It is a decision about one's roots in the past and responsibilities in the present. Even in affirming one's membership in the Jewish people, one is drawn to inquire into the distinctive life of that people.

In the modern period some Jews have offered purely "national" definitions of Judaism, stating that to be a Jew is simply to belong to a people, like other peoples. Schweid sees this definition as restating and not escaping the trap of modern alienation. All peoples acquire direction and vitality from their history, culture, and sacred sources. They are formed by their culture, just as they also author that culture. Individual identity and creativity are nourished by the fullness of culture that a person appropriates.

The path of return of the individual Jew ultimately points toward an encounter with the Jewish religion. For Schweid, the national and cultural elements of Jewish identity are inextricably bound to religion. There is no Jewish people without Torah, which has always been the abiding source of Jewish culture. The individual who chooses to be part of the Jewish nation and believes that that choice must be expressed in distinctive ways of life that have developed over history eventually turns to the Torah to discover what it has to offer.

The open encounter with Torah is also the last stage in the path of return of the Jewish person, whom Schweid calls the cultural Jew, who is actively involved in the life of the Jewish people and its heritage.[13] The label *cultural* designates a Jewish identity that seeks to live in continuity with a variety of expressions of Jewish life from the past but rejects the religious bases of these expressions.

Schweid understands the reasons for the historical coalescence of this secular Jewish identity, and he respects its strengths and accomplishments. The vitality of this definition is indisputable because the majority of Jews of the present generation who have a positive relationship to Judaism have it in virtue of the appeal of Judaism as a culture. Significantly, most of those individuals who worked for the establishment of the modern state of Israel were motivated and guided by this viewpoint.

Schweid's insistence that these Jews reexamine their relationship to Judaism rests on his argument that the cultural standpoint lacks a way of maintaining continuity with that past, giving a fullness to Jewish life in the present, or providing a platform for Jewish creativity. The cultural Jew has no criteria for selecting what aspects from the Jewish tradition to appropriate into his or her life. A person chooses something rather than something else just because he or she, in some sense, likes it. This process of selection from the past unavoidably leads to distortions. When past expressions of Jewish life are taken out of the environment of religious values, ways of life, and institutions that gave birth to and sustained them, the result is a false, cosmetic repetition. Finally, even the appropriation of such profound elements of the past as the land of Israel, the Hebrew language, and the Sabbath and Jewish holy days has not resulted in an experience of the wholeness of Jewish life in the state of Israel or a confidence in the emergence of new, authentic Jewish creations in the future.

Schweid proposes two ways that returning Jews of today can readdress the religious tradition and answer their longing for a full Jewish life. Minimally, he asks for a positive attitude toward religion as the expression of the highest values of Jewish culture. He also has dedicated much of his work to exploring the meaning of Torah, the mitzvoth, and the divine covenant, expanding the possibilities for authentic lives of faith (*emunah*).

Schweid sees a positive attitude toward religion as supplementing and widening the secular Jew's view of himself or herself, rather than as a repudiation of this view. Mature secular humanism is not blind to the human struggle with meaning or the notion that people have responsibilities to each other. An appreciation for religion can arise out of an openness toward religious experience and thought as expressions of this quintessential quest for meaning. It also develops out of the recognition that every person owes a debt to those who contributed to the cultural and historical traditions that give form to individual and collective life.[14]

The returning Jew has not established a new relationship to religion unless the stance of openness and appreciation is concretized through a decision to be obligated by at least some elements of Torah. At the outset, the obligation towards Torah can be met by appropriating its central themes: the rejection of idolatry, including its modern expressions, and the affirmation of one's responsibility for oneself, the neighbor, the society, and the natural environment.

The Life of Faith

Judaism remains inaccessible to many modern Jews when it is presented, as it often is, as a closed system of acts and doctrines. In this case Jewish belief is judged by the unhesitating ability to affirm that all of the Torah was received directly from God (*torah min ha-shamayim*) and that everything in it is to be taken as historical truth. Correspondingly, Jewish practice is seen as a fixed body of laws or mitzvoth that must be accepted totally and all at once.

Schweid regards the insistence that Jewish faith demands the affirmation of *torah min ha-shamayim* as stemming from a form of fundamentalism.[15] The insistence arose as a defensive response to the emerging historical and critical consciousness that marks the modern period. More important, this response rejects the possibility that there can be a bridge between the two cultures—secular and Jewish—that constitute the inescapable environment for the vast majority of Jews. In speaking of an alternative path that could bridge these cultures, Schweid has offered a phenomenology of Jewish belief, focusing on a dynamic understanding of Jewish faith, the mitzvoth, and even Judaism itself.

Jewish faith is not an assent to doctrines. It is trust in someone whom the believer has encountered and who has given assurances or promises about the future. The Bible, which remains the basis of Jewish faith today, indicates that the someone who is encountered, that is, God, has the power to fulfill promises and can be trusted to abide by them. God is known by humans through the divine actions of creation, revelation, and redemption. God's will is seen in the commandments, and when a person obeys them he or she feels God's presence as love. The Bible, then, insists that human life is fulfilled through a relation to God, expressed in a life of response to this moral will.[16]

What, then, are the mitzvoth, which religious Jews live with and returning Jews seek to appropriate? The mitzvoth are a developing body of commandments. They are in the full sense divine commandments or directives. Schweid once defined a mitzvah as a "directive whose source is in a divine authority whose presence we are in at the moment we give our obedience as an act of free will."[17] In fulfilling a mitzvah the Jew is responding to the divine presence that lies behind the directive. If the individual finds that a particular commandment has no meaning in the context of his or her free answer to the divine address, that person is not obliged to act. What is important, in a broader vision, is that the individual seek to be open to the possibility of hearing each mitzvah and to reaching out to it. Thus the returning Jew must be in a process, through study and action, of widening the body of those mitzvoth to which he or she can respond.[18] The goal of that process is to achieve a life of Torah, where God's call engages the Jew not just at special times but for his or her whole life.

Being prepared to reply to a divine directive requires more than just the individual's intention. It is also important that those who teach and interpret the directive help make it accessible to those who hope to fulfill it. Schweid has often criticized the rabbis who have the duty to interpret Torah for failing to be responsible to those who seek to find their way back. He believes that the interpreters of Torah have not honestly sought to make it alive to the non-Orthodox majority, by listening to their quests, understanding their situation, and considering the consequences of decisions as they affect the whole people.[19]

The most developed statement about the nature of Judaism is found in the monograph on the universally acclaimed historian Gershom Scholem. This statement focuses on Scholem's contention that Judaism cannot be defined in terms of a single worldview, religious experience, or way of life. Schweid begins his reply with a portrait of the Bible as a revolutionary document that overturns the reigning mythic view of the universe and the stance of idolatry that corresponds to it. The Bible witnesses to the religious notion that God is a "supernatural personality ruling the forces of nature."[20] Although the mythic view makes the gods part of these forces and bound to them, the Bible affirms that there is a moral power who stands free from all mechanical causality. When the believer stands in true relation to this power, his or her life is infused with freedom and meaning. Schweid finds, however, that idolatry leads either to a false security issuing out of the belief in humans' power to control and dominate or to an immobilizing despair that prevents one from seeing the future except as ruled by laws of necessity.

In all times, Judaism retained at its core this biblical notion, along with a historic myth that "includes the stories of the creation, the patriarchs, the wanderings in the desert, the settlement of the Land, the construction of the Temple, the monarchy, the decline and the destruction."[21] Based on this myth, the rabbis developed a religion "centering on the manifest way of life governed by study of Torah and the fulfillment of its ordinances."[22] As the Jewish people experienced historical crises, they extended and developed their understanding of the relationship between God and his people. Even biblical religion was not naive or unreflexive. It knew of times when God's presence and direction were missing. Its response was to ask that the people make fundamental changes in their hearts, that is, a religious turning or *teshuvah*. Later in history, the notion of the completion of God's plan through a messianic future emerged.

Zionism and the Jewish State Today

There is a powerful political dimension to Schweid's philosophical work. Of course, the Jewish philosophical endeavor, which includes a concern with and responsibility for the concrete life of a people, necessarily contains this dimension. In the modern period, many Jewish philosophers either explicitly or implicitly argued that the condition of being dispersed throughout the world did not inhibit the vitality of Jewish existence. Eliezer Schweid, in contrast, constructs a philosophy around the return of the Jewish people to the land of Israel.

The passionate commitment to the Zionist enterprise and to the present state of Israel is not so much a theme within Schweid's life and work as it is both the point of departure and the spirit that motivates everything. For he believes that only through Zionism can individual Jews fulfill their responsibility to the people as a whole and the Jewish community solve the problems that beset it. In this view, Zionism encompasses all areas of national life: the political, economic, social, linguistic, and cultural. His formulation of the goals of Zionism testifies to an extraordinary vision: "to bring a scattered people home; revive its national language as a vernacular and as a language of total creativity; lay societal and economic foundations, at the same time transform the Jewish collectivity's occupational patterns; crystallize social and daily-life forms; and create political frameworks."[23]

Two features of his thought that I have not noted earlier are diagnostic of the strength of this commitment and the resources for Jewish thought that he finds through it. Schweid does not hesitate to argue in continuity with the confidence exhibited by Zionist thought before the last two decades that there is no future for the Jewish people outside the land of Israel.[24] Additionally, he can honestly address the meaning of the Holocaust for Jewish life without seeing the need for this terrifyingly destructive event to give positive content to Jewish identity or education. For him, choosing life, that is, choosing the fulness of Jewish life opening for those who live in Israel, is the most authentic response to the Holocaust.[25]

Schweid is heir to the cultural stream within the Zionist movement. For him, Zionism was not just a rebellion against "Judennot," Herzl's phrase for the persecution and oppression that the Jews were experiencing in Galut. Schweid has written that the Jew who comes to Judaism because of outside pressure, rather than being motivated by an inner necessity, will see Zionism as nothing more than a form of assimilation.[26] It is rather "the problem of Judaism," that is, the stagnation of Jewish communal life, upon which he focus as a Zionist thinker. His goal has been to explore the conditions necessary to create a new Jewish culture that retains the essence of continuity with the past and finds a proper balance between traditional contents and what is positive in modern secular culture.[27] Schweid has often been critical of the generation of the founders who failed to provide the means for creating and expressing the life of the soul and the spirit.[28] Finally, Schweid's work indicates a deep sensitivity to the early religious Zionists, who saw the movement as the only way to give new life to a religious tradition burning low and under siege in the changing conditions of Galut.

Some of the most significant sources of Schweid's thinking about the critical questions that beset the state of Israel are found in this extended series of critiques of major thinkers within the Zionist movement. These critiques almost take the form of dialogues, in which Schweid probes past standpoints unearthing both the failures that have led to current crises and the overlooked insights that might point in new directions. With the problem of the renewal of full Jewish communal life as his point of orientation, Schweid has offered incisive criticisms of the work of Ahad Ha-Am, Rabbi Abraham Isaac Kook, and Gershom Scholem.

The difficulties that Schweid sees in the thought of the influential secular Zionist Ahad Ha-Am are used to diagnose the flaws in cultural Zionism as well as in the current standpoint of many secular Israelis.[29] Ahad Ha-Am, who is usually recognized as the father of cultural Zionism, believed that the religious foundation of the Jewish community would eventually dissolve through its contact with the emerging secular environment of the nineteenth and twentieth centuries. He also recognized that authentic Jewish life must be built on some elements from the religious life of the past, and he sought to glean from it such contents as the Sabbath, holidays, marriage laws, Hebrew language, and love of the land of Israel. Schweid has contested this effort to establish continuity with the past, finding it partial and ultimately manipulative. According to Schweid, only a sense of being obligated to the past, and not just choosing desirable features from it, can provide a foundation which is of one whole texture and also has the ability to generate new forms. Further, as we have seen, the sense of being obligated necessitates an open encounter with Judaism, Torah, and the mitzvoth.

Schweid finds more substance in the writings of Hayim Bialik and A. D. Gordon,[30] for they sought to approach the depth of religious life rather than just find a substitute for it. Bialik thought that the relevance of Judaism could be made alive through aggadah, and he hinted at bringing the fullness of national life to the Torah. Gordon is appreciated by Schweid for his attempt to establish a contemporary halakah, that is, a way to enable the community to take shape in Israel.

Schweid finds some of the obstacles to a revived religious life in Israel encapsulated in the religious philosophy of the chief rabbi during the mandate period, Abraham Kook.[31] Schweid firmly disputes the judgment of many modern Orthodox Jews in Israel that Kook's ideas present a true way to bridge the religious-secular split in that nation. On one hand, Kook had a toleration and appreciation for the secular Zionists who were laying the foundations for the return of the Jewish people to the land of Israel. He saw secular Zionism as a necessary stage in the development of the people, one that had a role in the divine plan. On the other hand, according to Schweid, Kook's Kabbalistic reinterpretation of secular Zionism does not contribute concrete solutions to actual problems in the here and now. It does not reach out to understand the point of view, experiences, and hopes of secular Jews but counsels a religious toleration that is to remain in force until wayward secular Jews renounce their errors.

The thought of Rabbi Chaim Hirschensohn is often contrasted with that of Rabbi Kook in Schweid's corpus.[32] The book *Democracy and Halakhah* explicitly lauds the insights of Hirschensohn as unique, fertile efforts seriously to address the modern experience of the Jewish people, including its spiritual and cultural renaissance in Israel.[33] Hirschensohn sought to understand the historical process that led to secular Zionism, such as the Haskalah movement and the entry of Jews into Western political and cultural life. He struggled with such challenges as the emergence of the social sciences, the new historical consciousness, biblical criticism, and democracy. Through this struggle, Hirschensohn's own understanding of Judaism and Torah were changed, but the rabbi did not fear this development. He believed, as did Maimonides, that there could not be a contradiction between Torah and the positive achievements of the human spirit.[34]

There are four aspects of Schweid's positive evaluation of Hirschensohn that are directed into the current religious-secular struggle in Israel. First, Hirschensohn regarded Torah as the dynamic, developing basis for the life of a nation. The interpreters of Torah have a duty to prevent a cleavage between it and the people by renewing Torah according to the conditions and needs of the Jewish people. Second, he examined not just the conclu-

sions of precedent-setting halakic decisions of the past but asked
about the religious-moral principle behind the decisions. In this
way, he viewed halakah as a positive moral and religious expression that sought to address modernity, rather than as a body of
prohibitions warding off the new.[35] A conception of halakah in
harmony with the modern world is the basis for Schweid's innovative call to regard all those realms of Jewish life in Israel in
which a national-cultural foundation is being built as opportunities for expanding the scope of the mitzvoth as divine directives.[36]

Third, though many religious Israelis insist that democracy is
antithetical to Torah and a Jewish state, Hirschensohn discussed
the spirit common to both. He viewed the covenantal basis for
Torah as the free choice of the people, and he believed that only
through the uncoerced decisions of Jews today would Torah once
again become the foundation for all.[37] Fourth, Schweid is
extremely sympathetic to Hirschensohn's hope for a sincere
debate, in fact, a "battle of peace," between religious and secular
Jews to decide the nature of the Jewish state. Hirschensohn trusted
that this battle would force religious Jews to explicate the moral
relevance of Torah, while respecting and replying to their opposite partners. Secular Jews would come to realize that the Torah
expressed a set of options to the spiritual, cultural, and even
political crises that the Jewish settlement in Palestine faced.[38]
Schweid has often expressed his desire for such a dialogue
replacing the climate of mutual hostility, self-righteousness, and
political manipulations that fashions the present debate.[39] He does
not wish for or foresee a full agreement between the two sides, but
he thinks that more dialogue might stimulate a consensus about
self-definition and ways of life.

In analyzing some crucial postulates that underlie the prolific
investigations of Jewish mysticism by Gershom Scholem,
Schweid is brought to formulate perhaps his most important
philosophical work. The contest between Schweid and Scholem is
not about some arcane matter: it concerns the possibility of Jewish
religious renewal in our time. Integral to this question of renewal
are such fundamental issues as the nature of Judaism, the character
of its continuity over history, the essence of the crisis that
modernity poses, and the direction that an authentic reaction
must take.

In *Mysticism and Judaism according to Gershom G. Scholem,*

Schweid restates, refines, and clarifies major themes from his earlier corpus. As we have seen, Scholem contended that there was no abiding essence to Judaism, expressed as a worldview, religious experience, or way of life. Schweid rightly noted that this view allowed Scholem, along with the most revolutionary side of Zionist ideology, to affirm that there is no limit to what may stand as a legitimate part of Jewish creativity.[40] Schweid acknowledged and prized the varieties of Jewish life from the biblical period to our own, but he still insisted that there is a core to that multiplicity. Explicitly addressing the issues of essence and continuity, he wrote:

> The scholar who ponders the secret of the Jewish religion's continuity and singularity ... will find it in the historical myth of the Bible and the early rabbinic sages, and in the religious experience that comes to expression in the way of life based on that historical myth, namely, the life of *Torah* and divine ordinances. This is the thread of continuity that runs from the Bible and prophecy to the enterprise of early rabbinic sages, from the works of early rabbinic sages to the creations of the medieval sages, from the creations of these sages to the products of the Jewish religion's sages and thinkers in the modern age.[41]

The core of this excitingly bold statement is the contention that the "life of Torah and divine ordinances," that is, the life of halakah, was and remains essential to the continuity of Jewish life in the past and present. Of course, this is one of the unifying themes of Schweid's entire undertaking.

Equally as challenging to Schweid are Scholem's statements that dispute the legitimacy and efficacy of Jewish philosophy and theology as a whole; and here, again, many contemporary religious and secular Israelis concur with Scholem. Scholem regarded medieval and modern Jewish mystical movements as the only authentic responses to changes in the intellectual, social, and political environment occurring during these periods. In opposition, Schweid believed that mysticism ignored these changes, rather than seriously struggling with them. It was through Jewish philosophy and theology that Jews came to an understanding of the developing nature of their new environments and formulated systems that sought to bridge the old and new. Although he recognizes that no thinker or system of thought can, on its own, create a viable foundation for a community, Schweid sees the role of Jewish thought in this quest as irreplaceable. He argues:

> From the medieval period up to the present day, the Jewish people has been mostly located within the realm of a western culture which is based on scientific thinking and the accumulation of scientific knowledge. The people sought to participate in the culture of its environment, to exist in this environment and to make its contribution, while also preserving its individuality and uniqueness.... We can state categorically that from the tenth century, it became apparent to Jewish thinkers that philosophy was vitally necessary for the continuity of Jewish culture's integral development—insofar as Judaism did not relinquish its aspiration to remain the comprehensive culture of a people.[42]

In essence, both Scholem and Schweid realized that the religious structure of Jewish communal life was shattered in the modern period. Scholem believed that only through a miraculous reemergence of Jewish mysticism could a religious foundation for the Jewish community be reconstructed. He ruled out any other possibility, through his paradoxical insistence that authentic Jewish religious life must be founded on a fundamentalist belief in *torah min ha-shamayim*, coupled with his view that all such religious expressions are mere fossils from the past. Schweid recognized that these views were shared by many secular Israelis, who ridicule Jewish orthodoxy as anachronistic but also deny the legitimacy of any "modern" Jewish religious movements. He took issue with the view that only a fundamentalist stance toward Torah was authentically Jewish and explored paths that could lead toward contemporary individual and communal religious renewal.

Although Franz Rosenzweig was a non-Zionist, he is for Schweid an outstanding representative of those who fulfilled the tasks of modern Jewish philosophy.[43] Rosenzweig attempted to translate the religious myth, categories, and experience of Judaism for Jews living in the twentieth century. Like Schweid, he focused on the need for religious renewal because he saw religion as the core of the identity of the indivudual and the culture of a people. Further, both developed a positive and expansive view of halakah as God's call to integrate increasing dimensions into the life of the covenant. Still, Schweid's appreciation for Rosenzweig's efforts is mitigated by his judgment that Rosenzweig was able only to present a remedy for the individual's alienation, not a basis for a community, and that he removed the Jewish people from the arena of human history.

Schweid's critique of Ahad Ha-Am, Rabbi Abraham Kook, and Gershom Scholem indicates one method that he used to address issues now current in Israeli life. He also wrote a great number of pointed essays for this purpose. In his response to the changing life of this community, one particular development in his thought comes to light. Whereas in the decades of the 1960s and 1970s Schweid parried with the ideology of the dominant secular group, in the last decade he has increasingly been attentive to elements within the often self-righteous religious camp. Schweid sustains both poles of his critique and vision by maintaining that each side has need of the other.

He has chronicled the obvious move toward extremism in many religious communities within Israel. Growing numbers of religious Jews have isolated themselves from the nonreligious, questioned the validity of the modern democratic state, and sought to force compliance with their own needs and views, all by appealing to religious principles. Schweid has carefully but very firmly pointed out that religious Jews must accept joint responsibility as citizens of the state, that earlier religious authorities did not regard the democratic state as a threat to Judaism or the halakic life, and that nonreligious Jews also have consciences and principles that must be respected.[44]

Repeatedly Schweid has argued that a "battle of peace," of debate and dialogue, is necessary because neither secular nor religious Jews can live in the Jewish state without the other party.[45] Secular Israelis require a relationship to Judaism and to religious Jews to strengthen their tie to the Hebrew language, to their sacred sources—especially the Bible—to the historical and national symbols that unify the people, and finally, to help legitimate their right to the land of Israel. Religious Israelis must be reminded that in the last two hundred years secular Jews have been the most creative and now provide, through the state, the conditions that allow religious communities to survive and flourish. Schweid finds himself forced to state the obvious, that Jews cannot have a modern state of their own without secular knowledge and technology.

Schweid regards it as a misconception to propose that there are actually two monolithic camps in Israel. Within Israel there is a striking and healthy multiplicity of conceptions of the proper character of the Jewish state. He has often expressed displeasure over the course of events in the early history of the state, when the variety of small voluntary communities and associations of the Yishuv period was replaced by a centralist policy that transferred the task of building up the land to state agencies. The renewal of Jewish communal life, on the contrary, should be accomplished through the development of similar communities, according to Schweid. The state must thus encourage "every Jewish community to interpret, each in its own way and according to its perceptions, the Jewish meaning of its way of life and to express this interpretation in intellectual, literary, artistic creativity, and even in life styles."[46]

Eliezer Schweid's quest to make earlier ways of life and patterns of thought accessible to his contemporaries aligns him with some of the endeavors of such modern Jewish philosophers as Hermann Cohen, Franz Rosenzweig, Martin Buber, Abraham Heschel, and Emil Fackenheim. Like them, Schweid recognized that there could not be a mere repetition of the past and that a reactionary or fundamentalist position toward Torah was a totally inadequate response to modernity. The alternative path of Cohen, Rosenzweig, Buber, Heschel, and Fackenheim has elements in common with that phenomenology of Jewish belief, description of Torah in terms of covenant and historical myth, and substantial but fluid sense of halakah that I have detailed in Schweid's work.

Schweid excels at this existentialist endeavor to make the past accessible to Jews of his time. It is the only way that more than just a few of those born outside of an insulated religious community can reestablish contact with their religious tradition. Rosenzweig and Schweid, in particular, have given individuals the confidence that the will to return can be translated into a definite path of action. They did this by indicating that a person does not have to choose between a full life in the modern world and a life of Torah. First, they demonstrated that the Jewish experience of faith, that is, of listening to and freely answering God's address, transcends all historical periods. Second, they portrayed halakah not as a finished body of law but as a developing realm of concrete responses to the divine call.

Schweid has characterized the central issue of nineteenth- and twentieth-century Jewish thought as "the belief in *Torah* as an authority dictating a community's way-of-life."[47] Although this statement is generally valid, it underscores the features that distinguish his work from the other Jewish thinkers named above. No other Jewish philosopher in the modern period has directed his work into the concrete present life of Jewish communities in the manner of Schweid. Even the masterful educational writings of Rosenzweig do not match the extensive and innovative insights of Schweid. Nor have any of these thinkers wrestled as seriously with the issue of helping a community find a consensus concerning fundamental Jewish patterns of life.

The analyses and insights of Schweid stand as contributions not only to modern Jewish philosophy but to modern religious thought as a whole. Modern religious thinkers, that is, Christian and post-Christian philosophers and theologians, have customarily ignored Jewish philosophy, yet there are many areas of Schweid's work that could prove valuable to them. Among these are his investigations into the nature of individual identity, the dynamics of religious belief, the relationship between religion and secular culture, and the role of the calendar in community life.

It is difficult to assess the impact of Schweid's writings, although it is clear that very few religious leaders in Israel have seriously read him and that the impasse between religious and secular Jews only seems to be hardening over time. These facts do not indicate any fundamental flaw in his work. A philosopher cannot be faulted for not solving a society's problems, problems that stem from deep economic, political, and social processes. But it is legitimate to ask whether Schweid has fully understood the price of having a Jewish state. The communal polarization and politicization might be an inescapable consequence of a modern nation-state. The development of a central bureaucracy, defense establishment, and the like cannot be overlooked in their effect on Schweid's hopes for the creation of small pluralistic communities that are responsible, among other things, for their own educational institutions. He looks at the prestate period when such communities existed as models for a possible future. Yet is this a real possibility?

Only the future can reveal the full answer to this question. But it is indisputable today that nothing is more essential to the future Jewish character of the state of Israel than the religious dialogue and experimentation that Schweid has called for and that no Jewish philosopher has done more to pave the way for these than he has.

There is no more compelling witness to the creative emergence of contemporary Jewish philosophy in Israel than the writings of Eliezer Schweid. Decades earlier, Julius Guttman concluded his classic work *Philosophies of Judaism* with lines of sadness: "Jewish philosophy, which has been renewed in the last decades of the nineteenth century, has now reached its nadir. If it once more arises to continue its work, it will develop under entirely new conditions."[48] It now appears that the hope that underlies these lines for a new stage in the Jewish philosophical endeavor was not futile.

Notes

1. Eliezer Schweid, *Israel's Faith and Culture* (Jerusalem, 1976), [Hebrew], p. 9, and "The Thought of Eliezer Schweid—A Symposium," *Immanuel* 9 (Winter 1979): 92–93.
2. Eliezer Schweid, *The Solitary Jew and His Judaism* (Tel Aviv, 1974) [Hebrew].
3. Nahum N. Glatzer, ed., *Franz Rosenzweig: His Life and Thought* (New York, 1970), p. 135.
4. Eliezer Schweid, *A History of Jewish Thought in Modern Times* (Jerusalem, 1977), [Hebrew].
5. Eliezer Schweid, *Between Orthodoxy and Religious Humanism* (Jerusalem, 1977) [Hebrew].
6. Eliezer Schweid, *The Land of Israel: National Home or Land of Destiny* (Rutherford, 1985).
7. Ibid., p. 10.
8. Eliezer Schweid, *The Cycle of Appointed Times: The Meaning of Jewish Holidays* (Tel Aviv, 1984) [Hebrew].
9. Eliezer Schweid, *Mysticism and Judaism according to Gershom G. Scholem: A Critical Analysis* (Jerusalem, 1983) [Hebrew]. Quotations from the English translation by David Weiner (Atlanta, 1985), will be indicated by page numbers in parentheses.
10. "Thought," p. 94.
11. Eliezer Schweid, *Israel at the Crossroads* (Philadelphia, 1973), p. 77.
12. *Solitary Jew*, p. 17.
13. Schweid's most detailed analyses of the situation of the cultural Jew are found in *Israel's Faith and Culture*, p. 152–78; and Eliezer Schweid, *Judaism and Secular Culture* (Tel Aviv, 1981) [Hebrew], p. 221–48.
14. *Judaism and Secular Culture*, pp. 228–29.
15. *History of Jewish Thought*, p. 121.
16. See the essay "What Is Faith?" in *Israel's Faith and Culture*, pp. 11–67, and *Scholem*, pp. 29–30.
17. *Israel at the Crossroads*, p. 86.
18. Ibid., pp. 86–99.
19. Eliezer Schweid, *Between Judaism and Zionism: Essays* (Jerusalem, 1983) [Hebrew], p. 95, and *Israel at the Crossroads*, pp. 98–9.

20. *Scholem*, p. 29.
21. Ibid., p. 47 (94).
22. Ibid.
23. Eliezer Schweid, "Elements of Zionist Ideology and Practice," in Moshe Davis, ed., *Zionism in Transition* (New York, 1980), p. 239.
24. *Between Judaism and Zionism*, p. 256.
25. A good example of Schweid's treatment is "'Choose Life'—The Holocaust in the National Conscience," ibid., pp. 121–37.
26. *Judaism and Secular Culture*, p. 159.
27. Ibid., p. 22.
28. Ibid., p. 222; *Israel's Faith and Culture*, p. 185.
29. *Israel at the Crossroads*, pp. 69–83; *Judaism and Secular Culture*, p. 32–41.
30. *Judaism and Secular Culture*, pp. 60–66, 157–81.
31. *Between Orthodoxy and Religious Humanism*, pp. 31–33; Eliezer Schweid, *Democracy and Halakhah: A Study in the Thought of Rabbi Chaim Hirschensohn* (Jerusalem, 1978), pp. 159–70; *Judaism and Secular Culture*, pp. 110–42.
32. *Between Orthodoxy and Religious Humanism*, p. 43–46; *Democracy and Halakhah*, pp. 159–70.
33. *Democracy and Halakhah*, pp. 1–12.
34. Ibid., p. 36.
35. Ibid., pp. 102–3.
36. *Israel's Faith and Culture*, p. 176.
37. *Democracy and Halakhah*, pp. 59–89.
38. Ibid., pp. 168–69.
39. Ibid., pp. 169–70, and *Between Judaism and Zionism*, p. 105.
40. *Scholem*, p. 37.
41. Ibid., p. 68 (132).
42. Ibid., p. 66 (129–30).
43. Ibid., pp. 82ff–85. There is a discussion of Schweid's treatments of Rosenzweig in Michael Oppenheim, "The Relevance of Rosenzweig in the Eyes of His Israeli Critics," *Modern Judaism* 7 (May 1987): 193–206.
44. *Between Judaism and Zionism*, pp. 85–104; *Scholem*, p. 73.
45. *Democracy and Halakhah*, pp. 168–70; *Judaism and Secular Culture*, pp. 240–1.
46. "Elements of Zionist Ideology," pp. 248–49; see also *Judaism and Secular Culture*, pp. 246–47.
47. *Scholem*, p. 84 (159).
48. Julius Guttmann, *Philosophies of Judaism* (Garden City, N.Y. 1966), pp. 450–51.

FOR FURTHER READING

Works by Eliezer Schweid

Israel at the Crossroads. 1969. English trans. Philadelphia, 1973. This collection includes an important essay on Jewish identity. Several of the essays argue for the centrality of halakah for modern Jewish life and explore ways that nonobservant Jews can begin to appropriate halakah into their lives.

The Solitary Jew and His Judaism [Hebrew]. Tel Aviv, 1974. This book is Schweid's most systematic account of the nature of current Jewish solitariness and alienation and the way the situation can be overcome through identification with the family, people, culture, and religious sources of Judaism.

Israel's Faith and Culture [Hebrew]. Jerusalem, 1976. Among the important writings in this collection, one essay examines the nature of Jewish faith, and another powerfully critiques the cultural definition of Jewish identity.

Between Orthodoxy and Religious Humanism [Hebrew]. Jerusalem, 1977. Orthodox, Neo-Orthodox, Religious Zionist, and other twentieth-century streams of Jewish religious thought are examined in this work.

A History of Jewish Thought in Modern Times [Hebrew]. Jerusalem, 1977. This is a penetrating, insightful, and clear presentation of the course of modern Jewish thought, as well as an analysis of the issues and challenges that lie at its foundation.

Democracy and Halakhah: A Study in the Thought of Rabbi Chaim Hirschensohn [Hebrew]. Jerusalem, 1978. Schweid seeks to plumb the thought of this innovative religious Zionist to uncover some of the hidden resources of halakic thought in its confrontation with the challenge of the establishment of the modern Jewish state.

The Land of Israel: National Home or Land of Destiny, 1979. English trans. Rutherford, 1985. The meaning of the land of Israel for Jewish thought is chronicled by examining statements from all periods of Jewish history. Schweid demonstates that Israel represents both the promised land of religious hope and the tangible homeland of the Jewish people.

Judaism and Secular Culture [Hebrew]. Tel Aviv, 1981. An original statement about the nature of secularism and its impact on Jewish life is presented in this volume. The thought of Bialik, Y. Kaufmann, Kook, M. Kaplan, Gordon, Rosenzweig, and Guttmann is discussed in separate chapters.

"Spiritual Reorientation as a System of Thought," In *Israel Efrat: Poet and Thinker*, pp. 231–57. [Hebrew]. Tel Aviv, 1981. This essay is an insightful analysis of the "speech-thinking" of Franz Rosenzweig.

Between Judaism and Zionism: Essays [Hebrew]. Jerusalem, 1983. This collection focuses on the problems that have arisen since the Yom Kippur War in the overall relationship between Judaism and Zionism.

Mysticism and Judaism according to Gershom G. Scholem: A Critical Analysis [Hebrew]. Jerusalem, 1983. English translation by David Weiner (Atlanta, 1985). The encounter between Scholem and Schweid gives birth to the latter's most refined philosophical statement of the nature of Judaism and the possibilities for a continuity between past and present. This short monograph is essential reading for an understanding of the pivotal issues behind all of modern Jewish thought.

The Cycle of Appointed Times: The Meaning of Jewish Holidays [Hebrew]. Tel Aviv, 1984. The holidays are investigated to reveal the wholeness of Jewish culture, both as Weltanschauung and as a concrete way of life.

Works about Eliezer Schweid

"The Thought of Eliezer Schweid—A Symposium," *Immanuel* 9 (Winter 1979): 87–102. Israeli philosophers explore the main issues in the thought of Schweid in this record of a symposium held in 1978. In the course of these discussions, Schweid outlines the goals of his work and situates it in terms of other modern Jewish thinkers.

Oppenheim, Michael. "Eliezer Schweid: A Philosophy of Return," *Judaism* 137 (Winter 1986): 66–77.

———. "Paths of Return: The Concept of Community in the Thought of F. Rosenzweig and E. Schweid." In R. Aigen and G. Hundert, eds., *Community and the Individual Jew*. 1986.

———. "The Relevance of Rosenzweig in the Eyes of His Israeli Critics." *Modern Judaism* 7 (May 1987): 193–206.

Joseph Soloveitchik

DAVID SINGER

In the world of East European Jewish piety in which Rabbi Joseph
B. Soloveitchik was born—a world that remained permanently
fixed as his touchstone of Orthodoxy—theology as a formal
discipline counted for very little. Soloveitchik was heir to the
"Litvak" tradition, characterized by extreme intellectualism chan-
neled almost exclusively into study of the Talmud. Soloveitchik
observed on several occasions that his grandfather Rabbi Hayyim
"Brisker" (1853–1918)—a talmudic genius—happily combined
great intellectual prowess with simple piety; he was, in Soloveitchik's phrase, a "man-child." As for Soloveitchik's father,
Moses (1876–1941)—who preceded his son as chief talmudist at
Yeshiva University—we have it on good authority that he never
once glanced at Maimonides' *Guide of the Perplexed*, even while he
was endlessly absorbed in the study of Maimonides' halakhic
writings.

Soloveitchik's background, with its lack of interest in theological and philosophical issues, needs to be stressed at the outset
of this essay because there is a danger that focusing on Soloveitchik's theological *oeuvre* will distort our view of his career. It
must be borne in mind that Soloveitchik is first and foremost a
talmudist; that is where the greater part of his intellectual energies
have gone on a daily basis for more than eight decades. In recent
years, Soloveitchik's halakhic writings have begun to see the light
of day, and significant new additions in this area are to be
expected. Is it not possible, then, that Soloveitchik's most important legacy will be as a creative talmudist; that he will be seen as a

figure who carried to new heights the "Brisker" mode of talmudic analysis? Such a thought would certainly have gladdened the hearts of Soloveitchik's father and grandfather.

And yet Soloveitchik is more than a traditional talmudist. He has a thoroughly modern side, which is clearly expressed in his theological essays. Although Soloveitchik's Orthodoxy is never in question, it is an Orthodoxy that feels impelled to take itself seriously in the context of modernity. Hence not only is Soloveitchik engaged with various currents of modern thought—neo-Kantianism, existentialism, phenomenology, philosophy of science —but also he has attempted to make them part and parcel of his self-understanding as an Orthodox Jew. It is precisely this element that makes Soloveitchik's theological enterprise so fascinating and that, we may be certain, will constitute his theological legacy.

Soloveitchik was born in Pruzhan, Poland, on February 27, 1903. He was initiated into the Brisker method of Talmud study by his father, who was his one and only teacher until his late teens. When the family took up residence in Warsaw in 1920, Soloveitchik began to engage in secular pursuits; he studied with a series of tutors until he attained the equivalent of a *gymnasium* education. In 1925, Soloveitchik enrolled as a philosophy student at the University of Berlin, specializing in logic, metaphysics, and epistemology. Soloveitchik remained at Berlin for six years, capping his academic work with a doctoral dissertation on the neo-Kantian philosopher Hermann Cohen.

In 1932, Soloveitchik emigrated to the United States, becoming chief rabbi of the small Orthodox community in Boston. What made him an unusual figure was that he was fully at home in two very different intellectual milieus—the worlds of Torah learning and Western culture. Thus the traditionalist rabbi Abraham Kahane-Shapiro of Kovno could say of Soloveitchik in a letter written in 1931:

> The spirit of his illustrious grandfather, the leading rabbi of his time, Rabbi Hayyim Soloveitchik, rests upon Rabbi Joseph Dov Soloveitchik. Just like his grandfather, he, too, is a master of the entire range of Talmudic literature.... Happy is the country that will be privileged to be the home of this great sage. The sages have ordained him to be the true interpreter of all religious problems, and the halakhah shall always be in accordance with his rulings.[1]

At the same time, Soloveitchik was able to join with such prominent academics as Harry Wolfson and Solomon Zeitlin in a 1935 lecture series celebrating the Maimonides octocentennial; the titles of his speeches were "Maimonides and Kant on the Conception of Freedom of the Will and the Problem of Physical Causality in the Modern Theory of Knowledge" and "Maimonides' Philosophic and Halakhic View on Homo Sapiens and the Modern Philosophy of Value."

Upon succeeding his father as chief talmudist at Yeshiva University in 1941, Soloveitchik quickly gained renown in the modern Orthodox community. To many modern Orthodox Jews, the "Rav," as he was affectionately called, was a full-fledged cultural hero. After all, in addition to being a masterful talmudist, he had a Ph.D. in philosophy and maintained a strong interest in such diverse subjects as mathematics, science, Christian theology, and literature. Was this not living proof that the gap between Orthodoxy and modernity could be bridged—and in a creative manner? Honor followed honor for Soloveitchik, who remained on the Yeshiva faculty for more than four decades, training thousands of young men for the Orthodox rabbinate. Only in 1982 was Soloveitchik forced to retire because of poor health, effectively bringing his career to an end.

It is commonplace in discussions of Soloveitchik to bemoan the fact that he has published very little. Certainly one would have wished to see much more from his pen, particularly since it is reported that he has a large quantity of material ready in manuscript form but has been reluctant to release it. Yet Soloveitchik's number of publications has grown steadily over the years. Many of his essays are short, but others are quite lengthy, and four— "Halakhic Man," "The Lonely Man of Faith," "But from Thence Ye Will Seek," and "The Halakhic Mind"—constitute small books.

The discussion that follows will focus on four of Soloveitchik's essays—"Halakhic Man" (1944), "The Lonely Man of Faith" (1965), "But from Thence Ye Will Seek" (1978), and "Hark, My Beloved Knocks" (1961). Each merits attention in its own right as a creative contribution to Jewish theology. Taken together, they convey a sense of the range of Soloveitchik's theologizing with regard to both subject matter and methodology.

Soloveitchik's first weighty publication, and the one that played a crucial role in establishing the regnant image of him as the philosopher of halakhah, was "Halakhic Man." This essay is a pioneering attempt to explain the inner world of the talmudist in terms drawn from Western culture. To appreciate the ground-breaking nature of "Halakhic Man," it is necessary to bear in mind that virtually all modern efforts at constructing a Jewish theology have been based on the nonlegal sources of Judaism—aggada, philosophy, Kabbalah, and so on. Yet it is the halakhah that stands at the center of Jewish life. But to speak of the halakhah is to speak of the talmudist, the man for whom it is the breath of life. What is the nature of his endeavor? Why is he drawn to the halakhah? What does the talmudist experience as he labors over an intricate halakhic problem? Why is he convinced that in studying the details of often obscure laws, he is dealing with matters of ultimate religious importance? "Halakhic Man" is in a class by itself in the modern literature of Judaism in being centrally concerned with these questions.

At first glance, it would appear that the philosophical abstractions of neo-Kantianism are absolutely irrelevant to an understanding of the nature of the talmudist's endeavor. What possible connection could there be between talk about Being, a priori ideas, mathematics and science, and an appreciation of the labors of a man who pores over ancient texts so he can better understand the details of religious laws? Yet, amazingly, Soloveitchik manages with a single interpretive twist to make neo-Kantianism fully relevant to the analysis of talmudism. How does he do so? By arguing that the talmudist, no less so than the mathematician-scientist, makes use of an a priori system of ideas in approaching reality. In the case of the mathematician-scientist, the a priori system consists of the theorems and laws which he brings to bear in his research efforts. For the talmudist, the equivalent system is the halakhah, which is not only a set of behavioral norms but also—and more important—a logical, conceptual structure. As Soloveitchik expresses the matter:

> When he approaches reality, halakhic man comes with his Torah, revealed to him at Sinai, in hand. He engages the world with set laws and established principles. A complete Torah of precepts and laws guides him to the road which leads to existence. Halakhic man approaches the world well furnished with statutes, laws, principles,

and judgments, in an *a priori* relation. His approach is one which begins with an ideal creation and concludes with a real one. To what can this be compared? To a mathematician who fashions an ideal world, and uses it for the purpose of establishing a relationship between it and the real world.... The essence of the halakhah, which was received from God, lies in the creation of an ideal world, and in recognizing the relationship which holds between it and reality.... There is no phenomenon or object for which the *a priori* halakhah does not construct an ideal standard.[2]

Having posited a basic identity between the mathematician-scientist and the talmudist based on the methodologies they employ, Soloveitchik seeks to show that their general intellectual orientations are also strikingly similar. Thus he argues that the talmudist, no less so than the theoretical physicist, is engaged in "pure" research; he is a speculative thinker who is little interested in the practical consequences of his studies. The "ultimate" for the talmudist, Soloveitchik tells us, is "not the realization of the halakhah, but the ideal construction which was given to him at Sinai, and which stands forever." Or again: "Theoretical halakhah—not action; ideal creation—not reality represent the longing of the master of halakhah." Carrying his comparative analysis a step further, Soloveitchik maintains that the mathematician-scientist and the talmudist share a this-worldly outlook. The latter has no use for a separate transcendental realm because his beloved a priori halakhic principles exist specifically to be applied in the "real" (natural-sense) world. Finally, Soloveitchik points to a passion for quantification as a common characteristic of the talmudist and the mathematician-scientist; both scholars seek to translate infinity into "finite creations, delimited by numbers and mathematical measures."[3]

Given Soloveitchik's portrayal of the talmudist as the intellectual twin of the mathematician-scientist, it is not surprising that he focuses on creativity as the defining characteristic and supreme virtue of his hero. On the intellectual side, the talmudist is a great conceptualizer, who frames all reality within the a priori categories of the halakhah. On the behavioral side, the talmudist is a self-determining personality who uses halakhic norms to shape the direction of his life. The process that is at work here is neatly summarized by Soloveitchik in the following equation: "The realization of halakhah = the concentration of transcendence in the world = holiness = creation."⁴

Obviously, the talmudist, as he is portrayed in "Halakhic Man," is an exalted religious figure. Yet even this statement fails to do justice to the full extent of the claim that Soloveitchik puts forward on his behalf. The key point is that Soloveitchik's discussion of talmudism is developed within the framework of a typological analysis of human experience. He is dealing, in the first instance, not with things as they are, or even as they might be, but rather with pure possibilities of existence. Specifically, Soloveitchik posits two basic universal human types, "intellectual man" and "religious man." The former is characterized by a boundless zeal for explanation, by a vast determination to remove the unknown from the cosmos. The latter, in contrast, is held spellbound by the mystery of the universe, which points obliquely to the presence of a transcendental realm. Soloveitchik argues that it is in the talmudist— or as he is referred to typologically, "halakhic man"—that these two types come together. Thus he states:

> On the one hand ... his [the halakhic man's] countenance and expression are comparable to that of intellectual man, who, with the joy of discovery and the thrill of creativity, occupies himself with ideal constructions, and compares his ideal concepts to the real world.... Yet, on the other hand, halakhic man is not a secular, cognitive type, whose mind is not at all concerned with transcendence, but is bound only to temporal life. God's Torah has planted in halakhic man's consciousness both the idea of everlasting life and the yearning for eternity.... He is religious man in all his loftiness and splendor, for his soul thirsts for the living God, and these streams of yearning surge and flow to the sea of transcendence.
>
> The only difference between religious man and halakhic man is that ... they go in opposite directions. Religious man begins with this world and ends up in supernal realms; halakhic man starts out in supernal realms and ends up in this world. Religious man longs to ascend from the vale of tears, from concrete reality, to the mountain of God. He attempts to extricate himself from the narrow straits of the perceptible world and emerge into the wide-open spaces of a pure and pristine transcendental existence. Halakhic man longs to bring down transcendence to the vale of distress that is our world, and to transform it into the land of the living.⁵

Halakhic man, then, as a type, represents a synthesis of the hard-headed thinking of intellectual man and the passionate spirituality of religious man; halakhic man uses the intellectualism of the former to achieve the spiritual ends of the latter. If intellectual man and religious man are "ideal" types in terms of human potential, then halakhic man is the ideal "ideal" type!

Soloveitchik's engagement with neo-Kantianism in "Halakhic Man" is matched by his engagement with religious existentialism in "The Lonely Man of Faith." In the latter framework, he introduces us to the typological pair "Adam the first" and "Adam the second," who are also referred to, respectively, as "majestic man" and "covenantal man." Soloveitchik bases his analysis on the two versions of the creation story in Genesis (chapters 1 and 2), which are notably different in several ways. What the Bible is offering us here, Soloveitchik argues, are "two Adams, two men, two fathers of mankind, two types, two representatives of humanity."[6] Thus Adam the first–majestic man is creative, functionally oriented, and enamored of technology; his aim is to achieve a "dignified" existence by gaining mastery over nature. Adam the second-covenantal man, in contrast, eschews "power and control"; as a nonfunctional, receptive, submissive human type, he yearns for a redeemed existence, which he achieves by bringing all his actions under God's authority. Majestic man, in short, glories in the assertion of human will, while covenantal man seeks its extinction.

In "The Lonely Man of Faith," majestic man and covenantal man remain permanently at war with each other; there is no end to the conflict between them. Moreover, Soloveitchik insists that both exist simultaneously within every religious Jew and that God regards this situation as fit and proper. Why is this so? Why should the religious Jew not try to cast out secular majestic man from his inner being? Because, Soloveitchik argues—in what is certainly a key interpretive point of "The Lonely Man of Faith"—Adam the first's secularity has religious sanction, the stamp of God's approval; majestic man is created in the "image of God" and commanded to "fill the earth and subdue it." Thus Soloveitchik arrives at a "tragic" view of the nature of religious life as entailing a "staggering dialectic":

> [God] wants man to engage in the pursuit of majesty-dignity as well as redemptiveness. He summoned man to retreat from peripheral, hard-won positions of vantage and power to the center of the faith experience. He also commanded man to advance from the covenantal center to the cosmic periphery and recapture the positions he gave up

a while ago. He authorized man to quest for "sovereignty"; He also told man to surrender and be totally committed. He enabled man to interpret the world in functional, empirical "how" categories.... Simultaneously, He also requires of man to forget his functional and bold approach, to stand in humility and dread before the *mysterium magnum* surrounding him, to interpret the world in categories of purposive activity instead of those of mechanical facticity.[7]

How does loneliness fit into Soloveitchik's scheme? Loneliness, he argues, has its source in the covenantal man side of the human personality and reflects an "I" awareness of "exclusiveness and ontological incompatibility with any other being." Soloveitchik expands upon this point in the following way: "The 'I' is lonely, experiencing ontological incompleteness and casualness, because there is no one who exists like the 'I' and because the *modus existentiae* of the 'I' cannot be repeated, imitated, or experienced by others." Not surprisingly, existential loneliness is a source of pain; it evokes a sense of the "absurd," thus leading the individual to doubt his "ontological legitimacy, worth, and reasonableness."[8] It is something, Soloveitchik stresses, that must be overcome.

The individual overcomes loneliness by establishing a "covenantal relationship" with God and fellow humans. This mode of existence, Soloveitchik emphasizes, is unique to the covenantal man type within the individual because the majestic man side of the human personality never experiences loneliness. There is an irony in this, in that majestic man is by nature a "social being, gregarious, [and] communicative." His sociability, however, has nothing to do with the need for dialogue. Rather, it represents a "creative social gesture"; he joins forces with others because he believes that "collective living and acting will promote his interests"; he forges a functional community in which he can better display his dignity and majesty. At bottom, then, majestic man remains self-sufficient, "ontologically complete," even while living in a "natural community." In that community, Soloveitchik tells us, "Adam and Eve act together, work together, pursue common objectives together; yet they do not exist together. Ontologically, they do not belong to each other; each is provided with an 'I' awareness and knows nothing of a 'We' awareness.... The in-depth personalities do not communicate, let alone commune, with each other."[9]

If the majestic man type within the individual points him in the direction of the natural community, the covenantal man type prompts him down the path toward the covenantal community. It is in the latter mode of relationship that true dialogue is achieved and the circle of existential isolation is broken. Since covenant making takes place on two levels—between man and God and between fellow humans—it may be wondered which comes first. Soloveitchik's answer here is clear—the lonely individual has to reach out to God before he can open himself to other human beings. Paradoxically, though, this reaching out comes about through an act of "recoil," in which the covenantal man side of the human personality humbly submits to God's will. It is when covenantal man "lets himself be confronted and defeated by a Higher and Truer Being," Soloveitchik argues, that "finitude and infinity, temporality and eternity, creature and creator become involved in the same community. They bind themselves together and participate in a unitive existence." Having made an initial "sacrificial gesture" vis à vis God, the inner covenantal man now turns to fellow humans and repeats the act: he "give[s] away part of himself" in "surrender and retreat," with the result that true human companionship is born. What emerges from all this, in Soloveitchik's view, is a "community of commitments ... compris-[ing] three participants: 'I, thou, and He,' the He in whom all being is rooted and in whom everything finds its rehabilitation and, consequently, redemption."[10]

In "But from Thence Ye Will Seek," Soloveitchik presents still another theological blueprint, this one shaped by the structures of phenomenological analysis. Soloveitchik's aim in the essay is bold in the extreme: to describe, step by step, the God-man encounter. In its initial phase this encounter is characterized by a full-fledged dualism as represented by the "natural religious experience" and the "revelational religious experience." In the natural religious experience man, in freedom and creativity, searches the cosmos for traces of the divine. This process is successful to a degree, but it ultimately breaks down, leading to the revelational religious experience. Now it is God who extends himself to man, while man responds with feelings of terror and constraint. In the next phase of the encounter, labeled by Soloveitchik *"imitatio dei,"* the initial dualism begins to be overcome. What started out as a God-man relationship characterized by trust/fear becomes one of love/awe, and man begins to experience God's law—the halakhah—as his own. In the culminating phase, labeled by Solo-veitchik "*devekut*," man clings to God in passionate love, achieving thereby complete freedom and creativity.

Soloveitchik states unequivocally that Judaism endorses the natural religious experience, but it is ultimately found wanting. As he puts it: "Judaism knows that [the] cosmic encounter, despite its importance, greatness, and power, is insufficient."[11] Why is this so? Most basically, it is because God never fully reveals himself in the cosmos; part of Him always remains hidden. Thus, though the natural religious experience has its place in the religious quest, it inevitably ends in frustration. It is here that the revelational religious experience comes into the picture:

> Man's search for God expresses itself in an intellectual act. All men of knowledge search for God, but ... when they reach the final boundary of reality [they] are astonished and retreat. When they confront eternity, with its frightening distances that both draw and repel, entice and mock—they all cease their quest. Many are perplexed; many are overwhelmed and commit heresy. Only a few remain standing in the face of the patent mystery and await salvation from God, He whom they seek. Here is the breaking point and here there appears a revelation of God, that is beyond nature, beyond reality bounded by time and space.[12]

In the revelational religious experience God enters the human domain as an all-powerful judge, demanding complete obedience and self-sacrifice. It is precisely for this reason, Soloveitchik argues, that the revelational religious experience strikes terror in man and compels his assent to the divine norm. Nevertheless, freedom and creativity—characteristics initially associated with the natural religious experience—emerge once again as key elements of religious life through the observance of the ethical commandments of the Torah (for Soloveitchik, following the lead of Maimonides, this is *imitatio dei*) by means of which man begins to assimilate the divine qualities of freedom and creativity that are embodied in the created order. As a result of *imitatio dei*, then, there is the beginning of a harmonization between "decree and autonomous creativity, the yoke constraining man and sponta-neity, the awe of the revealed commandment and the splendid vision of complete free choice, the revelatory experience and the experience of freedom."[13]

It is in the *devekut* stage that the natural religious experience and the revelational religious experience become fully harmonized and freedom and creativity shine forth in all their splendor. Since *devekut* has a mystical connotation, it is important to note that Soloveitchik is not referring to *unio mystica*, the absorption of the individual into God. Rather, he intends a cleaving to God achieved through knowledge rooted in passionate love. But knowledge of what, specifically? Soloveitchik's answer is clear: knowledge of the halakhah. The halakhah, according to Soloveitchik, makes *devekut* possible in three ways: through the "supremacy of the intellect"—that is, as a corpus of law open to profound study; through the "elevation of the body"—that is, as a guide to religious practice; and through the "perpetuation of the divine word"—that is, as a chain of tradition embodying the voice of prophecy. Soloveitchik concludes:

> As man's understanding deepens and intensifies, the unity of the wonder of creation and the commandment of Sinai begins to show itself until it fills his entire being. To the degree that the unity of creation and Sinai becomes apparent to him, man overcomes his consciousness which had been divided between the rational and the revelational and impresses upon it the seal of unity and uniqueness. There is no difference between creation and Sinai except a directional one: the direction of the question and the direction of the answer. The former is filled with enigmas, while the latter proclaims the answer.[14]

"Hark, My Beloved Knocks" is much shorter than the other three essays, but it is no less ambitious in its theological aim. Here Soloveitchik deals with the perennial problem of the suffering of the righteous in the context of a discussion of the Holocaust and the creation of the State of Israel. Basic to his analysis is the distinction between "man of fate" and "man of destiny" and a logic of explanation and a logic of response. The man of fate is committed to a logic of explanation; he seeks, through a metaphysical-speculative approach, to provide a rational solution to the problem of evil. Such an approach, Soloveitchik argues, must ultimately fail, either by leading to skepticism or—perhaps worse—by denying the reality of evil. The man of destiny, in contrast, eschews a rational approach, seeking instead a logic of response. His aim is practical-ethical in that he aspires to transform evil and suffering into a source of goodness and merit. Soloveitchik states:

> Suffering comes to elevate man, to purify his spirit and sanctify him, to cleanse his thoughts of the dregs of superficiality and vulgarity; to refine his soul and broaden his horizons. A general principle: suffering—its purpose is to correct the flaw in man's personality.... Suffering appears in the world to contribute something to man, to make atonement for him.... Suffering obligates man to return in full repentance to God.[15]

How does this analysis apply to the Holocaust? Soloveitchik minces no words in underscoring the "absolute hiddenness of God's face" in the Holocaust—the withdrawal of God's special providence from the Jewish people—yet he states bluntly that there is no way to account for this—no logic of explanation. Why God permitted the Jewish people to suffer in the Holocaust must remain a mystery. What is clear, however, Soloveitchik stresses, is the logic of response that emerges from the Holocaust, the "duty of suffering man that arises out of his suffering":

> Our great rabbis have taught us: "Man is obligated to bless for evil as he blesses for good." Just as the good obligates man to engage in elevated action, and demands of the individual or the community creative acts and renewal, so does suffering demand improvement of the soul and purification of life.... In short, it is not man's task to solve the problem of the rational cause or purpose of suffering in all its speculative complexity, but rather the question of its amelioration in all its halakhic simplicity.[16]

Soloveitchik carries his analysis a step further by dialectically linking the Holocaust and the creation of the State of Israel. Just as the former testifies to the withdrawal of God's special providence from the Jewish people, Soloveitchik argues, so does the latter point to its renewal. Again, it needs to be stressed that Soloveitchik is concerned with a logic of response and not with a logic of explanation. Thus he sidesteps the issue of the role of the reborn Jewish state in the process of redemption. Instead, he focuses on the appropriate Jewish response to God's "knock" on the door of history—the establishment of the State of Israel in the aftermath of the Holocaust:

In the midst of a frightening night, full of the horrors of Majdanek, Treblinka, and Buchenwald, in a night of gas chambers and crematoria, in a night of the absolute hiddenness of God's face ... in this very night the beloved arose and appeared. The God who was hiding ... suddenly appeared and began to knock at the entrance to the tent of the bedraggled and bereaved companion, twisting and turning on her bed in ... the torment of hell. It is because of the banging and knocking at the door of the companion, clothed in grief, that the State of Israel was born![17]

God's knock, Soloveitchik contends, calls for a twofold response: first, an emphasis on the commonalities that bind all Jews together—the "covenant of fate"—and second, a renewed commitment to the full implementation of the teachings of the Torah— the "covenant of destiny."

What are we to make of Soloveitchik's theological enterprise as a whole? It should be evident from the foregoing discussion that Soloveitchik is not a systematic thinker—he does not put forward a single, coherent theological system. This point needs stressing because there has been a tendency on the part of some of Soloveitchik's disciples to maintain the contrary, to argue that he is a systematic thinker in the mold of Maimonides. To date, however, no evidence has been provided to sustain this claim, which is counterproductive in that it raises expectations about Soloveitchik's work that cannot possibly be fulfilled.

To say that Soloveitchik is not a systematic thinker is not to imply—in the least—that his work is therefore somehow inferior or of lesser interest. After all, Buber and Kierkegaard were not system builders, yet they were, by any accounting, world-class theologians. The strengths that Soloveitchik brings to the theological enterprise are plain to see: a brilliant mind, phenomenal knowledge, a powerful religious imagination, and a flair for passionate expression. These characteristics show themselves time and again in Soloveitchik's writings, and they evoke the reader's respect and admiration.

Soloveitchik constantly returns to square one in his theological essays—symbolized by the complete absence of cross-references between his various writings—but this makes his achievement all the more impressive. How many times can a religious thinker say something fresh and new? In Soloveitchik's case the answer seems to be as many times as he can pick up his pen. An instance is to be seen in "Confrontation" (1964), in which Soloveitchik finds in the biblical creation story not the two types of "The Lonely Man of Faith"—majestic man and covenantal man—but three—"natural man," "confronted man," and "doubly confronted man." The full range of types that Soloveitchik develops in his essays is astonishing; in addition to those already mentioned, there are "cosmic conscious man" and "origin conscious man" in "Majesty and Humility" (1978), "New Year man" and "Day of Atonement man" in "How Is Your Beloved Better Than Another?" (1963), "New Moon man" in "The Hidden and the Revealed" (1963), and "king-teacher" and "saint-teacher" in "A Eulogy for the Talner Rebbe" (1972).

At this point the phrase "square one" needs to be given greater specificity. In part, it refers to the mode of theologizing that Soloveitchik employs, which, as we have seen, can differ sharply from one essay to the next—neo-Kantianism, existentialism, phenomenology, and so on. It also refers to the uses that Soloveitchik makes of his basic theological materials. The careful reader of Soloveitchik's work will observe that certain key motifs and themes keep recurring but that they are treated in very different ways in the various essays. Perhaps the best example of this is the striking similarities/differences between "Halakhic Man" and "The Lonely Man of Faith." In both essays there are Adam I and Adam II types: Adam I—intellectual man and majestic man; Adam II—religious man and covenantal man. Whereas in "Halakhic Man" Soloveitchik's sympathy is clearly with the Adam I type, in "The Lonely Man of Faith" it is decidedly with the Adam II type. Moreover, in the former essay Soloveitchik ultimately brings his types together—as he does in "But from Thence Ye Will Seek"—whereas in the latter essay he resolutely refuses to do so. (To add to the complexity, in the introductory section of "Halakhic Man" Soloveitchik states explicitly that the two types can never be reconciled—something he proceeds to do in the main body of the essay.)

Given Soloveitchik's capacity for freshness and surprise, it is understandable that students of his work have had considerable difficulty in getting a clear fix of his overall theological position. During the lengthy period in which Soloveitchik was known largely for "Halakhic Man," it was taken for granted that he was a neo-Kantian in the mold of Hermann Cohen. With the publication of "The Lonely Man of Faith," however, it became evident that Soloveitchik had a strong existentialist bent. Yet an existentialist sensibility already shows itself in the introductory section of "Halakhic Man," as well as in "Sacred and Profane" (1945). Then there is "The Halakhic Mind," which appeared in 1986, but was actually written in 1944. In this essay, Soloveitchik gives the back of his hand to the same neo-Kantianism that he relies on in "Halakhic Man," which was published in 1944. Adding still further to the complexity is the question of the status of "But from Thence Ye Will Seek." This essay existed in draft form in the 1940s but was not published until 1978, by which time it had been considerably revised. Is this essay, then, to be seen as an early or a late work?

In attempting to arrive at a sense of the whole with regard to Soloveitchik's theological enterprise, scholars have taken a variety of tacks. Eugene Borowitz has argued that Soloveitchik simply changed his mind, first embracing neo-Kantianism and then existentialism. Aviezer Ravitsky has distinguished between Soloveitchik's approach to the general religious personality, which takes one form, and the halakhic personality, which takes another. Lawrence Kaplan has stressed language of publication as the key factor, arguing that Soloveitchik is addressing different audiences with different aims in his English and Hebrew essays. David Singer and Moshe Sokol have taken the position that the contradictions in the writings reflect the contradictions in the man—that Soloveitchik is a conflicted personality.

I suggest that his writings are addressed, first and foremost, to Rabbi Joseph B. Soloveitchik himself. Students of Soloveitchik's thought have noted that he never argues the premises of his faith—they are taken for granted. But Soloveitchik cannot take for granted that his is an Orthodoxy that can pass muster in the context of modernity. This is something that he must prove to himself time and again. Hence his repeated engagement with various currents of modern thought. By assimilating these currents to his own theological agenda—by making them part and parcel of his self-understanding as an Orthodox Jew—he is able to gain a sense of mastery and control over modernity. The stakes for Soloveitchik in this enterprise are extremely high: nothing less than his self-respect as an Orthodox Jew.

340 . Joseph Soloveitchik

One can see this process at work in "The Halakhic Mind," in which Soloveitchik draws on the findings of modern philosophy of science to make the case for religion as an autonomous cognitive sphere. His basic thesis is announced in the opening sentence: "It would be difficult to distinguish any epoch in the history of philosophy more amenable to the meditating *homo religiosus* than that of today." What arouses Soloveitchik's enthusiasm is modern philosophy of science's acceptance of "epistemological plural- ism," an acceptance based on such developments as the theory of relativity, quantum mechanics, and non-Euclidian geometry. Epi- stemological pluralism opens the way for the recognition of religion as an autonomous domain and therefore for the revitali- zation of the philosophy of religion. Soloveitchik states:

> The *homo religiosus* must regain his position in the cognitive realm. He is no longer the emotional creature, swayed by abstruse sentiments and ephemeral feelings; nor is he the ethical idealist in eternal quest for sanction and authority. He is a cognitive type, desiring both to understand and interpret. Reality, as the object upon which the cognitive act is directed, can no longer be the concern of the scientist and philosopher only, but also that of the *homo religiosus*. This does not mean that religion is about to repeat the errors of the Middle Ages and compete with science. It signifies only that knowledge is not the exclusive province of the theoretician of science; religion, too, has a cognitive approach to reality.[18]

One can well imagine the relish with which Soloveitchik makes this point.

It would appear, then, that Soloveitchik is, so to speak, pouring old Jewish wine into new Westernized bottles. But that clearly is not the whole story because the Westernized bottles end up affecting the flavor of the Jewish wine. By this I mean that Soloveitchik's exposure to currents of modern thought leads him to embrace—although there are contrary indications as well—key values of modernity. Certainly the reader of his essays, par- ticularly "Halakhic Man" and "But from Thence Ye Will Seek," is struck by the emphasis on freedom, creativity, self-actualization, and this-worldliness. In "The Lonely Man of Faith" Soloveitchik fully endorses the scientific and technological thrust of Western civilization: "Man reaching for the distant stars is acting in harmony with his nature which was created, willed, and directed by his Maker. It is a manifestation of obedience to rather than rebellion against God." In "But from Thence Ye Will Seek" and "The Lonely Man of Faith," Soloveitchik shows a keen appreciation of the category of the aesthetic as an aspect of religious experience. Finally, in "Hark, My Beloved Knocks" Soloveitchik gives his blessing to the modern Zionist enterprise and the secular State of Israel.

Although Soloveitchik's modernity can clearly be established, it is more implicit than explicit in his work. His essays contain no direct discussion of these matters and what they imply for the Orthodox community as a whole. That task now falls to the younger generation of Orthodox thinkers, who will have to take up where Soloveitchik left off. One thing is certain: the challenge of modernity will not go away.

Notes

1. Cited in Aaron Rothkoff, *Bernard Revel* (Philadelphia, 1972), p. 128.
2. Joseph Soloveitchik, "Halakhic Man," in Pinchas Peli (ed.), *In Aloneness, In Togetherness* [Hebrew] (Jerusalem, 1976), p. 64.
3. *Ibid.*, p. 101.
4. *Ibid.*, p. 156.
5. *Ibid.*, pp. 85–86.
6. Joseph Soloveitchik, "The Lonely Man of Faith," *Tradition*, Vol. 7, No. 2 (Summer 1965), p. 10.
7. *Ibid.*, pp. 49–50.
8. *Ibid.*, p. 22.
9. *Ibid.*, p. 23.
10. *Ibid.*, p. 28.
11. Joseph Soloveitchik, "But from Thence Ye Will Seek," *Hadorom* [Hebrew] (No. 47, 1978), p. 11.
12. *Ibid.*, p. 14.
13. *Ibid.*, p. 55.
14. *Ibid.*, p. 57.
15. Joseph Soloveitchik, "Hark, My Beloved Knocks," in Peli (ed.), *In Aloneness, In Togetherness, op. cit.*, pp. 339–340.
16. *Ibid.*, p. 342.
17. *Ibid.*, p. 354.
18. Joseph Soloveitchik, *The Halakhic Mind* (New York, 1986), p. 40.

FOR FURTHER READING

Works by Joseph Soloveitchik

A substantial portion of Soloveitchik's writings are in the Hebrew language and remain untranslated. Among works available in English, either in the original or in translation, are the following:

"Confrontation," *Tradition* 6:2 (Spring/Summer 1964). Soloveitchik's statement in opposition to interfaith dialogue.

Halakhic Man, Philadelphia, 1983.

The Halakhic Mind, New York, 1986.

"The Lonely Man of Faith," *Tradition* 7:2 (Summer 1965).

On Repentance, New York, 1984. This work was compiled by Pinchas Peli and is a series of profound meditations on the nature of repentance.

The Rav Speaks, Jerusalem, 1983. Five addresses on themes related to Zionism and the State of Israel.

Works about Joseph Soloveitchik

Critical literature on Soloveitchik is only beginning to emerge and develop. The following works are of special interest:

Borowitz, Eugene, "A Theology of Modern Orthodoxy: Rabbi Joseph B. Solo-veitchik," in *Choices in Modern Jewish Thought*, New York, 1983, pp. 218–42. A leading Reform thinker reflects on the significance of Soloveitchik's theological enterprise.

Hartman, David, *A Living Covenant*, New York, 1985, pp. 60–108; 131–59. A lover's quarrel with Soloveitchik's work, written by a former student and disciple.

Kaplan, Lawrence, "Rabbi Joseph B. Soloveitchik's Philosophy of Halakhah," in *Jewish Law Annual* 7, ed. by B. S. Jackson, New York, 1988, pp. 139–97. This is an important effort at establishing Soloveitchik's philosophy of halakhah.

Lichtenstein, Aharon, "Rabbi Joseph Soloveitchik," in *Great Jewish Thinkers of the Twentieth Century*, ed. by Simon Noveck, New York, 1963, pp. 281–97. This work contains valuable biographical information.

Ravitsky, Aviezer, "Rabbi J. B. Soloveitchik on Human Knowledge: Between Maimonidean and Neo-Kantian Philosophy," in *Modern Judaism*, 6:2 (May 1986), pp. 157–88. Ravitsky makes a serious attempt to situate Solo-veitchik's work in philosophical terms.

Singer, David, and Sokol, Moshe, "Joseph Soloveitchik: Lonely Man of Faith," *Modern Judaism* 2:3 (October 1982), pp. 227–72. This is a study of Solo-veitchik's writings, linking his ideas and personality.

Leo Strauss

HILLEL FRADKIN

Leo Strauss was born in Germany on September 20, 1899, in the town of Kirchhain in Hesse. Coming from an observant family, he received a traditional Jewish education as well as a secular education. For the latter he attended the Gymnasium Philippinum in Marburg, from which he graduated in 1917. Upon graduation he entered the German army and served until the end of World War I. For the next seven years Strauss pursued university studies at Marburg, Frankfurt, Berlin, Hamburg, Frieburg, and Giessen, principally in philosophy and secondarily in history.

In 1921 he received his doctorate from the University of Hamburg for a dissertation on the problem of knowledge in the philosophy of Jacobi, written under the direction of Ernst Cassirer. Strauss continued his studies and began to publish reviews and articles in two German Jewish journals, the *Judische Rundschau* and *Der Jude*. His publications were principally devoted to two subjects: Zionism, of which Strauss was an early adherent, and biblical interpretation. An article on Hermann Cohen's analysis of Spinoza's biblical interpretation published in 1924 brought him to the attention of Julius Guttman, then president of the Academy for the Science of Judaism in Berlin. He was offered a position at the academy, which he held from 1925 to 1932. At the academy he devoted himself to research on Jewish philosophy, and among his principal tasks was work on the academy's edition of the works of Moses Mendelssohn.. His contributions to this undertaking included translations of Mendelssohn's Hebrew works as well as introductions to several of his writings. During this period he also published his first book, *Spinoza's Critique of Religion.*[1] While in Berlin, Strauss became acquainted with many of the younger scholars active in either Jewish or philosophical studies and became closely associated with Alexander Kojeve, Karl Lowith, Hans-Georg Gadamer, Jacob Klein, and Gershom Scholem.

In 1932, Strauss received a fellowship from the Rockefeller Foundation for the Social Sciences in Germany and spent the first year of his grant in Paris doing research on medieval Jewish and Islamic philosophy. This work led to the publication in 1935 of a book on medieval Jewish thought, *Philosophy and Law.*[2] The second year he spent in England working on Hobbes. During this year he married Marie (Mirjam) Bernson.

With the advent of Hitler's government, Strauss decided not to return to Germany but to remain in England, and he spent the next three years at Cambridge, continuing his research on Hobbes. During this time he published his book *The Political Philosophy of Hobbes: Its Basis and Its Genesis.*[3] During this period he began to seek a permanent position in the United States. In 1937 he was appointed as a research fellow at Columbia University, but the following year he took an appointment at the New School for Social Research and remained a member of its faculty until 1948.

From 1949 until 1968 Strauss taught political philosophy at the University of Chicago. During this period he held visiting appointments at the University of California at Berkeley and the Hebrew University of Jerusalem. After retiring from the University of Chicago, Strauss taught briefly at Claremont Men's College before taking a position as the Scott Buchanan Distinguished Scholar at St. John's College in Annapolis, Maryland. Strauss died in Annapolis in October 1973. All of his immediate family except his wife, daughter, and son perished during World War II. Strauss is today survived by his daughter Jenny Strauss Clay, who is a professor of Classical Greek literature, and his son Thomas P. Strauss, who works for the U.S. armed forces in Berlin.

Strauss was the author of fifteen books and dozens of articles. Of those, the best known are the books on Spinoza and Hobbes and *On Tyranny, Natural Right and History, Thoughts on Machiavelli, Persecution and the Art of Writing,* and the *City and Man.*[4]

Leo Strauss is most generally known not as a contemporary Jewish thinker or even as a Jewish scholar but as a political scientist and in particular as a student and historian of the tradition of political philosophy. His published works typically were studies of individual authors or even single texts belonging to this tradition. The range of authors who attracted his interest was unusually broad. He published several works concerned with the origins of political philosophy, including studies of Plato, Xenophon, Aristotle, Thucydides, and Aristophanes.[5] He also wrote on several modern political philosophers, including Machiavelli, Spinoza, Hobbes, Locke, Rousseau, and Nietzsche.[6] In addition to ancient and modern thought, he published inquiries into medieval thought, including and most notably several studies on medieval Jewish authors such as Moses Maimonides and Judah Halevi.[7] The latter works are his best known on Jewish thought, although his studies of Spinoza are sometimes also seen as related to this field.

By his own account, the immediate purpose of this historical research, his principal work, was to establish the most accurate understanding of the thought of the principal figures and developments in political philosophy. Toward the beginning of his scholarly career, Strauss began to wonder whether the understanding of the history of political philosophy then current was satisfactory, and he attempted to submit this tradition to a fresh and thorough reinvestigation. The results of his research yielded new interpretations of important political philosophers such as Plato, Xenophon, and Machiavelli, as well as a new interpretation of the course of political philosophy as a whole.

Strauss pursued and offered his research as a contribution to historical scholarship and in conformity with the highest standards of such scholarship. For this reason and because his studies of Jewish authors form a relatively small portion of his published corpus, his role as a contemporary Jewish thinker is not immediately obvious.

Nevertheless, on several occasions, Strauss indicated that his work had an important relationship to and bearing on contemporary Jewish thought and its themes. These occasions included both public lectures (some of them later published) in which he addressed contemporary questions and his historical studies themselves, some of whose introductions or prefaces present extensive discussion of such themes.[8] The best known of the latter is the semiautobiographical preface Strauss composed for the

English translation of his book on Spinoza.[9] On these occasions, Strauss indicated that his historical research had not been motivated by historical or antiquarian curiosity but by contemporary concerns. This work was most immediately inspired by and ultimately intended as a response to a contemporary crisis or rather group of crises: the crisis of modern Jewish life in general and modern German Jewry in particular, of which a crisis in contemporary Jewish thought itself was a part. In Strauss's presentation, these problems were linked to a more general crisis of modern Western civilization. In Strauss's discussion of contemporary events and thought he addressed all aspects of these crises. His reflections on these matters form the first of his contributions to contemporary Jewish thought and the foundation for understanding the manner in which his historical research was related to it.

It is worth noting at the outset, however, one important conclusion of Strauss's reflections on the contemporary Jewish situation. He indicates that he became convinced that it was necessary to try to effect a recovery of the thought of the past, and in particular the history of political philosophy, and for that reason he undertook historical research. Viewed in this light, all of his historical research might be viewed as a contribution to contemporary Jewish thought. If there is some merit in this notion, at the outset it nonetheless appears paradoxical. It is somewhat more clear and useful to observe that Strauss came to regard the purpose of his work as the recovery of an accurate understanding of the twin sources of Western thought: Athens and Jerusalem, or classical philosophy and biblical revelation.[10]

Thus the foundations of Jewish thought represented one of the two central foci of his mature reflections and were expressed not only in the study of medieval Jewish thought but in interpretation of the Torah, in particular, though not exclusively, Genesis. Moreover, his thought aimed not only at the recovery of Athens and Jerusalem but also of an understanding of the tension between them. He suggested that the "core, the nerve of Western intellectual history, Western spiritual history, is the conflict between the Biblical and the philosophic notion of the good life ... [and] that this unresolved conflict is the secret of the vitality of Western civilization."[11] To the extent that the contemporary crisis threatened this vitality, his work was directly related to the contemporary situation.

In pursuit of this goal he found certain aspects of medieval Jewish thought, in particular the work of Maimonides and Halevi, to be the most useful and authoritative guide. Thus his studies of medieval Jewish thought occupy a more central role in his work and thought than their number might indicate. Seen in this light, the core of his thought may be regarded as a contribution to contemporary Jewish thought. Still, by virtue of its apparent anachronism, this notion too will appear paradoxical. Hence, for a proper appreciation of Strauss's contribution it is useful to begin with his other: his analysis of the Jewish crises of his times.

The Contemporary Crisis

Strauss referred to the contemporary crises as the "theological-political predicament," appropriating the terminology of Benedict Spinoza, and it is important to consider his usage of this term.[12]

As it emerges in Strauss's discussion in the preface of his book on Spinoza, the predicament in question referred to a complex of factors,[13] the most salient of which was the politically dependent and threatened situation of the German-Jewish community. The immediate source of danger to the German-Jewish community was the weakness of the Weimar Republic, the first liberal democratic regime in German history. As a liberal democratic regime in the classic sense, that is, of Spinoza, the first proponent of liberal democracy, it offered full political and civil rights to all citizens regardless of religion. In Germany, as everywhere else in Europe, liberalism thus understood had been the condition of the admission of Jews to full citizenship and their assimilation to modern political life and society. In Germany, although Jews were accorded greater rights in the course of the nineteenth century, they did not receive full political rights until the establishment of the Weimar Republic.

The founding of the Weimar regime represented the culmination of a long struggle to establish a liberal state in Germany, which had begun during the German Enlightenment of the eighteenth century. Though this goal seemed to have been achieved through the Weimar Republic, that regime, almost from its inception, appeared weak and unstable. Strauss concluded as early as 1925 that its weaknesses were or would prove to be fatal. This was the first respect in which Strauss found himself and other

German Jews in the grip of the theological-political predicament, for the weakness and ultimate demise of the Weimar Republic would surely have an adverse effect on the political and general situation of Germany's Jews. This fear was fulfilled only too soon.

If the political problem of the German-Jewish community was Strauss's most immediate concern, it was not his only or even his deepest concern. Strauss was conscious of the fact that the. weakness of the German-Jewish community was only the most extreme expression of the threatened character of Western Jewry. It was true that liberalism had established itself in other Western countries much earlier, and for this and other reasons, had deeper roots in their respective political traditions. Nonetheless he was deeply and fully conscious of the degree to which in Western culture as a whole, philosophical and intellectual support for liberalism had been and was continuing to be eroded. Germany offered the most extreme example through the emergence and influence of radical critiques of both modern liberalism and modern rationalism. These critiques, first presented by Nietzsche, were, during Strauss's early adulthood, associated above all with the work of Martin Heidegger. Although the expression of these radical critiques through moral relativism and existentialism had not yet been accepted everywhere and in every respect, Strauss expected the "new thinking," as it was then called, eventually to prove irresistible. This view was based on his thorough and deep study of the new teachings, which he thought derived their power from the fact that contemporary rationalism and even modern rationalism as a whole was fundamentally unable to respond. Indeed he found that many of his Jewish contemporaries, most notably Martin Buber and Franz Rosenzweig, adhered to these critiques, albeit adapted to a "Jewish" perspective, which may be termed Jewish existentialism.

The rise of Jewish existentialism was, for Strauss, one expression of the deep ambiguities in German and Western Jewry's vision of itself, which constituted another equally serious and long-standing aspect of the theological-political predicament. For the emergence of Jewish existentialism within German Jewry was only the latest expression of the struggle within modern German-Jewish thought over its posture toward modern liberalism. This was hardly surprising for a number of reasons. Among them was the fact that inasmuch as the history of modern Germany's resistance to liberalism had been prominent and vigorous, expressing itself in such movements as romanticism, nationalism, and modern anti-Semitism, it had forced the German-Jewish community to call into question its own prospects from and attitude toward liberalism, even while working for the political achievement of that liberalism.

The ambiguities in the German-Jewish situation, both external and internal, resulted in an unusually rich variety of distinctively modern Jewish movements: the modern Jewish enlightenment; all modern forms of Judaism: Reform, Conservative, and Modern Orthodoxy; the Science of Judaism; modern Zionism; and Jewish existentialism. At issue in these movements was, of course, not only the political condition of modern Jewry but its spiritual condition as well, that is, its distinctive identity and its self-respect. These movements, although originating among German Jews, were applicable to the situation of modern Jewry generally, and Strauss could and did consider them in this light, that is to say in the light of their ability to respond to the modern Jewish problem. His reflections on these expressions of contemporary Jewish thought represent the first of his contributions to that thought.

Contemporary Jewish Thought

Of the contemporary Jewish responses to the modern world, Strauss seems to have preferred Zionism. He was a Zionist in his youth and a lifelong supporter of Israel. He concurred in Gershom Scholem's view that the establishment of the state of Israel "procured a blessing for all Jews everywhere regardless of whether they admit it or not."[14]

Despite Strauss's appreciation of Zionism and its accomplishments, he also discerned limitations, both practical and intellectual, to the capacity of Zionism to provide a full solution to the modern Jewish problem. These limitations were to some degree characteristic of all contemporary Jewish responses, and their manifestation in other forms of contemporary Jewish thought were even more serious than those which affected Zionism. Rather than being solutions to the modern Jewish problem, they were a part of that problem. Strauss's role as a contemporary Jewish thinker thus first comes to light as a critic of contemporary Jewish thought. His critique might be summarized as follows.

Almost all contemporary Jewish movements had their origins in a certain disappointment or dissatisfaction with modern principles and their results, above all, modern liberalism. But such dissatisfaction was not limited to the Jewish world. Indeed, a principal cause of Jewish dissatisfaction was its non-Jewish counterpart, one important expression of which was the failure or incapacity to accept Jews on an equal footing. As a result of its own dissatisfactions with modernity, the non-Jewish world had formulated a variety of new bases for contemporary life and thought such as romanticism and historicism of all varieties, including existentialism.

When Strauss examined contemporary Jewish responses, he discerned that each in its own way represented a kind of imitation of non-Jewish movements. This was sure to cause grave problems, practical as well as intellectual, for it was unclear whether conceptions that originated in a desire to overturn liberalism could safely be employed as models for Jewish life. More important, this Jewish response extended the dependence of the Jewish community from the political to the spiritual realm, which, according to Strauss, was "the core of the predicament of German Jewry."[15]

Strauss's diagnosis of the problem of contemporary Jewish thought arose through and derived from detailed consideration of its specific forms. To illustrate what he meant more concretely, a few examples of Strauss's analysis will be useful. Let us return first to Zionism.[16] Strauss observed that Zionism had proclaimed and rested upon the important truth that liberalism could not provide full equality for Jews. At best, it could provide political equality. In its primary form, liberalism proposed the establishment of a sharp distinction between the public and private spheres. To the former, everyone, regardless of religious or social origin, would be admitted as an equal and on a nondiscriminatory basis, enjoying full political and legal rights. The private sphere, however, would lack any enforcement of equality and would permit, if it did not solicit, various forms of social inequality and discrimination. Dissatisfied with this state of affairs and uncertain even of its stability, certain Jewish political thinkers proposed the establishment of an independent Jewish community and thus founded Zionism.

Nevertheless, the original founders of Zionism continued to see the Jewish problem and its solution in liberal terms. They proposed to establish a modern, liberal, secular state. This proposal encountered several problems, which forced the program of Zionism to undergo a change. As a political movement, Zionism required support from the Jewish community, which it could gain only by appealing to traditional Jewish sensibilities and longings. This was, in some degree, a fruitful problem and solution for it pointed to the fact that the state as originally conceived by Zionism lacked the richness of traditional Jewish life. Cultural Zionism, which embodied this perspective, seemed to be a decisive improvement. Yet cultural Zionism achieved this advance by understanding traditional Jewish life or Jewish heritage "as a culture, that is, as a product of the national mind, of the national genius."[17]

This understanding was plainly borrowed from the contemporary European historical and romantic movements. In Strauss's view, such dependency was not its only liability. As an instrument of the Jewish tradition and heritage it was rooted in and dependent on a perspective that had not understood itself as the creation of the Jewish nation but as a divine gift, divine revelation. This presented some additional difficulties. Could the vitality of the tradition survive a transformation in the understanding of its roots? Might not this difficulty as well as other reasons require the transformation of cultural Zionism into religious Zionism? But did not religious Zionism need to understand itself first as Jewish faith and only secondarily Zionism? Considerations like these led Strauss to conclude that the eventual outcome of Zionism would be an uneasy compromise of modern and Jewish principles with the inevitable contradictions. This precluded the possibility of seeing in Zionism the complete solution to Jewish problems and hopes or to the limitations of liberalism, which was also an uneasy compromise. All this did not deprive Zionism, in Strauss's view, of its nobility and great merits, but it did lead him to observe that as a practical matter it also required a greater appreciation of the dignity and merits of liberalism.[18]

Considerations like the ones outlined above with respect to Zionism pointed in the direction of another kind of Jewish response: a return to Jewish faith or tradition.[19] Indeed, such an alternative was apparently available in the new form of thought proposed and elaborated by several older German-Jewish contemporaries such as Martin Buber and Franz Rosenzweig, which may be termed Jewish existentialism.

Rosenzweig was, of course, the leading figure in German-Jewish thought, and Strauss studied his and Buber's thought closely. Ultimately he rejected the path they outlined. It is evident from Strauss's analysis that his reasons for demurral derived not from Jewish existentialism's appeal for faith and tradition but from the grounds on which it was based and the form it took as a consequence.

As Strauss understood Jewish existentialism, its call for a new way of thinking partook of and was partially grounded in the contemporary critique of modern rationalism. Hence to understand the problem Strauss discerned with Jewish existentialism it is necessary to see it within the context of existentialism in its entirety. The existentialist critique was understood by Strauss and his contemporaries, including the existentialists, not merely as a departure from modern rationalism but as its natural and necessary outcome. Modern rationalism was seen to have achieved its culmination and perfection in the form of thought known as historicism.

The most general and fundamental premise of historicism is the view that all forms of human thought, including all forms of philosophy, are essentially an expression of the historical context in which they arise and are inevitably limited by that context. The claim of all earlier forms of philosophy to be objective and rational was thus invalid. In its own earliest forms, this consequence was avoided by historicism through the assertion that the historical process was rational and was now adequately grasped by nineteenth century thought. Such claims were advanced in different ways by Hegel and Marx, but these claims proved difficult to maintain and were ultimately rejected. With the denial of the rationality of history itself, all claims of rationalism appeared to be empty, for the existentialist critics of historicism were themselves historicists, that is, they accepted the historically limited character of human thought.

For such radical historicists, the consequence of this outcome of modern Western thought was the condition termed nihilism. The latter referred to the fact that a consequence of this perspective was the view that there was no human understanding of human good or evil that had any rational or objective grounding. Everything that men looked up to, judged themselves by, or pursued was nothing more than an expression of their desires, passions, and prejudices, in a word their values, which were based solely on the faith men placed in them. The great variety of such values, which had emerged over the course of human history, was a function of, if not exactly explicable through, the continuous but mysterious development of human consciousness. Being mysterious, they were the arbitrary dispensations of that history. Among those dispensations was contemporary thought, which had finally revealed this fundamental arbitrariness.

It was now known that all human thought and endeavor were fundamentally meaningless. Man was confronted with the abyss, his true situation, which meant that human life was predicated on decision and choice but lacked any basis on which to ground that choice. Nihilism was the present and fundamental human condition.

The first important aspect of the provenance and character of existentialism within the Jewish context was that the defeat of modern rationalism seemed to lead naturally to a new appreciation of reason's ancient rival, faith. Indeed, the collapse of modern rationalism seemed to leave man only faith with which to understand and face his situation. For the critique of modern rationalism shared in common with modern rationalism itself the conviction that modern rationalism was *the* perfection and culmination of rationalism in all its forms. For Buber and Rosenzweig these circumstances pointed to a new departure for faith in and adherence to biblical revelation.

Strauss was deeply impressed by the critique of modern rationalism and persuaded of its force, at least insofar as it was a critique of modern rationalism and not rationalism as a whole. For Strauss too, this critique reopened the question of the past and a return to faith.

Nevertheless, Strauss discerned difficulties in Jewish existentialism that derived from its provenance in existentialist thought. The first was that there was more than one form of existentialism. Most important in the contest was the Jewish existentialism of Buber and Rosenzweig and the atheistic existentialism of Martin Heidegger. Each was offered as *the* appropriate interpretation of the implications of the critique of rationalism or the current human condition of nihilism. This implied that it was not immediately clear where the existentialist critique led and its consequences for faith. In considering this competition, Strauss observed reluctantly that Heidegger had a deeper and more thoughtful command of contemporary thought than either Buber or Rosenzweig. The superior abilities and attainments of Heidegger did not, however, simply settle the issue. For Strauss observed that there was merit in the claim of the Jewish exist-entialists that atheistic existentialism as a form of philosophy now rested on unevident or willful belief. Given the primary character of philosophy as the search for truth on the basis of what is evident to man, this amounted to the defeat of philosophy, even its final defeat, in its age-old struggle with faith. Philosophy's role should be and could only be to accept tutelage from faith and religious experience.

Strauss's ultimate difficulty with Jewish existentialism was that its proponents seemed unwilling or incapable of following their own advice. For so far from bringing the teachings of faith to philosophy, it was a school of philosophy itself. Indeed, instead of simply elaborating biblical faith and its conceptions, it brought to bear upon them the categories of contemporary thought, among them the categories of atheistic existentialism. A specific example, but one far-reaching in its impact, was the attempt by Jewish existentialists to assert that biblical revelation, like existentialism, taught that the human situation was simply an abyss and that man faced a world in which no security was to be found. In Strauss's view, however, understanding biblical teaching in this manner represented a far-reaching modification of biblical teaching which owed its inspiration not to Sinai, but to Nietzsche and Heidegger. Although the Bible perhaps teaches that man can find no security through his own endeavor, that "for the prophets there is no refuge and fortress except God, ... the security afforded by God is everything."[20] As Strauss observed, the controversy between Jewish and Heideggerian existentialism seemed to be degener-ating "into a race in which he wins who offers the smallest security and the greatest terror."[21] In such a context, Strauss predicted that Heidegger would be the winner. Strauss observed further that even to the extent that contemporary circumstances marked the "victory of orthodoxy," the accomplishment of that victory "through the self-destruction of rational philosophy was not an unmitigated blessing, for it was a victory, not of Jewish orthodoxy, but of any orthodoxy, and Jewish orthodoxy based its claim to superiority to other religions from the beginning on its superior rationality (Deut. 4:6)."[22] It might be true, as Jewish existentialists seemed to claim, that the new philosophy was grounded in willful belief, but it seemed to owe as much to willfulness as to the obedient faith biblical revelation demanded. Thus Jewish existentialism seemed incapable of articulating a real alternative to contemporary philosophy that would be truly grounded in biblical revelation and have as its task the meditation upon and elaboration of its teachings. Moreover, insofar as it endorsed the premises of contemporary existentialism, it could not oppose, if it did not actually assist in, the victory of orthodoxy as such, that is, philosophically grounded political and/or religious fanaticism.

Progress or Return

Such reflections on the problems of contemporary Jewish thought led Strauss to wonder whether what was really called for was a genuine and unqualified return to the past. Strauss was aware of the fact that this was largely considered to be an impossibility both by contemporary Jewish and non-Jewish thought. Still he wondered "whether what seems to be an impossibility is in fact only a very great difficulty."[23]

More specifically, he wondered whether the alleged impossibility of such a return did not rest on a half-forgotten and thus unevident and unexamined confidence in progress. Strauss was aware that the original and primary modern belief in progress had been shattered by modern intellectual and political developments, including contemporary existentialism. Yet he wondered whether it was not ultimately retained, even within existentialism itself, through the latter's confidence that it was the necessary outcome of all previous human thought and the necessary basis of all present and future human thought. He thus wondered whether the contemporary and radical critique of human thought might not be insufficiently radical and critical and therefore whether it was not necessary to submit its own premises to a critical analysis. To accomplish this it was necessary to call every notion of progress into question, which could be accomplished only by undertaking a thorough and unprejudiced investigation of the thought of the past. It was with this goal and in this spirit that his historical researches were undertaken.[24]

Seen in this light, it is evident that Strauss's historical researches might be regarded, and were perhaps intended to be understood, as a form of contemporary thought. Their historical contribution resembles and responds to the historicizing tendencies of the greatest contemporary or near contemporary thinkers of Strauss's era such as Nietzsche and Heidegger. Moreover, Strauss gave clear if relatively quiet indications that while pursuing his historical research he did not cease to reflect on and refine his understanding of the challenge of contemporary thought.

It is evident that the task Strauss set himself was a monumental undertaking, not only because it embraced the entire tradition of Western thought but because it was obliged to address the tradition with little if any authoritative guidance. For Strauss noted, "With the questioning of traditional philosophy the traditional understanding of the tradition becomes questionable."[25] It is also evident through the large number of books and articles and the multiplicity of subjects, authors, and texts that make up Strauss's corpus. Therefore, the summary of his thought, necessary here, can and will only imperfectly indicate the character of his reflections and conclusions.

Two aspects of Strauss's thought are of immediate help in delineating its general outlines. The first is his concentration on the study of one particular branch of philosophy, political philosophy. This was not a matter of personal or scholarly taste. It arose in the first place from his reflections on contemporary thought and in particular the fact that through contemporary developments philosophy had been called into question not merely as the source of knowledge about any particular subject but as such, i.e. as an activity.

This brought to light the fact that the fundamental question philosophy had perennially faced, if not always consciously and explicitly, is its status as a way of life. Upon reflection, this question proved to be a special and perhaps the highest case of a general question: what is the best way of life or the good life simply? Strauss noted that this question formed the highest theme of morality and politics, thus pointing to the centrality of moral and political reflection and therewith the philosophic centrality of the tradition of political philosophy.

Although the place and role of political philosophy within the tradition of philosophy as a whole had sometimes been over-looked, particularly in contemporary understanding, Strauss confirmed his insight and intuition through the course of his research. This confirmation took the form of a second general conclusion that a radically new reflection upon and answer to moral and political questions was what had launched modern philosophy and indeed modern life. Strauss discovered or rediscovered these origins in the thought of Niccolò Machiavelli.[26]

Through his study of Machiavelli, Strauss concluded that there was a deep and radical divide between modern and premodern thought which was based on Machiavelli's radical reorientation of moral and political reflection. This reorientation was founded in a new view of the place of reason in human nature and human life, a paradoxical view according to which human rationality was grounded in human irrationality. This insight enabled Strauss to understand why modern rationalism had collapsed and been replaced by irrationalism.[27]

Strauss's explanation of the course of modern thought and his elaboration of its historical development and consequences permitted him to concretize the suggestion that the problem of contemporary thought might be traced to and perhaps limited by questionable modern premises and therefore that it might be possible and useful to return to the thought of the past. For Strauss's interpretation of modern thought led to the conclusion that its course and the developments of modern life related to it did not arise as the arbitrary dispensation of a mysterious historical process. Rather, they were the result of a philosophic program or decision or a change in political philosophy that was neither simply philosophically necessary nor in light of its outcome self-evidently politically desirable.

Strauss was thus able to turn to the past and in particular to premodern thought being open to the possibility that it might still have some force as a guide or basis for the contemporary human situation.

Strauss's Jewish Studies

From the perspective of the Jewish situation or crisis, and in light of the problems of contemporary Jewish thought, this implied an attempt to elaborate biblical revelation's view of the world and the best human way of life that would be faithful to its original conception. Among the efforts this obviously entailed was a fresh investigation of the Bible or Torah, which found expression in several articles and lectures. But for guidance and instruction in this effort, Strauss also turned to the great Jewish thinkers of the Middle Ages, above all Maimonides and Halevi.[28]

At first, this procedure seems puzzling or to entail significant problems not unlike the difficulties Strauss discerned in Jewish existentialism. For as everyone knew, or seemed to know, medieval Jewish thought and its interpretation and elaboration of the biblical perspective were mediated by and ultimately dependent on the influence of an alien form of thought—classical Greek philosophy.

Thus Strauss's focus on medieval Jewish thought might seem to be exposed to objections similar to ones he had himself raised with respect to Jewish existentialism. Strauss denied that on the basis of his new understanding of medieval Jewish thought or more precisely medieval Jewish rationalism, an understanding that departed dramatically in form, method, and substance from the view of modern scholarship.[29]

To begin with, Strauss observed from both his study of medieval Jewish texts and modern historical scholarship devoted to them that the latter, despite its claims to historical accuracy, had failed to observe the phenomena of medieval Jewish thought faithfully. It had, to borrow Strauss's characterization of his own early study of Spinoza, understood these texts "too literally because [it] did not read [them] literally enough."[30]

These texts proclaimed immediately and everywhere that they were composed in a manner quite different from contemporary writings, practicing a mode of composition referred to as esotericism. The purpose of this mode of writing was to conceal certain important views from the majority of readers and to reveal them only to that class to whom they were appropriate. The medieval Jewish authors themselves attributed their pursuit of esotericism to the requirements of both the Jewish law and their subject matter. They also indicated that the literary consequences of these requirements were highly unusual and complicated.

Although all of Strauss's scholarly predecessors could not help but be aware of the explicit esotericism of medieval Jewish authors, Strauss concluded that none of them had taken these pronouncements seriously enough. One expression of this failure was the habit of taking the most "philosophic" utterance of these authors as their true view or more generally of believing that all such authors had a "philosophy." Strauss observed that this mode of understanding had more to do with current convention than with the perspective of these authors. It was a literalism that flew in the face of certain other and very literal facts about these texts, literary and substantive. To remedy the deficiencies of our understanding of these texts Strauss devoted enormous labor in observing, elaborating, and explicating their literary characteristics.[31]

The most general and immediate fruit of these labors was the discovery or rediscovery of the fact that the great works of medieval Jewish thought, above all Maimonides' *Guide of the Perplexed*, were not philosophic books in the precise sense of the term but Jewish books. This meant to say that the basic and abiding premise of books like the *Guide* was that there was a fundamental and ineradicable difference between the grounds of philosophy and biblical revelation, and it was the grounds of the latter that were stipulated as primary. These basic characteristics expressed themselves in such things as the fact that the subject of Maimonides' *Guide* was not philosophy but the "science of the Law," or "true science of the Law."[32]

According to Strauss, such books indeed might make use of philosophy, even very extensive use of philosophy, including and most importantly the radical probing and questioning of the premises of biblical revelation. This did not, however, mean that they were philosophic books in the medieval, i.e. strict sense of the term. They began by regarding divine revelation as authoritative, as the beginning point rather than, as philosophy did, from what is evident to all men everywhere. The consequence of their use of philosophy was the radical clarification of the character of biblical revelation. As a result, such books proved to be the most authoritative commentaries on the Bible. The understanding they provided was the best basis and guide for a reelaboration and appreciation of the biblical perspective and provided the soundest possible basis for any serious return to the Jewish thought of the past. Despite the very different form Strauss's own biblical commentaries took, he acknowledged their great debt to the insights provided by medieval Jewish thought.[33]

Moreover there is an additional way in which, according to Strauss, medieval Jewish thought escapes the difficulties of contemporary Jewish thought. Strauss argued, that in the course of exploring the differences and tensions between philosophy and biblical revelation, medieval Jewish thought brought to light an important ground common to both, the theme or problem of divine law. The most striking feature of this account was the claim that law or divine law was a primary, perhaps the primary, problem for classical philosophy, a view alien to contemporary understandings of classical philosophy. Nevertheless, liberated from "the traditional understanding of the tradition," Strauss was able to confirm this view for himself by a fresh study of classical thought.

This confirmation revealed that despite the conflict between biblical revelation and philosophy, they did share a common ground to which revelation had an equal if not greater claim. Indeed, their conflict necessarily presupposed this common ground in the theme of law. For this and other reasons, Strauss was not obliged to understand such roots as medieval Jewish thought had in classical philosophy as the introduction of alien considerations. He could also entertain and pursue the possibility that the recovery of the understanding of the conflict between philosophy and revelation could be the key to the recovery of the "vitality of Western civilization." Precisely what Strauss meant by this statement is, unfortunately, far from clear. The twin foundations of premodern thought still offered different views or answers and thus remained in conflict. Moreover, modern thought and particularly the world it had engendered was a massive contemporary fact. Hence despite and even because of the force of premodern thought, the immediate practical impact of a "return to the past" and even its propriety remained problematic.

What is most immediately clear about what Strauss proposes is the following: it is not only the answers men give that are constitutive of their ways of life but the questions they seek to address. His work had shown that the fundamental question of premodern thought was the question of the best way of life. It also showed that modern thought was grounded in the attempt to turn away from this and related questions. It had undertaken this effort because of its recognition that premodern thought had been unable to provide an absolutely definitive answer to these questions and in the hope that the ones it would pose would be soluble. This, however, had not been the outcome. Rather, modern thought had effectively collapsed. Premodern thought, however, had not. It was both possible and necessary to readdress the question of the best way of life. In doing so, one had access not only to a different form of thought but to the primary experience of man. As a result, however unclear the meaning of the past might be at present, it provided access to a firmer foundation than all the constructions of modern thought, which were now revealed to have been built in sand, and shifting sand at that.

For the Jewish situation, this meant a way of life grounded in the pursuit of the questions raised and addressed by such men as Maimonides and Halevi and the elaboration of the answers provided by the Torah. Strauss's own life offers an example of such a life of reflection and meditation.[34]

Today it is relatively easy to see the contemporary importance of Leo Strauss's reflections, if only in part. That part which is most evidently helpful is his analysis and diagnosis of contemporary Jewish problems, including the problems of contemporary Jewish thought. The problems he observed in the contemporary Jewish situation have not disappeared or been solved but have only increased in extent and gravity. The only problem of Strauss's youth that has disappeared is that of German Jewry, which as Strauss observed was not solved but annihilated. Strauss now seems to have been unusually prescient about the depth and characteristics of the contemporary Jewish crisis.

Perhaps the most obvious contemporary example is the degree to which Strauss foresaw and analyzed the problems that would attend the State of Israel. The complications and tensions arising from the relationship between Zionism and Judaism come increasingly to the fore within Israel as the central spiritual and political dilemma of the state or the theological-political predicament of the Zionist enterprise.

This conflict would not, it is safe to say, alter Strauss's appreciation of Israel and Zionism but would confirm his conclusion concerning it: "Finite, relative problems can be solved; infinite, absolute problems cannot be solved. In other words, human beings will never create a society which is free from contradiction. From every point of view it looks as if the Jewish people were the

Chosen People, at least in the sense that the Jewish problem is the most manifest symbol of the human problem insofar as it is a social or political problem."[35]

A somewhat less obvious if increasingly evident example is the growing impact of existentialism, especially Heideggerian existentialism. As Strauss predicted, this has ceased to be simply a German phenomenon and now appears under a variety of forms such as deconstruction, regnant everywhere in the Western world, including, of course, the English-speaking world. This is particularly significant insofar as the latter is the most ancient home of modern liberalism and the current home of the world's largest Jewish community.

This situation has been greeted with equanimity and even enthusiasm by the majority of intellectual authorities, Jewish as well as non-Jewish. Nevertheless, it presents deep problems and liabilities. For here and now, just as in pre–World War II Germany, this form of thought denies that any principles, including those of liberal democracy and Judaism, have any ultimate intellectual force. All are understood merely to be one or another species of ideology. Such force as they have is a function of the will or commitment invested in them.

The influence of this mode of thought does not offer particularly happy prospects. For Jews the problems it presents are twofold. The transformation of the support for liberal democracy from a matter of principle to a matter of will makes the continuation of liberal democracy a function of the convictions, or for most practical purposes the habits, of the greatest political force. As a minority, Jews never have and never will constitute such a force in and of themselves. Such was always the case, but heretofore they could appeal to their fellow citizens on the basis of principles thought to be binding on all. With the rejection of the principles of liberal democracy they have lost or are losing the grounds of that appeal.

Liberal democracy has suffered many setbacks in the last century, and all have had serious consequences for the political condition of Jews. It is safe to say, however, that a serious change in the character of American political principles would constitute the greatest and perhaps final defeat of modern liberalism and present a very grave threat to the Jewish community. For unlike other countries, such as Germany, where liberalism was an innovation and had to struggle to establish itself, the United States was founded as a liberal democracy and has always been such. Its failure to maintain its original principles would be modern liberalism's ultimate defeat.

The impact of existentialism is not, of course, limited to the non-Jewish world but is increasingly felt within Jewish thought and life. This presents several problems. As Strauss observed, at its root are premises alien to Jewish thought. It also, by denying the force of principle, presents the possibility that Jewish thought and life will become an ever more changing and empty pastiche so that the American Jewish situation may soon come to resemble that combination of political and spiritual dependence Strauss identified as the predicament of German Jewry.

The equanimity and receptivity of some Jews in the face of these developments is for obvious reasons somewhat surprising, but only somewhat. It is in part a testament to the enormous power of that development in contemporary intellectual life which Strauss described as the "the victory of orthodoxy, of any orthodoxy through the self-destruction of rational philosophy." Unfortunately, its force is so great that it has permitted Jews to overlook or neglect Strauss's observation that "Jewish orthodoxy based its claim to superiority to other religions from the beginning on its superior rationality."[36]

Such circumstances constitute the latest embodiment of the theological-political predicament and call for the deepest possible reflection. Whether or not such reflection can affect the material condition of contemporary Jewish life, there is something Jews may do which is entirely in their hands: prepare themselves to understand and face this predicament. For such a task Leo Strauss is one of the most important guides.

Among the many reasons for this is Strauss's deep study of and reflection on the deepest sources of contemporary thought and understanding, its force and temptations, above all the thought of Martin Heidegger. In particular, Strauss probed the significance of the fact that Heidegger's thought claims to be the fulfillment not only of philosophy but of man's religiosity and religious longings.

In a lecture devoted to Heidegger, Strauss once summed up the peculiarly atheistic religiosity or peculiarly religious atheism of Heidegger in the following way. "Being as Heidegger understands it may be described crudely, superficially and even misleadingly (but not altogether misleadingly) by saying that it is a synthesis of Platonic ideas and the Biblical God: it is impersonal as the Platonic ideas and as elusive as the Biblical God."[37]

Seen in this context, Strauss's attempt to respond to the contemporary Jewish and Western crises might be described crudely, superficially, but not altogether misleadingly as follows. The investigation of the thought of the past permits the emergence and elaboration of the view shared by both classical philosophy and biblical revelation that the strictly knowable God will be impersonal and the distinctly personal God will be mysterious. It is this agreement that was the original grounds of the pursuit and fulfillment of Western man's religious longings no less than his philosophic eros, the plane of the Torah's claim to be wisdom in the sight of the nations, no less than Socrates' claim to have a certain kind of human wisdom. Perhaps, then, in this sense the thought of the past may offer some immediate prospect of an alternative Jewish response to the contemporary crisis as well as the prospect of the future vitality of the West.

Notes

1. Published as *Die Religionskritik Spinozas als Grundlage Seiner Bibelwissenschaft: Unter-suchen zu Spinozas Theologisch-politischem Traktat* (Berlin, 1930); English trans. *Spinoza's Critique of Religion* (New York, 1965).
2. Published as *Philosophie und Gesetz: Beitrage zum verstandnis Maimunis und seiner Vorlaufer* (Berlin, 1935). English trans. *Philosophy and Law: Essays toward the Understanding of Maimonides and His Predecessors*, trans. Fred Baumann with a foreword by Ralph Lerner (Philadelphia, 1987).
3. *The Political Philosophy of Hobbes: Its Basis and Its Genesis* (Oxford, 1936). Foreword by Ernest Barker. Reissued with a new preface, Chicago, 1962.
4. *On Tyranny: An Interpretation of Xenophon's Hiero* (New York, 1963); *Natural Right and History* (Chicago, 1953); *Thoughts on Machiavelli* (Glencoe, Ill., 1958); *Persecution and the Art of Writing* (Glencoe, Ill., 1952); *The City and Man* (Chicago, 1964).
5. *The City and Man, On Tyranny, Xenophon's Socratic Discourse: An Interpretation of the Oeconomicus* (Ithaca, 1970); *Xenophon's Socrates* (Ithaca, 1972); *The Argument and the Action of Plato's Laws* (Chicago, 1975); *Socrates and Aristophanes* (New York, 1966).
6. *Thoughts on Machiavelli* (Glencoe, Ill., 1958); *Natural Right and History* (Chicago, 1953); *What Is Political Philosophy* (Glencoe, Ill., 1959); "Note on the Plan of Nietzsche's *Beyond Good and Evil,*" *Interpretation* 3 1973.
7. See Bibliography under Jewish Studies.
8. Many of Strauss's public lectures have been collected and published under the title *The Rebirth of Classical Political Rationalism: An Introduction to the Thought of Leo Strauss*, selected and introduced by Thomas L. Pangle (Chicago, 1989). It contains both previously published and unpublished lectures. See in particular Parts I and Part III, especially "Progress or Return."

. 9. This preface was reprinted as a chapter of Strauss's *Liberalism, Ancient and Modern* (New York, 1968), as "Preface to Spinoza's Critique of Religion."
10. See "Progress or Return," in *Rebirth of Classical Political Rationalism.*
11. Ibid., p. 270.
12. "Preface," *Liberalism*, p. 224.
13. Ibid., pp. 224–27.
14. Ibid., p. 229.
15. Ibid., p. 227.
16. Ibid., pp. 227–30.
17. Ibid., p. 229.
18. Ibid., p. 230.
19. See ibid., pp. 231–139.
20. Ibid., p. 234.
21. Ibid., p. 235.
22. Ibid., p. 256.
23. Ibid., p. 231.
24. See in general "Progress or Return," in *Rebirth of Classical Political Rationalism.*
25. "Preface," *Liberalism*, p. 234.
26. "Niccolò Machiavelli," in Leo Strauss and Joseph Cropsey, eds., *History of Political Philosophy*, 3d ed. Chicago, 1987.
27. *Philosophy and Law*, p. 4, n. 1.
28. Ibid., pp. 3–10.
29. *Persecution and the Art of Writing*, chapter 2, 3, and 4.
30. "Preface," *Liberalism*, p. 257.
31.. Among the fruits of these labors are *Persecutions and the Art of Writing* and "How to Begin to Study *The Guide of the Perplexed*" in Maimonides' *Guide of the Perplexed*, trans. Shlomo Pines (Chicago, 1963), reprinted in *Liberalism.*
32. See esp. "How to Begin to Study *The Guide of the Perplexed.*"
33. "Progress or Return," in *Rebirth of Classical Political Rationalism*, p. 253.
34. For a fuller discussion of Strauss' study of medieval Jewish Thought see Fradkin, H., "Philosophy and Law: Leo Strauss as a Student of Medieval Jewish Thought" *The Review of Politics*, 53:1 pp. 40–52, South Bend, 1991.
35. "Preface," *Liberalism* p. 230.
36. Ibid., p. 256.
37. "An Introduction to Heideggerian Existentialism," in *Rebirth of Classical Political Rationalism*, p. 46.

FOR FURTHER READING

Works by Leo Strauss

"Preface" to *Spinoza's Critique of Religion*, New York, 1965. Reprinted in *Liberalism, Ancient and Modern.* Strauss' intellectual autobiographical statement.

The Rebirth of Classical Political Rationalism: An Introduction to the Thought of Leo Strauss, Chicago, 1989. Selected and introduced by Thomas L. Pangle. An especially helpful collection of lectures on general aspects of Strauss' thought.

Natural Right and History, Chicago, 1953. Strauss' general treatment of the history of political philosophy and in particular the problem of justice.

What Is Political Philosophy?, Glencoe, IL, 1959. This collection includes essays dealing with the problem of political philosophy, as well as modern political philosophy.

Liberalism, Ancient and Modern, New York, 1968. A collection of essays within the overall framework of liberalism and its various interpretations.

The City and Man, Chicago, 1964. A good introduction to the general character of Strauss' interpretation of classical philosophy, containing essays on Plato, Aristotle, and Thucydides.

Jewish Studies

Philosophy and Law: Essays toward the Understanding of Maimonides and his Predecessors, Philadelphia, 1987. This is Strauss' earliest work on medieval Jewish thought and includes a critique of modern scholarly approaches.

Persecution and the Art of Writing, Glencoe, IL, 1952. A collection of five essays, whose subjects are Maimonides, Halevi, Spinoza, and the literary problems of interpreting medieval Jewish thought.

"Progress or Return." A series of lectures delivered at the B'nai B'rith Hillel Foundation, University of Chicago, 1952, and published in its entirety in *The Rebirth of Classical Political Rationalism*, Chicago, 1989, pp. 227–70.

"How to Begin to Study Medieval Philosophy." *The Rebirth of Classical Political Rationalism*, Chicago, 1989.

"How to Begin to Study *The Guide of the Perplexed*" in *Maimonides' Guide of the Perplexed*, Chicago, 1963, pp. xi–lvi. Translated by Shlomo Pines, and reprinted in *Liberalism, Ancient and Modern*, New York, 1968. Strauss' most extensive treatment of Maimonides' thought and the means for understanding its themes and problems.

"On the Plan of *The Guide of the Perplexed*." *Harry Austryn Wolfson Jubilee Volume*, Jerusalem, 1975, pp. 775–791.

"Maimonides Statement on Political Science." *Proceedings of the American Academy for Jewish Research* 22:115–30. Reprinted in *What Is Political Philosophy*, Glencoe, IL, 1959.

"Jerusalem and Athens: Some Preliminary Reflections." In *Studies in Platonic Political Philosophy*, Chicago, 1983.

"Notes on Maimonides' *Book of Knowledge*," *Studies in Platonic Political Philosophy*, Chicago, 1983.

"Notes on Maimonides' *Letter on Astrology*," *Studies in Platonic Political Philosophy*, Chicago, 1983.

"Notes on Maimonides' *Treatise on the Art of Logic*," *Studies in Platonic Political Philosophy*, Chicago, 1983.

"Introductory Essay for Hermann Cohen, *Religion of Reason Out of the Source of Judaism*," *Studies in Platonic Political Philosophy*, Chicago, 1983.

"On the Interpretation of *Genesis*." *L'Homme: Revue Française d'anthropologie* 21:1, pp. 5–36, Paris, 1981. [With French translation.]

Works about Leo Strauss

Deutsch, Kenneth L. and Nicgorski, Walter (editors), "Special Issue on Leo Strauss," *The Review of Politics*, South Bend, 1991.

Pangle, Thomas L., "Editor's Introduction," in *The Rebirth of Classical Political Rationalism: An Introduction to the Thought of Leo Strauss*, Chicago, 1989. Selected and introduced by Thomas L. Pangle.

Pangle, Thomas L., "Introduction," *Studies in Platonic Political Philosophy*, Chicago, 1983.

Pippin, Robert, "The Modern World of Leo Strauss" *Political Theory* 20:3, pp. 448–472, Newbury Park, 1992.

Tarcov, Nathan and Pangle, Thomas L., "Epilogue: Leo Strauss and the History of Political Philosophy," in *History of Political Philosophy*, 3d edition, eds. Leo Strauss and Joseph Cropsey, Chicago, 1987.

Elie Wiesel

ALAN L. BERGER

Elie Wiesel has influenced the post-Holocaust landscape more than any other contemporary Jewish thinker. Wiesel, whose works are permeated by *Ahavat Yisrael* (love of the Jewish people), bears witness to the philosophical and theological uniqueness of the *Shoah* for Jewish life and thought. His writings testify for the lives and dreams of the 6 million victims of the *Shoah*, expose the cruelty of their killers, and reveal the indifference of the onlookers. Wiesel's works raise a host of questions: What kind of God allows the murder of His Chosen People? What is the role of human compassion in redeeming the world? How can the Jewish people relate to the world after Auschwitz? Wiesel, as author, teacher, and messenger, has become synonymous with the contemporary Jewish situation. His insights are stamped with the authenticity of personal witness: Holocaust survivor, present at the creation of the modern State of Israel, and reporter of the spiritual rebellion of Soviet Jewry. Wiesel personifies both the despair and the hope characteristic of the diaspora. His life and works are marked by paradox. A European-born Jew, he exerts enormous influence on American Jews and Christians. Profoundly and essentially Jewish, his works and insights reverberate in much of the best of contemporary Christian theology. Firmly committed to the uniqueness of the Holocaust, Wiesel seeks to elucidate its universal implications.

Biography

Wiesel was born on September 30, 1928 (*Simchat Torah*), in Sighet, Transylvania, the only son of Shlomo and Sarah (there were three sisters, Hilda, Beatrice, and Tziporah). Wiesel's father, although an emancipated Jew (he did not have a beard), served as a communal leader in Sighet and was religious and Jewishly literate. He was fond of cantorial music, and helped his son study Talmud and Kabbalah but insisted that the boy also learn secular subjects such as astronomy, Hebrew literature, and psychology. Shlomo Wiesel forced his son to study modern Hebrew. Wiesel's mother-tongue was Yiddish, although he knew Hungarian and Romanian. Sarah Wiesel was a highly cultured person who read German literature and yet was an ardent follower of Wizsnitz Hasidism. Wiesel reports that her dream was for him to be "both a Ph.D. and a rabbi." As a youth Wiesel lived in a Jewishly insulated world, attended heder and yeshiva, read the Bible, was steeped in Hasidism, and fervently believed in the coming of the Messiah. Wiesel was deeply influenced by the tales he heard from his Hasidic grandfather Dodye Feig, a disciple of the Wizsnitzer rebbe. Years later Wiesel lovingly recreated these stories in his widely acclaimed book *Souls on Fire* (1972). In 1944 the Jews of Sighet were deported to Auschwitz, where Wiesel lost his parents and youngest sister, Tziporah. This shattering experience formed the basis for his stark memoir *Night* (English edition, 1960), which has become a classic of Holocaust literature. The only one of Wiesel's works that directly engages the catastrophe, it reveals Nazism's absolute assault on the Jews and Judaism's covenantal worldview. The flames of Auschwitz consumed Wiesel's pre-Holocaust religious innocence. "The student of the Talmud, the child that I was," he writes, "had been consumed in the flames. A dark flame had entered into my soul and devoured it." His subsequent interrogations of God, which assume various forms of a *din Torah* (divine trial), and man are based on the realization that the *Shoah* is without historical or theological precedent. Wiesel himself views *Night* as the foundation for all his subsequent works.

After liberation, Wiesel refused to return to Sighet and, along with four hundred other child survivors of Buchenwald, arrived in France. There he studied French, the language in which he writes, and supported himself in a variety of ways: as camp counselor, choir director, tutor, and translator. He studied French literature, philosophy, and psychology at the Sorbonne and the University of Paris. In France he began reading non-Jewish sources and was influenced by the works of Albert Camus, Fyodor Dostoevski, André Malraux, Friedrich Nietzsche, and Jean Paul Sartre. The French Catholic writer François Mauriac encouraged Wiesel to write and contributed the foreword to *Night*. In addition to classical and Hasidic Jewish sources, Wiesel acknowledges his admiration for the work of Franz Kafka. Consequently, Wiesel, not unlike Martin Buber and Abraham Joshua Heschel, weaves a Jewish tapestry whose strands contain both Hasidic and existential sources. The result for Wiesel, however, is far greater than the sum of its parts. His insights, frequently expressed in aphoristic form, distill the complexity of contemporary Jewish existence.

Wiesel vowed not to speak or write of the Holocaust for a decade. "Long enough," he recalls, "to learn to listen to the voices crying inside my own. Long enough to regain possession of my memory. Long enough to unite the language of man with the silence of the dead." During this time he traveled to India, where he wrote a treatise on asceticism in Judaism, Christianity, and Hinduism. He became disillusioned with asceticism, however, when observing the disinterest to suffering in India. While there, Wiesel studied English.

During the late 1950s and early 1960s Wiesel traveled widely in his capacity as a journalist for Israeli, French and American newspapers. In 1963 he became a naturalized American citizen. A master teacher, he lectures worldwide. Wiesel's lectures at the 92nd Street YMHA are delivered to standing room only crowds. He published twenty-five of these lectures as *Sages and Dreamers: Biblical, Talmudic, and Hasidic Portraits and Legends* (1991). In 1972 Wiesel became Distinguished Professor of Judaic Studies at City College in New York. Since 1976 he has been the Andrew W. Mellon Professor in the Humanities and University Professor of Religious Studies at Boston University. Three years later he was appointed chairman of the United States President's Commission on the Holocaust, becoming chairman the following year of the United States Holocaust Memorial Council. Wiesel is also the recipient of numerous literary, teaching, and humanitarian awards from universities and organizations both in America and abroad. At a nationally televised White House ceremony on April

19, 1985, President Ronald Reagan presented Wiesel with the Congressional Gold Medal of Achievement. In accepting the award, Wiesel challenged the president to cancel a scheduled visit to the German military cemetery of Bitburg, where members of the SS were buried. Wiesel cited the talmudic dictum of speaking "truth to power." He spoke movingly of justice and memory, admonishing Reagan that the president's place should not be with the killers but with their victims. Wiesel's more than thirty books have been translated into several languages, including Dutch, Japanese, and Norwegian. The global impact of Wiesel's thought was formally recognized with the bestowal of the Nobel Peace Prize on December 10, 1986.

Wiesel's Writings

Wiesel's prolific writings assume many forms: cantatas, dialogues, dramas, essays, memoirs, plays, and novels, all of which he views as extensions of his teaching. These works address three basic issues: the Holocaust and its implications, a recreation of Hasidic tales, and an inspired examination of biblical personalities. A fourth category, works on the struggle of Soviet Jewry, dates from his book *The Jews of Silence: A Personal Report on Soviet Jewry* (1966). All of Wiesel's writings, however, form a *midrash* on the *Shoah*, which the author terms the "dark side of Sinai." Wiesel then re-views all preceding Jewish history in light of the *Shoah*. His writings address a multiplicity of themes: Jewish identity, the possibility of covenantal Judaism after Auschwitz, the role played by Christianity during the Holocaust and the continuing plague of anti-semitism, the relationship of the Holocaust past to any possible human future, the moral obligation of post-Auschwitz literature, and the role of silence in communicating what happened to the Jews of Europe. Wiesel's writings in general, and his novels in particular, are highly symbolic, combining Jewish mystical and French existentialist motifs. Consequently, many readers have misunderstood his theological views. In addition, Wiesel's thought eludes the systematic tendency of traditional philosophical and theological speculation. His is, instead, a literary or narrative theology that is at its most penetrating when raising rather than answering questions. Wiesel as storyteller can ask, and keep on asking, about those issues which lie at the core of post-Auschwitz Jewish existence. Referring to the Holocaust, for example, he observes, "I'm afraid of anyone who comes with a theory, a system, based on that experience. I am suspicious; I don't want theories. I believe the experience was above and beyond theories and systems and philosophies. What remains is the question: How, What and Why?"[1]

The Centrality of the Shoah

Wiesel compares the impact of the Holocaust on Jewish existence to God's Revelation at Sinai. Auschwitz is, for Wiesel, the "most important event in Jewish history and in human history; with the possible exception of Sinai." From the deadly combination of mass death and human indifference, Wiesel believes that a "new philosophy of Jewish existence" based on the experience of the *Shoah* is required. The *Shoah*'s implications are devastating. As Sinai created Jewish life and established guidelines for human behavior, so the Holocaust was designed to obliterate this life and these values. "Auschwitz," writes Wiesel, "signifies death—total, absolute death—of man and of mankind, of reason and of the heart, of language and of the senses. Auschwitz is the death of time, the end of creation; its mystery is doomed to stay whole, inviolate."[2] It is against this background that Wiesel attempts his task of outlining the post-Holocaust contours of covenantal Judaism. Consequently, his works may be seen as nothing less than an attempt at beginning history again by addressing the changed nature of Judaism's basic paradigms. Wiesel boldly emphasizes this conviction, observing, "In the beginning there was the Holocaust. We must therefore start all over again."

God and History: The Covenantal Quandary

Wiesel's understanding of Jewish history reflects the seriousness with which he takes the continuing validity of classical Judaism's covenantal assertions. "As a Jew," he observes, "you will sooner or later be confronted with the enigma of God's action in History." The ancient covenantal promise bound together the choosing God and His chosen people. In return for the Jewish people's protection of God's Torah, God pledged to assume responsibility for protecting the Jewish people. The covenantal paradigm assumes that historical events are undergirded by a sometimes hidden but always divine meaning. Historical events were seen as indicators of divine approbation or disapproval. Prophetic Judaism, seen in this light, was the paradigm for a Jewish theology of history. Wiesel, who frequently cites Jeremiah as well as Job, is heir to this prophetic understanding of history, which is rooted in the questioning of God. Consequently, Wiesel views the Holocaust as a total assault on this biblical understanding of the relationship between historical events and covenantal meaning. Wiesel radicalizes his view, contending that "for the first time in our history, this very covenant was broken. That is why the Holocaust has terrifying theological implications. Whether we want it or not, because of its sheer dimensions, the event transcends man and involves more than him alone. It can be explained neither with God nor without Him."[3] But Wiesel's radical assertion does not mean that covenantal Judaism has come to an end. His subsequent position reflects, instead, an embrace of paradox.

For Wiesel, the "essence of Jewish history is mystical and not rational." Against all logic, Jews and Judaism have persisted in persisting. This mystery is, for Wiesel, "matched only by the Jews' will to survive" in a world that would be more comfortable without them. Wiesel's understanding of the post-*Shoah* covenant rejects such claims of traditional theodicy as the biblical notion of "punishment for sin" (*mipenei hataeinu*) and its more philosophical formulation of suffering as a "reproof of love" (*yessurin shel ahavah*). Instead, his novels reflect the consequences of what the sixteenth-century Kabbalist Isaac Luria termed *shevirat ha-kelim* (the breaking of the vessels), an act that implicitly viewed evil as an element within the divine. This cosmic catastrophe did, however, have a possible remedy. For example, the human task, according to the Lurianic Kabbalah, is to assist God by striving for *tikkun*, a continuous act of mending or repairing the world by raising divine sparks that fell to earth when the vessels broke. By successfully completing this task, asserted Luria, one can bring about the coming of the Messiah. Wiesel has been deeply influenced by the Kabbalistic paradigm. He attests that his Holocaust fiction is "first of all a story of night which the Kabbalah calls *shvirat hakelim*—the breaking of the vessels—that something happened at the origin of creation, a cosmic cataclysm. Our story is of the same nature. Something happened a generation ago, to the world, to man. Something happened to God. Certainly something happened to the relations between man and God, man and man, man and himself."[4]

God and Man: The Covenantal Response

Wiesel's post-Auschwitz narrative theology articulates a position that acknowledges the reality of despair but rejects the view that claims God is dead. Wiesel's covenantal response, however, simultaneously challenges the unshaken faith of an orthodoxy that sees nothing theologically exceptional emanating from the *Shoah*. Concerning the former, Wiesel's 1970 response to Richard Rubenstein deserves attention. "How strange," said Wiesel, "that the philosophy denying God came not from the survivors. Those who came out with the so-called God is dead theology, not one of them had been in Auschwitz. If you want difficulties, choose to live *with* God. Can you compare today the tragedy of the believer to that of the unbeliever?!" The real tragedy, the real drama, is the drama of the believer."[5] Commenting on the certitude of the pious, Wiesel wrote, "If God is an answer, it must be the wrong answer. There is no answer." In *Night*, for example, Wiesel recalls that while in Auschwitz he was forced to watch a young boy being hung. Amid the metaphysical and moral chaos of the death camp, Wiesel remembers responding to the question, "Where is God now?" Wiesel heard a voice within him answer, "Where is He? Here He is. He is hanging here on this gallows." Wiesel's quarrel with God has not diminished, but it has assumed a more subtle form. In his fifth novel, *The Gates of the Forest* (English translation, 1966), for example, Wiesel inextricably binds the destiny of God and man. On one hand, Gregor, the main character, says the *Kaddish*, the mourner's prayer, which Wiesel describes as "that solemn affirmation, filled with grandeur and serenity, by which man returns God his crown and his scepter." The book's epigraph, however, suggests a more intricate relationship between God and man. There Wiesel writes, "God made man because he loves stories."[6] The paradox is that God must eternally listen to tales from the kingdom of night which implicate the Creator of the universe. Wiesel's 1988 novel *Twilight*, situates this divine-human relationship in an upstate New York psychiatric clinic whose patients identify with biblical characters, including God. Raphael

Lipkin, scholar of mysticism and sole survivor of his family which perished in the Holocaust, travels to the clinic searching for the whereabouts of his long lost and mysterious friend Pedro who saved his life during the *Shoah*. At the clinic Raphael interrogates, yet ends by affirming, God. But the way to approach the post-Auschwitz God is by moving closer to man.

Wiesel's gradual theological evolution does not, however, mean that he exonerates God. Instead, Wiesel's image is of a post-Auschwitz deity whose position has been unequivocally compromised. Wiesel, like Job, affirms God but doubts divine justice. The question in Wiesel's works is not, Can there be a Judaism without God? To this query Wiesel answers a resounding no. Rather, the threat to Jewish life and theology resides in the existence of a God who lacks justice. Commenting on his post-Auschwitz understanding of chosenness, for example, Wiesel contends that the Jews may very well be on a "suicide mission." This is the motivation lying behind Wiesel's statement, "My disputation with God still goes on. To me it (the *Shoah*) was an injustice on a theological scale, on a universal scale. God was silent, and therefore His silence was unjust."

The relationship of man to an unjust God is highly complex. Part of the profundity of Wiesel's view on the matter lies in his refusal to permit God's injustice to deter man's belief in the divine. This "protest from within" is a well-established one in Judaism, having biblical, rabbinic, and Hasidic antecedents. In *A Jew Today*, Wiesel cites an episode recorded by an unnamed chronicler from the Middle Ages which provides another example of such protest. It is the tale of Jews who refused to abandon their faith and were exiled from Spain during the reign of Ferdinand and Isabella. The motley group was deposited on a deserted beach and abandoned. Among them were a husband and wife and their two children. The group suffered from hunger and thirst, and their number slowly decreased. As Wiesel poetically writes, "They were four to fall asleep; they were three to rise." On successive mornings, the father dug graves and said *Kaddish* for his wife and his older son. When his younger son died, the father dug a grave and addressed God: "Master of the Universe, I know what You want—I understand what You are doing. You want despair to overwhelm me. You want me to cease believing in You, to cease praying to You, to cease invoking Your name to glorify and sanctify it. Well, I tell you: No, no—a thousand times no! You shall not succeed! In spite of me and in spite of You, I shall shout the *Kaddish*, which is a song of faith, for You and against You. This song You shall not still, God of Israel." And, adds the chronicler, "God allowed him to rise and go, farther and farther, carrying his solitude under a deserted sky." This tale, which is told by Solomon Ibn Verga in his martyrology *Shevet Yehuda* (1520s), illustrates the protest from within that characterizes Wiesel's view of the post-Holocaust relationship between God and man. In Wiesel's words, "One can be a very good Jew, observe all the *mitzvot*, study Talmud—and yet be against God. *Af al pi khen velamrot hakol*—as if to say: You, God, do not want us to be Jewish; well, Jewish we shall be nevertheless, despite your will."[7]

The Paradox of Post-Auschwitz Literature

Can one write about the Holocaust? Reflecting his immersion in the Jewish mystical tradition, Wiesel contends that in transmitting the event one betrays it. The *Shoah* has destroyed language. Wiesel asserts that he "writes against words" because "by its uniqueness the holocaust defies literature." The teller of tales should, instead, convey what happened in the same manner that the Talmud was taught, "transmitted from mouth to ear, from eye to eye." It is in this context that one can begin to understand Wiesel's contention that a theology of Auschwitz is blasphemous and a novel that purports to be about Auschwitz is either not a novel or not about Auschwitz. Yet Wiesel continues to write, and his understanding of the function of literature after Auschwitz deserves careful attention.

Wiesel's novels are offered as testimony. They are written with the bold hope of "saving mankind." The writer, his message, and his view of literature's role are intimately bound to the Holocaust experience. All of his literary figures, their judgments, and ours, must be made against the ominous omnipresence of the *Shoah*. For Wiesel writing is an act of correcting injustice. Consequently, it is not so much a question of whether Wiesel's novels "work," in the literary sense of plot, character, and mood. Although his novels do work in this way, to read them so is to see the trees and miss the forest. The real question is far more profound. Have his readers been transformed? Faithful to his Hasidic beliefs, Wiesel knows that tales have the power to change people. Consequently, the post-Auschwitz writer no longer has the luxury of writing to entertain. Rather, the writer as witness has an altogether different purpose; his mission is to "disturb, alert, awaken, warn against indifference to injustice." Does Wiesel's literature of testimony compel realization that Auschwitz marked a historical turning point, that, in his words, "What died at Auschwitz was not only man, but the idea of man?"[8]

For Wiesel, writing assumes multilayered meanings. It is, on one level, an attempt to "wrench" Holocaust victims from "oblivion." "To help the dead," writes Wiesel, "vanquish death." Perhaps one can, even for a moment, recreate a smile, a tear, or even an entire community. Consequently, Wiesel's novels frequently blur the lines between history and legend. His underlying assumption is the presentness of the past and the mystical bond between all Jews, the dead, the living, and those yet to be born. This assumption emerges with great eloquence in Wiesel's prize-winning novel *A Beggar In Jerusalem* (1970), which was written in part as a reflection on the relationship of Israel's triumph in the Six-Day War to the Holocaust. David, the main character, has a vision in which a preacher observes that Israel defeated its enemies "because its army, its people, could deploy six million more names in battle." The dead of the Holocaust past, in other words, ensure that Israel will win, thereby making possible a Jewish future.[9]

Writing is also Wiesel's way of engaging in a dialogue with his reader, which he compares with that between man and God. Extending Buber's observation, Wiesel writes, "Whenever one man speaks to another, ultimately he involves God." Writing also has salvific import; it is a way of beginning history again. Just as the Talmud was written after the destruction of the second Temple, so now in the wake of the *Shoah*, a new Talmud must be written "to accentuate the new beginning." Wiesel's is, in fact, a "literature of new beginning." He explains what he means: "Just as a religious Jew says *tehillim* every day, we tell our tale every day, again and again, always the same tale, except we begin it anew and shall never end it." Consequently, after the Holocaust there is no longer the possibility of art for art's sake. All literature must be written with the *Shoah* as background.[10]

Memory and Identity

Jewish identity in the age of Auschwitz is a complex issue, one with resonances that are at once personal and national, existential and theological, intensely individual yet fraught with great historic consequences. Wiesel views memory as the key to Jewish identity in the post-*Shoah* world. Memory is endowed with an ontic nature. "If we stop remembering," attests Wiesel, "we stop being." Consequently, memory involves far more than an act of individual consciousness. This appears with special pathos in Wiesel's 1992 novel *The Forgotten*, which tells the tale of Elhanan, a survivor who is losing his memory to Alzheimers. Before the inevitable occurs, he must transmit his memory of the *Shoah* to his son Malkiel who, in turn, travels to the Romanian village of his father's childhood where he encounters truths enabling him to confront the Jewish past and embrace his people's destiny. *The Forgotten* is Wiesel's most clearly wrought portrait of the possibilities and limitations involved in transmitting survivor memory to the second generation witness. Memory, for Wiesel, is the linking of the Jewish generations. "Because of our memory," he observes, "our ranks are thicker, and the density of our experience more exalting."

For Wiesel, *K'lal Yisrael* (the community of Israel) bears both a physical and a metaphysical dimension. Linking this view to memory of the *Shoah*, Wiesel makes both a negative and a positive assertion. First, he writes, "Anyone who does not actively, constantly engage in remembering and in making others remember is an accomplice of the enemy." This is followed by a call to conscience as well as identity: "Conversely, whoever opposes the enemy must take the side of his victims and communicate their tales, tales of solitude and despair, tales of silence and defiance." Distinguishing sharply and irrevocably between survivors and nonwitnesses, Wiesel nevertheless contends that all Jews who seek Jewish and human authenticity must listen to, be transformed by, and in turn, transmit tales of the Holocaust. Here again Wiesel reflects his faithfulness to the Hasidic tradition, which compared the telling of tales to a sacred act. But this is not only a Jewish issue. Wiesel is thinking about all mankind. Memory bears universal salvific weight. For example, the past is a "shield for the future" in the sense that "tales of the Holocaust can prevent a universal holocaust." The Holocaust, in Wiesel's view, can serve either as an end to history's devastation or as a "momentous warning of things to come." Everything depends on Jewish identity, which for Wiesel means Jewish memory.[11]

The Role of Silence

To accomplish his task, Wiesel employs silence the way conventional authors use words. He observes, for example, that he entered literature "through silence"—not the silence of indifference or concealment but the silence of revelation. In *One Generation After*, for example, Wiesel writes that "silence, more than language, remains the substance and the seal of what was once their [the victims] universe, and that, like language, it demands to be recognized and transmitted." Wiesel, here, as elsewhere, reflects his indebtedness to mysticism in which silence plays a crucial role. Always at home in the Bible, Wiesel knows what God said at Sinai but wonders about the silences between words. How did God communicate this silence? Wiesel observes, "This is the silence I tried to put in my work, and I tried to link it to that silence, the silence of Sinai."[12]

Silence is in the title of Wiesel's first book, *Un di Velt Hot Geshvign* (*And the world was silent*). Published in Buenos Aires in 1956 in Yiddish, the book indicts the world's silence during the Holocaust. But it holds aesthetic import for Wiesel's subsequent novels. The 1956 book contains 800 pages. Subsequent editions were much shorter. In 1958 a greatly compressed version of the book was published as *La Nuit* (*Night*) in Paris. The American translation of *Night* is a 120-page memoir. From this experience Wiesel learned that condensing, distilling the essence—silence— is the plumbline of post-Auschwitz literature.

Wiesel explores the theme of silence throughout his work, but especially in his novel *The Oath* (1973). Here the dialectic between speech and silence assumes added post-Holocaust urgency. The sole survivor of a pre-Holocaust pogrom breaks his vow of silence to save the life of his young interlocutor. Silence would have been better, but no one has the right to deprive another of the chance to live. *The Oath* illustrates the tension between words and silence, and the silence of words that characterize Wiesel's narrative theology. Addressing this tension, Wiesel told an interviewer, "I say certain things not to say other words. I write a page and the absence of the Holocaust in it is so strong that the absence becomes a presence."[13]

Messianic and Mystical Responses

For Wiesel, response to Auschwitz remains the single most vexing issue confronting humanity. Although the Holocaust as a historical event ceased in 1945, it continues to take its toll. "One can die in Auschwitz," writes Wiesel, "after Auschwitz."[14] He explores and rejects the options of despair and suicide. Instead, Wiesel suggests that the Jewish tradition provides models of response. He sees such paradigms in mystical madness and in messianism. But both of these models need to be altered in light of Auschwitz.

Wiesel distinguishes three forms of madness: clinical, political, and mystical. Rejecting the first two, he emphasizes the distinctiveness of the third. Mystical madness is associated with redemption and the bringing of the Messiah. It is a madness that affirms faith in God and in man, in spite of (*af al pi khen*) God and man. Mystical madness is based on a prophetic model that insists on upholding the covenantal standard no matter how degenerate a given political climate has become or how absurd the human situation appears. This madness is, in any case, preferrable to the "sanity" of a world in which gas chambers and crematoria can operate with impunity. Wiesel has observed that one has to be mad to seek to change mankind but that there is no other choice. It is, of course, not accidental that mystics and madmen and messianic seekers populate Wiesel's novelistic worlds. Mystical madness is tinged with ambiguity. It is always the mad ones, for example, who announce both the truth of Auschwitz and the hope for the Messiah.

Wiesel's post-Holocaust view of the Messiah simultaneously reflects the millennial passion of the Jewish people in exile and deepens and humanizes the meaning of the Messiah. Wiesel told a 1977 interviewer, "There is something about the Messiah in every one of my tales: in every one of my beggars, my teachers, my wise men, my princes." Wiesel's understanding of messianism is, like all his work, steeped in classical sources. The traditional Messiah, according to the Talmud, is to appear to a generation either wholly guilty or totally without blame (*Sanhedrin* 98a). What does Wiesel mean by messianism? According to Maurice Friedman, Wiesel's is a "messianism of the unredeemed." This messianism underscores the "need to remain human in a world which is inhuman." Wiesel's Messiah is not a transhistorical being but every person who behaves humanely toward other humans. Wiesel's main character in *The Gates of the Forest* observes, "The Messiah isn't one man, Clara, he's all men. As long as there are men there will be a Messiah."[15]

Wiesel, however, is fond of citing the Midrash concerning a new *Sefer Torah*. According to the legend, "Ever since the prophet Elijah ascended into heaven, all he does is go around the world as a chronicler, collecting tales of Jewish suffering. And when the Messiah will come, we are told, Elijah will give him his chronicles, his book of Jewish suffering, and that book will become the new *Sefer Torah*. That book will become the Torah, the New Law, the Messiah's Law. Thus the Messiah will remember our suffering."[16] Wiesel's more developed messianism is based on the act of waiting. *The Fifth Son* (1985), a novel he dedicates to his son and, by implication, all other children of survivors as well as those seeking to walk a post-Holocaust Jewish path, advocates a messianic patience in the face of an unredeemed world.

The Holocaust: Unique and Universal

Wiesel views the Holocaust as the greatest tragedy in Jewish history. Only the Jews were "ontologically threatened." Wiesel has, in a characteristically poignant aphorism, stated the unique position of the Jewish victims. "Not all victims were Jews," he writes, "but all Jews were victims." Wiesel does not intend to forget or dishonor the other victims, but he wishes to underscore that the situations were different. Jews were murdered because of their birth. In a murderous inversion of biblical chosenness, the Nazis became godlike, deciding, in the words of the *Yom Kippur* liturgy, "Who shall live and who shall die." In the *Akedah* (the sacrificial binding of Isaac) of the Holocaust there was no angel to stay the hand and no ram to substitute for the Jewish people. The Holocaust is, for Wiesel, *sui generis*.[17]

Wiesel as an acute and sensitive student of, and participant in, Jewish history is concerned that the uniqueness of the Holocaust will in time become blurred and then forgotten. At first, survivors spoke of the 6 million Jews. Then some people said that others were killed as well. The new formula became 11 million victims, 6 of whom are Jews. Wiesel's concern is that if this progression continues, the next step will be to speak of 11 million. "If everyone suffered," he observes, "then no one suffered." For Wiesel, the distinction is between Jewish victims of the Holocaust and victims of World War II.[18]

The *Shoah* has universal implications, but they reside in its Jewish uniqueness. The survivors' remembering is, for Wiesel, an act of generosity," aimed at saving men and women from apathy to evil, if not from evil itself." Those who are unable to deal with the Holocaust's Jewish specificity aid the murderers by taking "away from the dead the only thing left to them—their Jewishness and their uniqueness." "Don't they," queries Wiesel, "deserve at least that?"[19]

Elie Wiesel's Impact

Wiesel's impact on contemporary Jewish thought has been enormous. He is widely perceived as a *moreh hador* (teacher of the generation), a bridge between an unspeakable past and an un-knowable future that will be forever clouded by that past. Wiesel's thought has considerably enriched Jewish and Christian theology. His model of the post-*Shoah* covenant, for example, has engendered a "school" of neo-Orthodox theologians, most notably Emil Fackenheim and Irving Greenberg, whose works have been deeply influenced by Wiesel's writings. Many in the field of literary criticism have found Wiesel's works and insights indispensable in their own confrontations with the *Shoah*. This same observation is equally valid for Christian theologians with integrity enough to examine the role played by the teachings of their own tradition in paving the way for the *Shoah*. Wiesel's writings have become an indispensable starting point for anyone wishing to think seriously about the *Shoah*'s theological and moral implications. His teachings have as well a remarkable ecumenical attraction that serves to sensitize contemporaries to the reality of evil and suffering and to the continuing pain of Holocaust survivors and their children.

All of Wiesel's writings, his explorations of biblical figures, the

Hasidic movement, Soviet Jewry, and the threat of a nuclear holocaust, reveal his conviction that, on one hand, the unity of Jewish history and the linkage between Jews everywhere must be viewed through the prism of the Holocaust. On the other hand, his works simultaneously convey the growing relationship between the Jewish catastrophe and universal history. Concerning the former, Wiesel attests that authentic Jews are those who embrace a collective memory. He believes "man to be the sum total of his own experiences and those of his predecessors. We were all at Sinai, and in Egypt before that. We all saw the Temple in Jerusalem, both in its splendor and in its flames. We were all in Spain at the time of the Inquisition. We were all in Treblinka."[20] Consequently, his books dealing specifically with the Bible such as *Messengers of God* (1976), *Images from the Bible* (1980), and *Five Biblical Portraits* (1981) speak of the ancients as contemporaries. Their experiences are paradigmatic for subsequent generations of the House of Israel. Wiesel contends, for example, that Isaac is the first survivor and that the tale of the *Akedah* is "the most timeless and relevant to our generation." But there is more. Referring to Cain and Abel, Wiesel observes, "Only today after the whirlwind of fire and blood that was the Holocaust, do we grasp the full range of implications of the murder of one man by his brother, the deeper meanings of a father's questions and disconcerting silences."[21]

Wiesel's retelling of Hasidic tales is accomplished from an insider's perspective and emphasizes both his indebtedness to the Jewish mystical tradition and the enormity of what was lost in the *Shoah*. Although most of his novels are written in the Hasidic manner and all contain Hasidic teachings, three are specifically devoted to the lives and teachings of certain key *zaddikim* (mystical leaders of the Hasidim): *Souls on Fire: Portraits and Legends of Hasidic Masters* (1972), *Four Hasidic Masters and Their Struggle against Melancholy* (1978), and *Somewhere a Master: Further Hasidic Portraits and Legends* (1982). He notes the similarity in the historical conditions that gave rise to eighteenth-century Hasidism and the situation of post-Auschwitz humanity: "Our people had to start over again building upon ruins and unite surviving individuals and decimated communities." Furthermore, with the absolute collapse of reason, people now, as then, need something—or somebody—to bestow meaning so as to avoid despair. Hasidism's stresses on the sacredness of man and the necessity of reaching God through human relations makes it the perfect antidote for an age that has so blemished the notion of life's sanctity. Teaching by means of tales and legends rather than abstractions, the Hasidic movement strove to unite rather than divide people. Wiesel also emphasizes that friendship (*dibuk haverim*) and laughter are crucial to Hasidism. He remembers that during the *Shoah* the Jewish people had no friends and that laughter is a physical expression of spiritual rebellion. The Hasidic imprint is also found in Wiesel's emphasis on messianic waiting.

Retelling the legends and tales of *zaddikim* such as Israel Baal Shem Tov, Nachman of Bratzlav, Menachem-Mendl of Kotzk, Rebbe Pinhas of Koretz, the Holy Seer of Lublin, Moshe-Leib of Sassov, Naphtali of Ropshitz, and others, Wiesel views their teachings and behavior in light of the flames of Auschwitz. To cite but two of numerous examples, he reports the famous "Friday night" incident when Menchem-Mendl of Kotzk extinguished the *shabbat* candles and retreated into twenty years of solitude. After reviewing the various explanatory hypotheses for this antinomian act, Wiesel offers an alternate reading. "Could he have foreseen," asks Wiesel, "that one hundred years after his retreat another fire would set the continent ablaze, and that its first victims would be Jewish men and women abandoned by God and by all mankind?"[22] Wiesel offers a similar explanatory midrash for the atypical behavior of Rebbe Pinhas of Koretz, who may have had a premonition of the German liquidation of Koretz's ghetto.

Wiesel's engagement with Russian Jewry involves both personal reportage (*The Jews of Silence*, 1966) based on his visit to the then Soviet Union a year earlier, a novel, *The Testament* (1980), and a play, *Zalmen, or the Madness of God* (1974). He views the spiritual rebellion of Soviet Jews as exemplifying the protest against both God and man necessary in a world that permitted Auschwitz. The title of his first work is meant as well as an indictment of Western Jewry, which has not, in Wiesel's view, marshaled sufficient support for their Russian counterparts. (Of course, the dramatic dissolution of Communism far outpaces current predictions. Nevertheless, Western Jewry does seem responsive to the very real dangers faced by the Jewish community in the Commonwealth of Independent Nations). *The Testa-*

ment is a fictionalized account of Stalin's murder of Jewish writers in which Wiesel stresses the mysterious continuity of Jewish identity, which frequently operates even against the conscious wish of individual acculturated Jews. Wiesel's play underscores the need for moral madness in a world of moral criminals. The intensity of his involvement with the spiritual uprising of Russia's Jews is seen in Wiesel's insistence that "If I should be remembered—I would hope it would be as a messenger of the young Jews of the Soviet Union."[23]

What is the relation of the *Shoah* to the non-Jewish world? Wiesel, who has frequently been called the "messenger of the dead," addresses this question in a variety of ways, by speaking, teaching, and writing and by his activities on behalf of oppressed and persecuted people everywhere. He views the Holocaust Memorial Museum in universal terms; it is to serve as a warning to all humanity. Symbolically, Auschwitz made Hiroshima possible. The *Shoah*'s Jewish specificity reveals the catastrophe's universal significance. Consequently, for Wiesel memory is not only a response to indifference but contains salvific import. "Memory," he observes, "may perhaps be our only answer, our only hope to save the world from the ultimate punishment, a nuclear holocaust." Wiesel sees the *Shoah*, therefore, as a lightning rod for the human race. Telling tales of what happened during the kingdom of night is thus a desperate attempt to save the world from a final destruction. He is clear on the warning function of the Holocaust Commission. "We do not have this Commission simply to remember but to warn. Last time it was the killing of the Jews, then the attempt to annihilate humanity itself. Between the two came the sin of indifference. Today when we hear the word 'holocaust' it is preceded by the word 'nuclear.' We hope this mission is a beginning. For if we forget, the next time indifference will no longer be a sin. It will be a judgment."[24]

Wiesel believes that "existentially the world has turned Jewish." This remark was made in the context of the Jewish people having lived on the edge of extinction for two thousand years; their fate was in the hands of others. Now, with the advent of nuclear bombs, the entire world knows what it means to have one's fate determined by unseen hands resting on hidden buttons. Yet Wiesel fights against despair. He views this struggle as the essence of the writer's task. He told a 1972 interviewer that

"Albert Camus said, 'In a universe of misfortune one must create happiness.' That is what I am trying to do—to create a meaning in a universe that has no meaning." It surely is not accidental that Wiesel's most sustained novelistic treatment of this issue comes in his book *The Fifth Son*, which is dedicated to the second generation (children of survivors). Here Wiesel has Ariel, son of survivors and himself a college professor, state: "From afar I glimpse the immense shadow, not unlike a monstrous, poisonous mushroom, linking heaven and earth to condemn and destroy them." But Ariel is a teacher, and his message and warning will continue to be given and to be heard. All of Wiesel's writings and stories can be seen as his self-described attempt to "make Jews better Jews, Christians better Christians, and men a little bit warmer so they do not feel crushed by their own solitude."[25]

There are, however, certain difficulties with Wiesel's view. For example, his insistence that the Holocaust teaches nothing has been challenged on a variety of fronts, not the least of which is his own attempt to articulate its universal implications. Second, by equating the *Shoah* with an eternal mystery, he prejudges the value of historical scholarship in making genuine contributions to our understanding of events. Wiesel's position also appears anathema to Orthodox Judaism, which does not see the Holocaust as a question about God but rather views it as an example of human evil. Many in the Orthodox community think that Wiesel's literary recreations fly in the face of halakhic (normative) Jewish prescriptions about the uniqueness of divine revelation and about God's relationship to history, as well as man's relationship to the divine. The image of God present in Wiesel's works may also be challenged for being too subjective. Wiesel's theology of history may be poetic, but it has little to do with classical Judaism. His belief that a philosophy of Judaism can emerge from the experience of the *Shoah* also appears suspect to those for whom the redeeming God of Sinai is the salvific paradigm. Moreover, Wiesel's critique of the lack of action on the part of the American Jewish community during the war seems to overlook the political weakness of the community at that time. Because he is a mystic, moreover, Wiesel's point of view will elude the grasp of some. His symbolism may be too secret, his silence too silent.

Wiesel has, nevertheless, made substantial and long-lasting contributions to the discussion of post-Auschwitz Judaism. No one has done more to etch the memory of the tragedy into human consciousness. Moreover, Wiesel's insistence on the moral role of the artist is a welcome and necessary antidote to contemporary literary nihilism. His ability to question God from within the tradition, however, is what makes Wiesel's voice so resonant. In *One Generation After*, for example, Wiesel writes a prayer in his diary: "I no longer ask You to resolve my questions, only to receive them and make them part of You." Wiesel's theological fervor enhances his complexity.

His insights into the relationship between Jewish history and Jewish destiny serve to heighten awareness of moral responsibility. He asks in a characteristically disarming way, what right he has to put an end to three thousand years of Jewish history by refusing to have children. Moreover, Wiesel has written on Jewish identity in a manner that makes it a Jewish obligation to remain Jewish by testifying and telling the tales of the *Shoah*. In so doing, he asserts, Jews make the world more human. In the final analysis, Wiesel's work is a powerful comment on the existential and theological quandaries that face those who, after Auschwitz, are committed to walk the covenantal path and find themselves torn between the demands of ancient and modern worlds.

Notes

1. Harry James Cargas, ed., *Harry James Cargas in Conversation with Elie Wiesel* (New York, 1976), p. 106.
2. Elie Wiesel, *A Jew Today*, trans. Marion Wiesel (New York: Vintage Books, 1979), p. 234.
3. Elie Wiesel, "Jewish Values in the Post-Auschwitz Future," *Judaism*, 16 (Summer 1967): 291.
4. Cargas, ed., *Cargas in Conversation with Wiesel*, p. 85.
5. Elie Wiesel, "Talking and Writing and Keeping Silent," in Franklin H. Littell and Hubert G. Locke, eds., *The German Church Struggle and the Holocaust* (Detroit, 1974), pp. 271, 274.
6. Elie Wiesel, *Night*, trans. Stella Rodway (New York, 1969), p. 76; Wiesel, *The Gates of the Forest*, trans. Frances Frenaye (New York, 1982), p. 225 and Epigraph.
7. Elie Wiesel, *A Jew Today*, trans, Marion Wiesel (New York, 1979), p. 164; Wiesel, "Jewish Values in the Post-Holocaust Future," p. 299.
8. Wiesel, *A Jew Today*, p. 171; Irving Abrahamson, ed., *Against Silence: The Voice and Vision of Elie Wiesel* (New York, 1985), 3:161; Wiesel, "A Personal Response," *Face to Face* VI (New York, Spring, 1979), 36; Wiesel, *Legends of our Time*, trans. Steven Donadio (New York, 1982), p. 190.
9. Elie Weisel, "Why I Write," trans. Rosette C. Lamont in Alvin Rosenfeld and Irving Greenberg, eds., *Confronting the Holocaust: The Impact of Elie Wiesel* (Bloomington,

1978), p. 206; Wiesel, *A Beggar in Jerusalem*, trans. Lily Edelman and Elie Wiesel (New York, 1985), p. 202.

10. Cargas, ed., *Cargas in Conversation with Wiesel*, p. 6; Abrahamson, ed., *Against Silence*, 1:325.

11. Abrahamson, ed., *Against Silence* 1:368; 2:104; 3:177; Wiesel, "A Personal Response," 37; Abrahamson, ed., *Against Silence*, 3:153.

12. Wiesel, "Why I Write," p. 200; Wiesel, *One Generation After*, trans. Lily Edelman and Elie Wiesel (New York, 1982), p. 198; Abrahamson, ed., *Against Silence*, 1:273.

13. Abrahamson, ed., *Against Silence*, 3:243.

14. Wiesel, *One Generation After*, p. 169.

15. Maurice Friedman, *Abraham Joshua Heschel and Elie Wiesel: You Are My Witnesses* (New York, 1987), p. 233; Wiesel, "The Gates of the Forest."

16. Irving Abrahamson, ed., *Against Silence*, 1985, 3:47.

17. Abrahamson, ed., *Against Silence*, 3: pp. 146, 172.

18. Abrahamson, ed., *Against Silence*, 3:156; 3:314.

19. Abrahamson, ed., *Against Silence*, 3:161; 1:207.

20. Abrahamson, ed., *Against Silence*, 57.

21. Elie Wiesel, *Messengers of God: Biblical Portraits and Legends*, trans. Marion Wiesel (New York, 1976), pp. xiii–xiv.

22. Elie Wiesel, *Souls on Fire: Portraits and Legends of Hasidic Masters*, trans. Marion Wiesel (New York, 1972), p. 254.

23. Abrahamson, ed., *Against Silence*, 3:316.

24. Abrahamson, ed., *Against Silence*, 1:162.

25. Abrahamson, ed., *Against Silence*, 1:255; 3:213; Wiesel, *The Fifth Son* trans. Marion Wiesel (New York, 1985), p. 219; Abrahamson, ed., *Against Silence*, 2:152.

FOR FURTHER READING

Works by Elie Wiesel

A Jew Today, New York, 1979. Translated by Marion Wiesel. This work is the focal point of Wiesel's collections of dialogues, essays, and reflections. The book contains powerful statements on the nature of Jewish identity, the Jewish mission to the world, and penetrating moral critiques of contemporary society.

Evil and Exile, with Phillippe de Saint-Cheron, Notre Dame, 1990. This book reports six days of interviews Wiesel granted to the French journalist. Wiesel reflects on the survivor mission, the Sh'ma Yisrael prayer as one of defiance, and the meaning of the Holocaust for world history. He also provides an evocative look at his relationship to the State of Israel and the nature of Jewish-Christian relations after Auschwitz.

From Kingdom of Memory, New York, 1990. These reminiscences constitute a verbal collage of Wiesel's concerns. His essay on belief reiterates the author's long-held view that what happened in the kingdom of night eludes articulation. The book also contains riveting dialogues between the child and his grandparents and the child and the mob. Wiesel's Nobel Address and Lecture emphasize that, like Job, contemporary Jews must see that faith is at heart a rebellion and that memory compels the Jewish people to have hope beyond despair.

Legends of Our Time, New York, 1968. Translated by Steven Donadio. A series of reflections based on Wiesel's premise that after Auschwitz there is need for a new type of mythopoetry based on the assumption that "some events do take place but are not true; others are—although they never occurred." In his essay "A Plea for the Dead," Wiesel decries the obscenity of blaming the dead for their own murder.

One Generation After, New York, 1970. Translated by Lily Edelman and Elie Wiesel. In this collection of essays, twenty-five years after the catastrophe, the author wonders if society has learned any moral lessons. He concludes in the negative. His essay "To a Young Jew of Today," however, emphasizes the centrality of the Holocaust for the Jewish identity of all Jews, even those born after the event.

Paroles d'étranger: Textes, Contes, Dialoques, Paris, 1982. This collection reveals the wide range of Wiesel's concerns and how they are linked by his reading of Jewish history. Consequently, whether he is describing the Hasidic ambience of Brooklyn or the suffering of the Cambodian people, the author's outlook is pervaded by a sense of moral urgency and a desire to protest all forms of injustice. Wiesel states the post-Auschwitz Jewish theological quandary in writing that whoever praises God for Jerusalem and fails to interrogate Him about Treblinka is a hypocrite.

The Six Days of Destruction, with Albert H. Friedlander, Mahwah, NJ, 1988. Subtitled "Meditations toward Hope," this volume addresses Wiesel's greatest fear, the fear that the Holocaust will be forgotten. Thus in a reversal of the Biblical paradigm of the six days of Creation, the present volume retells the story of the fate of European Jewry through the eyes of individual Jews who are, in fact, all the *Shoah's* victims. The book concludes with specially written *Yom HaShoah* liturgies for both Jewish and interreligious communities; the latter written by Eugene J. Fisher and Rabbi Leon Klenicki.

Works about Elie Wiesel

Abrahamson, Irving, ed., *Against Silence: The Voice and Vision of Elie Wiesel*, 3 vols., New York, 1985. This is an indispensable collection of Wiesel's lectures, interviews, dialogues, reviews, and other works. From now on every serious study of Wiesel's thought must refer to this work.

Berenbaum, Michael, *The Vision of the Void: Theological Reflections on the Works of Elie Wiesel*, Middletown, CT, 1979. A study of Wiesel acknowledging his centrality as post-Auschwitz thinker, while arguing that he radically erodes traditional Jewish faith in suggesting an additional covenant.

Brown, Robert McAfee, *Elie Wiesel: Messenger to All Humanity*, Notre Dame, 1983. A sensitive and moving reading of Wiesel's novels by a prominent Protestant thinker. Brown, who served with Wiesel on the U.S. Holocaust Memorial Council, demonstrates the universal implications of the Nobel laureate's works.

Cargas, Harry James, ed., *Harry James Cargas in Conversation with Elie Wiesel*, New York, 1976. A wide-ranging discussion that includes both biographical information and philosophical ruminations. Among the crucial issues discussed are Wiesel's understanding of the writer's post-Holocaust role and the influence of Jewish mysticism on his works.

Cargas, Harry James, ed., *Responses to Elie Wiesel: Critical Essays by Major Jewish and Christian Scholars*, New York, 1978. This important collection of essays reflects Wiesel's impact on the interfaith community of scholars. Especially revealing are conversations with Lily Edelman and the book's editor in which Wiesel speaks about his obsession to transmit the Jewish tale and the meaning of Jewish identity after the Holocaust.

Cargas, Harry James, ed., *Conversations with Elie Wiesel*, South Bend, IN, 1992. The second edition of Cargas' 1976 work contains eight additional interviews. Wiesel offers keen insight on various crucial issues including the relationship between Jewish particularity and universal human meaning, the father/son theme in his writings, and responding to Holocaust deniers. Wiesel defines a Jew according to three relationships: to God, to the Jewish People, and especially to memory.

Fine, Ellen, *Legacy of Night: The Literary Universe of Elie Wiesel*, Albany, 1982. An excellent study, perhaps the best, of the literary themes such as the concept of the "dead town," the "witness and his double," and the idea of the "surviving voice" which permeate Wiesel's novels.

Friedman, Maurice, *Abraham Joshua Heschel and Elie Wiesel: You Are My Witnesses*, New York, 1987. A humane and personal treatment of two of twentieth century Judaism's most significant thinkers. The book is especially helpful in understanding Wiesel's importance for diaspora Jewry. Friedman, the noted Buber scholar, contends that Wiesel's is a message for all contemporary humanity.

Rosenfeld, Alvin, and Irving Greenberg, eds., *Confronting the Holocaust: The Impact of Elie Wiesel*, Bloomington, 1978. A collection of essays that grew out of a symposium held at Indiana University. The topics reflect interdisciplinary, international, and interfaith efforts; the focus is on both literary themes and theological issues. The text includes a personal statement by Wiesel, "Why I Write."

Roth, John K., *A Consuming Fire: Encounters with Elie Wiesel and the Holocaust*, Atlanta, 1979. This work examines the impact of Wiesel's thought on Christians of conscience and the entire fabric of American religious life. The author argues that authentic post-Auschwitz Christians need to follow Wiesel's model of contending with God.

Michael Wyschogrod

DAVID R. BLUMENTHAL

Michael Wyschogrod has distinguished himself in three areas: as a contemporary philosophical theologian, as a spokesperson within modern Orthodoxy, and as an active participant in Jewish-Christian dialogue. Each of these areas must be examined to obtain the broad picture of the man.

Biographical Sketch

The facts of Wyschogrod's life are rather straightforward. He was born in Berlin in 1928 and was educated in the Hildesheimer school system there. His family fled to America in 1939 and, after a period in public school, he attended Yeshiva Torah Vodaath, an Orthodox school. In 1946, he began attending City College of New York, where he majored in philosophy. He went on to Columbia University to complete his Ph.D. in 1953. During his undergraduate and graduate years, he studied at Yeshiva University with Rabbi Joseph Soloveitchik. After completing his Ph.D., Wyschogrod embarked upon a career of teaching. He is currently professor of philosophy at Baruch College in New York.[1]

Wyschogrod is married to Edith Wyschogrod, a well-known philosopher, who has specialized in French phenomenology, having worked on Levinas and now on Derrida. They have two grown children.

As a Contemporary Philosophical Theologian

Wyschogrod's magnum opus is *The Body of Faith: Judaism as Corporeal Election* (New York, 1983; hereafter page references are given in the text). The book is Israel-centered. It is written out of the existence of the Jewish people; it is not an intellectualist, scholastic enterprise. *The Body of Faith* has one thesis: that the Jewish people is the dwelling place of God in the world; all the rest is commentary, a series of meditations on the scandal of chosenness in the light of reason, the Holocaust, Hegel, Heidegger, the State of Israel, Christian Scriptures, Barth, Buber, and traditional Jewish texts.[2]

Right at the beginning, Wyschogrod sets forth the basic metaphor, and it recurs with considerable literary power: that light implies darkness and darkness implies light. Philosophically this means that the light of reason or consciousness has two limits. First, reason is embodied, that is, it is contained within the limits of human perception and thought. Reason does not exist independent of human experience but through it. The body mediates reason. Second, reason must come up against the holy, which is itself not a form of reason. The holy is an awareness, a type of consciousness, which humans must experience. After experience, they can think about, or reason about, the holy. But holiness itself precedes reason or is not a part of reason. The existence of these limits on reason does not lead to despair but to a sense that, in human existence, light and darkness, consciousness and embodiedness, reason and experience are inextricably intermingled.

This metaphor of intertwined light and darkness lays the ground for the assertion that God's choosing a body, the seed of the Jewish people, is part of the reality of creation as God intended it. God chose the embodiedness of creation in general and of the Jewish people in particular. Embodied chosenness is structural to creation, to being. For this reason, "delicatessen Judaism" or the "Jewish face" is as much a part of the body of Israel as Jewish intellectualism and spirituality, even though the former do not seem to meet the criteria of light (26–27).

Wyschogrod ponders this embodied chosenness in the perspective of biblical Protestant theology, the Holocaust, and Eastern religions: [1] God chose the seed of Abraham, not because he rejected idolatry but because God loved Abraham. In a sharp appeal to Karl Barth, the great Protestant theologian of this century, Wyschogrod demands that these biblical indications of God's will be taken seriously. [2] Interpreting the Holocaust, Wyschogrod argues that the absolutism of Hitler's war against the Jews, the hatred of Jews that had no bounds, means that Hitler was really at war with God, trying to destroy God's embodied presence in the world. [3] Arguing against the otherworldly religion of Buddhism and Christian Scriptures, Wyschogrod notes that the measure of God's love is children, not eternal salvation. Abraham is offered seed, not escape from this life (123). History, not eternity, is God's arena. Redemption is political, not spiritual (178).

Wyschogrod then turns to Heidegger, regarded by many as the most influential philosopher of the twentieth century. Wyschogrod acknowledges and interprets Heidegger's Nazism (158–60), but he also offers a threefold biblical-theological critique of Heidegger's ontology: being in Heidegger is purely numinous or transcendental; it is not personal. Heidegger's being is monistic and hence transcends even God. And being purely ontological, it is without a sense of right and wrong; it is deethicized or amoral. All these qualities are completely incompatible with the loving, concrete presence of God as taught by traditional Judaism.

Wyschogrod then deals with deontology, which is Heidegger's activist program for living within his ontology. Deontology advocates a breaking of being by action (155–60). It calls for a sanctioning of violence as the only means of breaking out of the monistic ontology into life. Heidegger roots his ethics in deontological violence. This explains, in part, Heidegger's accommodation to Nazism. Again Judaism, which understand all being as created being, does not agree. Violence which breaks creation denies creation; this is sin.

Turning to and arguing against existentialist philosophies of despair and cynicism, Wyschogrod points out that the death of an animal means more to us than the breaking of a rock, and the corpse of a human being has more sanctity than the corpse of an animal; that is, some things mean more to us than others. Theologically stated, God's presence is more intensely present in some things than in others and, for that reason, they mean more to us than others. Put another way, God's presence lends meaning to our existence and protects us against meaninglessness (115–16).

Wyschogrod critiques Buber as too impersonal. Given the anthropopathism of biblical and rabbinic tradition, God cannot be demythologized (84, 169–72).

Acknowledging the need for the law and for interpretation, Wyschogrod notes that election transcends the law because God did not choose a teaching but a people. He then points to "the disobedience of orthodox Judaism," which has allowed the law to become self-sufficient, weakening the sense of responsibility to the God Who elected the people, not just to the revealed law (184–90, 207, 213). Wyschogrod does not give specific examples of this cult of the law in contemporary orthodoxy; he should have. A straightforward condemnation of specific practices (the question of who is Jew, the status of non-Orthodox Jews in Israel, the use of Nazi epithets by Jews to describe other Jews) would have made his point very clear and relevant.

Finally, "authenthic Judaism must be messianic Judaism. Messianic Judaism is Judaism that takes seriously the belief that Jewish history, in spite of everything that has happened, is a prelude to an extraordinary act of God by which history will come to its climax and the reconciliation between God and man, and man and man, realized. Messianism is therefore the Jewish principle of hope.... Beyond that, messianism is the principle of life in Judaism, preventing the past from gaining total hegemony over the present. Because there waits in the future a trans-formation of the human condition such as has never been known before, the past has only limited significance as a guide to the future" (254–56).

If there is a second major thesis in *The Body of Faith*, it is contained in chapter 3, though it is also scattered throughout the book. It is that "to believe in God is to have a psychological relationship with God" (91). This includes thinking about God but also having feelings about God, negative as well as positive. Our relationship with God calls upon the whole of the human personality—trust, suffering, prayer, love, anger, fear, and so on. Similarly, the God of biblical and rabbinic religion is anthropo-pathic. God too has a personality and experiences trust, suffering, love, anger, even fear, weakness, and frustration. This personal dimension of God's embodiedness is best seen in the term used by traditional Jews to address God: Hashem (literally, the Name) but used in an intimate, relational sense (92). God and humankind also share unpredictability as a character trait. Wyschogrod leaves some questions open: God knows loneliness and companionship, but can God know the companionship of sexuality? God knows fear for creation, but can God know the fear of death?

The Body of Faith is a very deep and complex book. Its very structure appears to wander over an irregular map; it needs to be read more than once, and not all at once. But there are also basic criticisms: [1] What is the relationship between election and revelation, between the body and the law? More needs to be said. [2] What is the status of Jewish non-Orthodox theologies? What truth value do they have? [3] What is the truth status of non-Jewish religions and their role in God's embodied history of redemption? [4] The book does not reveal the dimension of personal piety which is crucial to Jewish religious self-understanding.

Finally [5], women have pointed out that Wyschogrod's book is extraordinarily androcentric. The main image is the seed, not the egg; the body, not the womb. The God is the God of the patriarchs, and not the matriarchs. Revelation and tradition derive from men, not women. Women have charm and produce children, not spiritual or intellectual works. In the concentric circles of closeness to God, women are further removed than men. Indeed, the entire structure and language are very authoritarian, patriarchal. Wyschogrod pleads guilty: the feminist issue was not on his mind as he wrote this book over ten years; he favors the old-fashioned ways of being and expression, even though women are certainly as much a part of the embodied presence of God as men.

As a Spokesperson within Orthodoxy

Wyschogrod, who has been a member of the editorial boards of *Tradition* (the organ of American Orthodoxy) and *Judaism* (a nonsectarian publication), sees himself primarily as a philosopher-theologian and differentiates himself from others as follows: Irving Greenberg is an important leader in Jewish communal affairs but has no special training in philosophy. David Hartman has philosophical training and tends toward the classical philosophic Judaism of Maimonides. Joseph Soloveitchik, although earlier trained in philosophy, is primarily a halakhist and very high-level interpreter of Jewish texts. Wyschogrod's own contribution, then, is in the interstice between contemporary philosophy and Jewish existential theology.

There is great diversity within American Orthodoxy today. There is the Orthodoxy of Yeshiva University, urging a mixture of secular and Jewish learning, Hebrew-speaking, strongly Zionist. And there is the ultra-Orthodox yeshiva world, urging a rejection of secular learning, Yiddish-speaking, and non-Zionist, even anti-Zionist. (Interestingly, the *Artscroll* press occupies a middle road. It produces work in English yet the material is ultra-Othodox. The press has even produced two versions of its prayerbook, one with the prayer for the State of Israel, which is sensitive to the Zionist element, and one without, rejecting the Zionist element.) Wyschogrod considers the "return to Judaism" movement as part of the general swing from the Enlightenment. Any return is to be welcomed, but in the long run, the movement will not be statistically significant though exceptional individuals will be involved in it.

As a Zionist, Wyschogrod regrets that he did not stay in Israel when he taught there at Bar Ilan University in 1957–58 and was offered a position. He does not believe anyone is authorized to say whether the State of Israel is a messianic state, and he would feel better if the official formula of the Israeli rabbinate that the State of Israel is "the beginning of the growth of our redemption" would read "may it be the beginning of the growth of our redemption." Wyschogrod also points to the danger of messianic fervor which is blowing in the wind in today's political climate. Contemporary Jews who go to settle in Israel go there to settle in the land of Israel and not in the State of Israel, that is, they go to settle in a place that has religious, not just historical, significance. There is thus a subtle messianic nuance to such settlement. Jews who refuse to trade land for peace do so on messianic grounds; this is dangerous.

Wyschogrod is not against all accommodation though he feels that only those who must actually give up land should make the decision. Nonetheless, peace and saving lives, both Jewish and Arab, is more important than sovereignty over the land in pre-messianic times. And that is the point: these are premessianic times and hence Orthodox Jews should be willing to trade peace for land.

Wyschogrod also feels that, though there will be civil protest by Jews against policies of the Jewish state and even against the acts of other Jewish groups, there will be no open civil war among Jews, no matter how bad things get. Naturally, one ought to be sensitive to Palestinian suffering, but as long as their expressed wish is to eradicate the Jewish state, one must be very, very cautious.

The most serious question facing modern Orthodoxy is the question of truth. The Torah is truth, but Orthodoxy does not always face other issues of truth: the genesis of the text of the Talmud or the Tanakh or the evidence of archaeology. Orthodoxy must be in the forefront of those reverently seeking truth.

The second most serious question is the one of religious certainty. It is a complex issue. First, too many Orthodox Jews are too secure, and there is no security before God. God is a God of surprises; we must expect the unexpected from the living God. Furthermore, because God is a God of surprises, His Torah cannot be frozen into rigid orthopraxy. Second, excessive security brings with it an arrogance of Torah, a looking down on those who have less knowledge of the law, a derogation of others who are also God's chosen people. Third, this overly secure and arrogant attitude of many Orthodox Jews seems to be the flip side of the fact that an overwhelming percentage of Jewry has ceased being Torah-observant. The drop away from halakhic living by so many Jews seems to have paralyzed many of those who remain. This constellation of attitudes, Wyschogrod feels, is a serious problem within modern Orthodoxy.

As an Active Participant in Jewish-Christian Dialogue

Wyschogrod has been very active in the area of Jewish-Christian dialogue. He was a senior consultant on interreligious affairs for the Synagogue Council of America, a consultant on Jewish and interreligious affairs for the American Jewish Congress, and the director of the Institute for Jewish-Christian Relations of the American Jewish Congress. He has been on the editorial boards of the *Journal of Ecumenical Studies* and *Kirsche und Israel*. He has taught at the Heidelberg College of Jewish Studies, at the Theological Faculty in Lucerne, at the Kirchliche Hochschule in Wuppertal, and at Princeton Theological Seminary.

Wyschogrod has also served as a Jewish consultant to various Vatican committees and to the Presbyterian church. He has coedited three books in this area: *Jews and "Jewish Christianity"* with David Berger (New York, 1978); *Das Reden vom einen Gott bei Juden und Christen* with Clemens Thoma (Bern, 1984); and *Understanding Scripture: Explorations of Jewish and Christian Traditions of Interpretation* with Clemens Thoma (New York, 1987). He has published numerous articles and book reviews in this field, and a sizable portion of *The Body of Faith* is devoted to reading the corporeal election of the Jews over against Christian sources.

This interest derives from Wyschogrod's early work on Kierkegaard (*Kierkegaard and Heidegger: The Ontology of Existence* [London, 1954; reprinted New York, 1970]). Having been brought up in Germany, Wyschogrod is fluent in German and hence has been able to maintain multilingual contacts. He feels that his particular strength is that he can present traditional Judaism in a way that is understandable to Christians without significant distortion. Using the language of the other enables dialogue because Christians have their own categories, which need to be addressed if two-way conversation is to take place.

Asked whether this discussion is a dialogue of the elites or whether it has enough practical significance to head off another Holocaust, Wyschogrod maintains that no one knows how to prevent another Holocaust. But he feels, first, that Christians today are more likely to have a positive picture of Jews and Judaism than in any other time in Christian history. He also thinks that, were there a sudden surge in virulent anti-Semitism, Christian resistance would be greater, not only because of the ongoing dialogue but also because of the Holocaust and the study of the Christian roots of anti-Semitism that that has provoked. Finally, he feels it is irresponsible to play the insulted and injured party and walk away from dialogue as, for example, Eliezer Berkovits has done. It is also religiously impermissible because one must always be ready to help a person who wants to repent, even a non-Jew and even if the repentance is not perfect.

Wyschogrod thinks that the posturings and the political, negotiatory nature of dialogue is discouraging. But there are encouraging signs too. The only way to deal with this aspect of dialogue is to be honest. Wyschogrod and I served together as consultants to the Presbyterian church in writing its recent document on

Christian-Jewish relations, and, though the final document is not what we had hoped for theologically or politically, the dialogue in the various committees did enable us to point out that, theologically, God's covenant with the Jews is for progeny *and* for land and that, politically, the secure, continued existence of the State of Israel is the litmus test of Jewish existence and loyalty. A truly dialogic document in Christian-Jewish relations cannot be written today if it ignores these issues, no matter how theologically elegant or politically astute such an attempt may be.[3] Similarly, Wyschogrod's continuing work with the Catholic church, in spite of its nonrecognition of the State of Israel, has, he feels, the long-range effect of establishing contacts, of education, and of sharing—and no one knows what the future holds.

Finally, the impulse to dialogue is also rooted in theology:

> As a father, God loves his children and knows each one as who he is … because a human father is a human being … it is inevitable that he will find himself more compatible with some of his children than others and, to speak very plainly, that he will love some more than others … it is also true that a father loves all his children so that they all know of and feel the love they receive, recognizing that to substitute an impartial judge for a loving father would eliminate the preference for the specially favored but would also deprive all of them of a father. The mystery of Israel's election thus turns out to be the guarantee of the fatherhood of God toward all peoples, elect and nonelect, Jew and gentile. (*Body*, 64–65)

The truth status of Christianity within Judaism is not a fashionable question, but it is an important one. Traditional Jewish thought is divided, and Wyschogrod hopes to devote his next book to that subject.

Conclusion

One can quarrel with Wyschogrod on many issues; no oeuvre is so complete that it cannot be challenged. Yaakov Elman has put the Orthodox critique clearly in saying that Wyschogrod did not address an Orthodox audience in the traditional way: he did not touch base with the classic sources, frequently not citing his rabbinic references. He did not indicate his "party allegiance" within the Orthodox community. He did not locate himself in the spectrum of traditional Jewish philosophy. He did not deal with specifically halakhic issues. His emphasis on the renewal of Jewish art is frivolous. And he did not use a Jewish publisher. These are not serious criticisms.

Arnold J. Wolf has put the liberal critique well: Wyschogrod has not properly appreciated the positive effect of the Jewish alienation from traditional culture. Wolf does not say it, but I suspect he would reject the divine origin of Jewish particularity (at least in the sense in which Wyschogrod means it) and he would not accept the halakhic dimension of Wyschogrod's thought. (See note 2 for the reviews by Elman and Wolf.)

I, too, have indicated the open questions in Wyschogrod's oeuvre. But his pointing to the undiluted particularity, in the flesh, of the Jewish people, his indication of the theological roots of that particularity, his return to the anthropopathic understanding of God, and his willingness to engage contemporary philosophy and Christianity on their own grounds on these Jewish subjects is a contribution to modern Jewish thought. It has earned Wyschogrod a place among the Jewish thinkers of this century.

Notes

1. This article is based on an extended interview I had with Michael Wyschogrod at his office in December 1987. I am grateful to him for his time and for permission to use material from that interview.

2. *The Body of Faith* has been extensively reviewed. I call the reader's attention to three: Yaakov Elman's Orthodox perspective, "Election without Faith, Judaism without Mitzvot," *Judaica Book News* (Fall–Winter 1984), pp.8–10, 56–58; Arnold J. Wolf's Reform perspective, "Wyschogrod's Book *The Body of Faith*," *Sh'ma*, April 27, 1984, pp. 103–4; and David Blumenthal, *Association for Jewish Studies Review* 4 (Spring 1986), pp. 116–21.

3. The Presbyterian document went through several stages. As originally conceived and written for the southern church (Presbyterian Church in the United States), the document was stunning, theologically and stylistically. It had three major moments, from a Jewish point of view.

   First, the relevant sections of the document began by asserting the continuing nature of God's covenant with the Jewish people and went on to admit that God also has a continuing covenant with the Jewish people for the land of Israel, even though the boundaries vary in the biblical sources. The document then proceeded to distinguish between the covenant of land and sovereignty over the land. The former is valid even without Jewish sovereignty over the land; the latter is valid only as long as the covenant is kept faithfully. The document concluded the relevant section by an acknowledgment of God's call to justice to all persons and peoples, Jew and Gentile, Israeli and Palestinian. Throughout, the appeal was largely to verses in the Bible and to the theological logic of covenant. The differentiation of land, state, and justice was very helpful, and it is to be regretted that it was lost in later drafts of the document.

Second, Christians regard the covenants of the Hebrew Scriptures to have taken on a universal dimension in their Christian form; Jesus is sent to all humanity. The document thus interpreted the election of the particular Jewish people as "the harbinger of God's universal call to peoplehood in Christ." But it went a step further and drew a similar parallel between the particular land of Israel and "the sign of God's intention for a peaceable kingdom for all people ... an earthly, geographical, political place where one can be safe and secure, free from pressure and coercion ... a home, a means of life, a source of wealth, and a place where individuals can become a people." This was the first Christian theology of land that was not spiritualized into an otherworldly concept. It was a historical moment in Christian theology. The document's position also provided a Christian root for the claim of the Jewish people to the Holy Land. And the document's position provided a theological basis for asserting the claim of all peoples (including the Palestinians and the Israelis) for land, defined in its broad sense. It is to be most regretted that this was lost in later drafts.

Third, the document explicitly repudiated the mission to the Jews and explained that "witnessing" or "evangelizing" must take the form of personal Christian behavior and open nonproselytizing dialogue. This too was lost in later versions. Such are the vagaries of interfaith dialogue.

No one person or persons could take credit for the document in any of its forms. But I think that Wyschogrod's and my presence was a help on these as well as on other issues.

The document was published in revised form by the (unified) Presbyterian Church in the U.S.A. as "A Theological Understanding of the Relationship Between Christians and Jews."

FOR FURTHER READING

Works by Michael Wyschogrod

The Body of Faith: Judaism as Corporeal Election, Minneapolis, 1983. This is clearly Wyschogrod's most important work. In it he argues that the chosenness of the Jewish people is not an abstract concept but one inherent in the body of Jews, scandalous as this has been over the centuries.

Kierkegaard and Heidegger; The Ontology of Existence, London, 1953. One of the first studies of Kierkegaard's influence on Heidegger.

Works in General Philosophy

"Heidegger; The Limits of Philosophy," *Sh'ma* 12 (April 2, 1982), pp. 80–83. In this very important piece, Wyschogrod gives the biographical details of Heidegger's Nazi connection and anti-Semitism, including his post-war record. This is in contrast with the philosophical critique in *Body of Faith*.

"Sartre, Freedom, and the Unconscious," *Review of Existential Psychology and Psychiatry* 1 (Fall 1961) pp. 179–86. An analysis of Sartre's critique of the Freudian unconscious.

"Heidegger: Ontology and Human Existence," *Diseases of the Nervous System* 22 (April 1961) pp. 540–546. This is a technical philosophical essay dealing with Heidegger's views on the relationship between metaphysics and philosophical anthropology.

"Will in Psychology and Philosophy," *Encyclopedia Americana* 28, pp. 770–72, New York, 1962. An examination of the origin of the concept of will in Augustine and later Christian theology.

Jewish-Christian Issues

"Buber's Evaluation of Christianity: A Jewish Perspective," in Hayim Gordon and Jochanan Bloch, eds., *Martin Buber: A Centenary Volume*, Tel Aviv, 1981, pp. 403–17 [Hebrew]; pp. 457–72 [English]. This essay presents a sympathetic appraisal of Buber's work on Christianity. This is contrary to much of Jewish scholarly opinion which is decidedly cool, if not negative about Buber's work in this area.

Das Reden vom einen Gott bei Juden und Christen, with Clemens Thoma, Bern, 1984. This work grows out of several years of study with the Catholic faculty of Lucerne. The interplay of text and tradition is particularly well done.

"Israel, the Church and Election," in John Oesterreicher, ed., *Brothers in Hope*, New York, 1970, pp. 79–87. Discusses election in Judaism in relation to the understanding of that concept in the church.

Jews and "Jewish Christianity," with David Berger, New York, 1978. Explains the Jewish attitude toward "messianic Judaism" and Christianity.

"Judaism and Evangelical Christianity," in Marvin Wilson and A. James Rudin, eds., *Evangelicals and Jews in Conversation*, Grand Rapids, 1978, pp. 34–52. Wyschogrod addresses briefly such themes as the common sacred text of the Bible, the link of land and people, the law, the interrelationship of faith and works, and the divisive issue of the Messiah.

"The Law, Jews, and Gentiles: A Jewish Perspective," *Lutheran Quarterly* 21, (November 1969) pp. 405–15. Focuses on Paul's critique of biblical law and the Jewish response thereto.

"A New Stage in Jewish-Christian Dialogue," *Judaism* 31 (Summer 1982), pp. 355–65. A review essay of recent Christian evaluations of Judaism.

Contemporary Jewish Issues

"Agenda for Jewish Philosophy," *Judaism* 11 (Summer 1962), pp. 195–99. Discusses issues likely to be central to Jewish philosophy in the 1980's and 1990's.

"Faith and the Holocaust," *Judaism* 20 (Summer 1971) pp. 286–94. This is a significant critical review of Emil Fackenheim's approach to the Holocaust.

"Lebanon: A Loss of Confidence," *Sh'ma* 13 (March 18, 1983), pp. 72–73. Wyschogrod here takes a clear stand (together with others) on the morality of the war in Lebanon. It is part of the communal dimension of his theological enterprise.

"Some Theological Reflections on the Holocaust," *Response* 25 (Spring 1975) pp. 65–68. Evaluates critically the tendency to make the Holocaust fundamental to Jewish faith.

"Symposium: The State of Orthodoxy," *Tradition* 20 (Spring 1982) pp. 80–83. Evaluates tendencies in contemporary Orthodoxy, especially the exclusive focus on halakha.

About the Contributors

A. ZVIE BAR-ON is Professor Emeritus of the Hebrew University of Jerusalem. A participant in the guerilla- and regular warfare against Nazi Germany, he was awarded the Red-Star orden by the Soviet government. In 1957 he won the Ben-Gurion prize for an essay on Plato's philosophy. His recent publications include *The Categories and the Principle of Coherence* and *Philosophers Then and Now* (in Hebrew).

ALAN L. BERGER directs the Jewish Studies Program and teaches in the Department of Religion at Syracuse University. Among his books are *Crisis and Covenant: The Holocaust in American Jewish Fiction, Methodology in the Academic Teaching of the Holocaust* (Associate Editor), and *Bearing Witness to the Holocaust: 1939–1989.*

DAVID BIALE is the Koret Professor of Jewish History and Director of the Center for Jewish Studies at the Graduate Theological Union in Berkeley, CA. He is the author of *Gershom Scholem: Kabbalah and Counter-History* and *Power and Powerlessness in Jewish History*, both of which won the National Jewish Book Award. He just published *Eros and the Jews: From Biblical Israel to Contemporary America*, a study of Jewish views of sexuality and marriage.

DAVID R. BLUMENTHAL is the Jay and Leslie Cohen Professor of Judaic Studies at Emory University in Atlanta. His early work encompassed medieval Jewish thought; his later work has been in Jewish spirituality and includes: *Understanding Jewish Mysticism* (2 vols.), *The Place of Faith and Grace in Judaism*, and most recently, *God at the Center*.

RICHARD A. COHEN is Aaron Aronov Chair of Judaic Studies and Associate Professor of Religious Studies at the University of Alabama. He has published numerous articles on twentieth century continental philosophy, and is author of *Elevations: The Height of the Good in Levinas and Rosenzweig.*

DAVID G. DALIN is Associate Professor of American Jewish History at the University of Hartford, and a Senior Fellow at the Institute of Religion and Public Life in New York City. His books include *From Marxism to Judaism: The Collected Essays of Will Herberg* and *American Jews and the Separationist Faith: The New Debate on Religion and Public Life.*

ELLIOT N. DORFF is Provost and Professor of Philosophy at the University of Judaism in Los Angeles, and also teaches Jewish law at UCLA School of Law. Rabbi Dorff's books include: *Jewish Law and Modern Ideology, Conservative Judaism: Our Ancestors to Our Descendants, A Living Tree: The Roots and Growth of Jewish law,* and *Mitzvah Means Commandment.*

DAVID ELLENSON is I.H. and Anna Grancell Professor of Jewish Religious Thought at the Hebrew Union College-Jewish Institute of Religion, Los Angeles. He has written numerous scholarly essays and reviews and is author of *Tradition in Transition: Orthodoxy, Halakah and the Boundaries of Modern Jewish Identity* and *Esriel Hildesheimer and the Creation of a Modern Jewish Orthodoxy.*

HILLEL FRADKIN is Visiting Lecturer at the University of Chicago and Vice President of The Lynde and Harry Bradley Foundation. His major articles include "The 'Separation' of Religion and Politics: The Paradoxes of Spinoza," *The Review of Politics*; "God's Politics: Lessons from the Beginning," *This World*; and, "Philosophy and Law: Leo Strauss as a Student of Medieval Jewish Thought," *The Review of Politics.*

DAVID HARTMAN is Professor of Jewish Philosophy at the Hebrew University, Jerusalem and is founder and Director of the Shalom Hartman Institute in Jerusalem. He has twice won the National Jewish Book Award for the Best Book on Jewish Thought for *Maimonides: Torah and Philosophic Quest* (1977) and *A Living Covenant: the Innovative Spirit in Traditional Judaism* (1985).

JOCELYN HELLIG is senior lecturer in World Religions, Department of Religious Studies, University of the Witwatersrand, Johannesburg, South Africa. In addition to her works on Richard Rubenstein, she has published articles in scholarly journals and chapters in books in the fields of Holocaust theology, the causes and dynamics of anti-Semitism and the religious expression of South African Jews.

EDWARD K. KAPLAN, Professor of French and Comparative Literature and Research Associate of the Tauber Institute for the Study of European Jewry at Brandeis University, is currently writing an intellectual and cultural biography of Abraham Joshua Heschel. He has published articles on Heschel, Thomas Merton, Martin Buber, and Howard Thurman, and various works on 19th- and 20th-century French poets.

STEVEN T. KATZ is Professor of Jewish History and Thought in the Department of Near Eastern Studies at Cornell University. His works include: *Jewish Philosophers*, *Jewish Ideas and Concepts*, *Post-Holocaust Dialogues*, which won the National Jewish Book Award in 1984; *Historicism, the Holocaust and Zionism*; *Mysticism and Philosophical Analysis*; *Mysticism and Religious Traditions*; and *Mysticism and Language*. He is also the editor of *Modern Judaism*.

MENACHEM KELLNER holds the Sir Isaac and Lady Edith Wolfson Chair in Jewish Thought at the University of Haifa. He is the author of *Dogma in Medieval Jewish Thought*, the translator of Isaac Abravanel's *Principles of Faith*; and the editor of *Contemporary Jewish Ethics*, *The Pursuit of the Ideal: Jewish Writings of Steven Schwarzschild*, and of a critical edition of Isaac Abravanel's *Rosh Amanah* (forthcoming).

LORI KRAFTE-JACOBS is an adjunct member of the faculty in the Department of Philosophy and Religion at George Mason University. Dr. Krafte-Jacobs is the Associate Editor of *The American Journal of Theology and Philosophy* and author of *On Feminism and Modern Theological Method* (forthcoming).

MICHAEL OPPENHEIM is an Associate Professor and Chair of the Department of Religion at Concordia University in Montreal. He has published a number of articles in the areas of modern Jewish thought and contemporary Jewish identity, and is the author of *What Does Revelation Mean for the Modern Jew.*

CHARLES M. RAFFEL holds the Erna S. Michael Chair in Jewish Philosophy at Yeshiva University's Stern College for Women and has published essays and reviews in the fields of ethics and Jewish philosophy. Dr. Raffel has been actively involved in adult education, lecturing throughout the country on topics of Jewish interest and concern.

STEVEN SCHWARZSCHILD, who died in 1989, was Professor of Philosophy at Washington University (St. Louis). He served as editor of *Judaism* from 1960–1969, and published widely in the area of modern Jewish thought. Among his most significant publications are: *Franz Rosenzweig (1886–1929) – Guide to Reversioners* (London, 1960), and his collected Jewish writings, *The Pursuit of the Ideal*, edited by Menachem Kellner.

KENNETH SEESKIN is Professor of Philosophy and Chair of the Philosophy Department, Northwestern University, and also serves as the Director of the Jewish Studies Program. He has written about ancient Greek philosophy, Jewish philosophy, and the history of philosophy; and his books include: *Dialogue and Discovery: a Study in Socratic Method, Jewish Philosophy in a Secular Age*, and *Maimonides: A Guide For Today's Perplexed.*

DAVID SINGER is director of research for the American Jewish Committee and editor of the *American Jewish Year Book*. His essays and reviews have appeared in a wide variety of periodicals, including *Commentary, Modern Judaism, New Republic,* and *Tradition*. He is currently at work on an intellectual biography of Rabbi Joseph Soloveitchik.

MOSHE SOKOL is Associate Professor and Chairman of the Philosophy Department at Touro College in New York City. The author of numerous articles on Jewish ethics and philosophy, he has recently edited a volume of essays entitled *Rabbinic Authority and Personal Autonomy*.

Index

The interested reader may wish to examine other works in this series:

Great Jewish Thinkers of the Twentieth Century
Edited by Simon Noveck

Contents

© 1963, 1985
ISBN: 0-910250-06-5; 0-910250-07-3 (pbk.)

Concepts that Distinguish Judaism

Edited by Abraham Ezra Millgram

Contents

The Jewish Vision of God and Man

A Tradition in Transition

© 1964, 1985
ISBN 0-910250-00-6; 0-910250-01-4 (pbk.)

Frontiers of Jewish Thought

Edited by Steven T. Katz

Contents

© 1992
ISBN: 0-910250-20-0; 0-910250-21-9 (pbk.)